Colonial Saints

Colonial Saints

DISCOVERING THE HOLY IN THE AMERICAS, 1500–1800

EDITED BY
ALLAN GREER
AND
JODI BILINKOFF

Routledge
New York • London

Published in 2003 by
RoutledgeFalmer
29 West 35th Street
New York, NY 10001
www.routledge-ny.com

Published in Great Britain by
RoutledgeFalmer
11 New Fetter Lane
London EC4P 4EE
www.routledgefalmer.com

Routledge is an imprint of the Taylor & Francis Group.
Printed in the United States of America on acid-free paper.

10 9 8 7 6 5 4 3 2 1

Library of Congress Cataloging-in-Publication Data

Colonial saints : discovering the holy in the Americas, 1500–1800 / edited by Allan Greer and Jodi Bilinkoff.
    p. cm.
    Includes bibliographical references and index.
    ISBN 0-415-93495-8 — ISBN 0-415-93496-6 (pbk.)
    1. Christian saints—Cult—America—History. 2. America—Church history. 3. Christian hagiography. I. Greer, Allan. II. Bilinkoff, Jodi, 1955–

BX4659.A45 C65 2003
235'.2'097—dc21

2002032982

Contents

List of Illustrations vii

Preface ix
Allan Greer

Introduction xiii
Jodi Bilinkoff

Part 1 CULTURAL MIXING 1

1. St. Anne Imagery and Maternal Archetypes in Spain and Mexico 3
   Charlene Villaseñor Black

2. Querying the Spirit: The Rules of the Haitian *Lwa* 31
   Joan Dayan

3. Diego de Ocaña's Hagiography of New and Renewed Devotion
      in Colonial Peru 51
   Kenneth Mills

4. Old Bones and Beautiful Words: The Spiritual Contestation between Shaman
      and Jesuit in the Guaraní Missions 77
   Dot Tuer

5. St. Anthony in Portuguese America: Saint of the Restoration 99
   Ronaldo Vainfas

Part 2 HOLY WOMEN, HOLY MEN 113

6. Francisco Losa and Gregorio López: Spiritual Friendship and Identity Formation
      on the New Spain Frontier 115
   Jodi Bilinkoff

7. In the Shadow of the Cloister: Representations of Female Holiness in
   New France   129
   Dominique Deslandres

8. Isaac Jogues: From Martyrdom to Sainthood   153
   Paul Perron

9. Martyred by the Saints: Quaker Executions in
   Seventeenth-Century Massachusetts   169
   Carla Gardina Pestana

10. St. Palafox: Metaphorical Images of Disputed Sainthood   193
    Antonio Rubial García

Part 3 THE USES OF THE SACRED   209

11. Writing a Relic: The Uses of Hagiography in New France   211
    Julia Boss

12. Iroquois Virgin: The Story of Catherine Tekakwitha in
    New France and New Spain   235
    Allan Greer

13. "Redeemer of America": Rosa de Lima (1586–1617),
    the Dynamics of Identity, and Canonization   251
    Kathleen Ann Myers

14. Mexico's Virgin of Guadalupe in the Seventeenth Century:
    Hagiography and Beyond   277
    William B. Taylor

Select Bibliography   299

Contributors   305

List of Illustrations

Figures

1-1   Bartolomé Esteban Murillo, *St. Anne Teaching the Virgin Mary to Read*   7

1-2   Bartolomé Esteban Murillo, *Holy Family with a Little Bird*   9

1-3   Andrés de la Concha, *Holy Family as "los Cinco Señores"*   15

1-4   Diego de Pesquera, St. Anne Triplex.   16

1-5   Juan Correa, *Nativity of the Virgin Mary*   18

1-6   Elena Baca, *Portrait of My Grandmother*   23

10-1   Miguel Cabrera, *Allegories of the Virtues of Palafox*   198

10-2   Anonymous, *Juan de Palafox on Mount Carmel with Friars and Nuns*   199

10-3   Luis Berrueco, *The Life of St. John of God*   201

10-4   Anonymous, *Miracle of St. Nicholas of Tolentino*   202

10-5   Cristóbal de Talavera, *Father Baltasar Alvarez*   204

10-6   José de Ibarra, *Adoration of the Eucharist*   205

10-7   José Joaquin Magón, *Patrocinio de la Inmaculada Concepción*   206

13-1   Rosa de Lima, "The Mercies" (*Las Mercedes*) and
"The Mystical Stairway" (*La Escala Mística*)   266

Preface

For me personally, the process leading up to the publication of *Colonial Saints* has been a rewarding journey of exploration. As a specialist in the French colonization of Canada, I started out with a curious document, the life story of a Mohawk convert to Catholicism, Catherine Tekakwitha, written in the seventeenth century by a French Jesuit missionary. The text was clearly an exercise in hagiography, a genre that had not died with the waning of the Middle Ages but had, as I quickly discovered, continued to thrive in the centuries that followed the European "discovery" of America. The plot thickened when I found that Tekakwitha's life story had been translated into Spanish and published in Mexico. Traveling to Mexico City to find out more about how and why this sacred biography from the Far North had made its way into the heart of Spanish America, I looked up Antonio Rubial García at his office on the magnificent campus of the Universidad Nacional Autónoma de México. A generous scholar, well known for his studies of art, religion, and society in colonial Mexico, Antonio proved to be the perfect guide as I took my first faltering steps in the Mexican archives. He also put me in touch with another North American who had recently contacted him for advice on a similar topic. This was Jodi Bilinkoff, a historian of Catholicism in peninsular Spain, who, like me, was making a first foray into Latin American history in pursuit of the emigrant holy man Gregorio López.

From Antonio and Jodi I was soon introduced to other researchers interested in holy lives and representations of saintliness, in Brazil, the Caribbean, South America, Quebec, and Mexico. Two facts became clear: first, there was a wealth of material relating to hagiography and the cult of saints here in the "New World"; second, a substantial number of scholars was at work on these sources, but they tended to be isolated from one another by the barriers of language, discipline, and nationality. Since a few of us were carrying on a stimulating conversation through the medium of e-mail, it seemed logical to organize a live meeting and bring together historians, literary scholars, art historians, and anthropologists with a common interest in saintly lives in the Western Hemisphere. Accordingly, I arranged a conference at the University of Toronto in May 2000 and invited specialists from Mexico, South America, and Europe, as well as North Americans working on topics related to saints and their cults.

Though organized on a modest scale, the meeting attracted unanticipated media attention, including an article in the *New York Times,*[1] an encouraging sign that interest in the saints of an earlier age was not confined to a narrow circle of academic specialists. The title of the conference, "Colonial Saints: Hagiography and the Cult of Saints in the Americas, 1500–1800," emphasized its substantive focus, but the event also was designed to bring scholars together in unaccustomed configurations and to cultivate new interdisciplinary and international connections, not to mention fostering linkages between academics and nonspecialists. In discharging this integrative mandate, the conference was a great success, thanks in no small measure to the positive and receptive spirit of all those involved. Unfortunately, it was not practical to publish all the papers presented at the Toronto conference, so Jodi and I as coeditors have had to take only a sample for inclusion in this volume.

I hope readers will appreciate our use of "the Americas" as the geographical framework defining our approach to colonial cultural history. It is more conventional to organize scholarship under headings such as "Latin America," "North America," "The Caribbean," or even "The Atlantic World," but we have opted, quite deliberately, for a hemispheric scope. Historians of slavery have long been accustomed to thinking at the level of the "New World," but for reasons I cannot fathom, such an approach is still fairly rare in other fields of scholarship, notably religion.[2] We gain a fuller understanding of the colonization process in one region of the Americas, it seems to me, when we consider it in the context of the hemisphere as a whole. By that means, common themes become more visible, as do instructive points of contrast.

Many individuals and agencies contributed to the Colonial Saints conference and to this book; I wish to record my heartfelt thanks to all of them. The University of Toronto, and especially University College, hosted the event and helped to underwrite it financially. Funding also came from the Social Sciences and Humanities Research Council of Canada, the Connaught Fund, and the French consulate in Toronto. My Toronto colleagues David Higgs, Isabelle Cochelin, Paul Perron, and Carolyn Podruchny played a vital role in planning the conference, while Pam Gravestock handled all the practical arrangements with superhuman skill and sangfroid. Translators Alexandra Luce, Irene Marques, and Paolo Horta built bridges to connect our four languages. Special thanks go to Natalie Zemon Davis for her comments and concluding remarks, all of them displaying her characteristic blend of penetrating insight and warm encouragement.

I wish to take this opportunity also to acknowledge the indirect contribution of those scholars whose work on saints and hagiography in the colonial Americas has played such an important part in making this book possible: Leila Algranti, Lucia Bergamasco, François-Marc Gagnon, Serge Gagnon, Teodoro Hampe Martínez, Fernando Iwasaki Cauti, Asunción Lavrin, Luis Millones, Ronald Morgan, Luiz Mott, Guilherme Pereira das Neves, Stafford Poole, Pierre Ragon, Elizabeth Rapley, Manuel Ramos Medina, Daniel Reff, and Mario Valdés.

For me, working with Jodi Bilinkoff has been a rare privilege. With her in North Carolina and me on leave in England, *Colonial Saints* has provided the occasion for an extended e-mail conversation during the course of which I learned a great deal. And Jodi's inexhaustible supply of good humor made the editorial process a pleasure from start to finish. She and I were assisted by the imperturbable Gwendolyn Rice in Toronto; we are both very grateful to Gwen for her monumental efforts in editing and preparing the manuscript. Thanks also to Rich Haney, wonder-working patron saint of computers.

In the final stages of transforming a collection of papers into a book, Jane Harrison made an invaluable contribution. Karen Wolny, publishing director at Routledge, has been consistently enthusiastic about our project; we are deeply appreciative of her encouragement. And we thank our family members for their exemplary patience and unconditional support.

Allan Greer
January 2002

NOTES

1. Chris Hedges, "When Armies of Conquest Marched In, So Did Saints," *New York Times,* February 12, 2000.
2. Two recent books on the religious aspects of colonization have already blazed a trail for us: Fernando Cervantes and Nicholas Griffiths, eds., *Spiritual Encounters: Interactions between Christianity and Native Religions in Colonial America* (Lincoln: University of Nebraska Press, 1999); and Susan Dinan and Debra Meyers, eds., *Women and Religion in Old and New Worlds* (New York: Routledge, 2001).

Introduction

Every society has its heroes, persons of extraordinary virtue and valor who are held up as models for admiration and emulation. Traditionally for Christians these have been saints, figures whose lives of service and sacrifice have rendered them worthy of veneration after their deaths, and efficacious as intercessors between individual believers and the divine. From the earliest days of the faith, Christians recorded and circulated the stories of holy exemplars both orally and in written texts. By the high Middle Ages, hagiographies, or the lives of saintly persons, were composed in vernacular languages and avidly read by clerics and laypersons alike. The advent of the printing press in the later fifteenth century only enhanced the popularity of this literary genre, at once biography, sacred history, and didactic guide for behavior.[1]

Scholars with a European focus have long been interested in saints as well, regarding them as potent indicators of values and aspirations, and as barometers of change over time. In this more historical and ethnographic, as opposed to theological, approach, "saint" has come to mean any figure regarded as saintly or exemplary to a community of believers, not only someone officially canonized by the Catholic Church. Scholarship in history, literature, art history, and other disciplines has found rich food for reflection in textual and artistic expressions of devotion to the saints. Studies of the peculiar literary conventions of "sacred biography," examinations of the cults and pilgrimages surrounding the physical remains and plastic representations of saints, analyses of the political dynamics of canonization, inquiries into the gender ideals embodied in stories of male and female saints—these are but a sample of the varied approaches to the subject in its Old World Christian context.

Hagiography is by no means a peculiarly medieval genre; arguably it reached its apogee in the early modern period, when the printing press hugely expanded the availability of texts and when a resurgent Catholic Church encouraged the cult of saints in reaction to the Reformation (and while they attacked the traditional cult of saints, Protestants still managed to develop their own version of hagiographical narratives). And it was just at this time, as images and stories of ancient and more recently deceased spiritual heroes were proliferating across Catholic Europe, that Spanish and Portuguese navigators, followed not long after by French, English, and Dutch, were making contact with the Americas and their indigenous peoples. With contact came a series of invasions, both military and spiritual, as well as the establishment of colonial settlements. The colonizers came brandishing swords, guns, and crosses, but also the battle cry of Santiago, statues of Our Lady, books on the lives of Catherine of Siena and Anthony of Padua. Thus the saints of the Old World were introduced to—and often imposed on—the New.

Until recently, this hagiographic dimension of the colonization of the Americas excited little curiosity beyond the ranks of the devout. Now, however, scholars in and of Latin America and French Canada are beginning to respond to the exciting possibilities the saints afford anyone interested in probing the mysteries of colonial culture. Many of the themes considered by Europeanists—gender ideals, political conflict, art, and popular devotion—present themselves for the consideration of Americanists, but in addition, a whole series of specifically American issues ("American" in the broad, hemispheric sense) arise. These latter issues have to do with questions of colonial identity and protonationalism, but above all, they revolve around the fundamental issues of race and class that were thrown up by the impact of European colonization on Indian peoples and enslaved Africans.

As Spanish, Portuguese, and French settlers and missionaries came to lands that were new to them and to Christianity, they encountered indigenous peoples and enslaved Africans who had their own belief systems, their own experiences of the holy, their own "saints." Over decades of missionization, resistance, conversion, accommodation, fusion, and reinterpretation new religious forms emerged, incorporating traditions from both sides of the Atlantic. To study the saints of the New World during the centuries of European colonization is to contemplate the "spiritual conquest" of the Americas to be sure, but also the American "conquest" of Christianity.

While important work has been going forward on New World saints and hagiography, discussion has sometimes been limited by a certain compartmentalization by country, language, and discipline. The aim of this volume is to bring together the work of scholars from across the Americas and representing a range of scholarly fields. Our contributors focus on South America, North America, and the Caribbean; some of them normally write in French, Spanish, or Portuguese, others in English; yet they share a number of substantive interests and methodological preoccupations.

The mixing of peoples and cultures that became such a central feature of colonial American societies is examined by a number of contributors. We are largely dependent on the colonizers and their written texts in Spanish, French, Portuguese, and English for accounts of the past, but the sensitive readings offered by these scholars allows us to hear echoes of other voices, in Quechua, Aymara, Huron, Guaraní, Tupí, Nahuatl, and Haitian Creole.

For example, many essays in this collection highlight the experience of Catholic missionaries. As priests worked to bring a foreign, Old World religion to the New World, they often found themselves compromising, negotiating with, accommodating, and even showing a grudging respect for native peoples and traditions. In the process of converting, they were themselves, to some degree, "converted." Thus Antonio Ruiz de Montoya, in the case studied by Dot Tuer, had to master not only the language of the Guaraní in Paraguay but also the ways of their shamans, and adopt them to successfully compete against these rival practitioners of the sacred. Kenneth Mills shows how Diego de Ocaña came to appreciate that the dark-skinned Virgin of Guadalupe could hold a special meaning for Andean converts who "loved her a lot because she was of their color."[2] And the clerical promoters of the Iroquois Catherine Tekakwitha in New France, and later supporters in Mexico, Allan Greer explains, used her remarkable path from conversion to saintliness to insist on the "spiritual potential of natives."[3]

As the teachings of the missionaries interacted with native and African beliefs, practices, and discourses, new religious forms emerged. The cults of saints and other holy figures provide a lens with which to examine these fascinating processes of conversion, syncretism, and resistance, to witness a Christianity "remade" on American soil. For example, in Haiti, the Catholicism of the French colonizers and the manifold African traditions of the enslaved population clashed and combined to form the complex culture of vodou. Joan Dayan discusses how the Danbala wedo, an ancient African snake spirit, took on new meanings for Haitian believers when identified with St. Patrick, a saint associated with both snakes and the trauma of slavery and exile. This "dialogue between saints and spirits" could lead to unexpected results, such as the association of a Creole love goddess with the Virgin Mary.[4]

Female saints and indigenous goddesses intersected in colonial Mexico, too. Charlene Villaseñor Black suggests that St. Anne, the mother of Mary and grandmother of Jesus, a beloved figure in late medieval Europe, came to enjoy even greater popularity in New Spain, where she was identified with the Aztec goddess Toci, or "Our Grandmother." Black suggests that the embrace of St. Anne/Toci by native Mexicans indicated their acceptance of certain European Christian models of sanctity, but also their resistance to the missionizing project and their struggle to retain traditional religious beliefs and social structures.

Dot Tuer and Ronaldo Vainfas follow this line of analysis as well. Tuer uses the figure of San La Muerte, at once Guaraní god of death and suffering Christ, to illustrate "the ways in which Christian beliefs were received and mediated by indigenous peoples."[5] St. Anthony of Padua (or Lisbon) had an extraordinary career in Portugal's overseas empire. Vainfas demonstrates the amazing malleability of saints, showing how in this case, Tupí Indians, Afro-Brazilians, European settlers, and a Congolese prophetess and her followers all invoked the aid of a medieval Portuguese friar, and adapted his cult to fit their spiritual and political needs.

The interaction between St. Anthony and his petitioners points to a basic underpinning of devotion to saints, the need of individuals for counsel and assistance in a harsh and confusing world. A deep desire for intercession and redemption animates the intense, sometimes intimate relationship believers maintained with holy persons, living or dead. Women pleaded to St. Anthony for a marriage partner and to St. Anne for a successful childbirth. Spanish settlers in Mexico appealed to the hermit Gregorio López, and to portraits of the exemplary bishop Juan de Palafox in times of illness and adversity, as French settlers in Canada approached the holy woman Jeanne Le Ber and the relics of missionaries martyred in struggles with hostile Indians.

This yearning for personal mediation with the divine was not, of course, new or unique to the Americas in the colonial period, although stories such as the one recounted by Diego de Ocaña of the miraculous rescue of miners in Potosí by the Virgin of Guadalupe remind us of time and place. There were miners in Europe, but they were not Quechua or Aymara-speaking Indians, and not forced to extricate ore from a mountain of silver.

However, just as compelling as the personal dimension is the role of saints and their cults in the creation of collective identities. Stories of saintly figures and physical manifestations of the holy—pictures, statues, contact relics, bodily remains, and even the books in which sacred histories were written—could serve as repositories of faith and memory for communities in the process of formation on American soil.

Several contributors focus on these issues of identity and exemplarity for European immigrants as they attempted to establish communities in unfamiliar, sometimes harsh new lands. Julia Boss examines the significance of relics and written accounts of martyred missionaries for settlers in New France, texts and artifacts that became tangible expressions of what it meant to be Catholic and colonial. Jodi Bilinkoff suggests that Gregorio López, New Spain's "First Hermit," and his companion, the priest Francisco Losa, served as exemplars of otherworldliness and virtuous behavior for the groups of Spanish immigrants deemed most in need of such models, laymen and secular clerics. As St. Anthony of Padua underwent his metamorphosis from gentle thaumaturge and restorer of lost objects to manly patron of military campaigns and restorer of lost sovereignty, he became a powerful symbol of national identity and imperial aspirations for Portuguese, both on the peninsula and in Brazil. Carla Pestana shows how even in non-Catholic settings "holy" individuals stood at the forefront of debates over what constituted "true" religion and "godly" communities. In colonial Massachusetts, Puritans, determined to preserve their constituted community of "the elect" against outside threats, persecuted Quaker missionaries, as, ironically, they themselves had been persecuted by Anglicans back in England.

For persons of European descent born in one of the American colonies, or Creoles,[6] saints and their cults proved instrumental in their efforts to prove that their homeland, while only recently Christianized, was just as blessed and beloved by God as was the Old World. The holy persons, images, relics, and spaces found in the colonies could be construed as "sites of divine presence and favor," and imagined as both causes and effects of America's greatness.

The convergence of religious faith, pride of place, and an evolving sense of Creole distinctiveness from the European metropole can be seen in two of the New World's most famous devotions, to the Virgin of Guadalupe, in Mexico, and to Rose of Lima, in Peru, the subject of essays by William Taylor and Kathleen Myers, respectively. For the American-born priests writing "lives" of the revered Marian image of Guadalupe, the fact that the Mother of God had appeared on a hillside outside Mexico City demonstrated conclusively that this region had been graced by the Virgin, hailed as "our sovereign American lady" *(nuestra soberana criolla)*. The 1671 canonization of the Peruvian-born Rosa de Santa María, which gave the New World its first "official" saint, was a source of enormous pride for Creoles generally, and for residents of Lima in particular. For them, her sanctity proved two fundamental truths: that America had now reached "parity with the Old World," and that America played an "essential role in the history of the universal Catholic Church."[7]

Saints and their cults also spoke to the fundamental, if fraught, issues of gender, sexuality, and the body. A number of contributors examine narratives of saintly lives as forms of discourse that both molded and reflected the attitudes of women and men in colonial societies. Essays by Allan Greer, Kathleen Myers, and Dominique Deslandres explore models of Christian womanhood as represented by figures such as Catherine Tekakwitha, Rose of Lima, and Marie de l'Incarnation. The male clerical promoters of pious laywomen and nuns situated them within a tradition well known to Europeans, stressing their virginal purity, ascetic denial, and extreme bodily mortifications. Conventional as were these tropes, however, hagiographers clearly recognized the novelty of the New World setting. Rose of Lima was hailed by one effusive devotee as having aided in the conquest of America, her "virtuous fragrance . . . [having] converted into a paradise of holy delights this previously barbarous jungle. . . ."[8] A Jesuit marveled that the Ursuline Marie de l'Incarnation and other French women could "lose the fear associated with the weakness of their Sex, cross so many seas and live among the savages" in Canada.[9]

The story of Catherine Tekakwitha combines issues of race, gender, and sexuality in a volatile mix. As Greer shows, for most Europeans the terms "Indian woman" and "nun" represented irreconcilable binary opposites. The conviction that native women could not control their sexual appetites, and fears about racial mixing or "hybridity" in general prevented Indians from achieving full membership in religious communities during most of the colonial period. Persuading Europeans of the personal holiness and indisputable chastity of Catherine, an Iroquois convert, and then, by extension, the potential for this sort of life for any native woman truly graced with a vocation for the cloister required nothing less than a hagiographical tour de force.

Moralists also developed models of pious Christian masculinity, turning once again to the saints in their efforts to influence male attitudes and behavior. Charlene Black traces the changing textual and iconographic depictions of St. Joseph, from a doddering old man and peripheral figure to a virile young man, a strong and skilled carpenter who played a central role in the upbringing of Jesus, his "stepson." She relates this to efforts made in the sixteenth and seventeenth centuries to bolster the authority of fathers in the nuclear family and to encourage men to take more responsibility within the household. Jodi Bilinkoff looks at an extraordinary example of male bonding, the intense spiritual friendship between Gregorio López and Francisco Losa in early colonial Mexico. On this occasion, it seems, the message of service and sacrifice contained in their story, a much-needed "antidote" in a frontier society characterized by violence and greed, outweighed any concerns about the effective inversion of the usual hierarchical relationship between priests and laymen. The texts studied by Dot Tuer and Paul Perron as well speak to issues of male gender construction, designed as they were to present missionaries such as Antonio Ruiz de Montoya and Isaac Jogues as heroic, and encourage younger men to follow in their footsteps.

At the center of ideologies of gender and sexuality resides the human body, conveyor of manifold meanings. In both contrast and counterpoise to the intact body of the consecrated virgin was the brutalized body of the martyr. Narratives of missionaries killed by hostile "pagans" came to hold special significance for Catholics in New France, for example, connecting them with the early Christians of sacred history and creating the foundational texts necessary for a new church in a new world. Paul Perron's unflinching analysis of the torture and death of Isaac Jogues reminds us that violence lay at the very heart of the colonizing project.

Carla Pestana, in her examination of Quakers executed in Puritan Massachusetts, shows how, in this non-Catholic case, too, the martyr's body served as a transmitter of messages. While Quakers, like other Protestants, scorned the Catholic cult of the saints, the ability of their condemned missionaries to maintain calm demeanors and peaceful faces up until their final moments on the scaffold was read throughout the Anglo-American world as proof of the authenticity of their witness. Stories of Quakers willing to die for their faith, and showing amazing fortitude in the face of persecution and death, thus resemble many Catholic martyr accounts from the New World, but there is at least one important difference: the appearance of a woman, Mary Dyer, in the usually masculine roles of missionary and martyr.

Examining saints and the sacred in the Americas also forces us to confront a most unholy legacy of conquest and colonization: the body enslaved. In a world in which Europeans bought, sold, stole, shipped, possessed, and disposed of Africans and others as things, we should not be surprised that hunters of runaway slaves in Brazil would appeal to St. Anthony, the traditional recoverer of "lost objects," to aid them in their grisly work. It was to escape slave-hunting incursions of this sort that Antonio Ruiz de Montoya led thousands of Guaraní converts to safety in northern Argentina, an effort that may have proved more significant to his Indian followers than his "spiritual conquest" of rival shamans.

The interplay between slavery and spirituality forms the focus of Joan Dayan's essay on vodou in Haiti. As French colonizers used laws to render people "embodied property,"[10] prohibit miscegenation, and tie laborers to backbreaking work on the land, Haitians turned to the spirits as allies in acts of cultural resistance, to evoke their African roots and insist on their personhood. Ironically, in Haitian Creole the word *lwa* means both "law" and "god" or "spirit"—for Dayan, a cunning coincidence that suggests how the oppressed could use the latter to subvert the former.

Finally, saints, far from being static icons, provide windows on events in the larger world around them, and offer ways of charting change over time. Nearly every essay in this volume explores the myriad links between the sacred and the political in the colonial Americas.

Ronaldo Vainfas, for example, traces the cult of St. Anthony over the centuries, but also considers his significance during a precise moment in Luso-Brazilian history, the decades between 1580 and 1640. In this period, when Portuguese sovereignty was threatened by Spanish monarchs and Dutch corsairs, the saint emerged as a military hero, vanquisher of enemies and restorer of national pride and territorial integrity. In his analysis of the meanings and uses of Juan de Palafox, Antonio Rubial García shows how the figure of an exemplary bishop (d. 1649) from Puebla, Mexico, became enmeshed in the complex ecclesiastical and royal politics of the eighteenth century. The prelate's disputes with influential Jesuits and other adversaries during his lifetime guaranteed that after his death camps of supporters and opponents would face off, each using Palafox's image as a "political flag." The ensuing clash of ideologies and personalities would effectively sabotage canonization efforts despite the popularity of the bishop's cult in Puebla.[11]

Political and intellectual developments in the late eighteenth and nineteenth centuries would ultimately lead to the dismantling of the colonial system, profoundly altering religious practice and discourse in the Americas. William Taylor situates his reconstruction of early devotion to the Virgin of Guadalupe within debates over a nascent "Creole consciousness" or "protonationalism" that eventually assigned a prominent role to the Marian image during Mexico's War of Independence of 1808–10. Woven throughout Joan Dayan's exploration of vodou spirituality is the tortured history of Saint-Domingue/Haiti, from French colonization through independence in 1804, to the virtual reenslavement of many of its people by a military regime in the mid-nineteenth century.

The Puritans of Massachusetts, who had congratulated themselves for ridding their colony of dangerous heretics from 1659 to 1661, faced increasing criticism of their decision in subsequent decades. During the American Revolution, Carla Pestana notes, a society on the verge of becoming a nation built upon "rights" rather than a community built upon "godliness" looked back to the execution of Quakers as an unforgivable act of intolerance. Mary Dyer and her companions were hailed now, not as martyrs to their faith, but as champions of "religious freedom" or "freedom of conscience."

Examining the sacred in the New World reveals fundamental truths about the colonial experience: extraordinary acts of courage, unspeakable moments of brutality, poignant struggles for individual and collective identity, the transmission of old faiths and the creation of new ones. These essays, we hope, will deepen our understanding not only of the saints but also of their believers, the peoples of the Americas, in all their complexity and humanity.

Jodi Bilinkoff

NOTES

1. On the near-universality of "saints" see Richard Kieckhefer and George D. Bond, eds., *Sainthood: Its Manifestations in World Religions* (Berkeley: University of California Press, 1988). Thomas Heffernan points out that the genre of hagiography has one of the longest continuous histories, "beginning with St. Luke's rendering of St. Stephen's martyrdom in Acts and having no de facto end . . ." in *Sacred Biography: Saints and Their Biographers in the Middle Ages* (New York: Oxford University Press 1988), 15–18.
2. Kenneth Mills, "Diego de Ocaña's Hagiography of New and Renewed Devotion in Colonial Peru," 61.
3. Allan Greer, "Iroquois Virgin: The Story of Catherine Tekakwitha in New France and New Spain," 234.
4. Joan Dayan, "Querying the Spirit: The Rules of the Haitian *Lwa*," 48.
5. Dot Tuer, "Old Bones and Beautiful Words: The Spiritual Contestation between Shaman and Jesuit in the Guaraní Missions," 79.
6. The Spanish originally applied the term *criollo* to slaves of African ancestry born in America, but later extended its meaning to cover Spaniards born in the colonies. The French version of *criollo* is *créole*, and it tends to have a similarly dual sense: depending on the context, it can mean a white or a black person born in the New World. *Créole* took on an additional, linguistic, sense in the French Caribbean, where it applies to a colonial language, with French vocabulary and some African grammatical structures, spoken by islanders of African descent.
7. Kathleen Ann Myers, " 'Redeemer of America': Rosa de Lima (1586–1617), the Dynamics of Identity, and Canonization," 258. See also Antonio Rubial García, "St. Palafox: Metaphorical Images of Disputed Sainthood," 192, on Palafox and Puebla; Jodi Bilinkoff, "Francisco Losa and Gregorio López: Spiritual Friendship and Identity Formation on the New Spain Frontier," 115, for the cult of Gregorio López concentrated in the area around Mexico City; Dayan, "Querying the Spirit," on the role of "Creole spirituality," 42, note 14, in the making of the "Haitian community," 45, note 16; Marie de l'Incarnation on aura of holiness "in the air" of New France, quoted in Dominique Deslandres, "In the Shadow of the Cloister: Representations of Female Holiness in New France," 145, note 73.
8. Quoted in Myers, " 'Redeemer of America,' " 258, note 32. See also Mills, "Diego de Ocaña's Hagiography," on the Virgin of Guadalupe as "la Conquistadora," 51.
9. Paul Le Jeune quoted in Deslandres, "In the Shadow of the Cloister," 136, note 22, see also her discussion of how religious women in New France regarded themselves as "missionaries" and "apostles," 136–137.
10. Dayan, "Querying the Spirit," 31.
11. Antonio Rubial García, "St. Palafox," 192. Other essays touch on conflicts related to ecclesiastical and secular politics at the local level that could have wider implications. See, for example, Bilinkoff, "Francisco Losa and Gregorio López," on tensions between secular and regular clergy in New Spain in the late sixteenth century and the reforming efforts of Archbishop Moya de Contreras; and Greer, "Iroquois Virgin," on the controversy over the foundation of the Corpus Christi convent for noble Indian women in Mexico City in the 1720s.

Part 1

CULTURAL MIXING

1

St. Anne Imagery and Maternal Archetypes in Spain and Mexico

CHARLENE VILLASEÑOR BLACK

Believed by Catholics to have been the mother of the Virgin Mary and grandmother of Jesus, St. Anne enjoyed remarkable devotion in sixteenth-, seventeenth-, and eighteenth-century Mexico. Numerous colonial hagiographies, sermons, and devotional texts, as well as countless visual images, lauded her as the "Mother of the Mother of God" and the "most holy Grandmother of Jesus."[1] Many Mexican villages, chapels, churches, and missions were named after her. Today Anne remains a venerated saint in Mexico. Anthropologists recently documented thirty-one communities that celebrate her July 26 feast day, plus forty additional locales where Mary's Nativity is observed on September 8.[2] Thus, after the Virgin Mary, St. Anne is the most celebrated female holy person in Mexico. What is so remarkable about St. Anne's vigorous following in Mexico is that her cult attained popularity despite Spanish Church and Inquisition attempts to squelch such devotion. In fact, St. Anne's cult flourished in colonial Mexico at the very time it declined in importance in Spain. Why did the cult of St. Anne prosper in Mexico as it dwindled in Spain? Positing answers to that question, which take into account the creation of new hybrid cultural forms in colonial Mexico, is the goal of this chapter.

As in the case of many other important Catholic saints, the Gospels make no specific mention of St. Anne. The first textual references to her appear in the apocryphal *Protoevangelium of St. James,* from about 150 C.E., which opens with the story of Anne and Joachim as a prelude to the Nativity of

Mary. The widely circulating *Golden Legend* of Jacobus de Voragine, written in about 1260, elaborated on and popularized the *Protoevangelium* and other apocryphal tales about Anne, such as the *Gospel of the Pseudo-Matthew* and the *Nativity of Mary.* These early sources encapsulated the medieval construction of St. Anne's life. After twenty years of marriage to St. Joachim, a union that produced no offspring, an aged St. Anne miraculously conceived Mary during an embrace with her husband at the Golden Gate of Jerusalem, a wondrous series of events memorialized by the artist Giotto in his Arena Chapel frescoes. The Golden Legend also popularized the belief, apparently dating from the ninth century, that St. Anne was thrice married. According to this version of Anne's vita, after Joachim's death, she remarried two additional times, to men named Cleophas and Salome. With each husband she bore a daughter, all three of whom were named Mary. Belief in Anne's three marriages, or the trinubium, fostered by circulation of the *Golden Legend,* became widespread in Europe.[3]

In the West, St. Anne rose to prominence in the late Middle Ages. Her cult reached its height between 1450 and 1550, according to the scholars Kathleen Ashley and Pamela Sheingorn, authors of an important study of St. Anne as European cultural symbol.[4] William A. Christian Jr.'s research on Iberian popular devotion confirms the importance of St. Anne's cult in sixteenth-century Spain. His analysis of King Philip II's *relaciones topográficas* of 1575–80 in New Castile, a printed census of Spanish towns that included questions on devotional practices, demonstrates that after the Virgin Mary, St. Anne was the most popular female saint in sixteenth-century Spain.[5] She was widely hailed as the patron of the childless, women in childbirth, as well as a universal intercessor capable of intervening during outbreaks of the plague or threatening weather. In 1584 Pope Gregory XIII mandated universal observance of St. Anne's July 26 feast day in the Roman Catholic Church. Clearly, the lack of canonical church writings on St. Anne did not discourage devotion to her figure.[6]

Early Modern Spanish and Mexican devotional writers explained the absence of Gospel references to St. Anne by suggesting that just like the Holy Grandmother's womb, which had held the secret treasure of the most pure Virgin, the Bible, too, contained hidden treasures.[7] These treasures were revealed by sermons, devotional texts, and images of the saint. Five different image types representing St. Anne enjoyed popularity in Spain, all of which were transferred to Mexico during the colonization. These were the Holy Kinship and the Holy Family, St. Anne Triplex, the Nativity of the Virgin Mary, depictions of Sts. Anne and Joachim together, and St. Anne teaching the Virgin Mary to read. Visual readings of these various images demonstrate that all thematize Anne's maternality, to use Julia Kristeva's term denoting idealized fantasies of motherhood.[8] Thus all focus on her roles as mother, grandmother, and matriarch, depicting scenes of pregnancy, birth, and maternity.

According to one interpretation, late medieval portrayals of the Holy Kinship valorized the women of Jesus' family.[9] The scene represents the numerous members of the extended Holy Family, including the Virgin and Child, St. Joseph, and St. Anne, as well as Mary's apocryphal sisters, their husbands, and six children. A print of the theme forms the frontispiece to one of the most influential premodern Spanish hagiographies of St. Anne, Juan de Robles' *La vida y excelencias y miraglos de santa Anna y de la gloriosa nuestra señora santa maria fasta la edad de quatorze años: muy deuota y contenplatiua nueuamente copilada* (Seville: Jacobo Cromberger, 1511). A painting by Hernando de Esturmio of 1549 in the parish church of Santa María de la O in Sanlúcar de Barrameda also depicts the subject.[10] Typically, the Virgin, Child, and St. Anne appear in the foreground on a throne attended by the other daughters and their children. Their various husbands, all rendered as diminutive forms in hieratic scale, cluster together in the background, peering over the throne. According to Sheingorn, proliferation of the Holy Kinship was linked to attempts to trace Jesus' genealogy through matrilineal descent as well as to the valorization of the matriarchal extended family in Europe.[11]

Depictions of St. Anne Triplex, or *selbsdritt,* as it is more commonly known in northern European art, consist of an oversized St. Anne holding her daughter, rendered in hieratic scale, upon her lap, the latter with the infant Jesus in her arms. Such images serve as a synecdoche, or shorthand notation, for the extended clan of the Holy Kinship. Examples by Spanish artists are numerous in the fourteenth, fifteenth, and the first half of the sixteenth centuries.[12] By using hieratic scale, in which the most important figure is rendered as the largest, artists glorified Anne as the Holy Family's matriarch and emphasized Jesus' matrilineal descent.[13]

Scenes of the Nativity of the Virgin, which depict Anne after giving birth, glorified the saint's position as the mother of Mary as they provided visual testimony to her traditional role as patron of women in pregnancy and childbirth. The subject appears frequently in sixteenth-century Spanish art. Examples include paintings by Fernando Yáñez de la Almedina (Valencia, cathedral, 1507–10) and Juan de Borgoña (Toledo, cathedral, 1509–11), among many others. In Borgoña's fresco, St. Anne reclines in bed, weary from the labor of childbirth. An attendant offers a bowl of food to the saint, perhaps the *caldo* or soup recommended by Spanish medical doctors to be fed to women after giving birth. Frequently, female attendants prepare to bathe or swaddle the newborn Mary. Artists often included St. Joachim as an onlooker. Comparison between Early Modern Spanish medical texts and depictions of the Nativity of the Virgin suggest that such images reflect actual postpartum practices. Indeed, an important Spanish medical text from 1580 employed a print of the Nativity of the Virgin as its frontispiece.[14]

The earliest images of the Holy Grandparents, Sts. Anne and Joachim, together, appear to have been by-products of the cult of the Immaculate Conception, which rose to importance in the twelfth century. Depictions of Anne and Joachim embracing in front of the Golden Gate of Jerusalem attempted to visualize Mary's miraculous conception. Examples of the scene are plentiful in sixteenth-century Spanish art and include paintings by Pedro Berruguete (Becerril de Campos [Palencia], Santa María), Fernando Yáñez de la Almedina (Valencia, cathedral, 1507), Juan de Borgoña (Toledo, cathedral), Antonio de Comontes (Toledo, Concepción Francisca), Juan Correa de Vivar (Toledo, Santa Isabel de los Reyes), Vicente Macip (Segorbe, cathedral, c. 1530), and others.[15] In the sixteenth century, artists cut down depictions of the Tree of Jesse to depict only Anne, Joachim, and Mary, a new image designed to give visual form to the Immaculate Conception.[16] Suzanne Stratton has identified the first such depiction, a stained glass window in Granada Cathedral from about 1528.

Although the theme of St. Anne teaching the Virgin to read appeared infrequently in Spanish sixteenth-century art, three notable examples date from the seventeenth century, by Juan de Roelas (Seville, Museo de Bellas Artes, 1610–15), Bartolomé Esteban Murillo (Madrid, Museo del Prado, c. 1650) (figure 1-1), and the sculptor Juan Martínez Montañés (Seville, Convento de Carmelitas de Santa Ana).[17] All three artists depicted the child Mary seated at her mother's knee, before an open book. In the 1700s the subject became popular on both sides of the Atlantic, perhaps as a result of the Spanish Enlightenment promotion of reading.[18]

Figure 1-1

Bartolomé Esteban Murillo, *St. Anne Teaching the Virgin Mary to Read,* circa 1650.
Museo del Prado, Madrid.

These various images, numerous religious texts, and the record of
popular devotional practices provide eloquent testimony to Anne's position of honor in sixteenth-century Spain. St. Anne's heyday in Spain,
however, was about to end. Church reformers' writings as well as the visual
record suggest that attempts to suppress her cult in Spain began shortly

after the Council of Trent (1545–63). The Spanish campaign to down-play St. Anne's cult is surprising, particularly since Pope Gregory XIII mandated universal observance of her feast day for the entire Roman Catholic Church in 1584. Because of the unauthorized, vernacular nature of Anne's cult, however, some delegates at the Council of Trent, the church council convened in response to the Protestant Reformation, as well as later Tridentine reformers, regarded popular enthusiasm for St. Anne with suspicion.[19]

The first image to disappear from Spanish artists' repertoires was the St. Anne Triplex. Although I have found no specific critiques of the image or instructions to artists to cease its depiction, one imagines that commissions for the type dwindled after the Council of Trent for a variety of reasons. Reformers' call for a new religious art—an art of clarity that placed a premium on the creation of reality effects—surely caused interest in the hieratic, abstract theme of St. Anne Triplex to decline. Concerted attempts by Spanish theologians to trace Jesus' genealogy through his foster father, St. Joseph, may have further discouraged patrons from commissioning images designed to pictorialize Jesus' female forbears.[20]

The disappearance of St. Anne Triplex, its trio of grandmother, mother, and son, a referent of the extended clan, heralded the decline in Spanish depictions of the Holy Kinship. By the seventeenth century, Spanish Holy Families had undergone a major metamorphosis. Artists produced fewer scenes of the Holy Family with the Virgin's parents, Sts. Anne and Joachim, and concurrently they focused on the nuclear family. St. Joseph began to dominate the scene.[21] Murillo's *Holy Family with a Little Bird* (Madrid, Museo del Prado, c. 1650) (figure 1-2) exemplifies the newly reconfigured patriarchal nuclear Holy Family. In Murillo's painting, the powerful figure of the young St. Joseph is the focal point as he keeps a vigilant eye on the divine toddler, at play with the family dog. The demure Virgin, the traditional focus of such scenes, looks on modestly from the left background, winding thread for spinning.

In fact, after the Council of Trent, Church reformers explicitly banned representations of the Holy Kinship because they included the apocryphal "sisters" of Mary from St. Anne's second and third marriages and urged artists to depict only the nuclear Holy Family. The censors fretted about the historical "authenticity" of these sisters, a typical concern after the Council of Trent, but also about Anne's three husbands.

Figure 1-2

Bartolomé Esteban Murillo, *Holy Family with a Little Bird*, circa 1650. Museo del Prado, Madrid.

Reformers were eager to quash the idea of the trinubium. At best these multiple marriages presented an unseemly view of the mother of the mother of God. At worst, they cast doubt on the sanctity of matrimony and its status as a sacrament, a major issue of debate with Protestants. Thus, the trinubium, deemed unorthodox, was stricken from hagiographies.[22] The Spanish artist, art theorist, and *veedor,* or inspector, for the Spanish Inquisition, Francisco Pacheco, addressed the problem explicitly in a section of his treatise *The Art of Painting* titled "A Painting of St. Anne No Longer in Use":

> At one time, the painting of the glorious St. Anne seated with the most holy Virgin and her Child in her arms and accompanied by her three husbands, her three daughters, and many grandchildren, as it is found in some old prints, was very valid, of which today the most learned do not approve and which the most judicious painters justly reject, because, as Tertulian said: "Time increases wisdom and uncovers truths in the Church." Thus, today we see favored as certain and secure truth the single marriage of St. Anne and St. Joachim.[23]

Pacheco also weighed in on the appropriate portrayal of the Nativity of the Virgin, comparing several sixteenth-century variations of the scene. The great detail provided by Pacheco suggests the popularity of the subject in sixteenth-century Spain as well as the variation in its depiction. In a 1568 print by Cornelius,

> one sees St. Anne in a large bed, with fluttering curtains, with a melancholy countenance; two servants seem to be in conversation behind the bed and three other women, who, on their knees, put the nude holy child in something like a wood tub, washing her, half of her body uncovered, and the other servant, to one side, warming a cloth; a child angel, on its knees, with another cloth in its hands; another angel standing with a little basket of clothes, and another, half kneeling, unfolding the swaddling cloth.[24]

Pacheco praised a depiction "in a little painted panel from the predella of an altarpiece in San Lorenzo" in Seville by Pedro de Campaña: "the saint is in the bed and she has next to her chest, wrapped in cloths, the most holy child; St. Joachim seated next to the bed, dressed as he typically is painted, with tunic and mantle, and two servants busy with the appropriate tasks: one plucking a hen and the other sweeping the room."[25] Pacheco could not resist offering his own version of the scene, focused on the presentation of the newborn to the proud St. Joachim:

> I would present this story in this manner: St. Anne in the bed, seated, propped up on some pillows, with veil and white garments in linen, covered with a little blanket; one servant who brings her a plate with something to eat; St. Joachim seated at the head of the bed and another old woman who shows him the child wrapped in her little blanket; and the old saint looking at his most beautiful daughter with happiness and admiration.

Most significantly, Pacheco cautioned artists to depict the newborn Mary clothed, not nude, since "if we avoid nudity in the Christ Child, so, too, in the Virgin, his Mother, with even more reason, for being a woman."

The only major Spanish artist to depict the scene in the seventeenth century was Murillo, in a canvas dated to 1660 (Madrid, Museo del Prado).[26] Instead of portraying the presentation of the newborn to St. Joachim, as suggested by Pacheco, Murillo relegated Joachim to the shadowy left background, where he comforts his exhausted wife. The canvas instead emphasizes the bathing and dressing of Mary in the foreground. Murillo took care to depict the newborn carefully covered in white blankets.

Images of the Holy Grandparents, Sts. Anne and Joachim, also decreased in frequency in the seventeenth century, as artists and theologians created new depictions of the Immaculate Conception. In 1568 the Counter-Reformation art reformer Johannes Molanus, in his *Treatise on Sacred Images,* refuted popular belief that the conception of Mary resulted from her parents' embrace. In 1677 Pope Innocent XI banned belief in the Golden Gate episode altogether, lest beholders link the physical embrace with Mary's Immaculate Conception.[27] Like representations of the embrace, scenes of Anne, Joachim, and Mary, visual shorthand for the Tree of Jesse, also disappeared from artists' repertories, replaced by new portrayals of the Immaculate Conception that represented Mary alone. Pacheco described the Church-approved version of the image, his own painting of it dating from 1619 serving as a visual primer for the complicated, abstract symbolism (Seville, Museo de Bellas Artes).[28]

Despite being "beloved and admired by the faithful," the theme of St. Anne teaching Mary to read had no basis in historical fact in Pacheco's estimation.[29] The art theorist and Inquisition official Juan Interián de Ayala concurred in his influential text of 1730, *The Christian and Erudite Painter, or Treatise of Errors Frequently Committed in Painting and Sculpting Sacred Images.* He condemned paintings of St. Anne teaching the Virgin to read as "very absurd," since they depicted Mary as a young girl of seven or eight. According to the official Church-approved version of Mary's life, her parents had presented her at the temple at age three. "How could any say or paint of the same Virgin at the age of eight, or even at five, that her venerable mother taught her to read?" he asked. Furthermore, it was "very difficult to believe that Mary learned her alphabet at the tender age of no more than three years of age."[30]

But was more than a notion of historical accuracy at stake here? Is it possible that in the minds of the adoring faithful, these images posited for St. Anne a role in human redemption, a role at odds with official church teachings? In fact, reading is associated with the Incarnation, the moment when the "word" that is Christ became flesh, according to the Gospel of John, and Mary was frequently shown reading in representations of the Annunciation. A seventeenth-century reading primer begins with the text of the "Ave María" ("Hail Mary"), the church's most important prayer to Mary, based on the archangel Gabriel's words at the Incarnation. Thus, by teaching Mary to read, St. Anne prepared her daughter for these momentous events. Furthermore, the teaching scene implied the Virgin Mary's reliance on her mother's guidance. Interián countered that "there is no lack of those who affirm that neither her mother, nor any other teacher, taught Mary her letters, but that she learned them from the Holy Spirit."[31] By giving St. Anne such an influential role in the life of Mary, images of her teaching her daughter to read also challenged early modern Spanish parenting norms. Spanish humanists and period Church writers advised fathers to take more active roles in their children's education.[32]

After reaching its apogee in the sixteenth century, the production of new St. Anne imagery declined significantly. In the wake of the Council of Trent, Spanish church reformers endeavored to clarify St. Anne's life in an attempt to control popular notions about the blessed matriarch. In the seventeenth century, representations of St. Anne Triplex disappeared completely, scenes of the Nativity of the Virgin became uncommon, and depictions of St. Anne teaching Mary to read were infrequent. In scenes of the Holy Family, St. Joseph, the object of energetic Church promotion after the Council of Trent, gradually replaced St. Anne as the Church forbade representation of the Holy Kinship. Indeed, the textual and visual evidence suggest a campaign to suppress popular devotion to St. Anne in seventeenth-century Spain.

This campaign appears unique to the Spanish Catholic Church. In France, for example, the medieval cult of St. Anne enjoyed a resurgence in the seventeenth century, as witness numerous images of the saint produced by French Baroque artists.[33] Furthermore, in addition to the papal declaration of universal observance of St. Anne's feast day in 1584, in 1621 Pope Gregory XV encouraged devotion to Anne due to her popular appeal. As is well known, however, the Spanish Church and monarchy (its king and queen hailed as "the Catholic monarchs") did not flinch from disregarding papal policy. In 1621 Italy was on the verge of the Catholic Restoration, the period of triumph that marked the end of the austerities of the Counter-Reformation. Spain, however, remained in the grip of Tridentine social and cultural control until the 1650s. Significantly, two of the most memorable and unique Spanish seventeenth-century images of St. Anne, Murillo's *St. Anne Teaching the Virgin Mary to Read* (Madrid, Museo del Prado) (figure 1-1) and his *Nativity of the Virgin* (Paris, Musée du Louvre), both postdate 1650.

The suppression of St. Anne's cult in early modern Spain also may have been linked to its focus on her maternality. The cult's surge in the late medieval period coincided with the rise to prominence of an unparalleled number of female saints' cults. Social historians such as David Herlihy and others have linked these cults to European women's increased power in the family and within society.[34] In contrast, the early modern era witnessed the promotion of a number of important male saints, as well as frequent attempts to contain and control European women. Historians have amply demonstrated these trends in sixteenth- and seventeenth-century Spain.[35]

In fact, Spanish Tridentine reformers enthusiastically promoted the cult of St. Joseph the humble carpenter, earthly spouse of the Madonna, and foster father of Jesus. In the seventeenth century, his figure quickly overshadowed that of St. Anne. St. Joseph assumed all of the functions previously assigned to the grandmother of Jesus. Like Anne, he became a universal saint, recipient of all manner of petitions. He took over Anne's previous patronage of woodworkers. Most incredibly, St. Joseph also appropriated St. Anne's role as patron of infertile women and even mothers in childbirth.[36] In place of Anne, the powerful thrice-married matriarch of the Virgin Mary's large extended family, the early modern Church favored St. Joseph, beneficent emblem of fatherly authority. The shift in emphasis from St. Anne to St. Joseph can be detected clearly in images of the Holy Family from sixteenth- and seventeenth-century Spain.

Mexico, however, was a different story. Although beholden to the same Inquisition pronouncements promoting St. Joseph and censoring the imagery of St. Anne, Mexican artists created numerous images of the "most holy grandmother." This despite the declaration of St. Joseph as sole patron of Mexico in 1555, with special jurisdiction over the conversion to Christianity, a role he retained until 1746, when the Virgin of Guadalupe was elevated as his copatroness.[37] Indeed, Mexican devotion to the Holy Grandparents seems to have been widespread. In 1716, a friar preaching in Mexico City claimed that St. Anne had cured "more than 500 infertile women with her intercession and prayer. . . ."[38] The same friar also reported that St. Anne had miraculously gilded a chalice in a church dedicated to her.[39]

Although artists on both sides of the Atlantic were beholden to the same Inquisition pronouncements, read many of the same religious texts, and received similar artistic influences, sacred imagery in colonial Mexico differed in important ways from that produced in the metropole. While much colonial Mexican religious art follows general developments in Spain, notable variations suggest an independent evolution in the Americas. Examination of these differences provides a more nuanced view of artistic production in the Spanish Empire. Such images may even reveal native responses to colonization. In the case of Holy Family imagery, the differences between Spanish and Mexican artworks are dramatic. Many Mexican Holy Family images continued to depict the extended family throughout the seventeenth and eighteenth centuries, and accorded special importance to Sts. Anne and Joachim. In some instances, colonial artists persisted in characterizing the Holy Family as matriarchal in nature by placing the women of the family in positions of prominence. In fact, only about half of extant colonial Mexican Holy Family depictions privilege St. Joseph as paterfamilias in the manner of Spanish representations.

The Holy Family as "los Cinco Señores," or "the five lords or masters," which depicts the nuclear Holy Family of Mary, Jesus, and Joseph joined by Jesus' maternal grandparents, Sts. Anne and Joachim, enjoyed particular popularity in colonial Mexico. On November 11, 1726, in Mexico City, a preacher claimed to give the first sermon on the subject, revealing that the inaugural celebration of the Cinco Señores had taken place in 1725.[40] At the 1783 dedication of a church named in their honor in Tehuaca, Mexico, a sermonist who likened the members of the Holy Family to powerful and sovereign lords disclosed that the Cinco Señores enjoyed their own feast day, on January 19.[41] Mexican devotion to the five lords or masters appears to have been quite vibrant in the colonial period.

Mexican Holy Family depictions frequently privileged St. Anne, in contrast to Spanish renditions. A late-sixteenth-century painting by Andrés de la Concha of the *Cinco Señores* (Mexico City, cathedral) (figure 1-3) valorizes the women of the Holy Family by enthroning them, relegating Sts. Joseph and Joachim to the margins. Simón Pereyns' seventeenth-century *Virgen del Perdón* places St. Anne in the foreground on equal footing with St. Joseph (formerly Mexico City, cathedral). In one of Cristóbal de Villalpando's paintings of the *Cinco Señores* (Toluca, Museo de Bellas Artes, late seventeenth century), the women of the Holy Family appear

Figure 1-3

Andrés de la Concha, *Holy Family as "los Cinco Señores,"* late sixteenth century.
Cathedral of Mexico City.

front and center. In a 1722 version of the theme by Nicolás Rodríguez Juárez, St. Anne, Christ, and Mary are elevated on clouds in the center, with Sts. Joachim and Joseph flanking (Querétaro, Museo Regional). Representations of the Double or Earthly Trinity, which in Spain focus closely on the patriarchal nuclear family of St. Joseph, Mary, and Jesus, in Mexico frequently include the Holy Grandparents, Anne and Joachim.

Mexican depictions of the St. Anne Triplex include several versions attributed to Diego de Pesquera as well as at least two additional anonymous sculptures (figure 1-4; and Puebla, Santa Mónica). In a panegyric preached in honor of St. Anne in Mexico City in 1735, the preacher Juan Manuel de Estrada made a daring declaration that seems to have found inspiration in the image of St. Anne Triplex. He asserted that the communion wafer, which according to the doctrine of transubstantiation is transformed into Christ's literal body and blood during Mass, also becomes St. Anne's body, by virtue of her role as Jesus' grandmother. He proclaimed:

Figure 1-4
Diego de Pesquera, St. Anne Triplex, late sixteenth century. Cuauhtinchán convent, Puebla, Mexico.

Mary, flesh and blood from the entrails of Anne, is the same flesh and blood of Christ. . . . I will say it more clearly: so that the glory of the treasure of Anne does not remain hidden. The flesh and blood of Mary is the same flesh and blood of Anne, as her daughter and the richest treasure of her very entrails. The flesh of Christ, that his Majesty offers us to torture, in this Eucharistic Bread . . . is the very flesh of Mary: . . . thus, the flesh of Anne is the Sacramental flesh itself of Christ in the Eucharist. . . . Christ's flesh came from Anne's flesh, through Mary: so that the flesh of Christ is the flesh of Anne: and it is the flesh that his Majesty gave us to eat for our health in the Eucharist.[42]

This bold suggestion, which I have not seen in Spanish devotional texts, renders explicit in words the idea at the heart of images of the Triplex that visualize generational descent from Anne to Mary to Jesus.

The Nativity of Mary appears frequently in Mexican colonial art, especially in the seventeenth century, and closely re-creates Pacheco's prescription for the scene. An example by Juan Correa (figure 1-5: Mexico City, Pinacoteca Virreinal de San Diego, seventeenth century) was particularly influential. In Correa's painting, Anne reclines in a canopied bed as a servant brings her a bowl of soup. The emphasis is on the presentation of the newborn Mary to her father, St. Joachim, who occupies a prominent position in the right foreground. While the iconography does not depart from Spanish norms, Correa did introduce a significant New World variation—he depicted people of color in the scene, most notably the female figure in the background presenting the soup bowl. Interestingly, Correa was Afro-Mexican, and his numerous religious paintings are distinguished by the inclusion of people of color, and in particular, ethnic *angelitos.*

Another seventeenth-century version of the Nativity of the Virgin, by an unidentified artist (Tepotzotlán, Viceregal Museum), similarly valorizes St. Joachim by focusing on the presentation of the newborn. Anne lies propped up on pillows in bed as a servant woman, again a person of color, brings her a plate of food. The figures of Anne and St. Joachim are slightly oversized, a vestigial reference to the hieratic scale employed in medieval depictions. The seventeenth-century painting *Nativity of the Virgin* by Juan Sánchez Salmerón, originally in Mexico City's cathedral but now part of the Viceregal Museum in Tepotzotlán, also reserves hieratic scale in its depiction of Anne and Joachim. It, too, gives visual form to Pacheco's prescription.[43] A weary St. Anne reclines in bed as a maidservant

Figure 1-5

Juan Correa, *Nativity of the Virgin Mary,* seventeenth century. Museo Nacional de Arte, Mexico City.

presents her with a bowl of soup. St. Joachim is seated prominently in the right foreground. In the center foreground two women, one young and one old, admire the infant. In an eighteenth-century rendition by Juan Rodríguez Juárez, which forms a companion piece to a scene of the Presentation of the Virgin in the Temple (Tepotzotlán, Viceregal Museum), three maidservants, including a woman of color, prepare Mary's cradle, as another brings a bowl of soup to St. Anne. A servant presents the newborn child to the proud Joachim.

By re-creating actual postpartum practices and including contemporary details such as household furnishings, depictions of the Nativity of Mary spoke to women in a direct manner that encouraged them to identify with Anne's pregnancy and parturition experiences. In contrast, according to the church, the Madonna experienced a supernatural, problem-free pregnancy and miraculous, painless delivery, after which she still remained virginally intact.[44] St. Anne faced the normal difficulties of pregnancy, which Mexican hagiographers attributed to the work of the devil. One writer described how, given her age and years of infertility, Anne doubted the reality of her pregnancy. At other times, "the devil troubled her with frights and fears, and with a thousand melancholy and mournful fantasies," emotional states with which any woman who has felt the powerful hormones of pregnancy can identify. When a hurricane struck Anne's house, she nearly miscarried, but her strength, constancy, patience, and faith helped her withstand these trials. Finally, after nine months, the "long and sad night" of her infertility came to an end: "she felt in her womb a movement equal and similar in all ways to that felt by all mothers when they deliver themselves of the weight that they have carried in their entrails."[45] Images of the Nativity of Mary, which depicted a happy but exhausted postpartum St. Anne, as well as devotional texts about her birth experience, assured women of the valor and worthiness of childbearing.

Whereas in seventeenth-century Spain the depiction of Mary alone encircled by symbols of her purity represented the abstract concept of the Immaculate Conception, in seventeenth-century Mexico several different image types visualized the theme. In addition to the standard scene of the Virgin surrounded by Immaculist emblems as described by Pacheco, Mexican artists also depicted Mary joined to her parents by lily branches. Examples by Juan Sánchez Salmerón and others can be cited (Tepotzotlán, Viceregal Museum). In paired images of Anne and Joachim alone the holy grandparents are represented with lilies emerging from their chests, a truncated reference to the Virgin of the Immaculate Conception, as in two seventeenth-century paintings by an unknown artist now in the Viceregal Museum in Tepotzotlán. In two eighteenth-century pendants, another unnamed artist inexplicably transformed the lily into a branch of greenery. Apparently, as time wore on, artists lost the knowledge that the lily branch functioned as a notational shorthand for the Immaculate Conception. So, too, have contemporary worshipers and art historians. The catalog of the Tepotzotlán collection identifies the foliage as a laurel branch, a symbol of peace.[46] Entire series of paintings dedicated to the Holy Grandparents can be found in colonial Mexican churches, including an altarpiece in San Juan Bautista in Coixtlahuaca, and in churches in the exconvento of Churubusco (formerly from La Piedad) in the Federal District, and San José in Puebla. These altarpieces amply demonstrate the intensity of Mexican devotion to the Holy Grandparents.

Several distinctive variants of St. Anne teaching the Virgin to read appear in Mexican art. An unusual scene attributed to Baltasar de Echave Ibía dates from the seventeenth century (Mexico City, Pinacoteca Virreinal de San Diego). It represents St. Anne as a large, towering figure, a vestigial reference to hieratic scale, leading her daughter through a landscape. Both figures carry books. In an eighteenth-century painting by Francisco Eduardo Tresguerras, St. Anne teaches her daughter to read from a parchment scroll inscribed with Isaiah 7:14, the prediction of the Annunciation (Mexico City, Pinacoteca Virreinal de San Diego). The typical Spanish composition, in which Mary sits at Anne's knee before an open book, also appears. A print of the subject forms illustrates Joseph Francisco Valdes' *Vida de la Gloriosísima Madre de la Madre de Dios, y Abuela de Jesuchristo Séñora Santa Ana* (Mexico City: Herederos de Don Felipe de Zúñiga y Ontiveros, 1794).

Close visual readings of Mexican colonial images of St. Anne point to significant differences between Spanish and Mexican artistic production and raise intriguing questions. Whereas it is clear that in Spain the campaign to promote St. Joseph precipitated a marked decline in production of St. Anne's imagery in the early modern period, this campaign produced mixed results in colonial Mexico. Why were images of the extended Holy Family, which by their very definition diminished St. Joseph's importance, as well as images of the Holy Family as matriarchal, so common in colonial Mexico? Why do nearly half of extant colonial Mexican Holy Family depictions seem to privilege the women of the Holy Family? Was the Spanish church less successful in promoting its vision of the patriarchal nuclear Holy Family in the American colonies? These questions are especially puzzling, since after 1555 New Spain boasted St. Joseph as its patron and protector. Since Inquisition recommendations for religious imagery were identical in both Spain and Mexico, why did Mexican colonial artists demonstrate such enthusiasm for depicting St. Anne?

My strategy in positing answers to these queries is intended to refute common wisdom about Mexican art that explains iconographic anomalies such as the retention of St. Anne's imagery as mere expressions of the retardataire, "medieval" qualities of Mexican colonial cultural production. Conventional wisdom suggests that the persistence of extended matriarchal family imagery is typical of the retardataire style and iconography of art in the Spanish colonies. Specialists in the field have long characterized Mexican colonial art as medieval in nature, and thus the continuance of an older iconographic type would not be surprising.[47] Others would view this trait as indicative of the lower quality of Mexican art as well as a lack of sophistication by Mexican patrons and artists.

New avenues of exploration beckon. The persistence of a variety of Holy Family types, in particular those that privilege the family's women, indicates that the Inquisition and the Catholic Church had less control over the production of religious art in the New World than in Spain. Preliminary research on Mexican colonial art suggests that this is a promising hypothesis that will benefit from additional investigation. A recent study of print production in New Spain revealed little Inquisition oversight of Mexican printmaking. Similarly, a study of the imagery of St. Philip of Jesus, the first Mexican-born saint and patron of Mexico City, found negligible Inquisition involvement in regulation of the visual arts.[48] The great variety of colonial Holy Family images and the persistence of types discouraged by the Spanish church and Inquisition further suggest that oversight of religious imagery was less zealous in Mexico than in Spain. Even without widespread direct intervention, though, the Inquisition still fostered an atmosphere that discouraged radical departure from Church-approved imagery.[49]

Two additional lines of inquiry merit exploration. First, a partial explanation may be found by examining the social history of the Mexican family. Authorities on saints' imagery have convincingly argued that Catholic religious art is often in tune with the social reality of the family.[50] Since saints' images are often intended as models of behavior in Catholic societies, careful analysis can expand understanding of daily life. A second explanation will then be examined, St. Anne's conflation with the Aztec goddess Toci by indigenous converts to Catholicism.

The preference for the extended matriarchal family in Mexican Holy Family images may be traceable to the influence of indigenous family structures. Precontact native families and gender roles therein differed substantially from the early modern Spanish norm of the patriarchal nuclear family. In some ways, native kinship groups more closely approximated medieval European ideals, since they were large and varied in composition, consisting of extended family plus other nonblood-related persons. The Náhuatl word for "family," *cemithualtin,* or "those of one patron," corresponds to the people who share a living space, not a particular kinship group.[51] Male and female gender roles within the family also departed significantly from Spanish standards. In contrast to the model of male authority and female submission promoted by the Spanish colonizers, native Mexican men's and women's roles have been described as complementary in nature. In other words, native women enjoyed special status in the domestic sphere.[52] According to Louise Burkhart, native women's power and status in the home worried Spanish missionary friars, who viewed the native household as "a potential locus of subversion and resistance."[53]

Compelling textual evidence indicates that native Mexicans also favored the cult of St. Anne because it allowed them to continue religious practices to a revered Aztec deity, Toci, or "Our Grandmother," matriarch of the indigenous pantheon. The Franciscan friar Bernardino de Sahagún reported in the 1580s that native neophytes conflated Santa Ana with Toci in the village of Santa Ana Chiautempan. In 1611 the Dominican friar Martín de León complained that native converts in Tlaxcala continued to worship Toci while feigning devotion to St. Anne. He explained that they came to the Church of Santa Ana to worship "a goddess they called Tocitzin, 'Our Grandmother,' and even today they say that they celebrate the fiesta of Toci, or that they're going to Toci's temple. . . ."[54]

Significantly, St. Anne assumes many of Toci's guises in Mexico. Both figures are associated with maternality. Like the Aztec earth god-

Figure 1-6

Elena Baca, *Portrait of My Grandmother*, 1994. Albuquerque, artist's collection.
Photograph by Deliah Montoya.

dess, Anne is the patroness of midwives, of women in pregnancy and those in childbirth. As Tlazolteotl, Toci is represented giving birth, bringing to mind the numerous representations of St. Anne in the Nativity of the Virgin Mary.[55] Significantly, the feast of Mary's Nativity, celebrated

September 8, overlaps with celebration of Toci's feast in the eighth month of Ochpaniztli, which began on August 24 and lasted until September 13. The numerous colonial Mexican images of the Nativity of Mary should be understood within the context of this conflation of St. Anne and Toci, perhaps explaining the theme's great popularity in the colonial era.

The visual and textual evidence thus indicates that there was a limit to the colonizers' success in imposing a Spanish family ideology on Mexico. Although the Spanish could split up indigenous households, forcing them to conform to the model of the patriarchal nuclear family, Mexicans continued to elevate grandparents and grandmothers in particular to positions of honor, as they had done for centuries. Despite concerted attempts to impose European family ideals, centuries of indigenous attitudes toward family did not disappear easily.[56] Even today, contemporary Mexican culture values the extended family and accords a special place of honor to its matriarchs. The cult of St. Anne thus expands our understanding of the historical record and may even document Mexican resistance to Spanish colonial authority.

Echoes of the historical devotion to St. Anne and Toci as well as the importance of the grandmother archetype in Mexican culture can still be detected today. In 1978, the California Chicana artist Yolanda López created a modern Feminist Triplex, a touching triple portrait of her grandmother, mother, and self, all in the guise of the Virgin of Guadalupe. In the 1990s, the Nuevo Mexicana artist Elena Baca executed a series of moving portraits of her grandmother, after whom she was named[57] (figure 1-6). These two artists, as well as others, speak eloquently of the importance of their grandmothers in their lives, poignant contemporary echoes of a centuries-old devotion.

NOTES

1. Pedro de Ribadeneira, *Flos Sanctorum, o Libro de las Vidas de los Santos,* I (Madrid: Luis Sanchez, 1616), 493–94, "XXVI. de Iulio. La vida de santa Ana, madre de la madre de Dios," 493: "La vienauenturada santa Ana, madre de nuestra Señora santa Maria, madre de nuestro Señor Christo. . . ." On the same page: "la mayor loa que se puede dar a santa Ana, es llamarla Madre de la Madre de Dios, y abuela de Iesu Christo. . . . Abuela del hijo de Dios." Juan Manuel de Estrada, *Oracion Panegyrica de la Gloriosa Señora Santa Anna* (Mexico City: Joseph Bernardo de Hogal, 1735), 1: "la Gloriosa Santa Anna, Madre de la Emperatriz de Cielo, y tierra MARIA Santisima Nuestra Señora, y Abuela de Christo Señor Nuestro. . . ." Similar praises of Anne can be found in Juan de Robles, *La vida y excelencias y miraglos de santa Anna y de la gloriosa nuestra señora santa maria fasta la edad de quatorze años: muy deuota y contenplatiua nueuamente copilada* (Seville: Jacobo Cromberger, 1511); Valentina Pinelo, *Libro de las Alabanças y Excelencias de la Gloriosa Santa Anna* (Seville: Clemente Hidalgo, 1601); Fray Francisco de Lizana, *Vida, Prerrogativas, y Excelencias de la Inclita Matrona*

Señora Santa Ana (Madrid: Ioseph Fernandez de Buendia, 1677); Joseph de Espinosa Sotomayor, *Sermon Panegyrico en Glorias de la Señora Santa Ana, Fiesta, que en el Convento de San Juan Baptista de Metepec, celebró el dia 26. de Julio de este año de 1716* (Mexico City: Herederos de la Viuda de Miguel de Ribera Calderon, 1716); and Joseph Francisco Valdes, *Vida de la Gloriosísima Madre de la Madre de Dios, y Abuela de Jesuchristo Séñora Santa Ana* (Mexico City: Herederos de Don Felipe de Zúñiga y Ontiveros, 1794).

2. Imelda de León, ed., *Calendario de Fiestas Populares* (Mexico City: Dirección General de Culturas Populares, 1987). St. Anne's feast day is currently observed in the following Mexican locales: Hidalgo del Parral, Chihuahua; Santa Ana, Delegación Coyoacán, D.F.; Santa Ana, Delegación Cuauhtémoc, D.F.; Barrio Santa Anita, Delegación Iztacalco, D.F.; Santa Ana Tlacotenco, Delegación Milpa Alta, D.F.; Tláhuac (Barrio Santa Ana), Delegación Tláhuac, D.F.; Nazas, Durango; Santa Ana Michi, México; Santa Anita (Barrio Onal), México; Dolores Hidalgo, Guanajuato; Mochitlán, Guerrero; Santa Ana Ahuehuepan, Hildalgo; Tianguistengo, Hidalgo; Acatlán, Jalisco; Sirosto (Viejo y Nuevo, Uruapan), Michoacán; Turicato, Michoacán; Zacapu, Michoacán; Tenango, Morelos; Santa Ana, Oaxaca; Santa Ana Ateixtlahuaca, Oaxaca; Santa Ana del Valle, Oaxaca; Santa Ana Tavela, Oaxaca; Santa Ana Yareni, Oaxaca; Querétaro, Querétaro; Aquismón, San Luis Potosí; Moctezuma, San Luis Potosí; Santa Ana, Sonora; Sánchez Magallanes, Tabasco; Santa Ana Chiautempan, Tlaxcala; Soconusco, Veracruz; Vega de Alatorre, Veracruz; and General Pánfilo Natera, Zacatecas.

3. For the history of the development of Anne's cult I have relied on Kathleen Ashley and Pamela Sheingorn, eds., *Interpreting Cultural Symbols: Saint Anne in Late Medieval Society* (Athens: University of Georgia Press, 1990), "Introduction," 6–68, and esp. 6–27; James Orr, ed., *New Testament Apocryphal Writings* (London: J. M. Dent & Sons and Philadelphia: J. B. Lippincott, 1923); and Jacobus de Voragine, *The Golden Legend: Readings on the Saints,* 2 vols., trans. William Granger Ryan (Princeton, N.J.: Princeton University Press, 1993).

4. Voragine, *The Golden Legend,* I, September 8, The Feast of the Nativity of the Virgin Mary, 49ff. On the *Golden Legend*'s diffusion, consult Ryan's introduction, xiii. Approximately a thousand manuscripts of the text are still in existence. After the 1450s, the text circulated even more widely in printed versions. According to Ryan, "It has been said that in the late Middle Ages the only book more widely read was the Bible." For a discussion of the proliferation and diffusion of the Golden Legend via sermons and other sources in the late Middle Ages see Ashley and Sheingorn, "Introduction," *Interpreting Cultural Symbols,* 17.

5. William A. Christian Jr., *Local Religion in Sixteenth-Century Spain* (Princeton, N.J.: Princeton University Press, 1981). On the printed questionaire see p. 3. For Spanish chapels dedicated to St. Anne, p. 72; shrines dedicated to St. Anne, p. 123; Anne's popularity in sixteenth-century Spain, p. 123; observance of her feast day, p. 238; Anne's intercession against disease, pp. 43 and 94, and plague, p. 55; Anne's status in Spanish culture, pp. 37–38; devotion and vows to Anne, pp. 52–53, 240, 67–68; a miraculous image of St. Anne, p. 76; and Anne's patronage of sterile women, p. 245. Also consult Christian's appendix A, "Text of Madrid Vow to Saint Anne and Saint Roch, 1597"; and appendix B, "District and Regional Shrines, 1575–1580, New Castile."

6. On Pope Gregory XII see Ribadeneira, *Flos Sanctorum, o Libro de las Vidas de los Santos,* 494.

7. Juan de Torres, *Sermon Panegyrico en Glorias de la Señora Santa Ana, Fiesta, que en el Convento de San Juan Baptista de Metepec, celebró el dia 26. de Julio de este año de 1716* (Mexico City: los Herederos de la Viuda de Miguel de Ribera Calderon, n.d. [1716?]), folios 1–2. See also Ribadeneira, *Flos Sanctorum,* 493, and Juan Interian de Ayala, *El pintor christiano, y erudito, ò tratado de los errors que suelen comoterse freqüentemente en pintar, y esculpir las Imágenes Sagradas,* trans. Luis de Durán y de Bastéro (Madrid: Joachín Ibarra, 1782; original edition, 1730), II, 322.

8. The term is elaborated in Julia Kristeva, "Stabat Mater," in *Tales of Love,* trans. Leon S. Roudiez (New York: Columbia University Press, 1987), 234–63.

9. Pamela Sheingorn, "Appropriating the Holy Kinship: Gender and Family History," in *Interpreting Cultural Symbols,* 169–98.

10. The painting and its commission have been discussed by Carmen Calderón Benjumea, *Iconografía de Santa Ana en Sevilla y Triana* (Seville: Arte Hispalense, 1990), 48.

11. Sheingorn, "Appropriating the Holy Kinship," 169–98.

12. Manuel Trens, *María: iconografía de la Virgen en el arte español* (Madrid: Plus-Ultra, 1946); Werner Esser, "Die Heilige Sippe: Studien zu einem spätmittelalterlichen Bildthema in Deutschland und den Niederlanden" (Ph.D. diss., Rheinische Friedrich-Wilhelms-Universität, Bonn, 1986); and Calderón Benjumea, *Iconografía de Santa Ana en Sevilla y Triana* (Seville: Arte Hispalense, 1990), 48.

13. On the late medieval emphasis on matrilineal descent in Jesus' genealogy see Sheingorn, "Appropriating the Holy Kinship," 169–98.

14. Luis Lobera de Avila, *El libro del regimen de la salud,* vol. V, Biblioteca clásica de la medicina española (Madrid: Julio Cosano, 1923; original edition, 1551), chapter 14; Juan Alonso y de los Ruyzes de

Fontecha, *Diez Previlegios para mugeres preñadas* (Alcalá de Henares: Luys Martynez Grande, 1606), chapters 7 and 8, folios 92ff., 126ff., 160–63. Louis Haas, *The Renaissance Man and His Children: Childbirth and Early Childhood in Florence 1300–1600* (New York: St. Martin's Press, 1998), chapter 3; and Jacqueline Marie Musacchio, *The Art and Ritual of Childbirth in Renaissance Italy* (New Haven, Conn.: Yale University Press, 1999). Francisco Núñez, *Libro del parto humano, en el cual se contienen remedios muy útiles y usuales para el parto dificultoso de las mujeres, con otros muchos secretas a ellas pertenecientes y a las enfermedades de los niños* (Alcalá de Henares: Imprenta Real, 1580). The frontispiece is reproduced and Núñez's medical career discussed in Juan Luis Morales, *El niño en la cultura española*, I (Madrid: T.P.A., 1960), 139–41.

15. Suzanne L. Stratton, *The Immaculate Conception in Spanish Art* (Cambridge: Cambridge University Press, 1994), 20–28; and Calderón Benjumea, *Iconografía de Santa Ana en Sevilla y Triana,* 25–29.

16. Stratton, *The Immaculate Conception in Spanish Art,* 18–20.

17. According to Émile Mâle, images of St. Anne teaching the Virgin to read first appeared in European art in the fourteenth century. See Mâle, *L'art religieux de la fin du XVIe siècle, du XVIIe siècle et du XVIIIe siècle* (Paris: Armand Colin, 1951), 350. Spanish depictions of the subject seem to first appear in the sixteenth century, according to Calderón Benjumea, *Iconografía de Santa Ana en Sevilla y Triana,* 93. Two can be found in Seville and its environs: a sculptural relief on the tomb of Cardinal Hurtado de Mendoza carved by Domenico Fancelli Settignano in 1508–10 (cathedral, Seville), and an anonymous sculpture from the later sixteenth century in the Church of the Immaculate Conception in Villaverde del Río.

18. Calderón Benjumea, *Iconografía de Santa Ana en Sevilla y Triana,* 53.

19. See the discussion of the Council of Trent's stance on St. Anne in Sheingorn and Ashley, "Introduction," *Interpreting Cultural Symbols,* 43 and 47.

20. Discussed in my dissertation "Saints and Social Welfare in Golden Age Spain: The Imagery of the Cult of St. Joseph" (Ph.D. diss., University of Michigan, 1995), chapter 2, and in my book manuscript.

21. Two Castillian versions, by Juan Sánchez Cotán (Madrid, Carmelitas, before 1627) and Vicente Carducho (Madrid, Museo del Prado, 1631), give prominence to St. Anne at the expense of Joseph, who appears on the sidelines. Two Sevillian works by Antonio Mohedano (Seville, Museo de Bellas Artes, c. 1605) and a follower of Murillo equalize Anne and Joseph by placing them in the foreground adoring the Christ Child (Madrid, MacCrohon Collection). Other permutations of the extended family occur so infrequently as to make them unique. In canvases by El Greco and his follower Luis Tristán, the Holy Family appears with St. Anne (Toledo, Hospital de Tavera, c. 1590–95; and Seville, Lupiáñez Collection). In other paintings, El Greco includes St. John the Baptist in addition to St. Anne (Washington, National Gallery, c. 1595–1600; and Madrid, Museo del Prado, c. 1595–1600). In two Sevillian examples by Juan de Roelas and Zurbarán, the Holy Family appears with the Virgin's parents and the Baptist (Las Palmas, cathedral, 1607; and Madrid, Marquis of Perinat, c. 1625–30). In a single painting by Vicente Carducho, these figures are joined by St. Elizabeth (London, private collection).

22. On the depiction of the Holy Kinship in religious art see Johannes Molanus, *De Historia SS. Imaginvm et Pictvrarvm, Provero Earvm Vsv contra abusus* (Louvain: Lawrence Durand, 1619; first edition, 1568), chapter 28; *De Historia SS. Imaginum et Picturarum pro vero earum uso contra abusas/Traité des saintes images,* 2 vols., intro., trans., ed. François Bœspflug, Olivier Christin, and Benoît Tassel (Paris: Cerf, 1996), chapter 28.

23. Francisco Pacheco, *El arte de la pintura,* ed. Bonaventura Bassegoda i Hugas (Madrid: Cátedra, 1990), 580: "Pintura no usada de Santa Ana: En un tiempo, estuvo muy válida la pintura de la gloriosa Santa Ana asentada, con la santísima Virgen y su Hijo, en brazos y acompañada de tres maridos, de tres hijas y de muchos nietos, como en algunas estampas antiguas se halla; lo cual hoy no aprueban los más doctos y lo deben escusar, justamente, los pintores cuerdos; porque, como dixo, con razón, Tertuliano: "El tiempo aumenta la sabiduría y descubre las verdades en la Iglesia." Así, vemos hoy favorecido el único matrimonio de Santa Ana y San Joachín como verdad cierta y segura. . . ." Interián también rejected the trinubium (*El pintor christiano y erudito,* II, 322–23), as did Molanus (*De Historia SS. Imaginvm et Pictvrarvm,* chapter 28).

24. Pacheco, *El arte de la pintura,* 578–80: ". . . se ve Santa Ana en una bizarra cama, con las cortinas alzadas, con semblante melancólico; parecen dos criadas razonando detrás de la cama y otras tres mujeres que, puestas de rodillas, en una como tina de madera tienen la santa Niña desnuda, lavándola, descubierto el medio cuerpo, y otra criada, a un lado, calentando un paño; un ángel niño, de rodillas, con otro en as manos; otro en pie, con una canastica de ropa y otro, medio de rodillas, desenvolviendo una faxa. . . . Mase Pedro Campaña en un tablerito pintado, de un banco de retablo en San Lorenzo desta Ciudad: la Santa está en la cama y tiene junto a sus pechos, envuelta en paños, la santísima Niña; San Joachín sentado junto a la cama, vestido como se suele pintar, con túnica y manto y dos criadas ocupadas en los menesteres convenientes: una pelando una gallina y otra barriendo el aposento."

On p. 580: "Yo dispusiera esta historia desta manera: Santa Ana en la cama, sentada, arrimada a las almohadas, con tocas y ropas blancas de lienzo, abrigada con una mantellina; una criada que le lleva en un plato algo de comer; San Joachín sentado a la cabecera y otra mujer anciana que le muestra la niña envuelta en sus mantillas; y el Santo viejo mirando su bellísima hija con alegría y admiración. Advirtiendo, con esto, se huya, en todo caso, de pintar a Nuestra Señora desnuda (como hacen los más). Y esto es lo que dixe al principio que tenía que advertir en esta pintura; y si la escusamos en el Niño Jesús, en la Virgen, su Madre, con más razón, por ser mujer."

25. Campaña's painting has been identified by Calderón Benjumea as the one on the high altar of the parish of Santa Ana in Triana (Seville), *Iconografía de Santa Ana en Sevilla y Triana,* 36.

26. On the date and commission of the picture see Jonathan Brown, *Painting in Spain, 1500–1700,* Pelican History of Art (New Haven, Conn.: Yale University Press, 1998), 206.

27. Stratton, *The Immaculate Conception in Spanish Art,* 28.

28. Pacheco, *El arte de la pintura,* 656–58.

29. Pacheco, *El arte de la pintura,* 582 ("querida y admirada por los fieles").

30. Interián, *El pintor christiano y erudito,* II, 323: ". . . ser muy absurda la Pintura en que suelen representar á la Virgen de edad de siete, ú ocho años, junto á Santa Ana su Madre, quien en un libro que trae en sus manos, le enseña á deletrear, y los primeros rudimentos de las letras: lo qual en nngun modo es conforme á lo que se dice ya con unánime consentimiento, y parece confirmarlo la Iglesia con su dictamen sobre la Presentacion de nuestra Señora en el Templo. Pues afirmándose, que dicha Presentacion se hizo quando la Virgen tenia solos tres años ¿cómo podrá decirse, ó pintarse, el que á la misma Virgen, quando de edad de ocho, ó aun de cinco años, le enseñase á leer su venerable madre, siendo muy dificil de creér, que aprendiese las letras en la tierna edad de no mas de tres años?" Lizana, *Vida, Prerrogativas, y Excelencias de la Inclita Matrona Señora Santa Ana,* chapter XI.

31. Interián, *El pintor christiano y erudito,* II, 323.

32. Discussed in the following: Black, "Saints and Social Welfare in Golden Age Spain," chapter 4 (and in my book manuscript); Emilie Bergmann, "The Exclusion of the Feminine in the Cultural Discourse of the Golden Age: Juan Luis Vives and Fray Luis de León," in Alain Saint-Saëns, ed., *Religion, Body and Gender in Early Modern Spain* (San Francisco: Mellen Research University Press, 1991), 123–36; and Juan Luis Vives, *Instrucción de la mujer cristiana* (Buenos Aires: Espasa-Calpe, 1943).

33. Mâle, *L'art religieux de la fin du XVIe siècle, du XVIIe siècle et du XVIIIe siècle,* 346–53.

34. David Herlihy, "The Family and Religious Ideologies in Medieval Europe," in Tamara Hareven and Andrejs Plakans, *Family History at the Crossroads* (Princeton, N.J.: Princeton University Press, 1987), 3–17. Herlihy and others have convincingly argued that medieval hagiographies and religious images "respond" to the realities of households of the times. He writes (p. 14): "The history of medieval religion is thus intimately connected with the history of the family." Discussing familial images of saints' lives, he maintains (p. 13): "These familial images would have been totally ineffective, had they not reflected authentic domestic experiences and emotions." The overlap between lives of the saints and lives of real people is one of the major themes of Donald Weinstein and Rudolph M. Bell, *Saints and Society: The Two Worlds of Western Christendom, 1000–1700* (Chicago: University of Chicago Press, 1982), part 1. In the words of another scholar, "The function of religious paintings in conditioning religious and social attitudes cannot be overestimated." See Margaret Miles, "The Virgin's One Bare Breast: Nudity, Gender, and Religious Meaning in Tuscan Early Renaissance Culture," 32, in *The Expanding Discourse: Feminism and Art History,* ed. Norma Broude and Mary D. Garrard (New York: HarperCollins, 1992), 27–37. Recent postmodern theorizing has arrived at similar conclusions: Edith Wyschogrod, *Saints and Post-modernism: Revisioning Moral Philosophy* (Chicago: University of Chicago Press, 1990), esp. 25–30. According to Wyschogrod, although all hagiographies are constructions (even when they purport to record the life of a "real," documentable person), they must contain enough elements of facticity to make them believable to period readers.

35. See, for example, Mary Elizabeth Perry, *Gender and Disorder in Early Modern Seville* (Princeton, N.J.: Princeton University Press, 1990).

36. On St. Joseph see "Saints and Social Welfare," chapter 2; and Charlene Villaseñor Black, "Love and Marriage in the Spanish Empire: Depictions of Holy Matrimony and Gender Discourses in the Seventeenth Century," *The Sixteenth Century Journal,* 32 (2001): 637–67. On St. Anne's universality see the reference to Christian, *Local Religion,* in n. 5. For St. Anne's association with woodworking see Sautman, "Saint Anne in Folk Tradition," in *Interpreting Cultural Symbols,* 69–94.

37. Consult the following: *Concilio III Provincial Mexicano, celebrado en México el año 1585, confirmado en Roma por el Papa Sixto V, y mandado observar por el gobierno español en diversas reales órdenes,* 2nd ed., in Latin and Spanish (Barcelona: Manuel Miró y D. Marsá, 1870), 151, n. 2; Hermengildo Ramírez, M. J., "San José en la evangelización de América Latina," *Estudios josefinos* 45 (1991): 613–15; and José Carlos Carrillo Ojeda, M. J., "San José en la Nueva España del siglo XVII," *Presencia de San José en el siglo XVII. Actas del Cuarto Simposión Internacional (Kalisz, 22–29 septiembre, 1985)* in *Estudios josefinos* 41: 81–82

(1987): 631–32, 639–40. The elevation of the Virgin of Guadalupe as co-patroness with St. Joseph is detailed in Cayetano de Cabrera y Quintero, *Escudo de Armas de Mexico: Celestial Proteccion de esta Nobilissima Ciudad, de la Nueva-España, y de casi todo el Nuevo Mundo, Maria Santissima, en su Protentosa Imagen del Mexicano Guadalupe, Milagrosamente Apparecida en el Palacio Arzobispal el Año de 1531* (Mexico City: Viuda de Joseph Bernardo de Hogal, 1746).

38. Torres, *Sermon Panegyrico en Glorias de la Señora Santa Ana,* 2: "hizo fecundas mas de quinientas mugeres esteriles con su intercession, y ruego . . ."

39. Torres, *Sermon Panegyrico en Glorias de la Señora Santa Ana,* 2: "Digalo la Venerable Ana de San Augustin, que labrò Iglesia â Santa Ana con dineros, que por varias manos de almas devotas, le remitiò la Santa para la obra; y ya completa, deseaba vn Caliz para su fiesta, y aunque lo hallò curioso, pero no dorado; mas viendolo tan lindo, exclamò â Santa Ana con estas vozes: O Santa mia, quien tuviera dineros para dorar este Caliz para vuestra fiesta! Apareciosele Santa Ana, y poniendole en las manos vnos doblones de oro, quedó el Caliz curiosamente dorado."

40. Nicolas de Jesus María, *La Mano de los Cinco Señores Jesus, Maria, y Joseph, Joachin, y Anna. Panegirico de Sus Patrocinios, Predicado en la Dominica de èl, de N. Señor à 11. de Noviembre de 1725. en el Convento de Carmelitas Descalzos de S. Sebastian de Mexico* (Mexico City: los Herederos de la Viuda de Miguel de Rivera, 1726), dedicatoria and parecer (unpaginated).

41. Juan Anselmo del Moral y Castillo de Altra, *Sermon, que con Motivo de la Dedicacion, y estrenas de la Iglesia del Convento de Carmelitas Descalzos de la Ciudad de Tehuaca: En el dia, que el mismo Religiosisimo Convento Celebra la fiesta de los Cinco Señores, sus patronos, y Titulares de la dicha Iglesia, Predicó en ella, (el 19 de enero de 1783)* (1783; reprint, Puebla: Pedro de la Rosa, 1792), unpaginated dedicatoria: "la Sagrada Familia de Jesus, Maria, Joseph, Joaquin, y Ana; Poderosos Señores; Soberanos Señores . . ." Also see p. 7.

42. Estrada, *Oracion Panegyrico de la Gloriosa Señora Santa Anna,* 6: "MARIA carne, y sangre de las entrañas de Anna, es la misma carne, y sangre de Christo . . ." On p. 7: Dirélo mas claro: porque no se quede la gloria de el tesoro de Anna escondida. Es la carne, y sangre de MARIA, de la misma carne, y sangre de Anna, como Hija, y tesoro, que es, el mas rico, de sus entrañas mismas. La carne de Christo, que su Magestad nos offrece por majar, en este Pan Eucharistico: . . . es la carne misma de MARIA: . . . Luego la carne de Anna es la propria Sacramentada de Christo en la Eucharistia, que su Magestad Sacrosanta nos franquea por manjar en essa Mesa Sagrada de el Altar. . . . Tomó Christo carne de la carne de Anna, mediante MARIA: con que la carne de Christo es carne de Anna: y esta es la carne, que su Magestad nos dió á comer para nuestra salud en la Eucharistia."

43. *Pintura Novohispana. Museo Nacion del Virreinato, Tepotzotlán,* I (Tepotzotlán: Asociación de Amigos del Museo Nacional del Virreinato; and Americo Arte, 1992), 72.

44. Marina Warner has written the definitive study of Mary as mother in *Alone of All Her Sex: The Myth and the Cult of the Virgin Mary* (New York: Alfred A. Knopf, 1976), chapter 3. Also consult Juan de las Roelas, *Hermosura Corporal, de la Madre de Dios* (Seville: Diego Perez, 1621), folios 135ff. According to one sermonist, in contrast to normal women, forced to endure nine months of suffering, misery, and unhappiness during pregnancy as punishment for the fall in the Garden of Eden, Mary enjoyed a blessed and happy pregnancy. See Juan de Luna, "En la Fiesta de Nvestra Señora de las Nieues," in *Adviento, Natividad, Circvncision, y Epiphania de Nvestro Redentor. Con todas las Fiestas de nuestra Señora, y su Esposo San Ioseph* (Madrid: Juan de la Cuesta, 1608), 282: "pues que es lo que a todas las mugeres haze miserables, y infelices? el auer de traer nueue meses en su vientre con gran trabajo y molestia sus hijos, que esta fue la graue pena entre otras, que Dios le dio, por auerle ofendido . . . traeras essa carga pesada del hijo, y congojas nueue meses, porque como explican algunos sobre este lugar, sino pecara Eua, en formandose, y animandose la criatura, luego la pariera, y echara de si aquella pessadissima carga, que la hazia infeliz y miserable: esto pues que para las demas mugeres fue castigo, y miseria, que es traer tanto el niño en el vientre, para la madre del diuino Verbo Encarnado fue bienauenturança: y assi como a las demas esta grauedad hizo su vientre miserable, a sola la madre de Dios este traer su Hijo nueue meses en el vientre hizo su vientre bienauenturado. . . ." Not only was Mary's womb spared the discomforts and pain of pregnancy and childbirth, her breasts, too, avoided normal wear and tear. Although lactation deprived regular women's breasts of strength and substance, in the sermonist's estimation, Mary's miraculous milk, "milk from heaven," spared hers. In contrast to the "unhappy breasts" of other women, Mary's were fortunate and blessed. On p. 282: "lo mismo digo de los pechos, que dando leche se desustancian, mas los de Maria no, porque la leche fue milagrosa . . . leche del cielo . . . y ansi los de las demas mugeres infelices pechos, los de Maria dichosos, y bienauenturados y mas llamase el vientre desta Señora bienauenturado, porque trajo a Dios en el."

45. Valdes, *Vida de la Gloriosísima Madre de la Madre de Dios, y Abuela de Jesuchristo Séñora Santa Ana,* 127: "A este fin la tentaba con vanas desconfianzas sobre la realidad de su preñez, trayéndole á la memoria su avanzada edad, y la larga experiencia de tantos años que la certificaba de su esterilidad. . . ." On p. 128: "Otras veces la incomodaba con espantos, con sobresaltos, y con mil imaginaciones melancólicas y funestas, ordenadas todas á saltearle la voluntad y traerla á algun despacho, ó afecto desconcertado; pero resistia

fuertement la valerosa Matrona Ana todas estas diabólicas estratagemas. . . ." The tale of the hurricane is recounted on p. 131. On p. 202: "la noche larga y triste de tu esterilidad." On pp. 133–34: "sintió en su vientre un movimiento igual y semejante en todo al que sienten todas las Madres quando se descargan del peso que han traido en sus entrañas."

46. *Pintura Novohispana,* 123. My assessment that contemporary worshipers no longer know the original meaning of the lily stems in these images is based on informal questioning of worshipers in various Mexican churches.

47. Santiago Sebastián, Mariano Monterrosa, and José Antonio Terán, *Iconografía del arte del siglo XVI en México* (Zacatecas: Universidad Autónoma de Zacatecas, 1995), 11: "Como vamos a ver, en el México virreinal repercutieron las tradiciones medievales durante el siglo XVI. . . ."

48. Kelly Donahue-Wallace, "Prints and Printmakers in Viceregal Mexico City, 1600–1800" (Ph.D. diss., University of New Mexico, 2000); and Brendan R. Branley, "Felipe de Jesús: Images and Devotions" (M.A. thesis, University of New Mexico, 2000).

49. This interpretation has been inspired by Michel Foucault's discussion of the panopticon in *Discipline and Punish: The Birth of the Prison,* trans. Alan Sheridan (New York: Vintage/Random House, 1995; translation of original French edition of 1975).

50. Cf. n. 37.

51. See Louse M. Burkhart, "Mexican Women on the Home Front: Housework and Religion in Aztec Mexico," in *Indian Women of Early Mexico,* ed. Susan Schroeder, Stephanie Wood, and Robert Hackett (Norman: University of Oklahoma Press, 1997), 29.

52. Information on native family structures and gender roles is drawn from Schroeder, Wood, and Hackett, eds., *Indian Women of Early Mexico;* and in particular Burkhart, "Mexican Women on the Home Front," 25–54; Susan Kellogg, "From Parallel and Equivalent to Separate but Unequal: Tenochca Mexica Women, 1500–1700," 123–43, and Lisa Mary Sousa, "Women and Crime in Colonial Oaxaca: Evidence of Complementary Gender Roles in Mixtec and Zapotec Societies," 199–214; as well as Susan Kellogg, *Law and the Transformation of Aztec Culture, 1500–1700* (Norman: University of Oklahoma Press, 1995).

53. Burkhart, "Mexican Women on the Home Front," 52.

54. Fray Bernardino de Sahagún, *Historia general de las cosas de Nueva España,* III, ed. Angel María Garibay (Mexico City: Porrúa, 1981), 352–53. Fray Martin's report probably was based on Sahagún's text. Fray Martin de Leon, *Camino del Cielo en Lengua mexicana, con todos los requisitos necessarios para conseguir este fin, con todo lo que vn Christiano deue creer, saber, y obrar, desde el punto que tiene vso de razon, hasta que muerte* (Mexico City: Diego Lopez daualos, 1611), 96: ". . . la de Tlaxcalan Yglesia de Santa Ana por vna diosa que llamauan Tocitzin nuestra aguela, y oy en dia dizen que hazen fiesta à toci, ò van al templo de toci."

55. All information on Toci is drawn from the definitive study by Thelma D. Sullivan, "Tlazolteotl-Ixcuina: The Great Spinner and Weaver," in *The Art and Iconography of Late Postclassic Central Mexico,* ed. Elizabeth Hill Boone (Washington, D.C.: Dumbarton Oaks, 1982), 7–35.

56. According to Kellogg, in Mexico City, the Spanish colonizers eventually attained success in their campaign to Hispanize native family structures. By 1600, complementary gender roles and the extended kinship network, both of which increased women's standing in pre-Hispanic Mexico, had been replaced by the patriarchal, authoritative family of Spain. Native women's status continued to decline dramatically throughout the colonial period.

57. Discussed in my article "Sacred Cults, Subversive Icons: Chicanas and the Pictorial Language of Catholicism" in *Speaking Chicana: Voice, Power, and Identity,* ed. D. Letticia Galindo and María Dolores Gonzales (Tucson: University of Arizona Press, 1999), 134–74.

2

Querying the Spirit:
The Rules of the Haitian *Lwa*

JOAN DAYAN

He can be reached only through his body, and hence, in cases not capital, whipping is the only punishment which can be inflicted.

—Thomas Cobb, *An Inquiry into the Law of Negro Slavery in the United States of America*

He proves himself no specter, for he is visible in his flesh. Take away what he claims as proper to the nature of his body; will not a new definition of body then have to be coined?

—John Calvin, *Institutes of the Christian Religion*

In places that established slavery as an institution fundamental to the rights and identities of those who were not slaves, a unique blend of Cartesian doubt and sacred spirituality came into play. Throughout the Americas, under pressure of punishment without limits, the concept of personhood could be eliminated for the enslaved who lived in and through the body. In respect to civil rights and relations, slaves were not persons but things. Creatures of law, they were nonetheless dead to the law. What is this species of embodied property? On one hand, slaves had to be kept in their proper place as civil nonentities, gaining a legal will only to be punished when committing a crime. On the other, they were deemed, when it served the needs of their owners, as special properties that engendered sentiments of friendship, affection, and even esteem.

What kind of being is created by law when that entity is a slave? Worked at from the outside in: What kind of external world can exist for an object of law? Is lacking the ability to perform a civil act, to count in terms of civil rights and relations, something like losing a soul and keeping only a body, with or without limbs, as the law sees fit? I begin with these questions in order to deal closely with what is supposed to lie outside legal science. Outside the conceptual beliefs of Western legal faith stand the stubborn feet of spirits, the gods of those deemed primitive nondescripts. The *lwa* (Haitian spirits) did not inhabit a transcendent realm, nor were they "supernatural" in the usual sense of the term. Rather, the experience of serving the gods *(sevis lwa)* remained concrete. The *lwa* came into being through details and fragments, through the very things that might seem to hinder belief. Besides recalling Africa, these gods responded to the institution of slavery and to its peculiar brand of sensuous domination. A "historical streak" in these spirits reconstituted the shadowy gods of Africa as the daily, sometimes banal confrontations with the arbitrary power of the law.[1]

Vodou practice both absorbed and transformed the main ingredients of systemic deprivation, whether the curse of blood or the lure of property. Ghosts, creatures of the night, and other spirits, alternately embodied and disembodied, skinned or colored, articulated a genealogy of servitude. Moreover, what those in power called "sorcery" became an alternative history, a questioning turn by those deemed unable to think. The gods thus survived not as vestigial remnants but as bodies that held forth the promise of spirit, undoing and suspending the double categories of persons and property. For the *lwa* existed only because of matter, through the bodies of those they "mounted" or "possessed"; and in this extended, if somewhat archaic confrontation, these spirits turned their human vessels into embodiments of history.

Yet other bodies were also "possessed" by the transformative potential of the *lwa*—not only the living practitioners but the remote images of the Christian saints, frozen in time and reproduced in Catholic chromolithographs. In the transmission, as local spirits enter into the received figures of the saints, they affirm a broken but obstinate communion between past and present, colonizer and colonized. This identification between invisible spirits and the physical fact of the saints thus replaces a phantom ideal of the sacred with the empirical, verifiable body. That the subversive appropriation takes place between gods held in the mind and saints pictured on paper reveals how vodou's reenactment of history is also a reinvention of the sacred.

LAW'S MEMORY

That which was legally possible or impossible demanded the give-and-take between categories such as public or private, thing or self, physical or incorporeal. What laws became necessary for those who became masters and slaves? Once reduced to a special kind of property, slaves in the English colonies were to be governed as persons with wills of their own but fixed in their status as legal property, not an inferior kind of subject, as with the Spaniards. In French and Spanish law the slaves' subjectivity became central to the belief in conversion, to the promise that the soul of the enslaved remained free and unharmed, no matter the excesses committed on the body. British colonial law, rooted as it was in the rights of private property and privilege at common law, arguably resulted in harsher treatment of slaves.[2]

I take the 1685 *Code Noir,* or *Edict Regarding the Government and the Administration of the French Islands of America, and the Discipline and the Commerce of Blacks and Slaves in the Said Countries* and its double story as an exemplum for the transubstantiation of blood and gore into the seamless logic of law. One story created a servile body, destitute and incapable; the second summoned the brutalized but perfectible body. The redemptive boon was offered along with judicial destitution. The Code Noir granted official recognition to the slavery that had functioned for half a century without the king's seal. Though Jean-Baptiste Colbert, minister to Louis XIV, the Sun King, was influenced to some extent by the concepts of Roman canon law, he based most of the code on existing local slave laws and what he gleaned from consultations with French colonial authorities.[3]

Deprivation and exclusion form the basis of the code. Excessive rigor and excessive kindness work together to reduce what is most "human" about the slave. Though the master is obliged to feed, house, and clothe his slaves, the prohibitive measures of the code, through a series of exceptions and qualifications, permit brutality and the despotism necessary to enforce it. The power to exceed "humane" limits is implicit in these supposed regulations, as if one could qualify how much of the body can be mutilated, how much can be removed and still leave something that can be recognized as human. Quartering, hanging, burning alive, and other kinds of mutilation and torture were left to the courts. Methodical dispossession put forth as cautious care became the basis for the literal divestment necessary to turn humans into things.

The discourse on property contained in later articles gives us, though strategically delayed, the ground that supports all the other rules. "We declare slaves to be chattel and as such do they enter into the community having no consequence other than that of something mortgaged; they are to be equally divided by co-heirs, without preference to birth-right, nor shall they be subject to customary jointure, nor to feudal and lineal redemption. . . ." (article 44).[4] As chattels, things personal and movable, mere merchandise or perishables in the market, these bodies lose all familial ties in becoming property. An idea of redemption by lineage evolved and turned the rule of descent into the transfer of pigmentation, which fleshed out in law the terms necessary to maintain the curse of color. Emphasis on blood as conduit for the stain of black ancestry became more necessary as bodies of color began to merge, to lose the biological trait of blackness. The supremacy of whiteness now depended on a fiction threatened by what one could not always see but must fear: the black blood that would not only pollute progeny, but infect the very heart of the nation as well.

The fiction of civil death depends on the belief that so powerful are the rules of civilization and the prescripts of law that one can be dead when alive. Law can make one dead-in-life, and even determine when and if one is to be resurrected. Before slavery in the Americas and the codes that depended on the stain of black blood for the biological ignominy that stigmatized persons and justified their status as property, there had already existed a grid for producing noncitizens outside the bounds of civil society. How did civil death affect rights of property and privilege at common law? There were three principal incidents consequent upon an attainder for treason or felony: forfeiture, corruption of blood, and the extinction of civil rights, more or less complete. Of Saxon origin, forfeiture was part of the crime by which the goods and chattels, lands and tenements of the attainted felon were forfeited. According to the doctrine of corruption of blood, introduced after the Norman Conquest in 1066, the blood of the attainted person was held to be corrupt, so that he could not transmit his estate to his heirs, nor could they inherit.[5] According to William Blackstone in his *Commentaries on the Laws of England (1765–69)*, this inequitable and "peculiar hardship" meant that the "channel" of "hereditary blood" would not only be "exhausted for the present, but totally damned up and rendered impervious for the future."[6]

Unnatural or artificial death entailed a logic of alienation that could extend perpetually along constructed lines of racial kinship. Blackstone referred to natural liberty as "residuum," and he figured this residue of nature, the savage essence that must be ferreted out, as a stain. For the figurative distinction of civil and natural to function in the realm of action, the metaphor of corruption had to be grounded in would-be observable fact. Blackstone's language thus connected the figurative nature and the material body: "For when it is now clear beyond all dispute, that the criminal is no longer fit to live upon the earth, but is to be exterminated as a monster and a bane to society, the law sets a note of infamy upon him, puts him out of its protection, and takes no further care of him barely to see him executed. He is then called *attaint, attinctus,* stained or blackened."[7]

The deficiency of hereditary blood, and its consequences for the felon's descendants, became an alternative death penalty: not actual but civil death. Strict civil death, the blood "tainted" by crime, thus set the stage for blood "tainted" by natural inferiority. The racialized fiction of blood supplemented the metaphoric taint, not only defining property in slaves but also fixing them, their progeny, and their descendants in status and location. Though Blackstone denounced slavery, his description of the consequences of attainder promised a novel genealogical inscription of race that could be gotten from an old language of criminality and heredity. Blackstone described the king's pardon of an attainted felon as rebirth with a gothic twist. A king's pardon made the offender "a new man" with renewed "credit and capacity," but Blackstone warned that "nothing can restore or purify the blood when once corrupted . . . but the high and transcendent power of parliament." Once pardoned by the king, however, the son of the person attainted might inherit, "because the father, being a new man, might transmit new inheritable blood."[8] The restoration in blood or to blood, to be born again, even when not possible for the attainted himself who remained dead in law, devolved on the son, who could receive the transmitted new blood and thus incarnate the privileges of birth and rank his father had lost.

Such transmission or promise of purification would not apply to those who suffered the perpetual decimation of personhood and property understood as domestic slavery. Can we trace the idea of tainted blood, the most critical mechanism for exclusion in the slave laws of the Americas, back to the metaphysics of metaphorical blood and biological destiny? The composite rhetoric of disabling and protection necessary to the codification of legal bondage in the colonies reanimated legal precedent and gave new genetic capital to the principles of tainted blood, expulsion, and servility. Civil death remained distinct from other legal sanctions, since this concept and its attendant disabilities maintained both a strictly hierarchical order and the blood defilement on which that order depends. Corruption of blood operated practically as a severing of blood lines, thus cutting off inheritance, but also acted metaphorically as an extension of the "sin" or "taint" of the father visited on his children. If we treat blood and property as metaphors crucial to defining persons in civil society, then it is easy to see how "corruption of blood" and "forfeiture of property" could become the operative components of divestment. By a negative kind of birthright, bad blood blocked inheritance just as loss of property meant disenfranchisement. Yoked together as they are, these terms loosely but powerfully define types of slavery. Whether applied to the slave or the criminal, both are degraded below the rank of human beings, not only politically but also physically and morally.

THE LAW IS A WHITE DOG

During my last visit to Haiti, I heard a story about a white dog. Reclaimed by an *oungan* or *boco* who "deals with both hands," practicing "bad" magic, the dog appears as if skin bloated with spirit. Starving, its eyes gone wild, it appears late at night with its tongue hanging out. A friend called it "the dog without skin," but this creature was not a dog. Instead, when a person died, the spirit, once stolen by the *oungan,* awakened from what had seemed sure death into this new existence in canine disguise. We all agreed that no manhandled spirit would want to end up reborn in the skin of the dog. Being turned into a dog was bad enough, but to end up losing color— to turn white—seemed worse. In this metamorphosis, the skin of the dead person is left behind like the skin discarded by a snake. But the person's spirit remains immured in the coarse envelope, locked in another form, trapped in something not her own.

In presenting this white dog as model and code for understanding the rituals of law, I take spiritual belief as legal commentary and vice versa. The image of the dog skin that encases the spirit of the dead person can be related figuratively both to the civil body—the artificial person who possesses self and property, and to the legal slave—the artificial person who exists as both human and property. In the appearance of the white dog, the spirit of the natural person who has died haunts the living in a new skin. It is not simply a *baka,* an evil spirit wandering the earth in the form of cats, dogs, pigs, or cows. There remains something specific about the white dog of this story, not only the emphasis on color but also the spirit's desperate longing restrained in an envelope of skin. If the slave was understood to exist as a special species of property, the servile body that could be beaten to a pulp or kept intact, this dog invokes the double incarnation of brute body and lost soul, the empowered husk and the disabled gist of personhood. Like the sorcery that chains the spirit to dog flesh, the rules of slave law defined a legal body emptied of thought.

Let me push this story as far as it will go, giving blood, taint, and corruption their due. Historically nuanced processes of stigmatization have continued to ensure that the poor and the powerless are converted into so much material exposed to institutional degradation. Let us return for a moment to the legality of dispossession in the Code Noir. The passage out of Africa and into the Americas called for the creation of a servile body, unfit, incapable, and destitute. The rules for controlling slaves in the colonies depended on the enlightenment strategy by which humans ruled the universe of things, including, through a fantasy of reification, slaves. Could the piecemeal annihilation of the person have set the stage for the discourse of unending stigma that produced the juridical nonexistence of the person through degrees of deprivation, not only defining property in slaves but also permanently fixing them, their progeny, and their descendants in their status and location?

Civil death, in remaining crucial to our understanding of just how monstrous would be the legal annihilation of will, the juridical decimation of personhood known as domestic slavery, also helps us to understand how brutalization and what I've called "negative personhood" leaped across and superseded the European-imposed periodicities of such categories as colonial and postcolonial. The 1804 *Code Napoleon* or *Code civil des français* appeared in the same year that Jean-Jacques Dessalines declared the independence of Saint-Domingue. The Code Napoleon made all actions of the interdict "void in law."[9] In uncanny simultaneity, the French civil code that pronounced the juridical nonexistence of the person came into existence at the same time that Dessalines returned to the rules of the Code Noir to transform them in his 1805 Constitution. He made former slaves civil persons, endowed them with citizenship, and defined "citizens" as "blacks," no matter their color, as long as they were friends of Haiti.

The Code Napoleon brought unfreedom to the metropole at the same time that Dessalines proclaimed liberty in the former colony. The Code Napoleon provided for civil death by operation of law for the most serious criminal offenses. Genuine civil death for felony and treason resulted in the opening of the person's succession, dissolved his marriage, and deprived him of civil rights. Civil interdiction, however, could be pronounced under that code only in cases of imbecility, insanity, or madness. While France initiated anew the civil death and interdiction of certain citizens judged incapable or defective and thus deprived of the right to have rights, Haiti gave civil rights to slaves who had legally been considered nonpersons. The state of being dead in law, sustained through time in varying narratives of incapacitation, thus juridically sustained the potent image of the servile body necessary for the public endorsement of dispossession.

Slavery is an appropriate metaphor for the condition of the interdict, pronounced "civilly dead," because, like the slave, she cannot impose her will upon her life. The effect of such a judgment would be that not only the property but also the very will, body, and privileges of the interdict would be placed in charge of a curator. Like a dead person, the interdict is herself legally a cipher. She does not exist except through her curator, in whom she lives, moves, and has her being. The effect of interdiction is a radical dislocation of legal identity. Where does that displaced identity go? In the white dog, the slave who has no civil relation, the felon who is dead in law, the defective or imperfect human, and the naturally dead person are joined. The icon of brute matter that imprisons the spirit remains a way of understanding belief in Haiti. The vitality in this moving corpse is prelude to the paradoxes of a spirituality that both deprives and enhances: the convertibility that keeps vodou intact and resilient.

Let me urge a subtext to what I acknowledge as a mimetic bind: strategies of containment and exclusion that constructed the terrain for colonial reciprocity and mutual adaptability. Myths of blood and pleasures of property provided the terms for a modern concept of race. At the least, terms such as "corruption of blood" or "taint" could be forced into service of an ideology that underwrote the network of images for civility or sav-agery, ability or deficiency, natural or unnatural. Once the legal termi-nology of taint or disability was surcharged with racial prejudice, then the claim for personal rights became shifting and tentative, even paradoxical. For color, this appearance of a moral essence or transmissible evil could stand in society as both a threat and a curse, or finally, as justification for those so tainted. Like blood, color is fictitious, denoting primarily what is not observable, not fact but ideology. The concept of "blackness" had to be reinforced, made absolute and ultimately unchangeable against the prima facie evidence of fading color—the effects of that intermediate class of persons lightened by interbreeding. The strategy was to call the taint or stain "blood."[10]

But this ideology never died. The curse of color was encoded in law. If we make slavery as practiced in the Americas our hypothetical still point, then we can move back and forth from Paris to Haiti, and further, from medieval Europe to the Americas, from the fogs and fictions of ancient jurisprudence to the institution of slavery. These idioms of servitude look back to a myth of blood as legitimate pedigree and forward to an analyt-ics of blood reified as ineradicable stain. Can such rituals help us to under-stand what had been described to me as the "preternatural whiteness" of the dog without skin? The sin of the flesh and the fact of taint had to be made indelible through time. Those whites who intermarried could also be "degenerated" or "disabled" for the crime of misalliance. Once excom-municated from civil life, they formed yet another intermediate category of persons undone on the soil of Saint-Domingue. Moreover, as the rov-ing and palpable figure for what has not died, the dog's whiteness suggests the power of skin color, put on or removed, to determine status. In Haiti, the color obsession continues, distinguished as gradations of color from black to white, including mulatto, griffon, marabou, red-brown, brown, albino. The Haitian colonel Jean-Claude Delbau recalled the terror felt when during the 1990 American occupation of Haiti, "an inhabitant of Marigot, known in his village as a very dark black, suddenly changed skin and became completely white."[11] What might have seemed an ideal cult of whiteness was thus far more ambiguous than racist ideologues allowed: dark flesh turned white could also be monstrous.

How does the concreteness of vodou practice, its obsession with details and fragments, and its varying postures of service offer a colonial creolization that extends the experience of "possession" and "attachment" codified in legal narratives? As Christophine warned Antoinette in Jean Rhys's novel *Wide Sargasso Sea:* "No more slavery! She had to laugh! 'These new ones have Letter of the Law. Same thing. They got magistrate. They got fine. They got jail house and chain gang. They got tread machine to mash up people's feet. New ones worse than old ones—more cunning, that's all.' " In *Les Constitutions d'Haiti* (1886), Louis-Joseph Janvier described the Code Rural imposed by the military dictator Jean-Pierre Boyer, who governed Haiti from 1820 to 1843, as "slavery without the whip."[12] Not only did the Code Rural revive forced labor, it also defined a class called "cultivators," forced to work on the land. This category of persons included all who were not merchants or public functionaries.[13] The slippage between degrees of color, gradations of personhood, and the bounds of civility and savagery were sustained in the more or less unbroken momentum of law and history that carried servitude and disenfranchisement into the present. I have come to believe that the law in Haiti defeated the possibilities of creative ambivalence in colonial society. Legal thought relied on a set of fictions to sustain such precepts as the absolutist and physicalist concept of property: a fictive, and I would urge, supernatural domain grounded in the materials, the habits, and the usages of society.

If vodou and its *lwa* were responses to the institution of slavery, to its peculiar brand of sensuous domination, then we are dealing with two kinds of supernatural domains. The shock of creole society resulted in strange bedfellows, spiritual connections that had as much to do with legal science as theology. Dehumanization and bondage worked differently for those who were not accumulating property or trying to justify mastery. Slaves responded to the monsters they knew to be human, with an alternative epistemology, with ever-new embodiments of laws laid down, a discipline of mind ignored in many accounts of vodou.

What constitutes personal identity in vodou practice? Can we reconsider the notion of personhood in terms of the paradox inherent in defining a person as a thing but not treating her as a thing? Consider the three-part structure of Haitian identity. Though accounts are often contradictory, what matters is that the triad recalls the threat to the person who could be turned into a slave, alternately described as brute matter, dead thing, horse, mule, dog, or beloved object. Through these degrees of figurative denigration and literal dismembering, the institution thrived, ringing changes on persons, while it made money for those who trafficked in and owned human flesh. The *ti bon anj* or *petit bon anj* (the little good angel that is source of consciousness, affect, and will) depends on the *lwa* for protection, guarding against the thieving of personal identity so much a part of the institution of slavery and other strategies of dehumanization. The *gwo bon anj* (also called *lonb-kadav* or shadow corpse) is the double of the material body—something like the idea of spirit. The *gwo bon anj* can detach itself from the body, whether in dreams or when seized by a sorcerer, but the *ti bon anj* also risks dislocation. The *ti bon anj,* which makes up our personality or thinking matter, acts as if a container for the spirit. But without the *lwa* as support the *ti bon anj* can attach itself to anything, can be stolen by a sorcerer, can be turned into a zombie spirit or into a white dog. The third part of the person is the *ko kadav* or body corpse, the redoubled image of flesh and bones uninhabited by thought or will. To this nonhuman order the name matter belongs.

Ritualized decimation, the vodou answer to being dead in law, remains the zombie. If the dispossession accomplished by legal slavery became the model for possession in vodou—for making a person not into a thing but into a spirit—then the zombie remains as the reminder of legal incapacitation. Yet, as I have tried to show in the emblematic appearance of the white dog, the process of decreation, where humans become nonentities or alien specimens, takes many forms. It is as if with every experience of disability there came a need for more terse and ingenious expressions of derangement. Vodou, in responding over time to the arbitrary power of mastery, literalized these moments of memory in their gods and spirits. In short, like the law, vodou gives flesh to past narratives and life to the residue of old codes and penal sanctions. If the law energizes the unconditional maintenance of a servile order, then vodou returns to that servility and resurfaces transmuted. The raw materials of colonial legal authority and the divestment and stigmatization of Haitians at home and abroad remain the stuff of spiritual life.

LWA AND SAINTS

Could the rituals of vodou, either unwittingly or by design, have resulted in a colonial creolization that extends the experience of "possession" and "divestment" codified in legal narratives? Though the focus on corporeality and spectacular mutilation never stopped, once these practices resurfaced in Saint-Domingue the historically nuanced processes of stigmatization formed the lineaments of religious practices that defied and transformed these institutional remnants. My study of the materiality of vodou, its absorption of recalcitrant givens, leads me to view these practices not only as ritual reenactments of Haiti's colonial past but also as rereadings of the law. Etymology matters not only in sustaining the law but also in serving the gods. Vodou recapitulated the memory, themes, or arguments of colonial legal structures by repeating or reenacting them in ritual. In this sacramental exchange, the new covenant embodied in the *lwa* replaces the old "master." The *met tet* (master of the head) debunks the other mastery. The gods come up from the waters, and, entering their servitors, arrive not as imperishable but as supremely perishable.

Offering redemption from the curse of colonial law, the *lwa* substitutes this artificial death with a new life. As if repeating and transforming 1 Corinthians 3 ["a new covenant, not in a written code but in the Spirit; for the written code kills, but the Spirit gives"], a second, more sacred reproduction arises from the ruins of the written code. In Creole the word for law and god is the same: *lwa.* Those who ordained the *loi d'état* were countered by those possessed by the spirits. These reinterpretations tell a story of bondage more palpable than the precepts of law could have been. In other words, the difficult but abiding connection between the spirit and the letter is demonstrated by the particular ways in which ritual memory operates in vodou practice to constrain law. Like law itself, the spirits form the locus of embodied history, materializing dispossession and pointing to something crucial about this Creole spirituality. In inhabiting the blood of their devotees, the *lwa* replace the imagined "taint" with the sacred gist, redeeming the law of the oppressor. Not only do spirits embody the past, they also form the site where the present speaks to the future through acts of commemoration.

Nowhere does vodou inventiveness appear more emphatically than in the use of chromolithographs, or color prints, of the saints in venerating the *lwa.* The Haitian Duverneau Trouillot, in his 1885 *Esquisse Ethnographique, Le Vaudoun: Aperçu Historique et Evolutions,* judged vodou practices as atavistic remnants that would disappear under the weight of Christian civilization.[14] But Trouillot's celebrated "advantages of liberty" were never accessible to the Haitian majority. For them, the God, saints, and devils of French dogma, like the trinity of the law—life, liberty, and property—were remade on Haitian soil. These vestiges of theologies and texts, once reinterpreted by local uses and needs, articulated another history of the New World. When Catholic traditions joined with the attractions of African beliefs and cult practices, colonial taxonomies were stunned into a vital ambiguity. These kinds of slippages confounded the artificial and legal divisions of Saint-Domingue. Between Haitian independence in 1804 and the concordat between the French government and the Vatican in 1860, the Catholic Church had nothing to do with Haiti. During those years, religious forms and rituals developed that had been either forbidden or masked before the revolution. But even though the priests were gone, practitioners of what would become known as "vodou" remembered and retained Catholicism, just as before they had preserved the pasts of Rada, Congo, Ibo, or Nago spirits in Africa.

Whatever remained powerful in the minds of African-born and Creole slaves and free coloreds in Saint-Domingue resulted to a large degree from their encounters with Catholicism, even if deformed by abortive or hypocritical missionary efforts. Though the ornate trappings of Catholic ritual and its perversions (such as the legendary practice of baptizing in a punch bowl) were condemned as proof of a corrupt colonial clergy, these deformations of sacred calling ended up accelerating the religious beliefs and practices of slaves, who gave new meaning to the ceremonial scraps and put the spirit back in the letter. The persistent complaints of administrators and magistrates against the "contamination" of sacred relics with "profane" things has not been properly understood. For what has been seen either as subterfuge, a superficial and opportune observance, or impressionable and backward mimicry was rather evidence of a commitment and inventiveness that unsettled racist assumptions.

On the eve of the 1791 revolution in Saint-Domingue, the religious practices of slaves and free-coloreds who called themselves Christians threatened the colonial administration. Yet the proliferation of ordinances, decrees, and laws issued against not only vodou ceremonies but also against Church attendance were rarely obeyed. In the towns especially, ritual words and songs, the life of Christ, and the stories of the saints were eagerly adopted by those forbidden to become familiar with Christian doctrine. When slaves and free blacks shared in the observance of religious processions and saints' days, these practices reanimated the powerful substance of other beliefs, as well as refigured dispossession. After all, slaves were not only named after heroes, Greek and Roman gods, or days of the week, but also after Catholic saints. If newly baptized slaves could be renamed as saints, why couldn't their African spirits be identified with a saint? Moreover, the saints, often named and portrayed inconsistently by the priests, served as convenient vessels for the new gods. What was deemed only a superficial, sometimes parodic attempt at religious education gave the black inhabitants of Saint-Domingue what they needed to revitalize dead forms and hollow rituals.

When the slaves revolted in 1791, their already syncretic religious practices converged with the blood of the new dispensation. A study of the religious history of Saint-Domingue demands the give-and-take between cultures called "primitive" and those called "civilized." Far from carrying over some homogeneous and primordial "African" religion, the enslaved had already picked up bits and pieces of Roman Catholicism and Islam, which they structured in distinct ways into their religious practices. As Jean Price-Mars showed, not only were many of the first arrivals from the upper western coast of Africa Muslims, but also many of those from the kingdoms of the Congo, Angola, and Mozambique had already been affected by "Islamic propaganda" and "inculcated with Catholic ideas by the Portuguese, the first explorers of the African coasts, around the fifteenth century." Price-Mars concludes that quite possibly "the large majority of negroes torn from different places in Africa and brought to Saint-Domingue were pious peoples attached simultaneously to the Muslim and Dahomean faith, and even slightly Catholic."[15]

The bodies of the gods are invented and sustained in oppositional contexts. Not only do the ways of serving the *lwa* testify to local beliefs, they also reveal the fragmented devices of those who came to colonize. The devotee refers to *lwa* not only as "mysteries" or "the invisible ones" but also as "devils," "angels," and "saints," testifying to the crossing of terms that is so much a part of the transformative processes of vodou. In the twentieth century the church condemned what it called *le mélange,* the mixture of vodou and Catholicism—for example, vodou *lwa* identified with Catholic saints, and the absorption of the festivals of the Roman calendar by vodou adherents. There's an old saying in Haiti: "To serve the *lwa,* you have to be Catholic." During an "antisuperstition" campaign in 1941, a Catholic priest complained: "It is not we who have got hold of the people to Christianize them, but they who have been making superstitions out of us." But what the church had condemned as superstition was actually a continued and rigorous project of thought. Vodou's incorporation of Catholic representations into its life of the spirit validates the categories of mind and body.

Vodou, perhaps because of the absence of any unified superstructure and hierarchy, can best be described as a drama of transmutation. The *lwa* themselves form a family, and their mutual interpenetration reproduces and gives meaning to the Haitian community and its shared, supportive existence. Just as the old African gods undergo psychic translation into *lwa* once in Haiti, so the Catholic saints are Haitianized when they appear as chromolithographs on the walls or altars of the *ounfo* (temple).[16] The mutation of the saint expands the *lwa*'s traits, but also articulates the reciprocal abiding of human and god through a new understanding of the saints as cast in the same mold as the *lwa*. In the *lwa*'s altar room, or *bagui*, for example, the *lwa*'s favorite things are on display. These pieces of property are not only tokens of devotion preserved by the *oungan*, they also make up the lineaments and capture the idiosyncrasies of the *lwa*. On the walls hang the chromolithographs of the saints adopted and then redefined once in dialogue with the *lwa*.

The very idea of reciprocity—between humans and *lwa*, or between *lwa* and saints—is complex. Just as relations between humans and gods are not necessarily harmonious, so saints and *lwa* do not dwell together unperturbed. Let me return to the language of possession, or the *crise de lwa*—the moment when the god inhabits the head of his or her servitor. The "horse" is said to be mounted and ridden by the god, but this experience is not one of domination but a double movement of attenuation and expansion. In a sense, the appearance of the Catholic saints in the social and collective spectacle of vodou is as necessary to the spirits as are their human receptacles or mounts. For just as the *lwa* cannot be made manifest on earth without the person who becomes the vessel of embodiment, the *lwa* call to their devotees with the understanding that they also are reconstituted in the finite and visible emblems of the saints. A new understanding of spirituality occurs. Consider the superimposition of *lwa* and saint. When a person is "possessed," the gestures, facial expressions, voice, language, and accoutrements of the *lwa* change and adjust to the peculiarities of their devotees. Yet these products of a local imagination gain sustenance from the saints (or *sen*), who, along with the practitioners, corporealize the god's urges and give them a novel, doubly incarnate history.

What, then, does the human body of the pictured saint signify? Does it contain some extra element necessary to bring the *lwa* to mind? In redefining the saints as counterparts of the *lwa,* the saints begin to take part in a process of redefinition. Both liturgical and vodou histories are fleshed out through this dialogue. Can we define, with any precision, the way the correspondence works? And what is the history written on the bodies of the gods? What happened to the indigenous spirits when the mission of conversion to Catholicism goaded the Dahomean nature spirits into the anthropomorphized embodiments we now call *lwa?* In elaborating this idea, I take two examples: the venerable Danbala wedo, the Rada snake spirit born in Dahomey and transported to Haiti; and the varying emanations of Ezili, born on the soil of Haiti with no precedent in Yorubaland or Dahomey.[17]

Seen as a snake arching itself across the heavens in the path of the sun or as the rainbow, the beneficent Danbala, a spirit of fertility and one of the most ancient gods, was once celebrated in Dahomey as the great serpent who rises from the underworld to drink the fresh water of the streams. Moreau de Saint-Méry's 1797 description of the "cult of the snake," the earliest account of colonial vodou, presents the snake as the *vaudoux* in a box on an altar. The vodou "queen," as soon as she stands on the box, "becomes a new female python . . . penetrated by the God. She becomes nervous and her whole body goes into convulsions. Then the oracle speaks through her mouth; now she flatters and promises happiness, then she calls out in deep tones and screams reproaches. . . . All this is spoken in the name of the snake before this imbecilic troop. . . ."[18] This negative account of vodou as "sorcery" or "superstition" is crucial in understanding how vodou changed over time. The adoration of the snake in its literal form disappeared from the *ounfo,* and was often replaced by an egg and a snake in wrought iron, placed on the altar.

Danbala, "the master of the waters," presides over rivers, springs, and marshes. He is represented as a snake, arched in union with his female counterpart Ayida to form the rainbow. When possessed by Danbala, the human devotee hisses, slithers, and crawls through the *ounfo.* Yet Danbala also is identified with St. Patrick, the evangelizer of the Irish, represented in chromolithographs with two serpents under his feet and two others by his sides. In the chromo, St. Patrick, dressed as a bishop, holds a crosier in his left hand and stands near the shore of a river. Why would Danbala be represented by the saint who drove the snakes out of Ireland? What kind of correspondence is suggested when the vodou devotee uses the picture of St. Patrick crushing snakes underfoot?

This translation does not mean a perfect analogy between saint and spirit. Instead, the uneven, rough juxtaposition adds yet another narrative meaning to the Haitian spirit's history. There is a deeper meaning to the surface imagery. In choosing St. Patrick, Haitians did not simply choose a decorative icon for belief, for their attachment is to more than mere visuals. St. Patrick, of mixed Romano-British origin, was carried off by Irish pirates in A.D. 406 to become a slave among the still pagan inhabitants of that land. Legends abound concerning the bodily hardships of bondage, his sea journey to an unknown and wild land, his escape by ship to the Continent, and his return to Ireland to preach after being called to service in a dream. Let me pursue the way those instructed in the mysteries of the church might have understood these stories. Taken as a slave from his birthplace in a bondage Haitians knew, St. Patrick also made a sea journey that replicates the journey Africans made from Africa to the New World. Yet this Middle Passage was often inverted by slaves, who, in committing suicide or dying, believed they would return across the waters to their "native land." In St. Patrick's dual sea crossings, back and forth from bondage to escape, from one kind of freedom to another, Haitians remembered how their ancestors died into life, saved by descending into the waters and arriving reborn in Guinea.

Danbala also is born anew through the conjoining of Haitian spirit and Christian saint. What does this rebirth signify? Far from authorizing the split between a superficial Catholic image to hide authentic African belief, the correspondence makes explicit the deep meaning of an intimacy that thrives on noncoincidence, that lays bare the alternative history of vodou. Danbala, signifying both the snake crushed underfoot and the spirit rising up from the waters, materializes the abstract precepts of colonial law in an incarnation that destroys the imperial dichotomy of master and slave, victimizer and victimized, or colonizer and colonized. In this convertible process, Danbala both stamps out snakes and becomes the thing stamped out, speaking to his devotees as both master and mastered. He instructs them in a doctrine that displaces slavery into the place of ethics. What I call the law of vodou takes place in this locale of rearticulation, with spirit and saint reciprocally consigned to something that can no longer be called either "pagan" or "orthodox." Further, the biblical snake is laid bare as something other than evil, now holding the promise of knowledge that erodes the powerful dualisms of a dominant ideology.

In her varying manifestations, Ezili, the spirit or *lwa* of love, bears the extremes of colonial history. Most writers have turned to analogy in describing her. She is Venus. She is the Virgin. Known as "Black Venus," "Tragic Mistress," or "Goddess of Love," she is the *lwa* most bound to the harrowing reality of eighteenth-century Saint-Domingue. Served by her devotees with the trappings of libertinage—lace, perfume, jewels, and sweets—she carries the weight of a history where matters of luxury and abandon crossed with ideals of purity and grace.

In that unnatural situation where humans became property, love gained substance through time by a spirit that originated in the experience of domination. In that unnatural situation where humans became property as well as beloved objects, the mixed-blood or mulatto mistress signified the body that could join the conceit of love to the abandon of sensuous ecstasy. Moreau de Saint-Méry described the "Mulatresse" as "one of those priestesses of Venus." How, then, did this gorgeous emblem of decorum and lust emerge out of the fractured ruins of the past? Why did the spirit Ezili Freda, the pale and elegant lady of luxury and love, become identified with the Virgin Mary or the Mater Dolorosa (Mother of Sorrows)? What does it mean to serve this wayward spirit with the print of a young girl in a blue robe, wearing bejeweled earrings, necklaces of pearls and gold, and bracelets? Her arms are crossed over her heart, into which is thrust a gold dagger. Just as Ezili encourages the return to the entangled history of race and romance, so this representation emancipates the image of the Virgin from her spiritualization, returning her with gusto to the flesh-and-blood story of *her* passion. Not only does the superimposition of Mistress Ezili and Virgin Mary recall the incongruous origins of the cult of the Virgin, it also testifies to another repressed history: the syncretism of pre-Christian cults of willful goddesses and harlot saints, before they were idealized out of existence.

In this joining of Catholic image and Haitian spirit, there is no longer a space for pious compromise. Instead, in such rituals of service, notions of affection and attachment, as those of purity and virginity, adoration and degradation, are transformed. There are many Ezili, either regarded as members of the same family or as different manifestations of the same deity. Depending on region, ritual, *ounfo,* or individual devotee, her attributes and expressions vary. She possesses men as well as women, and both sexes take on her attributes and accede to her mystique of femininity. Yet even such generalizations as the "eternal feminine" are pulverized when she appears. Choosing women as well as men in "mystic marriage," the customary gendered relations between men and women no longer hold. Whether served in her garb of finery as Ezili Freda or as the black Ezili Danto (identified with the chromo of the black Mater Salvatoris, whose heart also is pierced with a dagger), or in the fury and violence of her other incarnations (such as Ezili ge wouj or Ezili-nwa-ka, or black heart, of the Petro family of spirits), she mimics and subverts the false idealizations of those who called themselves "masters," as well as exposing the hypocrisy inherent in the colonial relation. In this exchange of spirit and matter, the embodied *lwa* and the represented saint, the alleged disjunction between sacred and profane is suspended.

The two-way movement between magic and materialism, piety and incarnation, what Pierre Pluchon has called a "Creole Catholicism,"[19] is perpetuated by the dialogue between saints and spirits. Their mutual adaptability not only materializes but also legitimizes these sites of conflation as an extended allegory. In turning to the choice of specific images of the saints for representing their gods, we confront a cross-fertilization that defies any argument of superficial attachment to picture or ornament and takes us instead into an analytic of power. In the uneven reciprocity between the New World *lwa* and Old World saints, the doubling picked up on experiences that had been minimized in Catholic hagiography. This continued exercise makes history an integral part of the setting of belief.

NOTES

1. Joan Dayan, *Haiti, History, and the Gods* (Berkeley: University of California Press, 1995). Throughout this essay I will be elaborating on the arguments developed, 29–74 and 187–267.
2. See Elsa V. Goveia, *The West Indian Slave Laws of the 18th Century* (Barbados: Caribbean Universities Press, 1970), 25. She suggests that a respect for the rights of private property resulted in harsher treatment of slaves, recognizing the slave as "a person in a sphere far more limited than that allowed him in either Spanish or French law."
3. For an extended discussion of the regulated beneficence of the code and its logic of dehumanization see Dayan, *Haiti, History, and the Gods,* 199–212.
4. Ibid.

5. For an examination of the spirit of the law and the "legal fiction" of civil death, see Joan Dayan, "Legal Slaves and Civil Bodies" in *Materializing Democracy,* ed. Russ Castronovo and Dana Nelson (Durham, N.C.: Duke University Press, 2002). On the interpretive possibilities of this unnatural metaphor see Kim Lane Scheppele, "Facing Facts in Legal Interpretation," *Representations* 30 (1990): 42–77.

6. William Blackstone, *Commentaries on the Laws of England,* 4 vols. (1769; Reprint, Chicago: University of Chicago Press, 1979), 2: 253, 256.

7. Ibid., 4: 380.

8. Ibid., 4: 395.

9. Code Civil des Français, art. 502.

10. For a discussion of how Buffon's taxonomies of the species and his "imperceptible nuances" were transferred to the hybrid mixed-blood and the requisite taxonomies of color see the section on Moreau de Saint-Méry's systematizing of the conundrum of color in Saint-Domingue in Dayan, *Haiti, History, and the Gods,* 230–37. Moreau presented 11 categories of 110 combinations ranked from absolute white (128 parts white blood) to absolute black (128 parts black blood) in a series of lists of possible "nuances," a "colored nomenclature" that names anew those persons recast as products of an illicit mixture of blood.

11. Jean-Claude Delbau, *Société, culture, et médecine populaire traditionelle* (Port-au-Prince: Imprimerie Henri Deschamps, 1990), 207–10.

12. Louis-Joseph Janvier, *La République d'Haiti et ses visiteurs (1840–1882)* (Paris: Marpon et Flammarion, 1883), 32.

13. For a discussion of how the Code Rural reduced Haitians to slave status see Dayan, *Haiti, History, and the Gods,* 14.

14. Duverneau Trouillot, *Esquisse Ethnographique, Le Vaudoun: Aperçu Historique et Evolutions,* 26, 30–31, 37.

15. Jean Price-Mars, "Le Sentiment et le phenomene religieux chez les negres de St.-Domingue," in *Une Étape de l'evolution haitienne* (Port-au-Prince: Imprimerie "La Presse," 1930), 126–27.

16. Leslie G. Desmangles, *The Faces of the Gods: Vodou and Roman Catholicism in Haiti* (Chapel Hill: University of North Carolina Press, 1992), n. 3, 198. The author notes that these lithographs, printed in Mexico and in the Dominican Republic, are inexpensive and widely distributed.

17. For a discussion of what could be seen as a Haitian trinity that includes Ezili Danto, Ezili Freda, and Lasyrenn (the mermaid and water mama) see Karen McCarthy Brown, *Mama Lola: A Vodou Priestess in Brooklyn* (Berkeley: University of California Press, 1991), 220–57. See also Dayan, *Haiti, History, and the Gods,* 54–67; Joan Dayan, "Erzulie: A Woman's History of Haiti?," *Research in African Literatures,* 25, no. 2 (Summer 1994). Ezili figures in numerous classic works on vodou, including Alfred Métraux, *Vodou in Haiti,* trans. Hugo Charteris, with new introduction by Sidney Mintz (1959; reprint, New York: Schocken Books, 1971); Louis Maximilien, *Le Vodou haitien: Rite radas-canzo* (Port-au-Prince: Imprimerie Henri Deschamps, 1945); Maya Deren, *Divine Horsemen: The Living Gods of Haiti* (1953; reprint, Kingston, N.Y.: Documentext, McPherson & Company, 1989); Zora Neale Hurston, *Tell My Horse: Vodou and Life in Haiti and Jamaica* (1938; reprint, New York: Harper & Row, 1990), as well as works already cited.

18. M. L. E. Moreau de Saint-Méry, *Description topographique, physique, civile, politique, et historique de la partie française de l'Isle Saint-Domingue,* 3 vols. (Philadelphia: Chez l'auteur, 1797; new ed. by B. Maurel and E. Taillemite, Paris: Société de l'histoire des colonies françaises, 1958), 1: 65–69 for a complete description of this ceremony.

19. Pierre Pluchon, *Vaudou sorciers empoisonneurs de Saint-Domingue à Haiti* (Paris: Éditions Karthala, 1987), 38.

3

Diego de Ocaña's Hagiography of New and Renewed Devotion in Colonial Peru[1]

KENNETH MILLS

Diego de Ocaña was a Jeronymite alms collector and propagator of devotion who lived briefly but adventurously from about 1570 until 1608. As a representative of his monastery and the sanctuary of the miraculous image of the Virgin of Guadalupe in the Villuercas Mountains of Extremadura in western Spain, he and a companion, Fray Martín de Posada, traveled to the Spanish Indies in 1599. Among the royal privileges and entitlements conferred by a series of medieval and early modern Castilian monarchs on the Jeronymite guardians of Guadalupe was the right to send out agents such as Ocaña and Posada to inspect and spread devotion, and to gather alms to maintain a cult befitting the Mother of God and assist in the care of the thousands of pilgrims who flocked to the sanctuary each year. In the age of King Philip II, these questors or *demandadores* (as they were called) from the house at Guadalupe extended their field of operation beyond the Spanish and Portuguese heartlands and across the seas.

Ocaña and Posada crossed the Atlantic Ocean, passed through the Caribbean Sea and over the isthmus of Darién before sailing down the northwestern coast of South America as far as the port of Paita where Posada, the older man, already gravely ill, died in a rented room. Diego de Ocaña carried on alone, traveling through much of Spanish South America until 1605, at which point he passed north to New Spain, where he died in

Mexico City in 1608.[2] The cross-genre account of this journey, which Ocaña composed and illustrated principally, it seems, for Jeronymite and royal readers, is the starting point for any study of his life and significance.[3]

Ocaña, like many of his contemporaries, attached the utility and power of hagiography to places—to the "lives" of holy shrines and saints' images.[4] Accordingly, one can see Ocaña's reporting of his principal activities as a hagiographic rendering, an account of cultic beginnings composed by a founder, maker (or reformer, as the case may be), and first writerly champion of a series of images and shrines. As within a saint's vita, the personal and celestial often merge in Ocaña's account of his own thoughts and actions. The Jeronymite painted images of the Virgin of Guadalupe, but, to his understanding, he was only able to do so with the help of the Virgin herself. As he put it, she guided his paintbrushes. The same is true of the foundational narrative he builds: the sacred biographical beginnings of images are as likely to turn on Our Lady's interventions as on his or some other human initiatives. The stories of Ocaña's foundations in Peru accumulate through his manuscript, and, significantly, also are gathered together by the Jeronymite himself in a telling "chapter" within his work.[5] Just as a hagiographer would do amid his contemporary subject's various choices and life events, Diego de Ocaña recorded both what he had seen and what he wished to see. He sorted out details and protagonists, searched for the cues that would convince different readers, chose between obstacles, positioned solutions, and shaped his climactic episodes. He wrote to fasten down a sense of the cultic beginnings he had awakened and wanted to achieve. Inscribing beginnings that would persuade and endure meant attempting to influence not only the immediate consequences of his foundational actions but also the ways in which his images, and events surrounding them and their enshrinements, would be remembered.

I focus upon Ocaña's thoughts and actions in three of the urban settings in which he painted and enshrined holy images: Lima, Potosí, and Cusco.[6] In the coastal capital of Lima and in Cusco, the great highland city and former Inka center, the Guadalupan Jeronymite sought to recover power from existing, rival images of Our Lady of Guadalupe by asserting his monastery's authority over "copies" of the original image in satellite shrines, and over any alms collected in her name.[7] Ocaña's accounts of his reformative actions in Lima and Cusco surround his hagiographic climax, the reporting of his orchestration of fresh beginnings in the great silver-mining center of Potosí (in what is today Bolivia). To our eyes, his actions in Potosí can appear immediately more constructive in comparison with those taken in Lima and Cusco. Yet the fact that there were no "renegade" cults of Our Lady of Guadalupe for Ocaña to rival or correct in Potosí was, for him, more like a practical advantage to which he happily adjusted (after all, such a city teemed with other established and alms-hungry advocations of the Virgin and other images of saints within which to position his new cult). More critical issues were money and sizable populations from whom receptive devotees might emerge, and the importance of places such as Potosí (which seemed fairly to drip with money, people, and dramatic potential) to the mission of an itinerant fund-raiser, propagator of devotion, and community organizer such as Diego de Ocaña.

In mid September 1599, near Saña, in the valleys of Trujillo, Diego de Ocaña visited an already famous sculpted copy of the original image of Our Lady of Guadalupe. The statue was half a century old, having been carved in Seville at the request of Francisco Pérez de Villafranca Lezcano, an *encomendero* (Spanish settler entrusted with the labor and tribute rights over a specified group of Indians, in return for their protection, payment, and Christian instruction) and the son of one of the original Spanish founders of Trujillo. This *encomendero* had prayed to Our Lady of Guadalupe during an imprisonment in Peru, vowing that if he regained his freedom he would make a pilgrimage to her sanctuary in Extremadura to give thanks, and also that he would return to Peru with a faithful copy of her image to enshrine in a chapel. This he did, enshrining the image in a chapel in his *encomienda* by about 1560, before building a more permanent church and turning the foundation over to the care of the Augustinians in 1563.[8]

When Ocaña visited the shrine, he was impressed by evidence of fervent devotion and by the signs of the Augustinians' ability to beg sufficient alms to sustain their convent, themselves, and many pilgrims.[9] The place reminded him of the home cultivated by his own order in Spain. For like the Jeronymites at Guadalupe, the Augustinians were wealthy in income from "landholding, possessions, and the many alms given by those who pass through." And the image in their care had grown so famous for the miracles it had worked that, as Ocaña put it, "the people of Lima and the other Spanish towns [of the vast coastal region] are greatly devoted."[10] But any thrill he felt at coming upon so thriving a regional center of devotion to his beloved advocation dampened as he recognized the extent of the place's spiritual independence from the holy house and shrine in Extremadura. Neither in the northern coastal region nor in Lima was a thought being given to the original image of Our Lady of Guadalupe, and not a peso of alms was being sent to her Spanish home sanctuary.

When he came to write the final version of his manuscript, Ocaña represented his experience of the Augustinians' shrine, and some thinking time in nearby Saña, as kinds of seeds from which his principal foundational strategies would germinate and grow. In Ocaña's telling of his foundational adventures, it is a pivotal moment, a time of realization. He writes of abandoning any notion of founding a satellite shrine in nearby Saña that would respect the Extremaduran sanctuary's preeminence and assert his monastery's right to alms begged in the name of Our Lady of Guadalupe. The Augustinians and their image were simply too well established in the region. "I could do nothing in this town," Ocaña admitted, referring to Saña, "beyond empowering two people [to oversee collection and shipment] in case someone sought to make a donation to Our Lady of Guadalupe of the kingdoms of Spain in their last will or by some other means."[11]

Yet as powerless as he felt locally, his experience of the prosperous independence and lure of the Augustinians' coastal shrine heightened his focus upon what he might achieve in the far larger prize of Lima, a city that at the end of the sixteenth century already consisted of some twenty thousand people.[12] Moreover, as he told it retrospectively, Saña also marked the point at which he began to think more broadly, about what he might achieve even beyond Lima. His experience at the shrine of Guadalupe near Saña, he explained, "was one of the reasons . . . which moved me to set up chapels (hermitas) in Lima and in other parts." Within such chapels, Ocaña planned to position image copies that he himself would paint and see approved and enshrined. Around the images he would organize religious associations, festivals, and liturgical devotions, programs of preaching (in at least one setting, Potosí, in indigenous tongues as well as in the Spanish language), and, of course, systems of alms collection administered by hand picked stewards and designed to be protected in perpetuity. The sermons, as well as a cluster of hymns and a play composed by Ocaña himself, were to be peppered with miracle stories exemplifying the history and power of Our Lady of Guadalupe for diverse audiences.

The ultimate goal in Lima, as in other settings, would be a fresh beginning for a local cult of the Virgin of Guadalupe, which Ocaña could then champion as a founder and participant-teller. In pursuing this course, he consistently presented himself as a human conduit whom the Virgin guided to paint, to act, to write. Yet he simultaneously understood that, in more ways than were entirely comfortable, he was taking matters into his own hands. "I know full well," Ocaña explained to imaginable contemporary readers in Guadalupe and elsewhere,

> that there are, and will be, those in Spain who argue that it is not wise to make these images [as I have done]. But, for these reasons, they will begin to see their [the images'] importance. For now, and each year hence, from wherever there is a house and image of Our Lady of Guadalupe, many alms will leave the Indies [for the coffers of the monastery in Spain] which [otherwise] would have stayed. And now the majordomos [the stewards of the religious associations he founds]—who are like *demandadores,* and whom I leave [in their offices]—are masters of all [the alms gathered]. . . .

He held that any danger in the creation and proliferation of his portraits of the sculpted original would be outweighed by their local powers of attraction and careful administration. There should be no question of his aims and loyalties, he insisted; he served the monastery and Our Lady of Guadalupe, and the needs of her pilgrims, and he awaited nothing so much as the reward of his return to her holy sanctuary.[13]

His sense of a contest, the attempt to undermine the established appeal of the Augustinians' image and house, was not in the least concealed. And the chapel in Lima would be only a first move. Such a chapel, Ocaña reasoned, would

> take away people who would [then] not go along to that house [the one administered by the Augustinians] with their alms, but, rather, to those [chapels] which I founded, and to the images I made, so that memory of, and devotion to, the Spanish house would not be lost and all of the alms would go directly to Spain.[14]

Diego de Ocaña arrived in Lima on October 23, 1599. Finding influential support became a crucial early step in the viceregal capital, as it would be elsewhere. Ocaña requested, as per royal command, the appointment of a suitably devout and effective person from within the local establishment to assist and speed his efforts.[15] Blasco Fernández de Toro, "of proven nobility, a native of Trujillo in Extremadura, [and a] very rich man," fit the bill perfectly.[16] This would not be the last time Ocaña would secure the services and good example of an Extremaduran devotee of Our Lady as he got things started. Fernández de Toro became the first *mayordomo* of the new lay religious association of Our Lady of Guadalupe in Lima, the first to assume the responsibility of gathering alms for the monastery and shrine in Spain in perpetuity. He was, fittingly, also the first in the city to give alms—two hundred Castilian ducats—as an example to others. According to Ocaña's account, the man's ample gesture worked. The fledgling *cofradía* grew quickly among the upper stations of society in the city. The viceroy himself became the most high-profile early *cofrade,* and his joining became the cue for all the judges of the *audiencia,* and later the archbishop and the local inquisitors, all of whom climbed aboard and made contributions.

However necessary and gratifying these elite beginnings among Spaniards and Creoles (persons of Spanish descent, born in the Indies) were to him and the nascent advocation of Mary in this place, Ocaña clearly meant to move beyond the stages of authorization and sensational recruitment in Lima's palaces, in the interest of a cult that also might reach many other hearts. Ocaña, as I shall discuss below, was most articulate about appealing to indigenous peoples in discussion of his sojourn in Potosí, but the outlines of his search for a broader and deeper resonance are hinted at in these earlier moments in Lima. In the heat that began to envelop the region as Christmas and summer approached, Ocaña and Fernández de Toro crossed the city, going "house to house," he wrote, attracting all manner of people to the new *cofradía.*[17]

With his initial phase of authorization complete, and with key supporters and a *cofradía* in place, Ocaña set to painting an image of the Blessed Mary of Guadalupe to place as a focus for devotion. He sought a safe place for its enshrinement, and began the poly-faceted promotion not only of her Iberian and Mediterranean history and power but also of her connection to this American place in which she had arrived. He described his work and its immediate impact in Lima in a fashion he would go on to perfect in other places. Diego de Ocaña's painted images grew virtually three-dimensional:

I made a very fine and beautiful image, the same size as the one in Spain, painted on a canvas, upon which many pearls and precious emeralds were stuck, and to such a winning effect that the entire city turned up to see.[18]

A generous and timely donation to the Virgin of Guadalupe from a wealthy couple who were among Ocaña's most prized early recruits solved the problem of a home for the image. Not that he understood such actions—or even the plan that, as I noted above, Ocaña claimed had been hatching in his mind ever since his encounter with the coastal shrine of the Augustinians—to have been merely the products of his own good work or shrewdness. For here was a celestial sign, and a dramatic second act in his hagiography of Guadalupan devotion in Peru: the Virgin's opening and directing of two hearts toward the housing of Ocaña's first image for the viceregal capital. "Our Lady moved the souls of [the] two people, a husband and wife [Alonso Ramos Cervantes and Elvira de la Serna]," Ocaña wrote, to bequeath an *ermita* (*hermita,* a chapel and, in this case, center of devotion) worth ten thousand pesos on their lands just outside the city, on the road to Pachacamac.[19]

The chapel became the home of a painted image that Ocaña hoped would win over Lima and the entire coast of Peru. In his careful record of this image's early days, the Jeronymite stressed the mutually beneficial relationship between Lima's devotees and Our Lady of Guadalupe, a relationship that would be mirrored in the Jeronymite's systematic approach to the collection and apportioning of alms. He claimed that the people of Lima responded to the new image with "the greatest devotion (*grandissima devoçion*)," even offering six silver lamps. The Virgin, as intercessor before God, reportedly answered in kind, granting "many favors to the entire city."[20] This is all Ocaña reveals about miracles in Lima, for reasons I speculate on just below. But the words of the Dominican Reginaldo de Lizárraga, who visited the "church with the advocation of Our Lady of Guadalupe" a few years later (in 1605), and who explicitly compared what he witnessed there with what he observed in other churches, at least support Ocaña's picture of the image's vibrant start. Lizárraga's timing, and description of an image studded with precious stones and painted by a Jeronymite friar, make it clear that it was Ocaña's image he was viewing. He marveled not only at the striking ornamentation but also at the three existing altars and at the rich inlay in the walls of the chapel; further, there were, by his account, four priests who sang the *Salve* each Saturday in an attempt to keep up with the people's devotion. "Each day, they [the priests] say more than twelve masses there," Lizárraga wrote, noting also that it had also become customary for sailors in Lima to give alms to the image in this church before sailing from the port of Callao. He claimed that the people of the coastal region had already received a "thousand favors" from Our Lady and that devotion around this Marian image was on the rise.[21]

Ocaña would grow more specific about such signs of divine response in Potosí. In Lima, his contest with the Augustinians' rival image of the Virgin of Guadalupe appears to have obscured all else. Taking possession of the chapel "in the name of his convent" and enshrining a new image there prompted Ocaña to confident statements about the well-aimed blow he had struck against the Augustinians' shrine on the northern coast. "With this [act of foundation near Lima]," he gushed, "all the devotion to the other house was taken, and its name is already almost forgotten." Given the fact that devotion to the Guadalupan image of the Augustinians is known to have continued, Ocaña's words—even when grounded a little by Lizárraga's independent observations about the fervent beginnings at the *ermita*-church on the road to Pachacamac—are optimistic. Dreaming ahead was part of his work as the hagiographer of new devotion. As Ocaña well understood, and would demonstrate more dramatically in the highlands, establishing the Marian advocation of Guadalupe in a place called for precisely this kind of narrative encouragement of a wished-for reality through a distinct telling and retelling. He was inscribing the beginnings of a story.

After some eventful wanderings in Chile, Tucumán, and Paraguay, Diego de Ocaña spent almost three years, from July 1600 to June 1603, in the region of Potosí (with one stretch of some fourteen months in the city itself). Here, where no cult of Our Lady of Guadalupe existed at the time, his foundational adventure was different. In Potosí, to an extent seen in no other place, Diego de Ocaña was able to orchestrate a fresh beginning.

As I have noted, it was not as if there were no existing saintly contenders in this established colonial city. By the first year of the seventeenth century Potosí was a magnet to humanity, a city with well over a hundred thousand people (most of them native Andean laborers in and around the booming silver mining industry), and many other proven patrons were already in position. In the convent and church of San Francisco alone (and this temple, the most venerable in the city, would be chosen by Ocaña as the site for his image), there were active *cofradías* around a number of saintly images, both localized and more generalist in nature. Among the more storied in the former category was the Santo Cristo de la Veracruz (the Holy Christ of the True Cross), the striking, life-size image of an apparently dark-skinned Christ on the cross that was said to have appeared—in an exquisite, cross-shaped cedar box—at the doors of the primitive church one morning in 1550.[22] With devotees in Potosí and across a much wider Andean region, there was also Our Lady of Copacabana, the image of the Virgin of the Candlemas sculpted by the Indian artist Francisco Tito Yupanqui, enthroned in 1583 and under the sway of Augustinian evangelizers on the shores of Lake Titicaca since 1589. Yet these kinds of "rivals" would have been expected competition for Ocaña, elements of the kind of Catholic Christian religiosity he himself lived and represented. More pointedly, they populated the local, miraculous and image-based context, the devotional systems from which he might draw and that he might feed as he sought a niche for his newcomer, Our Lady of Guadalupe. The heterodoxy and spiritual independence (from originals) that some of these images shared with the Guadalupan images Ocaña had sought to rival on the northern coast, or replace in Cusco, were not his immediate concerns.

Diego de Ocaña took advantage of time he did not allow himself elsewhere, investigating Potosí and reflecting on his findings. He climbed the *Cerro Rico* (the signature conical mountain and site of much of the mining) and spent eight days talking with people there. After entering a mine, he wrote about the conditions for the some twelve thousand men who worked in the deepest galleries each day. "It seemed to me that I was in Hell," he concluded, picking up a trope among commentators on these mines that was already half a century old.[23] Stories of relentlessly blood-hungry mines fast became part of a persistently morbid lore in Potosí, a place of widows, Indian fear, and Spanish greed, a place in which mine inspectors cried for reform, in which cave-ins happened and people died. Ocaña could have availed himself of any number of potential sources on such matters.[24]

At core, Ocaña kept up his established way of proceeding, maintaining his particular alertness among the rich, pious, and influential. After an initial period of authorization and organization of key supporters, he painted an image of the Virgin of Guadalupe, embedding it with precious gems and emeralds collected from local women, just as before. With great fanfare, the image was carried through the streets to the church of San Francisco, where the Virgin-newcomer was greeted by the host of images of Franciscan saints before being granted pride of place above the *sagrario* in the main chapel.

Yet Ocaña's narrative of the contexts and effects of the enshrinement in Potosí also ventured from form, with the greater detail building toward a narrative culmination. The Jeronymite seems also to have derived special inspiration from the challenge of turning the Virgin of Guadalupe into a unifying religious symbol in so shocking and deeply divided a social setting as Potosí. The most remarkable dimension in Ocaña's account of his efforts in Potosí is the care he devotes to the conditions and emerging devotion of native Andeans in the city. The virtual silence about nonelite Indian devotees in Lima and Cusco begins to lift.

When Ocaña complained that his home-sanctuary in Guadalupe had neither acknowledged his remittances of alms nor responded to his repeated requests for *estampas* (authorized paper prints of engravings of the original miraculous image, which he might distribute in exchange for alms), he makes it clear that he did so with the popularity of these prints among Indians in mind. Even more exasperating to Ocaña was the discouragement he received from ecclesiastical officials when he sought permission to found a lay religious association devoted to Mary of Guadalupe among native Andeans in Potosí. For him, the problems of the prints and the *cofradías* of Indians rubbed together as a practical obstruction in a specific American place; an opportunity was being missed to build a more local and even domestic Christianity, and harm was falling only on native Andean Christians. "The Indians who are not gathered as *cofradía* members, because the bishops oppose me in this," Ocaña pointedly grumbled, "might at least take away a print."[25] Even Ocaña's reporting of the native people's "bad customs" are folded into the larger despair and wretchedness of their lives in the mines of Potosí, only making their new devotion to Mary of Guadalupe more noteworthy.[26]

It is not that Spaniards and Creoles are left out of the Jeronymite's vision of the future for the cult of the Virgin of Guadalupe in Potosí. They are attended to. But their membership is more assumed, when it is not downright disappointing. Even without the benefit of their own *cofradía* in her honor, Ocaña pointedly noticed, "the alms given by the native peoples outstripped those from the Spaniards."[27] He notes how Indian devotees had taken to calling the Virgin of Guadalupe "*la Señora Chapetona,* the new lady in the land."[28] These words issued from the same Ocaña who had passed up occasions to encourage an existing *cofradía* of Indians around an image of Our Lady of Guadalupe that he sought to displace in Cusco.

What was happening here? What accounts for the contrast, the differential attitude to nascent Indian faithful? Ocaña's activities and observations in Potosí—the wealthy place the alms gatherer had so anticipated, the place in which he resided longer than any single other setting in the Indies—were enjoying a heightened kind of telling. Perhaps Ocaña had grown partial to Indian mineworkers and their families whom he had taken the time to consider and watch grow devout, give alms, and gather around the new image he had painted and seen consecrated? More certainly, Potosí, and its Indian parishioners in particular, appear to have been fulfilling the needs of Ocaña the writer after the fact, his hagiographer's need for stirring, miraculous effect and edifying stories drawn from experience.

The image the Jeronymite painted and had adorned with jewels and emeralds (and immediately had authorized by the Extremaduran bishop of Charcas [and Ocaña's future patron] Alonso Ramírez de Vergara) was, as the reader will appreciate, entirely routine for Ocaña. Yet he described the new image here in a way that made it distinct from the images I have discussed above. As usual, and like most Christian imagemakers of his day, Ocaña sought to create what might be viewed as both a perfect replica and an extraordinary thing to behold.[29] But this time he fairly boasted of a certain aspect that calls for attention:

> Since I painted her a little dark *(un poquito morena),* and the Indians are like that, they said that That Lady *(aquella señora)* was more beautiful than the other images, and [that] they loved her a lot because she was of their color.[30]

It was not that Ocaña made his Virgin darker than the original (the face of the sculpted image of the Virgin of Guadalupe of Extremadura was, and is, famously dark); it is, as Jeanette Peterson has neatly observed, that he painted her slightly lighter, intentionally approximating the tone of the Indians' skin.[31] Ocaña's words about the color of the Virgin's skin in the image he had painted, and about the direct appeal to native Andeans, are revealing, especially when connected to the Jeronymite's strong reaction to the lack of *estampas* and the official denial of permission to found a *cofradía* of Indians in Potosí. They carry us closer to his intentions in the imperial city, and to the place his account of events there were meant to enjoy within his hagiographic account.

Ocaña notes that enthusiasm for the Virgin of Guadalupe was fanned in Potosí by at least two famous local preachers, the prior of the Dominican convent, Padre Fray Tomás Blanes,[32] and the Franciscan sermonizer and expert in the native Andean languages of Quechua and Aymara, Luis Jerónimo de Oré. Oré, in particular, was said to have addressed Indian congregations in their own tongue "every Sunday." On those occasions "he preached to the Indians of one or another miracle from this book of Our Lady of Guadalupe," a reference to Gabriel de Talavera's 1597 *Historia de Nuestra Señora de Guadalupe,* which Ocaña had carried to the New World as a principal inspiration and pastoral resource.[33]

The miracle stories selected from Talavera's *Historia* and employed by Blanes and Oré (not to mention Ocaña himself and other religious on other occasions), like the texts of the sermons, are not known from anything but Ocaña's summaries. Yet I believe that something of their content can be surmised by connecting these hints to a few sources that do survive, not least a play and twelve verses in praise of the Virgin's miraculous history and power, all of which Ocaña composed in Potosí. The *comedia* was put on at least twice, in Potosí in 1601 and in Chuquisaca in 1602 as part of the inspirational buzz and excitement sought by the *demandador*;[34] the hymns were sung by a student and choir of friars in the church of San Francisco at the time of his image's enshrinement.[35]

In brief, the play and verses can be understood as lyrical, performed encapsulations of a ready stock of miraculous information channeled from the Guadalupan miracle tradition, perhaps directly through Gabriel de Talavera's *Historia.*[36] Their author intended a transatlantic connection. Ocaña sought to impart a sense of the historic power of the Virgin of Guadalupe as an intercessor in an Old World while beginning the task of joining that sense of her power to the new setting of Potosí. He traded in an established polemical and miraculous tradition, and also in the purely human drama and power of the miracle tales of captives freed from grief and suffering under the Moor. Such messages may have inspired and refreshed people of Spanish descent and Hispanicized upbringings, but in the differently packaged forms of a viewable dramatic performance and, even more important, in native-language sermons, they also reached determinedly beyond such people, toward the Indian mineworkers and their families. Words and categories that had meant one set of things in the Reconquest and post-Reconquest atmospheres of intermittent war, pirate raids, prisoners, and slavery in the Iberian and Mediterranean worlds acquired pointed new meanings and value in the Andes. Different kinds of pain are evoked, new chains clank, and the Virgin offers succor amid the danger and drudgery of the mines and the tribute obligations, the Indians' colonial captivity.[37]

By Ocaña's account, a receptive and facilitating environment for the Virgin of Guadalupe had been carefully nurtured in Potosí. And it was during the festivities immediately following the enshrinement of the painted image in San Francisco that embryonic devotion is said to have brought its answer. The Virgin of Guadalupe, via God, responded with miracles. Diego de Ocaña's account reached its height in the reporting of "just two miracles"—that is how Ocaña put it. And they were not just any miracles: there was one for each of the key social communities in Potosí, the Indian and the Spanish, and each event had been investigated and authorized by an ecclesiastical *ordinario,* Ocaña stressed, " in accordance with the guidelines of the council."[38]

Both of Ocaña's miracle narratives, only the first of which I shall summarize here, recalled the patterns of older stories from the miraculous record kept by the Jeronymites in Guadalupe and from the compilation made by Talavera.[39] Yet into these patterns considerable local details were carefully tipped. The first of the two miracle stories involved the miraculous healing of a Spanish child stricken with a mysterious affliction. The boy, whose condition had deteriorated until he had become "like a dead thing" *(como una cossa muerta),* lived in the household of Juan Díaz de Talavera. The message was clear to any who cared to consider it, for Díaz de Talavera was the *síndico* of the convent of San Francisco, an influential local magistrate *(veinticuatro del cabildo),* lay agent, and crucial supporter who had not only funded the making of the new image but also whom Ocaña had chosen the *mayordomo* to oversee the spread of devotion and gathering of donations for the Virgin of Guadalupe. After nine days of watching the boy's condition worsen, the child's aunt, Anna de Salas, and another woman, María de Saldivia, covered the boy in a shroud and carried him to the base of the altar before the new image in the church of San Francisco. There, in front of many witnesses in the church, the women prayed fervently to Our Lady of Guadalupe to revive the child, only to see the boy come back to life. Within two days he was recovered, though very thin from his ordeal. Ocaña implied that, after this point, the child's gradual recovery of weight seemed linked to the rise in the people's veneration of the image that the miracle inspired.[40]

The story of the Spanish boy, while near to the thaumaturgical borderline between the common and the truly special,[41] was a classic tale of resuscitation. Even the story's principal local touch—that the child and the aunt and her friend were attached to the household of the chief *mayordomo* of the new *cofradía*—fitted snugly into an older pattern. The Virgin had often rewarded her chief servants in this way. Indeed, this common miracle type began, as it were, at a Guadalupan beginning, with the resurrection of the son of Gil Cordero, the cowherd to whom Mary had appeared in the sierra of Villuercas in the early fourteenth century and directed to her buried image.[42]

The second miracle attributed to Nuestra Señora de Guadalupe in Potosí in these days was a miraculous rescue of Indian mineworkers after a work-related accident. As with the first story, it is rather a stock type as contemporary miracle stories go.[43] Yet, even more than the first story, it betrays Ocaña's skills as a researcher of information and as player upon the expectations and needs of his audiences in Potosí.[44] One of the mining galleries on the *Cerro Rico* had caved in, and six Indian mineworkers were trapped beneath the rocks and earth. Five days of digging ensued, but the men still could not be reached. The Spanish mineowner was said to have appeared in the church of San Francisco, asking for a Mass to be said to Our Lady of Guadalupe. But he had come not out of devotion or genuine concern for the workers, Ocaña postulated with an undisguised directing of his readers' reactions, he was there because he had begun to worry about the compensatory payments he would need to make to the Indians' widows.[45]

When attempts to reach the mineworkers were abandoned after five days, the wives of the trapped men, along with many other Indian women, went back down to the church of San Francisco, "all of them weeping and crying out to Our Lady of Guadalupe," Ocaña reported, "pleading with her to watch over their husbands and keep them alive." Ocaña claimed that the *corregidor* (district administrator) in charge of affairs in Potosí was then moved by the Virgin of Guadalupe herself to go against normal procedure and order the women and others back up the mountain to resume digging for the trapped men. Meanwhile, the mineowner, who was not so moved, stayed behind in San Francisco. Ocaña claims to have gone up to the Spaniard and provoked an admission: Had he not come to the church on the day of the accident and entrusted Our Lady with the protection of the trapped men? The mineowner (who, for all his sins in this characterization, at least spoke forthrightly to the Jeronymite!) could not even claim credit for the request of the Mass; "it turns out that it was [made by] a friend of his," Ocaña added.

No sooner had the re-formed work party begun their digging than they began to hear shouts from within the mine. Not even a whisper had been heard in the whole five days of desperate excavations before this one. The trapped men, very much alive, now yelled out instructions to their wives. Ocaña offers a translation of what they are to have said "in their language": "Go to [the church of] San Francisco and pray to that Señora chapetona to get us out of here; she has been with us and she has given us water to drink from a porongo (a gourd)." The mineworkers were soon reached by their rescuers, and they are said to have climbed out of the collapsed mine "healthy and well," showing few effects of their ordeal.[46]

Ocaña's second miracle story tapped into the prevailing atmosphere of fear and death reported by contemporary mine inspectors and tellers of cave-in stories in Potosí. It is a well-observed narrative climax, getting local details and characters "right," an edifying story as persuasive and didactic as any of its kind in contemporary hagiography. There are Indian mineworkers "without hope" and left for dead in the mines, which in 1600 symbolized the Spanish extraction of wealth from America; there is a persistently selfish Spanish mineowner; there are Christian Indian women whose devotion is central and who, as prospective widows, might need paying; there is even, for good measure, a lone Spanish official who is reached by the Virgin and does not give up. And there is a rescue that could not have been brought by human measure.

Ocaña's message is delivered: while committed devotees of Spanish descent might take comfort in their miracle of the resuscitated boy, the Indians' newly kindled adherence to the image of the *Señora Chapetona* in the church of San Francisco wins the day. The Virgin of Guadalupe has noticed the native Andeans' plight and devotion, and the alms they could not afford to give. In their time of need, she has heard, and responds to, the prayers of the men in the collapsed mine and the women before her image; thanks to her apparition the mineworkers do not die, and thanks to her mediation, a miracle from God delivers them from death.

The stirring effect of this miraculous rescue and its retellings among the native Andeans in Potosí was, not surprisingly, stressed by Diego de Ocaña. "The Indians were so much moved," Ocaña writes, "that we could scarcely fit into the church of San Francisco."[47] And the miracle appears to have been pressed straight into duty (in the hopes of reaching even more Indians) by perhaps the most experienced and powerful local exemplarist: "the Very Reverend Father Luis Jerónimo de Oré preached of it [the miracle of the Indians' rescue] to all the Indians in their tongue," Ocaña wrote.[48]

"The Indians were so much moved," wrote Diego de Ocaña. How much is hopeful, hagiographic fantasy? How much of this maker-participant-teller's flight toward a miraculous climax in an exemplary pattern takes us steadily away from the reality of events in Potosí? While the questions are unanswerable in certain terms, Ocaña's report of a surge in devotion around the new image of the Virgin of Guadalupe, of crowds in the church of San Francisco, are borne out in a mundane document I have found preserved by the Franciscans in Potosí.

A memorandum dated November 14, 1600, and signed by seven friars (one of whom was the preacher Luis Jerónimo de Oré, who had taken the Virgin's miracle stories to Indians), states that a new image of the Virgin of Guadalupe had aroused such "devotion and crowds of people to the Masses and the *salves* on Saturdays" that significant changes were being contemplated in the church. The devotees of Mary of Guadalupe were regularly overfilling the chapel of the Immaculate Conception of the Mother of God. If this were allowed to continue, the older and established *cofradía* of the Limpia Concepción would have to be reaccommodated. Much might be offered the older lay association, but there was the vexing problem of prestige and precedence, the severe risk of causing an affront to the venerable *cofradía* if the friars attempted to free space to meet the enthusiastic response to the image of Our Lady of Guadalupe.[49]

There is not a whiff of triumph or boasting in this document, but rather some convincingly administrative hand-wringing, the sense of an earnest search for a resolution to a sticky internal challenge. The documentary fragment offers a glance behind the hagiographic peak in Ocaña's account of the rise in new devotion, a suggestion of people visiting and milling around the new image in Potosí that is as independent of the founder's orchestrating ink as one is likely to find. The Franciscans' memo does not mention the rescue miracle or any other, but it strongly suggests that in the month or so following events in October 1600, their church had indeed begun to fill with devotees of the new image painted by Diego de Ocaña. Like the Dominican Reginaldo de Lizárraga's recorded observations of fervent devotion in the new chapel of Our Lady of Guadalupe near Lima some five years after the enshrinement of Ocaña's image there (noted above), it suggests some real edges around the smooth of Ocaña's account, while illuminating at least the very immediate aftermath of the Jeronymite's activities.

Diego de Ocaña arrived in the former Inka capital of Cusco on August 24, 1603. He was warmly received at the monastery of San Francisco, where the friars were eager for news from their brethren in Potosí. Ocaña would stay a little less than two months, and be challenged in ways that recalled, at first, his experiences near Saña far more than those in the *villa imperial,* for he found in Cusco two existing images of Our Lady of Guadalupe. Critically, neither was in the power of a religious order in the manner of the existing image he visited on the northern coast. One of the Cuzqueño images of Mary of Guadalupe was in "the chapel of Don Melchor Inga [Don Melchor Carlos Inka]" in the church of San Francisco itself. The second image of Our Lady of Guadalupe was in church of San Blas, in the parish of Indians of the same name.[50]

Ocaña described both of the Cusco images as dating "from the time of Padre Fray Diego de Losal [del Losar]," a mostly mysterious Jeronymite predecessor from Guadalupe who had spent some twelve years as a *demandador* in the Andes,[51] without elaborating any more on what he may have learned about what had transpired between del Losar's time and his own. At first glance the discovery of surviving images from del Losar's earlier efforts would seem to have called for celebration by Ocaña. Moreover, these discoveries can appear to contradict Ocaña's repeated depiction of his predecessor as a man who had made no lasting impression. Yet, for Ocaña, what truly mattered was the kind of cultic survival, the kind of impression. What was wrong with the two Cuzqueño cults, in Ocaña's eyes, was simple: devotees had forgotten their obligation to the original image of Our Lady of Guadalupe and her Spanish shrine. Devotion and alms had become untethered. What had seemed so unreachable in the case of the image and shrine controlled by the Augustinians near Saña—and what had led him to enshrine and puff the fortunes of a new image he installed near Lima as the coastal rival—might be confronted more directly in Cusco.

Ocaña's own terms in describing his further actions shed light on his intentions. He writes of his attempt "to renew (renovar) the Spaniards' image, in order to renew, as well, devotion to and memory of Our Lady of Guadalupe."[52] The fate of the image in the parish of Indians of San Blas is not revealed or perhaps even known by Ocaña, but there is no missing the fact that he meant to displace it.[53] The demandador's sense of providing an overarching remedy for what he perceived as the problem posed by both of the images from the time of his predecessor is clear. He sought a transformation, an end for the two existing cults and a new beginning in which people would transfer their devotion to another image, a replacement that Ocaña himself would paint and see enshrined in the chapel of Don Melchor Carlos Inka and that the Jeronymite would ensure was properly sanctioned and supervised by new mayordomos. Ocaña's repeated use of the verb renovar, which I am glossing as "renew," in this instance is worth lingering over.[54] He did not use the word in contemplation of what could not be achieved near Saña or of what might be done in Lima (nor, for that matter, did he employ renovar in explaining similar actions in Ica, which I do not treat here). Ocaña was not engaged in the restoration of an existing image; he meant renovar in a more pointed, contemporary sense.

Ocaña set to painting a replacement image for Cusco, and thought carefully about how best to ensure the termination of devotion to the older images, and an awakened and enduring devotion to the new one. "To end all this [the devotion to the existing images]," Ocaña writes, "I made another image in this city and enshrined it in the same chapel."[55] His choice of the same chapel in which a cult to Our Lady had already strayed seems ill considered at first glance, but from Ocaña's point of view it was entirely consistent with the favor he showed to Franciscan convents and churches elsewhere (in both Potosí and Ica).[56] Besides, substituting one image for another was one thing, while outright suppression would be quite another: though he wrote nothing about it, perhaps Ocaña knew enough to fear the effects of too radical a move against the existing devotees of "the Spaniards' image" in the church of San Francisco in Cusco. Ocaña had noticed a silver lamp, filled with oil and burning continuously, in the chapel, endowed for perpetuity, and he was not to be distracted from the security offered by this established setting patronized by a wealthy Inka noble whom the Jeronymite appears to have seen no reason to distrust.[57]

Ocaña wrote of a triumph in Cusco that not only involved but also moved the people once again to bless (and ornament) a new image. He had gathered enough of the civic and ecclesiastical establishment on his side to fuel a memorable spectacle in service of his beginning. The story of another kind of new foundation, but with trademark elements, was being inscribed:

> With help of the things the people gave, I made a very beautiful image.
> And, with its many jewels, received from the people with much devotion,
> they carried it in procession all the way from the convent of Santa Clara to
> [the church and monastery of] San Francisco, which is to say from one side
> of the city to the other.[58]

The solemn procession saw special decorations; celebrations; and, according to Ocaña, daily Masses and *salves,* which drew crowds and lasted through nine days of festivities. On the night before the enshrinement, the *corregidor,* Pedro de Córdova Megia, commanded that all the streets, doorways, windows, church towers, and, above the city, even the ruins of the former Inka fortress of Sacsayhuaman be grandly lit up for the occasion. "It seemed as if the city was on fire," Ocaña wrote.[59] The bishop ordered all of Cusco's *cofradías* to march in welcome, and he himself blessed the new image of Our Lady before a new Mass was sung in the convent of Santa Clara, on the occasion of a sister taking the veil.[60] Consecration also brought the opportunity for preaching. Because the nuns were celebrating the festival of St. Francis, Diego de Ocaña preached on this holy subject before later (during the *novenario*) delivering two more sermons in the church of San Francisco, this time on his home subject of the history and power of Our Lady of Guadalupe.

The action can seem so different from what Ocaña pursued in Potosí. Did some Cuzqueños question or resent the replacement, the new and authorized image painted by this wandering Spanish friar, perhaps prompting them to turn to other saintly advocates or to an image of the Virgin of Guadalupe that someone had spirited away? Both of the images Ocaña found and displaced appear to have been venerated by current devotees. Around the image in the parish church of San Blas in 1603, Ocaña even reported that there was an existing *cofradía* of Indians, and also that "Spanish people attended for novenas."[61] In such circumstances there is no denying Ocaña's wresting of control in Cusco, the sharpness of what he did. "The image was placed in that chapel in which the other had been before," he wrote succinctly, and two new *mayordomos* were entrusted with the care of the image and the gathering and remittance of alms each year.[62] For him and, he trusted, for others, this was an act of renewal, a new beginning akin to the one in Potosí.

Although Diego de Ocaña could only bear to write about such matters indirectly, he had faced more than once the almost inescapable fate of his efforts as a propagator and reformer of Guadalupan devotion in the Indies. The shrine of the Virgin of Guadalupe attended by the friars of St. Augustine, near Saña, which he attempted to outshine with a chapel in Lima, like the veneration of existing images he faced down in Cusco, were signs of what lay ahead for his new sacred foundations. Even his arguably most promising cultic beginning in Potosí failed to develop as he intended. It was not long before Ocaña's careful designs wore down, and adjusted, more localized patterns of piety began to take their place. In all but one case (Chuquisaca, not treated in this chapter), his holy images were replaced in the settings he had arranged, and in all cases (including Chuquisaca) his *mayordomos'* successors faltered in terms of their set tasks, with remittances of alms to the Spanish sanctuary of Guadalupe apparently petering out within a few years of his departure.[63]

In the end, the resemblance between that which was attempted by Diego de Ocaña and by his predecessor Diego del Losar is striking. Ocaña left more traces of his thoughts and actions almost solely because he wrote about them. Even surviving written words proved impossible to fix as a single version, a fact perhaps best illustrated by the fate of the pinnacle of Ocaña's account, the miracle story from Potosí that dealt in the rescue of the Indian mineworkers. If Potosinos continued to tell the story recorded by Ocaña and preached by Luis Jerónimo de Oré, they would seem to have done so in ways that suited themselves, mixing its plot and details with other, similar stories such as the ones picked up and retold by Bartolomé Arzáns de Orsua y Vela in his early eighteenth-century history of their city.[64] The miracle narrative, like the new holy image at its center, slipped away from its first participant-teller to become the property of others, and not only people resident in the *villa imperial.*

In August 1601 Don Luis de Quiñones Osorio, a royal treasurer in Potosí, returned to Spain, and made a pilgrimage to the sanctuary of Our Lady of Guadalupe in Extremadura. He brought news of a miracle worked by God through the intercession of Mary in the mines of Potosí. In its transmission of the Virgin's (and Ocaña's) achievements in a far-off place to the center—through the process of being recorded in the miracle volumes in the archive of the Jeronymite monastery—the local miracle story was much changed. The details of Potosí fell away to meet the needs of the *santa casa* of Guadalupe. The local and the specific became abstracted in the interests of the universal and more generally powerful, or, put another way, in the interests of another local setting. There is nothing of the desperate rescue attempts, nothing of the work parties or mine inspectors, nothing of the gourd of water with which the Virgin sustained her desperate devotees—none of the ingredients that evoked local events, fears, and concerns. In the miracle volume testimony there is, rather, a story of pure miraculous transport, as from the dark of a Moorish dungeon to a just-departing ship in port. Within an hour of the Virgin's apparition to the men, they found themselves out of the collapsed mine, without a scratch.[65]

Quiñones de Osorio's pilgrimage had brought the story from Potosí back within a miraculous tradition much older and larger than itself—as the manacles and chains of former captives on the walls of the basilica or the dark *tablas* depicting miracles in the *mudéjar* cloister of the monastery would have reminded the bearer.[66] While the story could be said, in part, to have sprung from the traditions of this central shrine in the first place, it came from elsewhere. Diego de Ocaña had ensured that the miracle story, like the holy image he had painted in Potosí, was enmeshed within a particular American setting and the lives of its people. When the story of the rescued mineworkers was recorded in the miraculous catalog in the Spanish sanctuary, the balance that Ocaña had reached at the height of his hagiographic account was lost; one local purpose passed behind another.

NOTES

1. I will use the following abbreviations: AGI, Archivo General de Indias, Seville, Spain; AHN, Archivo Histórico Nacional, Madrid, Spain; AMG, Archivo del Real Monasterio de Guadalupe, Guadalupe, Spain; ABAS, Archivo-Biblioteca Arquidiocesanos "Monsignor Taborga," Sucre, Bolivia; ABNB, Archivo y Biblioteca Nacionales de Bolivia, Sucre, Bolivia; ACSFP, Archivo del Convento San Francisco de Potosí, Potosí, Bolivia; APDAL, Archivo de la Provincia de los Doce Apostoles de Lima, Lima, Peru; BE, Biblioteca del Escorial, El Escorial, Spain; BNM, Biblioteca Nacional de España, Madrid, Spain.
2. AMG, Códice 61 (Necrología de monjes, 1600–1747), fol. 7r.
3. Biblioteca de la Universidad de Oviedo, España, M-204, is untitled, but has been called the "Relación del viaje de Fray Diego de Ocaña por el Nuevo Mundo (1599–1605)."
4. See William B. Taylor's contribution to this volume, "Mexico's Virgin of Guadalupe in the Seventeenth Century." See also Thérèse Bouysse-Cassagne, "De Empédocles a Tunupa: Evangelización, hagiografía y mitos," in *Saberes y memorias en los Andes. In memoriam Thierry Saignes,* ed. Thérèse Bouysse-Cassagne (Paris: Institut des Hautes Études de l'Amérique Latine; Lima: Institut Français d'Études Andines, 1997), 157–212; Sofia Boesch Gajano, *Agiografia altomedioevale* (Bologna: 1976), 7–48; Donald Weinstein and Rudolph M. Bell, *Saints and Society: The Two Worlds of Christendom, 1000–1700* (Chicago: University of Chicago Press, 1982), esp. 166–93.
5. In what follows, I move often between the periodic narratives and his synthetic roundup. The latter is at "Relación," fols. 213r–215v, after Ocaña's account of his adventures in Potosí.
6. Ica and Chuquisaca (La Plata, the modern Sucre, Bolivia), in which Ocaña also painted and left images, must await another opportunity. On another image painted in Panama and left in Saña on the northern coast please see Kenneth Mills, "Diego de Ocaña, Holy Wanderer," in *The Human Tradition in Colonial Latin America,* ed. Kenneth J. Andrien (Wilmington, Del.: Scholarly Resources, 2002), 121–39.
7. These concerns had recently been reaffirmed as crucial matters of Catholic Christian faith both, expansively, by the Council of Trent (1545–63) and, more locally, by the late-sixteenth-century Jeronymite monastery of Guadalupe. The stipulations from the twenty-fifth session (December 3–4, 1563) of Trent can be studied in Norman P. Tanner, ed., *Decrees of the Ecumenical Councils* (London: Sheed & Ward; Washington, D.C.: Georgetown University Press, 1990) 2: 774–76. The influence of these Tridentine decrees can be traced to the Andes, especially in the first set of constitutions set down by the Second Provincial Council of Lima (1567–68), caput. 53: Quod sanctorum imagines sint omni decentia ac reverentia (see Rubén Vargas Ugarte, ed., *Concilios Limenses (1551–1772)* [Lima: S. A. Rávago e Hijos, 1951–54], vol. 1: 125) with confirmations by Lima's Third Provincial Council (1582–83), (Vargas Ugarte, ed., *Concilios,* vol. 1: 333 [Segunda action, cap. 25] and 366 [Quarta action, cap. 10]). On the motherhouse of Guadalupe's attitude, see below.
8. Ruben Vargas Ugarte, *Historia del culto de Maria en Hispanoamerica y de sus imagenes y santuarios mas celebrados* (Lima: Imprenta "La Providencia," 1931), 454–56.
9. On the Guadalupe of the northern coast from a later and supremely Augustinian point of view, Antonio de la Calancha, *Corónica moralizada,* ed. Ignacio Prado Pastor (Lima: Imprenta de la Universidad Nacional Mayor de San Marcos, [1638] 1974–81), esp. vol. 4, 1225–1385. Vargas Ugarte, working in part from Calancha, also relates some of the image's miracles; *Historia del culto,* 456–60.
10. "Relación," fol. 213v. Even allowing for Calancha's pride (see n. 9 above), the Augustinians' Guadalupe was the dominant Christian pilgrimage site on the northern coast in 1599.
11. "Relación," fol. 30r.
12. The viceroy's census of 1614 provides a rough estimate at best, but it put Lima's population at 25,454 persons, among whom were 10,386 people of African descent (5,587 women and 4,529 men); 9,616 people of Spanish descent (5,257 men and 4,359 women); 1,978 native Andeans (1,116 men and 862 women); 744 mulattoes (418 women and 326 men); and 192 mestizos (97 men and 95 women). See also Buenaventura Salinas y Córdova, *Memorial de las historias del Nuevo Mundo, Piru: Meritos, y excelencias de la Çiudad de Lima* (Lima, 1630) and useful discussion of contemporary population figures by Frederick P. Bowser in *The African Slave in Colonial Peru, 1524–1650* (Stanford: Calif.: Stanford University Press, 1974), 337–41.
13. "Relación," fols. 214v–215r.
14. "Relación," fol. 30r. Sebastián de Covarrubias Orozco defines an *ermita* as "a small place with a space apart as an oratory or small chapel, and a narrow corner into which he who lives there can withdraw," *Tesoro de la lengua castellana o española,* ed. Felipe C. R. Maldonado and Manuel Camarero (Madrid: Editorial Castalia, 1995), 486.
15. "Relación," fol. 56v. Ocaña included and signed his entire petition at fols. 56r–56v.
16. "Relación," fol. 56v. He also tells of attracting a rich and pious widow, Doña Jerónima de Orozco; fols. 59r–59v.
17. "Relación," fol. 57r.
18. "Relación," fol. 58r.

19. "Relación," fol. 57v. On the "hermita de Nuestra de Señora de Guadalupe," which Ocaña established on the edge of what was then the city of Lima: AMG Leg. 60, Escrituras de la fundación de la capilla de Nuestra Señora de Guadalupe en Lima, otorgada por Alonso Ramos Cervantes y Doña Elvira de la Serna, a favor de este Monasterio representado por Fr. Diego de Ocaña el año 1600, Lima, 2 de mayo de 1612. An eighteenth-century document in the Franciscan archive in Lima corroborates the arrangement, and raises the possibility that a Jeronymite convent might even have been entertained; APDAL, Registro A, parte 2, esp. fols. 556r–556v. Mons. Federico Richter, who has charted the vicissitudes of the Franciscan colegio into which Ocaña's foundation turned, asserts that the chapel-*cum*-colegio sat in the spot now occupied by the Palacio de Justicia in modern Lima; "El desaparecido Colegio de San Buenaventura de Nuestra Señora de Guadalupe de Lima (1611–1826)," *Anales de la Provincia Franciscana de los Doce Apostoles de Lima* 6 (1989), 30.

20. "Relación," fol. 58r.

21. Reginaldo de Lizárraga, *Descripción del Perú, Tucumán, Río de la Plata y Chile,* ed. Ignacio Ballesteros (Madrid: Historia 16, 1986), 115–16.

22. This Christ enjoys pride of place in the church of San Francisco in Potosí today.

23. "Relación," 168v, 170v.

24. See Luis Capoche's two contemporary cave-in stories, followed by other tales of terrible accidents in the *ingenios. Relación general de la Villa Imperial de Potosí,* ed. Lewis Hanke, Biblioteca de Autores Españoles, vol. 122 (Madrid: Ediciones Atlas, [1585] 1959), 158–59. Capoche was resident in Potosí in 1601: ABNB Cabildo de Potosí, Libros de Acuerdos, vol. 9, Potosí, July 24, 1601, fol. 171v. Within an extensive literature on Potosí see Laura Escobari de Querejazu, "Migración multietnica y mano de obra calificada en Potosí, siglo XVI," *Etnicidad, economía y simbolismo en los Andes,* ed. Silvia Arze et al. (La Paz: HISBOL, Sociedad Boliviana de Historia, Antropólogos del Sur Andino; Lima: Instituto Francés de Estudios Andinos, 1991), 67–83, and "Poblados de indios dentro de poblados de españoles. El caso de La Paz y Potosí," in *Pueblos de indios. Otro urbanismo en la región andina,* ed. Ramón Gutiérrez (Quito: Ediciones Abya-Yala, 1993), 317–80.

25. "Relación," fol. 159r–159v.

26. See "Relación," fols. 173v–176r.

27. "Relación," fols. 152v–153r, 159r–159v.

28. "Relación," fols. 159r, 163v.

29. David Freedberg, *The Power of Images: Studies in the History and Theory of Response* (Chicago: University of Chicago Press, 1989), esp. 109–12.

30. ". . . como yo la pinte un poquito morena, y los indios lo son decian que aquella señora era mas linda que las otras ymagenes, y la querian mucho porque era de su color." "Relación," fol. 163v.

31. Jeanette Favrot Peterson, "Shades of Blackness: The Virgin of Guadalupe from Spain to the Americas" (Bakwin Lecture at Wellesley College, unpublished paper).

32. "Relación," fols. 151v–152r.

33. "Relación," fol. 164r. Good orientation on Oré is Noble David Cook's introduction to Oré's *Relación de la vida y milagros de San Francisco Solano* (Lima: Pontificia Universidad Católica del Perú, [c. 1614] 1998). Gabriel de Talavera, *Historia de nuestra señora de Guadalupe* (Toledo: en la casa de Thomas de Guzmán, 1597).

34. On the accessibility of this play, Ocaña himself wrote that "whoever enjoys verse drama can read it [el que tuviere gusto la podra leer]," "Relación," fols. 192r–192v. The text of his "Comedia de N.S. de Guadalupe y sus milagros" duly appears as part of his description of the elaborate festivities in the regional capital, "Relación" fols. 235r–254r. See Teresa Gisbert's introduction to Diego de Ocaña, *Comedia de Nuestra Señora de Guadalupe y sus milagros* (La Paz: Biblioteca Paceña-Alcaldía Municipal [ca. 1600–1], 1957), also Theresa Gisbert, *Teatro virreinal en Bolivia* (La Paz: Biblioteca de Arte y Cultura Boliviana y Editorial del Estado, 1962), 20–25. The play also has been edited by Villacampa in *La Virgen,* 197–291 and by Álvarez (see Ocaña, *Un viaje,* apendice 6, 367–433), and it appears in Don Vicente Barrantes' handwritten copy (1880), wrongly attributed to "Fr. Diego de Prades [sic. Ocaña]": AMG Ms. B-104, fols. 5–102. See also Gretchen Starr-LeBeau's " 'The Joyous History of Devotion and Memory of the Grandeur of Spain': The Spanish Virgin of Guadalupe and Religious and Political Memory," in *Archive for Reformation History* (forthcoming) and, more broadly, Marie Helmer, "Apuntes sobre el teatro en la Villa Imperial de Potosí (documentos del Archivo de Potosí, 1572–1636), *Instituto de Investigaciones Históricas,* Universidad de Tomás Frias, vol. 2 (1960), 1–10.

35. "Relación," fols. 154r–157r; Ocaña, *Un viaje fascinante,* ed. Álvarez, appendix 3: 316–20.

36. On Ocaña's act of translation between miraculous contexts see Ocaña, "Relación," fol. 154v, fourth stanza. For more on this theme see my "Diego de Ocaña e la organizzazione del miraloso a Potosí" in *Il santo patrono e la città. San Benedetto il Moro: culti, devozioni, strategie di età moderna,* ed. Giovanna Fiume (Venezia: Marsilio Editori, 2000), 372–90, and, more broadly, Rafael Carrasco, "Milagrero siglo XVII," *Estudios de Historia Social* 36–37 (1986), 401–22, and William A. Christian

Jr., "De los santos a María: panorama de los devociones a santuarios españoles desde el principio de la Edad Media hasta nuestros días," in *Temas de antropología española,* ed. Carmelo de Lisón Tolosana (Madrid: Akal, 1976), 49–105, and "Recopilaciones de milagros en la red de santuarios españoles," in *Libro de los milagros de la Virgen de Orito,* ed. Anton Erkoreka et al. (Alicante: Santuario de Nuestra Señora de Orito y de San Pascual Bailón, 1998), 35–44. And on the sixteenth-century miracles of the Virgin of Guadalupe, esp. Françoise Crémoux, *Pèlerinages et miracles à Guadalupe au XVIe siècle* (Madrid: Casa de Velázquez, 2001).

37. "Relación," fol. 156v, tenth and eleventh stanzas.

38. "Relación," fol. 162v. Here Ocaña follows established procedures for the reporting and verification of miracles and apparitions, and made a bishop's authorization mandatory; *Decrees of the Ecumenical Councils,* ed. Norman P. Tanner (London: Sheed & Ward; Washington, D.C.: Georgetown University Press, 1990), vol. 2, 774–76, esp. 776. As William A. Christian Jr. has observed, the Tridentine norms, while strict, can be seen as "the continuation of the practice of many of the shrines in Spain as early as the mid-fifteenth century." See pioneering discussion by Christian in *Local Religion,* 103, 102–5.

39. The nine codices preserved in the Archivo del Real Monasterio de Guadalupe (AMG) record miracles reported by pilgrims who had traveled to the sanctuary to fulfill their vows and give thanks to the Virgin for benefits received between 1407 and 1722. Antonio Ramiro Chico, who is putting together a catalog of their contents, has surveyed the first six códices thus far. He finds five "predicaments" ["situaciones difíciles"] in which people most frequently sought the Virgin's miraculous protection: captivity or slavery; danger at sea; the cure of disease or illness; assistance in public or social strife; and, most broadly of all, rescue from all other manner of evil or danger. See Ramiro Chico, "Nueve códices de 'Milagros de Nuestra Señora de Guadalupe' " *Guadalupe* no. 669 (1984), 59–61, and, for his cataloging to date, nos. 669 (1984): 58–71; 670 (1984): 136–43; 672 (1984): 245–52; 676 (1985): 98–107; 680 (1986): 2–32; 696 (1988): 289–98. In the last quarter of the sixteenth century alone, hundreds of these miracle narratives, told by all sorts of people, were scrutinized for authenticity and recorded by the Jeronymite guardians of the sanctuary. Other extant Guadalupan miracle collections include BNM Ms. 1176 and BE Códice IV-a.

40. "Relación," fol. 162v.

41. Distinctions between miraculous resuscitations and simply amazing recoveries were also carefully observed in contemporary investigations of an individual's alleged sanctity and miracle-working. See the details of Francisco de San Joseph Suessa's investigations in 1615 into the purported miracles of the Franciscan Francisco Solano (1549–1610) in Peru; Noble David Cook, "Introducción," in Luis Jerónimo de Oré, *Relación de la vida y milagros de San Francisco Solano* (Lima: Pontificia Universidad Católica del Perú, 1998 [c. 1614]), xix–xx.

42. The earliest surviving account, from about a century after the purported event, is AHN Clero Códice 48 B (ca. 1400–1440), which appears to have been at least partly written by a Jeronymite friar named Alonso de la Rambla. But see also the more enthralling AHN Clero Códice 101 B (from the sixteenth century); the prefatory account of the discovery and shrine origins in AMG Códice 1, Milagros de Nuestra Señora de Guadalupe desde el año de 1407 hasta 1497; and the early chronicle, Diego de Ecija, *Libro de la invención de Santa María de Guadalupe; y de la erección y fundación de este Monasterio; y de algunas cosas particulares y vidas de algunos religiosos de él,* ed. Arcángel Barrado Manzano (Cáceres: Biblioteca Extremeña y Departamento Provincial de Seminarios de F.E.T. y de las J.O.N.S., [ca. 1514–56] 1953). A good framing discussion by Tomás Bernal García appears in *Guadalupe,* ed. Sebastián García y Felipe Trenado, 19–58.

43. See Michael E. Goodich, *Violence and Miracle in the Fourteenth Century: Private Grief and Public Salvation* (Chicago: University of Chicago Press, 1995). Treating sixteenth-century Guadalupan evidence, Françoise Crémoux, *Pèlerinages et miracles.*

44. "Relación," fols. 163r–163v.

45. "Relación," fol. 163r.

46. "Relación," fol. 163v.

47. "Relación," fol. 163v.

48. "Relación," fol. 164r.

49. ACSFP, Libro 1, Convento de San Francisco, Potosí, 14 de noviembre de 1600.

50. About two decades after Ocaña's stay in Cusco, the Carmelite Antonio Vázquez de Espinosa wrote of seven parishes of Indians, within which some fourteen thousand native Andeans (with many more in the city's environs) lived; *Compendio y descripción,* ed. B. Velasco Bayón (Madrid: Atlas, [c. 1620] 1969), 395, entries 1599 and 1601.

In his discussion of the Jeronymite's actions in the Andes, Arturo Álvarez misread Ocaña's note of the two existing images in Cusco and proceeded as if the image in the chapel of Don Melchor Carlos and the image in the parish church of San Blas were one and the same; *Guadalupe en la América andina,* 98, n. 20.

51. On Diego del Losar's mission, "Relación," fol. 214v.

52. "Relación," fol. 331r.

53. In brief, Ocaña's reticence seems connected to his fascination with the Inkas (by which I mean their pre-Hispanic history and imperial achievements, and their conquest by the Spanish [about both of which he read], and their elite descendants [whom he could see and about whom he could hear tell]) while in Cusco; they distracted him almost completely from consideration of the wider indigenous population of Cusco's colonial present. Kenneth Mills, "Cristianismo universal y la etnografía accidental en el Cusco colonial," unpublished paper delivered at "Cristianismo y el Poder en el Perú Colonial," Cusco, Peru, June 14–17, 2000.

54. See Sebastián de Covarrubias's first sense of *renovar* c. 1611 as "to make a thing like new." *Tesoro de la lengua,* 859.

55. "Relación," fol. 215v.

56. See discussion below, but also his reasons for preferring to leave images in Franciscan churches and convents at "Relación," fol. 357v.

57. The lamp at "Relación," fol. 331r, and mentioned also at 125r.

58. "Relación," fol. 331r.

59. "Relación," fol. 331v.

60. Contextualizing conventual life in this setting, Kathryn Burns, *Colonial Habits: Convents and the Spiritual Economy of Cusco, Peru* (Durham, N.C.: Duke University Press, 1999).

61. "[A] donde la gente española acudia a tener novenas," "Relación," fol. 215r.

62. "[Y] assi la pusse la ymagen en aquella capilla q. antes estava," "Relación," fol. 331v.

63. Kenneth Mills, "La 'Memoria Viva' de Diego de Ocaña en Potosí," *Anuario del Archivo y Biblioteca Nacionales de Bolivia* (1999), 197–241.

64. Lewis Hanke and Gunnar Mendoza, eds., *Historia de la villa imperial de Potosí* (Providence, R.I.: Brown University Press, 1965); among other examples, see esp. vol. 1, 303–5.

65. AMG Códice 8, fols. 85r–85v.

66. On the votive "grillos y cadenas" adorning the walls, inside and out, until the eighteenth century, see Carlos G. Villacampa, *Grandezas de Guadalupe,* 299. On the old *tablas* still present at the end of the sixteenth century, Talavera, *Historia,* book 4, ch. 3., fols. 192r–192v.

4

Old Bones and Beautiful Words: The Spiritual Contestation between Shaman and Jesuit in the Guaraní Missions

DOT TUER

In the northern Argentinean provinces of Misiones and Corrientes, where the grand Paraná River flows from Iguazú Falls to meet the Paraguay River and the indigenous language of Guaraní is still spoken by many as a mother tongue, a deep religiosity pervades the culture. In Misiones, once the site of the famous Jesuit missions or *reducciónes* (reductions), evidence of early conversion efforts are in ruins, covered by thick jungle foliage. In the capital of Corrientes, a colonial city founded in 1588, the spires of Jesuit, Franciscan, and Dominican churches remain signposts of a fierce evangelization. The cathedral harbors a vast (and undocumented) collection of wooden saints, many of which were carved in the 1700s by anonymous Guaraní artisans who learned their craft in the Jesuit missions. The oldest church, La Cruz del Milagro, houses a charred cross dating from 1592, a symbol of Christian supernatural power over attempts by hostile Indians to burn and destroy it. In the older neighborhoods of Corrientes, such as San Benito and Camba Cuá, household saints and virgins are paraded through the streets on religious holidays.[1]

While these Catholic icons are the visible legacies of a colonial project of religious conversion, there also exists a less visible but no less fervent veneration of folkloric saints such as San Lamuerte (the saint of death) that mix Guaraní and European influences.[2] A popular saint in the province of Corrientes and neighboring Misiones, San Lamuerte is traditionally made of human bone and carved by prisoners.[3] It comes in two versions. One is the Grim Reaper; the other, a small crouched figure that resembles the fetal position in which the Guaraní place their dead. The miniature Grim Reaper is used for protection and luck; Gauchos cover this version of the saint in silver and sew it inside the skin of their forearm.[4] The other version of the small crouched figure is kept in private homes and is passed through the female line of the family, who are responsible for maintaining an elaborate altar for its edification. Although San Lamuerte is not sanctioned by the church, local priests will sometimes acknowledge its existence as a form of Señor de la Paciencia. In order for San Lamuerte to achieve its considerable powers as an oracle and protector, it must be hidden inside the wooden figure of an official saint or Virgin and blessed unwittingly by a priest in a church on seven occasions.[5]

San Lamuerte serves as my theoretical amulet for the focus of this chapter—an analysis of shaminism and conversion strategies in Antonio Ruiz de Montoya's *La Conquista Espiritual del Paraguay,* an account of Jesuit missionary contact with the Guaraní written in the 1600s.[6] San Lamuerte, with his strange, illicit place in the litany of local saints, acknowledged but not officially sanctioned, half Catholic but also Guaraní, alerts us to the potential of a fluid world of spiritual exchange that underlies the visible codes of spiritual conquest, whether they be architectural or sculptural or textual. In turn, Ruiz de Montoya's *La Conquista Espiritual* reveals surprisingly porous boundaries between indigenous and Christian beliefs and visions. First published in Madrid in 1639 and one of the most widely read of the Jesuit accounts of the Paraguayan missions, it raises questions about the relationship between religious conversion and indigenous ritual. While the text is rhetorically structured as a first-person testimonial and ensconced within the Jesuit canon of mission texts, I want to suggest that nevertheless it can be read against the grain (in Gayatri Chakravorty Spivak's sense of literary sleuthing),[7] revealing a clash of world views that is at odds with traditional historical interpretations of the Jesuit mission project as either a benevolent but socially and culturally crippling paternalism or as a harsh pseudoplantation slavery for profit implemented under the cover of religious piety and zeal.[8]

As source material for the writing of colonial history, Montoya's account of his evangelizing activities raises important issues for the relationship between hagiography as an instructional text of religious conversion and its value as an ethnographic description of indigenous culture. While Montoya's and other Jesuit texts from the colonial period obviously view indigenous culture through the veil of Christian eyes (particularly in the manichean division of the world into the true God and pagan demons), what bleeds through this absolute conviction is the degree to which evangelization was subject to a negotiation between the spiritual realms of the Christian and the Guaraní. Through Montoya's descriptions of struggles over souls, he provides insights into the cultural dimension of the colonial periphery as a contact zone in which a blurring of boundaries between saintly conversion and shamanistic resistance occurs. In the same way that San Lamuerte unsettles the spiritual divide between Guaraní rituals of death and the Catholic cult of saints, so a reading of Ruiz de Montoya's *La Conquista Espiritual* against the grain dislodges assumptions about the ways in which Christian beliefs were received and mediated by indigenous peoples.

In part, my interest in Ruiz de Montoya lies in the fact that he provides one of the few extant texts on Guaraní culture of the colonial period outside of travelers' writings about Tupí-Guaraní and Tupinamba of Brazil, most notably Jean Léry's *Histoire d'un voyage fait en la terre du Brésil* (1578). Montoya is also interesting in that he was a creole, while most Jesuits undertaking mission work in Paraguay were from Europe. Born in Lima in 1585, he was the son of a Seville captain and a Peruvian woman.[9] His religious epiphany echoes that of Ignatius Loyola, who founded the Jesuit order in Paris in 1534 after renouncing a life as a soldier and adventurer. Montoya also led a dissolute life in Peru as a youth before beginning spiritual exercises in 1606 and receiving a vision of a field of pagans and transparent white-robed men that signaled the necessity of entering the order.[10] This mystic element of his faith, in which frequent visions of virgins and demons transported him to the spirit world, would remain with him throughout his life and inform his perceptions of the power of indigenous spirituality. After being ordained in 1611 in Santiago del Estero in northern Argentina, he traveled to Asunción to begin mission work in Paraguay, an administrative territory of the Jesuits that encompassed modern-day

Argentina, Bolivia, Uruguay, and southwestern Brazil as well as Paraguay. In 1622 he took his third set of vows at the Guairá mission of Loreta, in what is today Paraná Province in Brazil.

As a field missionary of the Jesuit order, Montoya entered a colonial region of the Spanish Crown already marked by a blurring of the boundaries between European and indigenous culture. Asunción, a strategic center of settlement and trade for the Spanish and a base for Jesuit missionary activities, was founded by Juan Salazar de Espinosa in 1537 after the garrison at Buenos Aires was destroyed by hostile pampa Indians. In the Guaraní territories of northern Argentina and Paraguay, the Spanish encountered a more hospitable climate of exchange and resources. Intermarriage as a form of strategic alliance was immediate and prolific, with the polygamous structure of Guaraní relations embraced by the Spanish. Martin de Barco Centenera's long historical poem *Argentina* describes Paraguay as "Mohamed's paradise" while Ruiz de Guzmán, a soldier on the Espinosa expedition, praised the Guaraní women as virtuous and beautiful.[11] In *La Conquista Espiritual* Ruiz de Montoya describes Asunción as having ten women for every man.[12] By 1600, indigenous food, beliefs, and customs were prevalent, and Guaraní had become the first language of the mestizo population. Due in part to the mixing of peoples and laxity of morals, the Jesuits were anxious to gather souls to be saved into missions remote from Spanish settlement.

From 1588, when the Jesuits first arrived in Asuncíon, until their expulsion from the Spanish colonies in 1767, they worked ceaselessly to create a linguistic, political, cultural, and economic territory of spiritual conquest. Within their administrative province of Paraguay, they founded and maintained a network of missions that stretched from the area of the Chiquito Indians north of Potosí in Bolivia to ill-fated outposts in Patagonia and the Gran Chaco. They studied indigenous languages and shaped a *lingua franca* from various dialects of Guaraní, publishing dictionaries, grammars, and catechisms, of which Ruiz de Montoya's *Tesoro de la lengua guaraní* (Madrid, 1639) and *Arte y vocabulario de la lengua guaraní* (Madrid, 1640) were among the most comprehensive.[13] The most famous grouping of missions, *las treinta doctrinas de guaraníes,* clustered between the Paraná and Uruguay Rivers in the Argentinean province of Misiones, became an object of fascination and speculation for Europeans. With communal structures of work and worship, elabo-

rate churches, and extravagant pageantry, the missions appeared to constitute a state within a state.[14] Voltaire's famous description of a Jesuit
mission in *Candide* speaks to the European perception of the avarice and
seemingly free hand the Jesuits had in organizing large tracts of Spanish
colonial lands:

> Candide was immediately shown into a shady retreat adorned with a pretty
> colonnade of green and gold marble, and trelliswork cages enclosing parrots,
> colibris, hummingbirds, guinea fowl and all sorts of other rare birds. An
> excellent meal had been served in golden vessels, and while the Paraguayans
> were eating corn from wide bowls in the blazing sunlight of the open fields,
> His Reverence the Commandant entered his arbor.[15]

While Voltaire's eighteenth-century satiric text imagined a feudal paradise of Jesuit overlords and docile serfs, the early years of the mission project in the 1600s were austere and politically volatile. As the founder of
some of the first missions in Guairá (in what is now Brazil east of São
Paulo), Montoya faced considerable resistance to his conversion project.
The missions were under continual threat from hostile Indians from the
Chaco and northern Paraguay, Portuguese slave-traders who swept
through the mission territory with armies of Tupí-Portuguese mestizos
known as the Mamelucos, and Spanish colonists who looked to the
Guaraní for *encomienda* labor.[16] Confronted with increasing military
incursions by the Mamelucos, the Jesuits decided to abandon the Guairá
missions in 1631. In an epic journey that contributed to his authority as
a spiritual leader of the Guaraní, Ruiz de Montoya led an exodus of
15,000 reduction Indians from Guairá to the present-day province of
Misiones. He describes in *La Conquista Espiritual* the hardships of this
messianic migration, marked by disease, starvation, and the death of more
than half the Indians.[17] After the forced transplantation of the Guaraní,
Montoya continued his fieldwork until 1637, when he was sent to Spain
to lobby for tax exemptions for the missions and the right of Indians to
bear arms. In 1641, while Montoya was still in Madrid, a battle fought
between the Guaraní armies under the command of the Jesuits and the
Mamelucos at Mbororé River established a line of defense against the Portuguese. By the time of his death in 1652, the reductions in Misiones were
well established and highly militarized. In 1710, a census count numbered
102,000 mission Indians.[18] Throughout the 1700s, the reduction Indians

would function as a reserve colonial defense for the Spanish Crown, conscripted for raids against the Portuguese fort of Colonia, hostile Chaco tribes, and colonist uprisings when necessary. By the 1750s, when the Guaraní Wars erupted in response to a demand by the Spanish Crown that a number of missions fall under Portuguese jurisdiction, it seemed to many in Europe that the Jesuits were indeed embroiled in an exercise of territorial sovereignty.[19] As Cacambo, the mestizo valet in *Candide* explains it:

> I was once a servant in the College of the Assumption, and I know the
> father's government as well as I know the streets of Cadiz. Their government
> is a wonderful thing. Their kingdom is already more than seven hundred
> fifty miles across, and it's divided into thirty provinces. The Fathers have
> everything, the people nothing; it's a masterpiece of reason and justice.
> I don't know of anyone as divine as the Fathers; over here, they wage war
> against the King of Spain and the King of Portugal, and in Europe they're
> the confessors of those same kings; here they kill Spaniards, in Madrid they
> send them to heaven. I find the whole thing delightful.[20]

Although the consolidation of the Jesuit network of missions by the 1700s enabled Voltaire to make a sweeping ironic assessment of their "kingdom" as a "masterpiece of justice and reason," Ruiz de Montoya describes a very different panorama in the 1600s. In the opening pages of *La Conquista Espiritual* Montoya writes of encountering "vast territories filled with wilderness, rugged terrain, dense forests and mountains" where "the Indians, in their old way of life, once lived in open or hilly country, or in forests and in clusters of up to five or six dwellings."[21] In turn, he asserts the importance of imposing Aristotle's *polis* over nomad space, claiming that through the efforts of the Jesuits, the Guaraní have "been brought into large settlements and, through the constant preaching of the gospel, transformed from country-dwellers into Christian citizens."[22] As one of the first missionaries in Paraguay, Ruiz de Montoya was instrumental in this transformation, founding eleven missions in Guairá from 1622 to 1628. In his establishment of these missions, Montoya followed instructions for town settlement based on the gridiron plan laid out by the Council of the Indies in 1573 and supported by Jesuit provincial ordinances.[23] Each mission was built as a closed rectangular fort in which at the head of the grid was the church, the Fathers' quarters (for two Jesuits), the common eating area, workshops for textiles, arms, art, and the jail. The Guaraní housing was laid out in long rows radiating verti-cally from the churches (which were often magnificently carved in stone and wood). The communal structure of agriculture, in which each fam-ily had a private plot *(abambá)* and a collective portion for the priests and God *(tupamba),* owes a debt to Incan social organization. The stonework also would appear to have been influenced by Incan masonry.[24]

The question of how the missions ordered space and time in relation-ship to the European values and to other colonial institutions, such as the city or the plantation, is an interesting one and not as transparent as sur-face appearances would suggest. The similarities and differences suggest that the Jesuit kingdom was less European and more transcultural than either the Jesuits admitted or the Europeans imagined. In Angel Rama's *The Lettered City (La Ciudad Letrada)*, a study of the relationship of colo-nialism in Latin America to the establishment of symbolic codes of archi-tecture and communication, he emphasizes the importance of the planned city as a key element in the reordering of space by the Spanish conquerors. Rama notes that unlike medieval towns, which were organically molded through usage and trade routes, Latin American cities were planned in advance according to the urban models of the Renaissance. The Americas presented the opportunity to impose an idealized city grid on a *terra incog-nita,* with the design of the central plaza based on Euclidean geometry and symbolizing a rationalization of space. The maintenance of this material and mental grid, according to Rama, was entrusted to *letrados* or "writ-ers," a privileged class of bureaucrats who were the mediators between the colony and the Crown, writing the reports to the king, and communicat-ing Spanish decrees and laws. Their capacity to manipulate symbolic lan-guages and codes permitted the imposition of an imperial imperative, which in turn was reinforced by a baroque order of visual signs. This play of visual and encoded language, argues Rama, enabled the seizure of space from the vast "nomad" lands of the New World and the naturalization of a colonial order.[25]

At first glance it would seem that the Jesuits repeated this strategy in the remote Paraguay region. There are, however, important differences. The rigidity and repetition of the mission plans belies the degree of fluid-ity and movement back and forth between the mission and the forest. Of note are statistics on the missions recorded by the Jesuits that reveal a vast disparity between the number of women (often listed as widows) and men in the missions—a ratio of approximately five to one.[26] While frequent incursions by hostile Guaycurú and Chaco tribes caused some deaths, it is highly probable that many of the men still lived in the forest, following traditional customs, while women chose to stay in the missions. Ruiz de Montoya's text records a number of instances in which the Guaraní come and go from mission settlements. For example, in one account of a Guaraní shaman, Montoya describes how "Taubici went to the reduction of San Igancio, where Father Simon Masseta was in charge, and began to establish himself among the Indians through his evil tricks. . . . When he left the reduction and took Indians with him during Corpus Christi the Jesuits warned they would be punished—after which enemies killed the cacique."[27] Similarly, the Jesuits also moved between the mission and the forest. In general, each mission was assigned two priests. One would stay in the settlement overseeing the communal work and tending to the sick; the other would wander the forest to bring back converts. In Jesuit culture, speech and not text was the primary symbolic code, with the Jesuits preaching to the Guaraní in both the forest and the mission church. The internal municipal organization of the missions was in the hands of caciques, who served as political mediators between the mission world and the nomad space of the forest. Rather than implanting settlements with vast uncontrolled territories in between, the imposition of the missions bled into the surrounding area and became a competing symbolic ordering of space with that of the colonial city.

As with the colonial city, it would seem that the plantation and the mission shared affinities in their coercive and organizational structures. However, the economic structure of the mission as a kind of communal enterprise of primitive accumulation and extraction differed from the economic colonial institutions of the *encomienda* and the plantation. Maté, a bitter herb drunk as a tea, was the cash crop that financed tribute to the Crown. However, it only grew in remote areas of the jungle, where it was harvested by expeditions of Indians. It was not domesticated until the eighteenth century and still had to be grown in *yerbales* far from mission settlements.[28] *Estancias,* which used slaves for labor, financed the urban Jesuit colleges and were separate from mission activity. The transculturation in plantation societies such as Cuba and Brazil, in which new cultural forms were forged from coercive mixing of peoples, had no parallel in the missions. Instead, with the expulsion of the Jesuits in 1767, the missions slowly disintegrated, and the Guaraní slipped away to the cities or back into the forest. While most historians (and anthropologists) attribute this to Jesuit paternalism (and thus the missions are framed as a failed experiment in acculturation), I would like to argue that it reflects the degree to which the Jesuits did not "fail" but inversely succeeded in incorporating Guaraní ritual codes and languages into their symbolic ordering of space and time.[29] Despite the seeming clarity of Montoya's separation of Christian settlement from the nomad space of the pagan forest, his descriptions of the conversion process and Guaraní resistance suggest that the missions existed in a murky realm between forest and clearing. In occupying this murky realm, the missions reflected the degree to which certain spiritual practices of the Guaraní mirrored those of the Jesuits.

In Guaraní culture, shamanistic powers are ordered around the role of speech acts as sacred, with powerful healers having the most developed gift of chants, or what the Guaraní term "beautiful words."[30] The "beautiful words" belong to the sacred realm of language that renders manifest a spiritual and embodied reality distinct from the visible world. In contrast to the everyday words used to describe a material universe, this scared realm of language uses metaphors and not nouns to designate common objects: tobacco smoke becomes deadly mist; the pipe becomes the skeleton of the mist.[31] All Guaraní have the potential to learn some of the beautiful words, although adolescents and some adults in rebellion against the spirits may be denied them. Most have learned one or two chants but have no potential to harness collective powers. Those who have the collective powers of healing and the capacity to divine the names of newborns are a second order of shaman called *paje,* a term now used in northern Argentina and Paraguay to refer to an underground practice of sorcery. The most powerful shamans are the *karai,* who could only be male and who lived apart from the community. They traveled constantly, often with an entourage of women, and were the only ones who could lead the Nimongarai, a feast when corn started to ripen and that brought all villages of a tribe together.[32] In the 1500s they led migrations of the Guaraní inland from Brazil in search of *la tierra sin mal* or (land without evil), an earthly paradise that the Guaraní believed lay west of their territories.[33] In a passage from Pedro Lozano's history of the Jesuit missions published in the 1700s, it is clear that the Jesuits recognized a shamanistic hierarchy and the existence of the *karai:*

The third kind of sorcery had much more authority than all the others, because it concerned a particular art known to very few. These, the boldest and most audacious, tried to convince the population that they were the sons of a supreme virtue, without terrestrial fathers, although they admitted being born of women. . . . They passed for authentic prophets in the eyes of the population, who saw some of their prophecies come true. They were believed to be saints, they were obeyed and revered like gods.[34]

E. Jean Matteson Langdon, in the introduction to his anthology on shamanism *Portals of Power: Shamanism in South America,* notes that the genealogy of the term "shamanism" comes from a Tungusic word describing ritual specialists whose activities include ecstasy, ritual flight, death, rebirth, journeys to the underworld and heavens, alliances with animals, and curing; their training includes trances, dreamwork, genealogy of secret languages, and plant identification.[35] While diverse scholars have investigated shamanism, Langdon proposes, and I would concur, that symbolic anthropology—with its concern for signification and representation in ritual—offers a useful perspective for an understanding of shamanism. Within symbolic anthropology, as exemplified by the work of Clifford Geertz or Victor Turner, the shaman is viewed as having a dual function in which his powers as a healer parallel his mastery of ritual. He is able to move between worlds, mediate disputes, mobilize the group, and direct economic and sometimes political activities. In his role as a mediator, Langdon notes that the shaman can lose his prestige through a confrontation with a more powerful shaman. Langdon argues that "shaman battles are an inherent part of this hierarchical ordering among them. The result of the loss of power signals the inability of the shaman to control the ecstatic experience, which marks the loss of his auxiliary spirits, as well as the power of his songs, and most often brings sickness, and, in some cases, even death for the shaman."[36]

The description of the shaman proposed by Langdon finds uncanny parallels in the activities of the Jesuit missionaries. In the mission, the Jesuits directed economic activities, functioned as healers, and moved seamlessly from the community to the forest. In the forest, like the *karai,* the Jesuits traveled alone; they also gathered communities together for special ceremonies. They spoke sacred words in their use of sermons, and engaged in shamanic battles to gather Guaraní souls to their missions. In terms of conversion, the Jesuits often called upon their own supernatural powers to combat those of the shamans.[37] Ruiz de Montoya is particularly interesting in this regard. Like the shaman whose visions signal power, he came to the Jesuit order through a series of mystic encounters with the spirit world, and continued to experience the ability to move between sacred and profane realms. In a passage from *La Conquista Espiritual,* Montoya describes how he and Father José Cataldino traveled to convince Indians to gather into large settlements in locations already designated for them. At one village they encountered a great sorcerer. Montoya recounts that his name was Taubici, meaning "devils in a row" or "row of devils"— which would suggest that he was a shaman, as the designation of "devil" in Jesuit texts is often used to describe the indigenous priest. Clearly from Montoya's description he was a powerful figure:

> He was extremely cruel; upon the slightest annoyance he would have Indians killed at whim, and so was held in awe and served at the merest hint of his thought. Shortly before our arrival he had an Indian killed because he had put him in charge of a sick little son of his and the boy had died. When he wanted to talk with the devil, he ordered everyone to get out of his house and to give it a wide berth all around. Four of his favorite girls would stay in his company. He would order part of the roof of his house taken off for the evil spirit to come in. Then the wretched fellow would have fits; his women would support him, holding his arms and head as he made wild faces and gestures. With these tricks and shams of his, he would afterward publish numerous lies about future events—some of which occasionally came true, having been gotten by hints from the devil.[38]

In the battles over prestige between the shamans and the Jesuits, Montoya's conversion accounts reveal a struggle around the spoken word in which the Guaraní shaman engaged in mimicry. Describing an encounter with the *cacique* Miguel Artiguaye, Montoya recounts that

> to gain greater prestige with his followers, he pretended to be a priest. In his private chamber . . . robed in . . . brilliant feathers and other adornments, he pretended to say Mass. He would spread a table with cloths and place upon them a manioca cake and show the cake and wine as priests do, finally eating and drinking everything. His vassals venerated him as a priest. His life was exceptionally scandalous as he had a large number of concubines. . . .[39]

Like the Jesuits, Artiguaye used gatherings as an opportunity to preach to the Guaraní. Montoya also writes of Artiguaye speaking against the Jesuits through a linguistic inversion in which the mission priests and not the shaman are the devils:

> The devils have brought us these men, for with new teachings they want to take away from us the good old way of life of our ancestors, who had many wives and servant women and were free to choose them at will. Now they want us to tie ourselves to a single woman. It is not right for this to go any further; we should drive them out of lands, or take their lives.[40]

Artiguaye also confronted the Jesuits themselves in the mission. Montoya describes Artiguaye as turning into a wild beast and shouting:

> You are no priests sent from God to aide our misery; you are devils from hell, sent by their ruler for our destruction. What teaching have you brought us? What peace and happiness? Our ancestors lived in liberty. They enjoyed all the women they wanted without hindrance from anyone. Thus they lived and spent their lives in happiness, and you want to destroy their traditions and impose upon us this heavy burden of being bound to a single wife.[41]

Whether this linguistic inversion is a result of Montoya's loose interpretation of Artiguaye's speech or Artiguaye's appropriation of Jesuit language is not ascertainable. What is clear is that a struggle over teachings and women occurred. In turn, Montoya describes how the shaman organized against the missions, whereby

> at daybreak a great racket and din was heard throughout the settlement— preparations for a war, drums, flutes, and other instruments. Three hundred warriors assembled in the town square, armed with shields, swords, bows, and great quantities of arrows, all splendid with rich painting and variegated feathering. On their heads they wore gorgeous feather crowns. The most elaborately decked out was the cacique Miguel. He wore a rich robe all of varicolored feathers very skillfully woven; on his head was a feathered crown.[42]

In this contestation for spiritual power, Montoya is triumphant, able to convince Miguel Artiguaye to leave the forest and join the mission. Yet even when the shamans capitulated, as Artiguaye did after his display of force, they still had the power of shape shifters, infiltrating and disrupting the sacred space of the priests. According to Montoya, they would frequently hide in the belfry and hum during the sermon, or ring the bell without warning. They also infiltrated the spiritual realm in the guise of priests, a form of symbolic inversion resulting in the literal transposition of the spiritual realms of the Guaraní and the Christian. Montoya describes this process as follows:

> In the reduction of Loreta five devils appeared. Four were dressed like ourselves in black cassocks, trimmed with tinselly bands, their faces very handsome. The fifth appeared in the form in which the Blessed Virgin is portrayed. However, as the devil is always a liar, even when counterfeiting the truth, his very deceptions betray the mark of his lie: the woman was carrying two children in her arms. The figures came up to a group of Indians. The latter halted at the sweet sound of their antiphonal singing as they walked along and imitated the tune of the litanies of Our Lady as sung in figured choral music in the churches there. The Indians noticed, however, that they uttered no praises or comprehensible words. They thought this must be something from heaven, to judge from their voices, ornamentation and beautiful faces. In all simplicity they asked them who they were. "We are angels from heaven," they replied; "we bring here the Mother of God, who is very fond of your Fathers." "Well, if that is so," said the Indians, "let us go to the father's house and the church." The simple folk thought they were sure to come and bring us something we would like very much. The devils replied: "It is not good for us to go to the Father's house; we will stay out here and assist them. We will speak to you slowly and teach you what you need to know and the Fathers do not tell you." At this, they disappeared.[43]

A hundred years later, Martín Dobrizhoffer, writing about Montoya and other Jesuit experiences in his *Account of the Abipones,* dismisses the shamans (whom he calls "jugglers") as frauds. Yet at the same time he acknowledges that a shamanistic ceremony of the Abipones where women speak to the dead had the power to convince Spaniards who lived among them "that the shades of the dead become visible at the call of a necromancer."[44] He also describes another battle of the shamans in which a flood is ascribed to the power of the Jesuits and thus the shamans lose prestige:

> This Pariekaikin in an oracular manner declared, that Father Joseph Brigneil had caused that rain for the advantage of his town, and that because he, Pariekaikin, did not choose to reside there, he had, out of revenge, directed the clouds with such art, that not a drop of rain reached his station. For they made no hesitation in accounting that Father a conjurer, because he happily and speedily healed the sick.[45]

Even Dobrizhoffer, for whom superstition is the source of the shaman's power, concedes that to evangelize, one must defeat the powers of the shamans. In this regard he cites the story of Montoya and his encounter with the bones of the shamans:

> What contests, and what trouble did they not cause to Antonio Ruiz de Montoya, the famous Guarany missionary! It was not till he had repressed the authority of the remaining jugglers, and commanded the bones of the dead ones, which were universally worshiped with great honors, to be burned in the presence of the people, that he converted an infinite number of savages to the Christian religion, and induced them to enter the colonies.[46]

The story of the bones, as told by Montoya, presents a fascinating blurring of Guaraní and Christian rituals and symbols. At a time when many of the Guaraní were deserting the mission, vanishing when the ringing of the bells signaled Mass on Sunday, Montoya learns from a young convert that they are flocking to the bones of venerated shamans hidden deep in the forest. In a curious inversion of the Calvary crosses, the Guaraní had placed "three dead bodies, on three hills, that talked; . . . warning the Indians against the Fathers' preaching."[47] Montoya finds a pagan boy in the forest who leads him to the three hills, where he discovers bones wrapped in hammocks "covered with two precious cloths of colored feathers."[48] In one of the hammocks he uncovers the bones of a famous shaman who had been dug up from a Christian church after the Guaraní heard him crying from his grave that he was suffocating. Montoya silences these bones that speak to the Guaraní by overseeing an exorcism in which the bones are removed from the forest and burned in the mission settlement. Montoya records his triumph over the bones as one in which the struggle for power was linked to a struggle over speech and naming:

> All the people were assembled in the church and were given a sermon. It dealt with the true God, with the worship owed him by his creatures, with the devil's artifices and impotence, and with the lies and deceit of magicians. . . . They cried aloud to God for pardon so feelingly and devoutly that we were moved to tears. After this one of the Fathers mounted a platform that had been erected on the square so that everyone, including women and children, could be undeceived by the sight of the cold bones. The Father displayed them, naming the persons whose bones they had been. It was amazing to see the people's rejoicing as they beheld this public discrediting of the great fraud regarding the corpses, which everyone had claimed were alive. They competed with one another to bring firewood for burning them. This was carried out in my presence, so that not a single bone could be carried off and

the lie thereby perpetuated. At this they took courage and showed us another recently dead boy. Though we had tried to baptize the person in his illness, they had concealed him, intending to build him a temple. He, too, underwent the penalty of fire. Once this disturbance was removed, the people came to church regularly, the pagans fervently requesting baptism and the Christian confession.[49]

While Montoya's account does not reveal how his actions were interpreted from the perspective of the Guaraní's worldview, a Jesuit account written more than a hundred years later confirms the importance of bones for an indigenous comprehension of their sacred realm. In Florian Pauke's account of San Javier mission of Santa Fe written in the mid-1700s, he describes how pagan Indians arrive at the mission with a large quantity of human bones that they have brought from the forest more than a thousand kilometers away. They request that the bones be buried in the mission cemetery, as some of their relations are buried there. Pauke replied that non-Christian bones could not be interred on sacred ground; rather than returning the bones to the forest, the Indians choose to rebury them outside of the church grounds near the mission.[50] Similarly, twentieth-century ethnographic research on the Guaranís' spiritual beliefs and practices has identified an important ritual significance for the preservation of bones. León Cadogan, a Paraguayan ethnographer who lived with the Mbyá-Guaraní of Guairá in the 1950s, recorded burial ceremonies that parallel the Guaranís' veneration of the bones in the 1600s. In his documentation of Mybá-Guaranís' cult of the bones, Cadogan describes how the Guaraní preserve the bones of the dead by burying the corpse in a bamboo basket. When the body is decomposed, the corpse is dug up and the bones preserved in a cedar container. "Beautiful words" or chants are pronounced to the bones to conjure the sacred realm and in hope of obtaining revelations linked to *la tierra sin mal.* According to León Cadogan, it is possible to go from one realm to the other without discontinuity—that is, to reach *la tierra sin mal* in human shape without dying—if the bones are venerated.[51]

Given the importance of the bones in Guaraní culture as objects of oracle power, Ruiz de Montoya's spiritual conquest over the bones can be understood as central to a shamanistic struggle over access to a sacred realm. By desecrating the bones of the Guaraní shaman, and speaking in their stead, he transposed Christian and indigenous spiritual worlds in much the same way that Artiguaye inverted the spiritual order when he practiced Mass in his private chamber. Through his acute sensibility of the indigenous spirit world and his religious zeal, he succeeded in appropriating the bones' power to speak, transforming the "beautiful words" of the Guaraní into the "fresh words" of the Christian faith. Whether or not this authority over the bones also extended to a cosmological equivalence between the Guaranís' belief in *la tierra sin mal* and the mission settlement is necessarily a question of inference. For the Europeans at the time, however, such an equivalence between evangelization and paradise was a direct one. Dr. Don Lorenza de Mendoza, who approved Ruiz de Montoya's *Spiritual Conquest* for publication in 1639, wrote in his foreword to the text of how Montoya led the Guaraní out of the wilderness to a "garden of celestial flowers and a new primitive church."[52]

Despite Montoya's dedication to the mission project, he was not to spend the last years of his life in the "garden of celestial flowers" he had so carefully cultivated. After leaving Paraguay in 1637 for Madrid, he spent a number of years in Spain defending Jesuit interests, and it was there that he penned *La Conquista Espiritual,* written in part as a strategic promotion of the Jesuit conversion project. Upon his return to Spanish America in the early 1640s he became embroiled in the ecclesiastical politics of Lima, and was delayed from returning to the missions by the task of representing and defending Jesuit interests to the viceroy. During these years he wrote a mystical guide to a spiritual inner life, *Firestone of Divine Love and Rapture of the Soul in Knowledge of the First Cause,* which remained in manuscript form until 1991.[53] While still stationed in Lima, his health began to deteriorate rapidly in 1652, and he died in April of that year. When the Guaraní in the reductions learned of his death, the epic journey he had undertaken with them from Guairá to Misiones twenty years before was reciprocated. In 1631 he had led the exodus of Guaraní like a *karai* leading his community toward *la tierra sin mal.* In turn, after his death, forty Guaraní traveled three thousand kilometers overland from the Loreta reduction in Paraguay to Lima to fetch his bones and return with them to Misiones, where the bones were laid to rest in Candelaria, now overgrown with jungle.[54] We cannot know, but only imagine, that perhaps those bones, like the ones Montoya had destroyed years before, spoke to the Guaraní from the spirit world.

As a linguist and a chronicler, Ruis de Montoya's written legacy has accorded him an important place in the Jesuits' historization of their mission project during the colonial period. In recent years his work on the Guaraní language has been greatly esteemed by anthropologists and linguists. Modern historians, however, have been more reluctant to engage his text as a documentary source—in part attributable, as Ernesto Maeder notes in his introduction to his annotated version of *La Conquista Espiritual,* to the objective difficulties that the text presents in its "casual chronology, its frequent admission of the supernatural, and its passionate style."[55] On the other hand, Ruiz de Montoya's religious fervor and his supernatural visions did not gain him entrance to the Jesuits' official litany of martyrs and saints. In Paraguay that ecclesiastical honor was reserved for Roque González (1575–1628), a native of Asunción and a contemporary of Montoya's who was canonized by Pope John Paul II in 1988. González, who like Montoya was an early field missionary and an adept linguist, was killed by Nezú, a Guaycurú shaman, while attempting to establish a reduction settlement in the Tape region of Uruguay. According to Montoya, witnesses reported that after killing González, Nezú donned his priestly vestments and "had babies brought before him and with his own barbarous rites attempted to erase the indelible character impressed upon their souls in the spirit of baptism."[56] Despite Nezú's attempt to reassert his authority over a sacred realm threatened by Christian conversion, when he returned to the funeral pyre the next day he heard González's heart speaking. Just as Montoya had sought to silence the bones, so Nezú and his followers sought to silence the heart. They removed it from the body of the priest, pierced it with an arrow, crushed the bones of the priest, and lit the remains on fire. Yet the heart, like the charred cross housed in *La Cruz del Milagro* of Corrientes, proved indestructible, "left like gold refined and purified by fire."[57] Taken to Rome in 1634 as the material evidence of his saintly status, González's purified heart was returned to Asunción in 1928.[58]

Unlike Roque González, whose death fits comfortably within a Christian tradition of martyrs and whose heart is still housed in the Jesuit college of Christo Rey in Asunción, Ruiz de Montoya died far from the "pursuit of wild beasts—the barbarian Indians,"[59] and his bones lie lost and forgotten in the ruins of the Jesuit missions. His ability to divine the shamanistic realm of the Guaraní and his role as the leader of an exodus of the Guaraní through jungle wilderness find biblical resonance with saintly visions and the exodus of Moses toward the promised land. At the same time, Montoya's spiritual interventions find equal resonance with the function of the powerful Guaraní *karai,* who presided over sacred words and led their people toward *la tierra sin mal.* As such, his saintly legacy is more akin to San Lamuerte's dissolution of boundaries between Christian and Guaraní spiritual beliefs than it is to the formal hierarchies of the Catholic Church. The Jesuit translator of his text into English, C. J. McNaspy, notes that Montoya's paranormal facility and his mystic encounters with diabolical possession may leave the modern secular reader uncomfortable. Similarly, one wonders if his descriptions of his battles with the shamans, in which inversions and mimicry are interchangeable between the two adversaries, also sits uneasily with the modern Jesuit scholar. The significance of his text for the historian of colonial contact, I maintain, lies precisely in this uneasiness. The power of his account, like that of San Lamuerte, who is hidden in the folds of the Virgin's skirt to be blessed, lies in a shamanistic vision buried in a Christian worldview of exorcism and devils.

José Rabasa, in his article "Writing and Evangelization in Sixteenth-Century Mexico," argues that the study of early missionaries "will enable us to (1) assess the practice, nature, and efficacy of conversion; (2) document different conceptualizations of indigenous religious beliefs; and (3) trace patterns in the transformation of native cultures." To his list I want to add a fourth point—in which the study of primary documents of cultural contact such as Ruiz de Montoya's *Conquista Espiritual* can suggest the ways in which interaction with indigenous spiritual beliefs also transforms a European worldview.[60] By reading Montoya against the grain, locating in his text an arena of instability within a missionary project and a correspondence between the roles of the Jesuit and that of the shaman, we can locate a blurring of boundaries between sacred realms and rituals that reveals a fluid arena of exchange. The degree to which this arena of exchange reflected conversion on either side is open to speculation, but what is clear is that when the Jesuits as speakers of the "beautiful words" left, the Guaraní looked elsewhere for shamans who could talk with the gods and listen to the bones.

NOTES

1. For a general history of Corrientes see Antonio Emilio Castello, *Historia de Corrientes* (Buenos Aires: Ultra Plus, 1984).

2. In addition to San Lamuerte, the other hybrid saint worshiped in Corrientes is Santa Librada, a black crucified woman. San Lamuerte is the more popular and underground of the two, reflecting in part a gradual diminishing of a strong African presence in Corrientes during the nineteenth century.

3. While San Lamuerte was traditionally carved from human bone, it is now made from wood or cow bone. When I purchased one from a small store in Corrientes last year, the saleswoman insisted, rather forcibly, that the saint was made from cow bone because the medical students no longer give cadavers to the artisans.

4. The origin of the use of San Lamuerte by Gauchos may be related to their own genealogy, which, although unclear, is traced by some scholars to a mixing of European immigrants and indigenous peoples during the colonial era. For the genealogy of the gaucho see Richard W. Slatta, *Gauchos and the Vanishing Frontier* (Lincoln: University of Nebraska Press, 1992).

5. There is little formal documentation of San Lamuerte. I obtained information about the saint through discussions with an artisan who carves the Grim Reaper version and a woman who maintains a private altar for the crouched figure version. In a videotaped testimony that I obtained of her and her San Lamuerte, she explains he has been in the family for more than two hundred years. He communicates to her through dreams and has foretold the future, including the death of her husband and the survival of her daughter in a motorcycle accident. A brief description of San Lamuerte is in Emilio Noya, *Imaginería Religiosa y Santoral Profano de Corrientes* (Corrientes: Subscretaría de Cultura de la Provincia de Corrientes, 1994). The belief in San Lamuerte in Misiones is recorded in Elsa Leonor Pasteknik, *Mitos Vivientes de Misiones* (Buenos Aires: Editoral Plus Ultra, 1997).

6. The full title of Ruiz de Montoya's text is *La Conquista Espiritual del Paraguay Hecha por los religiosos de la Compañía de Jesus en las provincias de Paraguay, Parana, Uruguay y Tape*. It was first published in Madrid in 1639. A definitive edition based on the original manuscript with annotated notes was published by Ernesto J. A. Maeder (Rosario: Equipo Difusor de Estudios Historia Iberoamericana, 1989). C. J. McNaspy, S.J., has produced a recent English translation, *The Spiritual Conquest Accomplished by the Religious of the Society of Jesus in the Provinces of Paraguay, Paraná, Uruguay, and Tape* (St. Louis: Institute of Jesuit Sources, 1993). For direct quotes from Montoya's text I have used McNaspy's published translation cited as *Spiritual Conquest.*

7. See Gayatri Chakravorty Spivak, "Subaltern Studies: Deconstructing Historiography," in her *Other Worlds: Essays in Cultural Politics* (New York: Routledge, 1988), 205.

8. These interpretations of the Jesuit missions were formulated in the late eighteenth and early nineteenth centuries by writers such as Voltaire and by travelers who visited the remains of the once-flourishing missions. For an overview and selection of various interpretations of the missions see Magnus Mörner, *The Explusion of the Jesuits from Latin America* (New York: Alfred A. Knopf, 1965).

9. Basic biographical information has been obtained from C. J. McNaspy's introduction to his translation of Montoya's text, based on Hugo Storni, *Catálogo de la Provincia del Paraguay* (Rome, 1980). See McNaspy, *Spiritual Conquest,* 11–24.

10. Ruiz de Montoya's report of his vision of the white-robed Jesuits is recorded in his *Carta de Comental,* written at about the time of his ordination. It is published in Guillermo Furlong, *Antontio Ruiz de Montoya y su Carta a Comental* (Escritores Coloniales Rioplatenses XVII, Buenos Aires: Ediciones Theoria, 1964). A translation is included as an appendix in McNaspy's *Spiritual Conquest* and titled "Report made by Father Antonio Ruiz de Montoya regarding graces received from our Lord," 194–204.

11. Martín Barco de Centenera's *Argentina, Conquista del Río de la Plata con otros acontecimientos de los Reynos del Perú, Tucumán, y Estado del Brasil* was first published in Lisbon in 1602. A version of the poem is in Pedro De Angelis, *Colecion de obras y documentas relativos a la historia antigua y moderna de las provincias del Rio de la Plata* (Buenos Aires: Imprenta del Estado, 1836–37). Ruy Díaz de Guzmán's account of the expedition up the Paraná River was finished in Charcas in 1612 and circulated in manuscript form until 1845. For a modern version of this account see Ruy Díaz de Guzmán, *Argentina* (Buenos Aires: Emecé Editores, 1998).

12. Antonio Ruiz de Montoya, *The Spiritual Conquest Accomplished by the Religious of the Society of Jesus in the Provinces of Paraguay, Paraná, Uruguay, and Tape* (St. Louis: Institute of Jesuit Sources, 1993), 30.

13. For a facsimilie edition of Montoya's Guaraní grammar first published in 1640 see Antonio Ruiz de Montoya, *Arte y vocabulario de la lengua Guaraní* (Madrid: Ediciones de Cultura Hispánica, 1994).

14. For an overview of Jesuit activities in Paraguay, the best source materials are Guillermo Furlong, *Misiones y sus pueblos de Guaraníes* (Buenos Aires: 1962) and Pablo Hernandez, *Organización Social de las Doctrinas Guaraníes de la Compañía de Jesús* (Barcelona: Gustavo Gil, 1913). Philip Caraman provides an adequate history in English that references some primary sources. See Philip Caraman, *The Lost Paradise* (London: Sidgwick & Jackson, 1975). One of the first Jesuit histories of Paraguay, published in Latin in 1673 by Nicolás Del Techo, remains a key text for information on the early Jesuit period. For a modern Spanish version see Nicolás Del Techo, *Historia de la provincia del Paraguay de la Compañía de Jesús por el P. Nicolás del Telcho* (Madrid: A. de Uribe y Cía, 1897). Some of the text is translated into

English in Awnsham and John Churchill, *A Collection of Voyages and Travels* (London, 1746). Most of the secondary material on the Jesuit missions has been written by the Jesuits themselves.

15. Voltaire, *Candide* (New York: Bantam Books, 1959), 53.

16. Hostile indigenous groups included the Guaycurú, Mybas, Abipones, Payaguás, and Tobas. For an overview of the indigenous presence in Paraguay and Argentina during the colonial period see Ernesto Maeder and Ramon Gutierrez, *Atlas Historico del Nordeste Argentino* (Resistencia: Conicet, 1994) and Branislavia Susnik, *Los Aborigenes del Paraguay: Etnología del Chaco Boreal y su periferia (siglos XVI y XVII)* (Asunción: Museo Etnográfico Andrés Barbero, 1978). For a general ethnographic study see Johannes Wilbert and Karin Simoneau, *In Their Own Words* (Cambridge, Mass.: Harvard University Press, 1992). The *encomienda* system granted Spanish colonists the right to use indigenous labor within a defined area for a certain number of days a year. It was open to great abuse and often amounted to tacit slavery. For a description of the *encomienda* see Charles Gibson, *Spain in America* (New York: Harper Torchbooks, 1966). In terms of the slave incursions from the São Paulo area eastward by the Mamelucos or *bandeirantes*, Philip Caraman estimates (based on primary sources) that between 1626 and 1632, sixty thousand Guaraní were sold in the slave markets of Brazil. See Caraman, *Lost Paradise*, 59.

17. Ruiz de Montoya, *Spiritual Conquest*, 105–10.

18. These are statistics compiled in a chapter on the Jesuits in Adalberto López, *The Revolt of the Comuñeros, 1721–1735* (Cambridge, Mass.: Schenkman, 1977), 36.

19. The Guaraní wars, portrayed in melodramatic grandeur in the Hollywood film *The Mission*, were fought as a series of skirmishes until a pitched battle was held at the *estancia* of Caaibaté on February 10, 1756. In the battle, more than fifteen hundred Guaraní were slaughtered, while the Spanish and the Portuguese sustained five casualties.

20. Voltaire, *Candide*, 54.

21. Ruiz de Montoya, *Spiritual Conquest*, 27.

22. Ibid., 30.

23. See M. W. Nichol, "Colonial Tucumán," in *Hispanic American Review* 18 (1938).

24. For architectural plans of the missions see Ernesto Maeder and Ramon Guitierrez, *Atlas Historico y Urbano de la Region del Nordeste Argentino: Pueblos de Indios y Misiones Jesuitcas.* Guillermo Furlong's exhaustive study on the missions, *Misiones y sus pueblos de Guaraníes*, contains detailed descriptions of daily activities based on published and archival accounts by Jesuits, including Antón Sepp's *Relación de viaje de las misiones jesuíticas*, first published in German in 1691; José Cardiel's *Declaración de la verdad*, first published in Latin in 1758; José Manuel Peramás's *La República de Platón y los guaraníes*, first published in Latin in 1791; José Sanchez Labrador's *El Paraguay Natural* (in manuscript form in the Jesuit archive in Rome) and his *El Paraguay católico* (first published in Buenos Aires, 1910), written in Spanish in the 1770s; and Martín Dobrizhoffer's *An Account of the Abipones*, first published in Latin and German in 1784, and then translated into English by Sara Coleridge (the poet's wife) in 1822.

25. See Angel Rama, *The Lettered City* (Durham, N.C.: Duke University Press, 1996), 1–50.

26. These are taken from census figures compiled for the years 1755 to 1765, Archivo de la Nacion, Buenos Aires. While these statistics are for a much later period than that under consideration here, they confirm accounts by Martín Dobrizhoffer in *An Account of the Abipones* that women sought refuge in the missions. Caraman also notes in *The Lost Paradise*, 135, that all missions had women's quarters after 1715.

27. Ruiz de Montoya, *Spiritual Conquest*, 47.

28. Maté is usually drunk in a gourd (also called a *maté*) with a silver straw (a *bombilla*). While its use was widespread in the colonial era and it quickly became a regional source of barter and a cash crop, early accounts suggest that before the conquest it was only used in sacred ceremonies. Montoya records that "I carefully enquired about its origin from Indians who were eighty or one hundred years old. I learned as a fact that in their youth the herb was not drunk or even known except by a sorcerer or magician who trafficked with the devil." See Ruiz de Montoya, *Spiritual Conquest*, 41. Eric Wolf discusses maté's economic importance in his book, noting that maté, unlike sugar or coffee, never achieved more than regional currency. See Eric Wolf, *Europe and the People without History* (Berkeley: University of California Press, 1982), 322.

29. Particularly harsh in his assessment is the Spanish naturalist Felix de Azara, who traveled in the mission area at the end of eighteenth century. His denunciation of the Jesuits' paternalism has shaped the dominant interpretation of the mission project in Argentina. See Felix de Azara, *Descripción general del paraguay* (Madrid: Alianza Ed. Quinto Centenario, 1990). For an overview of interpretations also see Magnus Mörner, *The Expulsion of the Jesuits from Latin America* (New York: Alfred A. Knopf, 1965).

30. The most important sources on Guaraní culture outside of early missionary accounts are anthropological ethnographic studies undertaken by León Cadogan in the 1960s, a lay ethnographer from Paraguay who was adopted by the Mybá-Guaraní. Preceding and parallel to Cadogan's extensive work on the Guaraní in Paraguay are a number of important studies published on the Guaraní in Brazil. Kurt Nimuendajú's classic study of the cosmology of the Apapokuva-Guaraní in Brazil was first published in 1914, while Alfred

Metraux lived with and studied the Guaraní in the 1920s. A contemporary of Cadogan, Egon Schaden has made important contributions to the field. See León Cadogan and Ayvu Rapyta, *Textos Míticos de los Mbyá-Guaraní del Guairá* (Asunción: Biblioteca Paraguaya de Antropología, 1997); Curt Nimuendajú, *Los Mitos de Creatión y de Destrucción del Mundo como Fundamentos de la Religión de los Apapokuva-Guaraní* (Lima: Centro Amazonico de Antropología y Aplicación, 1978); Alfred Metraux, "The Guaraní," in *Handbook of South American Indians,* vol. 3 (Washington, D.C.: Smithsonian Institution, 1963), and Egon Schaden, *Aspectos fundamentais da cultura guaraní* (São Paulo: Edusp., 1974). Branislava Susnik's *Los Aborigenes del Paraguay II: Etnohistoria de los Guaranies. Epoca Colonial* (Asunción: Museo Etnografico "Andres Barbero," 1990) provides a detailed sociological and historical analysis, drawing upon colonial and anthropological sources. Hélène Clastres has also combined these sources to write a superb analysis of Guaraní belief system that provides the best historical overview in English translation. See Hélène Clastres, *The Land-Without-Evil. Tupí-Guaraní Prophetism* (Urbana: University of Illinois Press, 1995). Two important recent studies with conflicting interpretations of Guaraní spirituality are the Jesuit Bartomeu Melia, *El Guaraní, Experiencia religiosa* (Asunción: Biblioteca Paraguaya de Antropología, 1991) and Alfredo Vara, *La Construcción Guaraní de la Realidad* (Asunción: Universidad Católica, 1984).

31. Hélène Clastres, *The Land-Without-Evil,* 74.
32. Nimuendajú was the first modern anthropologist to record the levels of shamanistic.powers. See ibid., 25.
33. Ibid., 49.
34. Cited in ibid., 30.
35. E. Jean Matteson Langdon and Gerhard Baer, eds., *Portals of Power: Shamanism in South America* (Albuquerque: University of New Mexico Press, 1992), 3.
36. Ibid., 16.
37. See Maxime Haubert, *La vie quotidienne au Paraguay sous les jésuites* (Paris: Hachette, 1967). See also Louis Necker, *Indios Guaranies y Chamanes Franciscanos* (Asunción: Biblioteca Paraguaya de Antropologia, 1990).
38. Ruiz de Montoya, *Spiritual Conquest,* 46.
39. Ibid., 53.
40. Ibid.
41. Ibid., 54.
42. Ibid.
43. Ibid., 64.
44. Martín Dobrizhoffer, *An Account of the Abipones, an Equestrian People of Paraguay,* vol. 2 (New York: Johnson Reprint Corporation, 1970), 73.
45. Ibid., 79.
46. Ibid., 80.
47. Ruiz de Montoya, *Spiritual Conquest,* 86.
48. Ibid., 86.
49. Ibid., 89.
50. Florian Paucke, *Hacia allá y para acá. Una estada entre los Indios Mocobíes 1749–1767,* 2 vols. (Buenos Aires: Tucumán, 1942), 2: 240.
51. León Cadogan, *Ayvu Rapyta. Textos Míticos de los Mbyá-Guaraní del Guairá,* 85–105.
52. Ruiz de Montoya, *Spiritual Conquest,* 27.
53. This text by Montoya remained in manuscript form until 1991, when it was published in Peru. See Ruiz de Montoya, *Sílex del divino amor,* Introducción, transcripci ón y notas de José Luis Rouillon Arróspide, (Lima: Pontificia Universidad Católica del Perú, Fondo Editorial, 1991).
54. McNapsy, Introduction to Ruiz de Montoya, *Spiritual Conquest,* 21.
55. Ernesto Maeder, Introduction to Antonio Ruiz de Montoya, *La Conquista Espiritual del Paraguay Hecha por los religiosos de la Compañia de Jesus en las provincias de Paraguay, Parana, Uruguay y Tape,* (1639), reprinted with annotated notes by Ernesto J. A. Maeder (Rosario: Equipo Difusor de Estudios Historia Iberoamericana, 1989), 9.
56. Ruiz de Montoya, *Spiritual Conquest,* 153.
57. Ibid., 154.
58. Cited in a footnote by C. J. McNapsy in Ruiz de Montoya, *Spiritual Conquest,* 215. Information on Roque González also can be found in Joseph N. Tylenda, *Jesuit Saints and Martyrs* (Chicago: Loyola Press, 1998).
59. Ruiz de Montoya, *Spiritual Conquest,* 29.
60. José Rabasa, "Writing and Evangelization in Sixteenth-Century Mexico," in Jerry William and Robert Lewis, *Early Images of the Americas: Transfer and Invention* (Tucson: University of Arizona Press, 1993), 66.

5

St. Anthony in Portuguese America: Saint of the Restoration

RONALDO VAINFAS

Of all Christian saints, St. Anthony had the strongest ties to Portugal and, partly for that reason, he had closer connections to Brazil than any other saint. He was born in Lisbon on August 15, 1195, near the cathedral in a house that is today a shrine. St. Anthony was born to a prominent noble family, the son of Martinho or Martim Bulhões and Teresa Taveira, and was given the name Fernando at baptism. Hagiographers recount that as a young man he was nearly seduced by a Jewish girl, but he managed to repel her advances by crossing himself. He remained chaste until the end of his life. Fernando attended the Lisbon Cathedral school and in 1210 concluded his studies in humanities and joined the Order of Canons Regular of St. Augustine at the St. Vincent Monastery. In 1212 he left for Coimbra and entered the Holy Cross Monastery, where he dedicated himself to the study of philosophy and theology. He specialized in Holy Scripture and was ordained a priest.

In 1209, a year before Fernando joined the Augustinian Canons, the Order of Friars Minor had been founded in Italy. It later became one of the most important medieval mendicant orders and may be considered the most significant work of St. Francis of Assisi. Ten years later, in 1219, five Franciscans came to Coimbra on their way to Morocco, where they were going on a religious mission. Fernando, then caretaker of the Holy Cross Monastery, offered them accommodation. The friars were later martyred by Muslims, and in 1220 Father Fernando witnessed their mortal remains pass through Coimbra. Deeply moved by the incident, he contacted the newly arrived friars at the Santo Antão of Olivais hermitage, requesting admission to the Franciscan order. When admitted, he took the name Anthony, probably in honor of St. Anthony the Abbot, known as Santo Antão in Portugal. So Father Fernando became Brother Anthony, soon to become the second most important member of the Franciscan order.

Friar Anthony, always a stout defender of the Christian faith, also traveled to Morocco on missionary work. During his stay there he fell gravely ill, risking his life in the name of God. On the return voyage, a violent storm forced the ship to the shores of Sicily, near the Strait of Messina, and thus the Italian career of Brother Anthony began.

He preached in Rimini, Faenza, Imola, Milan, and Bologna, and was especially celebrated for his great knowledge of theology. Francis of Assisi himself personally appointed him teacher of theology at the Bologna friars' school, a position he held for less than a year. In 1224 he traveled to the south of France, where he preached a sermon defending orthodox Catholicism against the so-called Albigensian or Catharist heresy. He also became a lecturer in theology at the University of Montpellier, a position he held until 1227, when he was appointed provincial of the northern Italian provinces. Finally, he settled at Padua. Francis of Assisi had died a year earlier and was canonized by the papacy in 1228. Friar Anthony continued his mission as preacher and lecturer until 1231, when he fell ill with fever, possibly through the effects of dropsy. The illness left him scarcely able to breathe. On Friday, June 13, he collapsed and died at age thirty-five. He was declared a saint by Pope Gregory IX in 1232 and was known thenceforth as either St. Anthony of Lisbon or St. Anthony of Padua.

A lecturer and a missionary, St. Anthony would be celebrated among Christians after his death for two other virtues that enhanced his popularity. First, he became known as a powerful thaumaturge, and his official hagiography recounts more than fifty miracles, including resurrections, control of natural phenomena, taming of wild animals, and curing of diseases. Also credited to him was the transformation of a frog into a cockerel and of a cockerel into a frog, actions performed to confuse a Cathar heretic. It is also reported that he had the power of bilocation and that he once bestowed the gift of speech on a baby so the infant could defend his or her mother's honor. The thaumaturgic career conferred on St. Anthony by his hagiography certainly contributed to his fame as a popular and domestic saint in the modern era. However, he is also renowned for his determined opposition to the Muslims, although it may be said that his actions in this regard were more rhetorical than practical. Above all, he has been revered for his struggle against the Albigensian heresy, a struggle conducted through itinerant preaching and scholastic debate. Therefore St. Anthony also was known as "The Hammer of Heretics," just as another famous saint, the Dominican Thomas Aquinas, was celebrated as "The Angelic Doctor" in recognition of his scholarly virtues.

St. Anthony's prestige as a great defender of Roman orthodoxy against heretical deviation had enormous importance during the Protestant-Catholic confrontation of the early modern period. For the Portuguese, his image as a warrior saint smiting heretics would be crucial in their struggle against the Calvinist Dutch in Brazil. The multidimensional nature of St. Anthony's reputation would be crucial to his role in the colonial setting.

In the popular Catholicism of the early modern period, St. Anthony had a domestic function associated with his aptitude for promoting marital matches. "Get me married, St. Anthony, get me married" is a refrain that runs through many prayers of the period. Yet this power to promote marriage is hardly mentioned in his hagiography or in authoritative reports on his thaumaturgic powers. The wonder-working gift that really stands out consistently is the power to recover lost objects and find missing people. This may be why he came to be regarded as a finder of spouses, for the line between the lost and the desired may be indistinct. St. Bonaventure, also another medieval Franciscan, had already appointed St. Anthony as *"membra resque perditas,"* and Antônio Vieira would refer to him as the *"deparador"* saint. This Portuguese word, now fallen into disuse, was used in the seventeenth century to mean "he who makes things appear" or, in other words, "he who finds the lost." Here was a saintly "discoverer."

The prestige of St. Anthony and the spread of his cult through Portugal and Brazil were extraordinary. According to Armando Mattos, fifty-seven hospitals (*hospícios* and *santas casas*) in Portugal named St. Anthony as their patron between the fifteenth and the eighteenth centuries;[1] by 1742 there were three hundred images of St. Anthony in the churches of the diocese of Lisbon alone.

In Brazil, St. Anthony's prestige also grew; with countless parishes, towns, and cities named after him, it would be fair to say that no other saint has lent his name to as many spots on the map of Brazil. By the end of the nineteenth century, 118 localities in Minas Gerais had been named after the saint from Lisbon. St. Sebastian followed, with 88 citations, and St. Anne, far behind, received only 27 citations. Between 1585 and 1650, a total of 8 of the 15 new Franciscan monasteries in Brazil honored St. Anthony's name; 4 of these were in the Northeast. St. Anthony was also named patron of 9 sugar mill chapels in Pernambuco, the same number dedicated to Our Lady of Rosario; St. John trailed behind. St. Anthony's reputation in Pernambuco was especially great, although it was hardly less important in other captaincies.

Throughout the colonial period, popular affection for St. Anthony rivaled devotion to Jesus Christ and the Virgin Mary. As the Holy Office grew more concerned with blasphemy in the second half of the sixteenth century—particularly after that milestone of the Counter-Reformation, the Council of Trent (1545–63)—Inquisitorial documents provide the best record of the participation of these holy figures in colonial daily life. Records of the first visitation of the Holy Office to Bahia and Pernambuco (1591–95) give detailed accounts of people cursing St. Anthony, even calling him a "crook," especially when he was unable to help them recover lost objects. Even in the 1540s, well before the Inquisitorial visitation took place, Pero do Campo Tourinho, a Porto Seguro landowner and captain who was constantly quarreling with the Franciscans in his captaincy, had been accused of saying that he would offer to Saint Anthony a "candle of shit."

However, curses against St. Anthony should not discredit the "advocate defender of lost causes" among Portuguese colonizers. On the contrary, they confirm his importance in daily life and people's great belief in his power to resolve everyday problems. Prominent among the evocations and imprecations were the issue of loss and the hope of recovering things. Thus the "*Responso das Coisas de Santo Antônio*," mentioned by Luiz Mott in an Inquisitorial case from Lisbon in 1694, must have been commonplace:

> Miraculous St. Anthony
> For the breviary you pray,
> For the cross you have carried,
> I beg you, St. Anthony, bring back
> What has been taken away (or lost, or gone)[2]

The last line varied according to the nature of the problem, indicating whether the saint was supposed to help recover objects that had been stolen or lost, or bring back a runaway husband or wife, fiancé or fiancée, lover, or slave. However, the *Responso* was proscribed by the official church.

From the realms of official and popular Catholicism, devotion to St. Anthony seeped into insurgent heterodox cults and rituals that were persecuted by the Inquisition. St. Anthony's name was associated with the main indigenous Santidade (the Santidade of Jaguaribe), a heretical aboriginal movement that flourished in Bahia at the end of the sixteenth century. The Santidade of Jaguaribe was a hybrid millenaristic movement, half Catholic and half Tupi. Its adherents challenged Portuguese colonization, defended indigenous traditions (primarily those of the Tupinambá), and fought against the colonizers and slavery. Its leader, Antonio, undoubtedly encouraged the Catholic-Tupinambá mixture in the rites of his sect. He had been indoctrinated by the Jesuits in a location known as Tinharé, in the captaincy of Ilhéus, but ran away to become the spiritual leader, or *Caraíba*,[3] of the movement. What could the Indian Antonio, who claimed to be the reincarnation of a Tupinambá ancestor, have learned about St. Anthony from the Jesuits? What could they have taught him about the patron saint of the illiterate, the thaumaturge, the divine saint, finder of lost things, the "discoverer saint"?

In the case of the *Santidade of Jaguaribe,* records confirming St. Anthony's presence are quite clear. However, Inquisition sources, especially those of the eighteenth century, indicate that this is not the case where certain Afro-Brazilian cults are concerned. The image of St. Anthony can be found in many records relating to the *calundus,* as well as in the *acotundá* of Minas Gerais.[4] The adoption of St. Anthony by certain Afro-Brazilians started in the colonial period, and he is perhaps still the principal saint of the *umbanda* in contemporary Rio de Janeiro because he is associated with the *exus.* For the *umbandistas,* the *exus* are intermediaries between the *orixás,* such as São Jorge/Ogum and Santa Bárbara/Iansã, and the terrestrial world. This syncretism becomes clearest on June 13, when both Brother Anthony's feast day is celebrated and the *umbanda* houses hold a great party for the *exus.*

The assimilation of St. Anthony by syncretic cults of non-Catholic origin may be understood, as Roger Bastide has suggested, as a phenomenon of cultural and religious resistance.[5] Paradoxically, the same saint venerated by many Brazilians of African descent also was adopted as a strong protector by the *capitães-do-mato,* men dedicated to capturing runaway slaves or *quilombolas*. As Luiz Mott has shown, St. Anthony was to these white Brazilians a "divine slave hunter." Masters upset by the loss of their slaves turned to this saintly finder, as did those who had lost objects, lovers, and the like. This essential trait of *membra resque perditas,* together with St. Anthony's military qualities, account for his enormous prestige, both in Portugal and its overseas empire.

Historically, there are no records of Brother Anthony engaging in military pursuits, though he did arm himself with words in the defense of the Catholic Church against infidels and heretics. Yet, at least in Brazil, St. Anthony of Lisbon would have a long career in arms, blessing forts and regiments and directly intervening in battles. St. Anthony's image would be decorated, promoted, and recognized for services rendered to the king, and it is probable that he superseded St. George, warrior saint par excellence, in Brazil. During the fifteenth century, St. George, an important saint for the Portuguese Avis dynasty, lent his name to many sites, including the famous African fortress of São Jorge da Mina. The union between the cross and the sword, which Charles Boxer viewed as typical of Iberian colonization, appeared very early in Brazil in the form of St. Anthony. For example, in the captaincy of Bahia, the church and the fortress were named Santo Antônio da Barra.

St. Anthony's military career in Brazil may well have started in this Bahian fortress, as he was incorporated into the regiment there as a private soldier at the end of the sixteenth century. The saint was later promoted to captain of the fort thanks to a petition from the local council of the city of Salvador. He was depicted as a soldier of the faith and a second lieutenant in both the Morro prison of São Paulo and the church of Mouraria.[6] In 1709 he earned the post of soldier in Paraíba; in 1717 he won the commission of artillery captain; in 1750 he was designated private at the request of the city council of Goiás. In several captaincies, military offices and awards were granted to St. Anthony's image, along with the corresponding pay.

However, what may seem strange from a contemporary point of view was a serious matter in those days, not only among popular classes, soldiers, and slaves, but also among the privileged classes of the colony. Brother Manuel Calado, in his *Valeroso Lucideno* of 1646, recounted how the residents of Recife gave Maurice of Nassau, the Dutch governor of Pernambuco from 1637 to 1644, the nickname "Santo Antonio" simply because he had given them freedom of worship and protected them from the Calvinist ministers, always ready to accuse the Pernambuco friars of idolatry.[7]

Thus we need to examine more closely the connection between the cult of St. Anthony and the military and political history of Brazil. To this end, special attention will be given to the Dutch triumph in the northeastern captaincies, which started dramatically in 1624, when the Dutch first laid siege to Salvador, whence they were expelled with great difficulty a year later, up to their successful occupation of Pernambuco in 1630. In fact, the Dutch occupied Pernambuco and other northeastern captaincies from 1630 to 1654; only then were they definitively expelled.

But if the context was dramatic in Brazil, it was even more so in Portugal. Problems started in 1578, when young King Sebastian (1554–78) decided to intervene in the disputes between local North African political leaders *(sheriffs)*[8] to reaffirm Portuguese influence in the region. This unfortunate initiative led to his death in the Battle of Alcácer-Quibir and the defeat of his large army. As he was not married and had no heirs, the Portuguese crown was conferred on the king's great-uncle, Cardinal Dom Henrique, whose main concern was to prevent annexation of the kingdom by Phillip II of Spain. In fact, after the cardinal's death in 1580, Portugal was forced to surrender, in spite of some internal resistance, and Phillip II of Spain became the new Portuguese king, beginning the so-called Iberian Union. Although most of the Portuguese nobility and clergy supported King Phillip's ambitions in Portugal and in overseas colonies, a deep resentment over the loss of national sovereignty spread among popular classes. Dissident nobles gathered under the leadership of Phillip's main opponent, the prior of Crato, also called Dom Anthony. During the final decades of the sixteenth and the beginning of the seventeenth centuries, rebel groups also arose from among the religious orders. Above all, the Society of Jesus became a major opponent of King Phillip, partly because the late King Sebastian had been educated by the Jesuits, but mainly because the new regime would greatly increase the power of the Inquisition in Portugal.

Therefore, early in the seventeenth century the Portuguese had to contend with both the Dutch, their explicit enemy overseas, and the Spanish, a more subtle enemy in its traditional role as rival for Iberian hegemony. One person was perhaps most responsible for St. Anthony's rising political status, as both patron saint of the Portuguese, and as the divine promoter of the wars of resistance. Antônio Vieira (1608–97) was born in Lisbon but moved to Brazil as a child. He was educated at the Jesuit College of Bahia and became one of the most important Jesuits in Luso-Brazilian history.

It is not the purpose of this chapter to explore the rich and multi-faceted career of the Jesuit Antônio Vieira, who legitimated African slavery to save the indigenous people from captivity, opposed the Inquisition on behalf of new Christians and even Jews, and who, after the Portuguese Restoration in 1640, became the ambassador of John IV in France and Holland. Nevertheless, there is one aspect of his biography that deserves more attention: his link with the Portuguese movement of prophetic millenarianism, which took root after King Sebastian's death in 1578. Vieira started his "Sebastianist" career during the last years of Castilian dominance with a sermon he gave in Bahia in 1634. In this sermon he established several analogies between King Sebastian and St. Sebastian, a martyr of the church. Alluding to the relationship between the hidden and the revealed when referring to the history of the saint, Vieira seemed to be stimulating hope that the king's power would be restored and the independence of the kingdom regained. According to the Jesuit, "the death of those who die in the name of God and for God is not what it seems, it is the image of Death hidden within the reality of Life." Vieira clearly supported Sebastianism in his inaugural sermon. As Jacqueline Hermann points out:

> The Hidden One (in the sermon) calls himself Sebastian and sacrificed himself in defense of the Christian faith. He was apparently allied with the enemies, and many of them took him for dead in a battle directed by the opponents of Christianity. But his appearance of death only confirmed the force of his life. . . .[9]

From his first sermon preached in the Royal Palace in 1641, Vieira defended the prophetic character of the *Trovas* (Ballads) attributed to a shoemaker called Bandarra, probably a new Christian who had been prosecuted by the Holy Office in the sixteenth century. Many considered these ballads the "Bible of Sebastianism," which foresaw the coming of a messianic Fifth Empire of the World.

In 1659 Vieira wrote the memorable *Letter to the Japanese Bishop, Hope for Portugal, Fifth Empire of the World,* a text that would involve him in serious problems with the Inquisition in the 1660s. This writing has been condemned for its "judaizing" and abuse of the Holy Scripture. The Inquisitorial trial, which landed Vieira in prison between 1665 and 1667, began in 1663. The *Letter to the Japanese Bishop* was an updated analysis of the *Ballads* of Bandarra, who, according to Vieira, had possessed a prophetic spirit and reaffirmed, among other things, the future emergence of a Fifth Empire, seated in Portugal and governed by the resuscitated emperor João IV. The *Letter to the Japanese Bishop* initiated Vieira's prophetic corpus and formed the basis for both his famous *History of the Future,* published in 1718, and the unfinished *Clavis Prophetarum.* In the *History of the Future,* Vieira took his messianic project for the implementation of the Fifth Empire of the World to the extreme. The Fifth Empire was described as a place filled with harmony and peace where all other religions and heresies were subject to the true Catholic faith for an undetermined period of at least one thousand years. *Clavis Prophetarum* was the culmination of Vieira's millenarian and messianic theological trilogy.

Vieira composed nine sermons entirely dedicated to St. Anthony. Of these, one was never delivered, and five were delivered in Brazil—one in Bahia and four in São Luiz. The others were delivered in Europe—one in Lisbon and two in Rome.[10] The first of these sermons, delivered in Bahia on June 13, 1638, must be understood in the context of the unfolding Luso-Dutch conflict in Brazil, and also as a prologue to the Luso-Spanish crisis in 1640. Vieira delivered the sermon in a church dedicated to St. Anthony on the same hill in Salvador where the decisive battle against the Dutch had been fought on May 16 of that same year. This battle definitively drove out the Dutch and frustrated their second attempt to conquer Salvador. In this bloody battle some five hundred soldiers under the command of Maurice of Nassau were killed and seven hundred wounded.

In a triumphant sermon Vieira recalled the Portuguese conflict against the Dutch. The text begins by praising the resistance of the people of Bahia, who took up arms and fought for forty days and forty nights. The sermon's focus, however, is an exegesis of the Second Book of Kings, narrating the siege of Jerusalem by King Sennacherib of Assyria (705–681 B.C.), and King David's successful recapture of the city under the protection of God. Comparing the siege of Jerusalem with that of Salvador, Vieira recounts the

events of the recent Luso-Dutch battle, arguing that the same divine intervention took place in both wars. The victory of Bahia over the heretics was
"the glory of all the saints," according to Vieira, but the defense of the city
had been the work of one saint alone: St. Anthony, to whom God had confided this task. Vieira proved his thesis by describing some moments of the
battle when the saint protected the Portuguese, even when it seemed that
all was lost.

> But he was not less worthy of admiration, as while the armed stronghold
> spontaneously surrendered, there stood St. Anthony's solitary trench, though
> quite ruined, exposed and almost leveling the ground, the only one showing
> signs of resistance![11]

Vieira had no doubt that St. Anthony had defended Bahia. By the
same token, he believed the saint would next free Pernambuco from the
heretics. "Restoration" was therefore the subject of Vieira's sermon, which
praised the victory in Bahia and urged the reconquest of Pernambuco.

Strictly speaking, the enemies in this conflict were the Dutch heretics.
But could the Jesuit have been referring to another enemy, the Castilians,
who had by then reigned in Portugal for more than half a century? Vieira
was very prudent and avoided celebrating the event as a Portuguese conquest. He limited his praise to the military victory of Salvador and celebrated the triumph of God and St. Anthony in general terms. Nevertheless,
a detail at the beginning of the sermon deserves special attention. The
preacher dedicated his text to *His Majesty*, studiously avoiding referring to
Phillip IV by name. He made a clear distinction between Portugal and
Spain when referring to the victorious monarchy. By 1638 the Iberian
Union had become quite weak, and thus the recapture of Pernambuco proclaimed by Vieira can be interpreted as connected to the struggle for the
restoration of Portuguese sovereignty in the Iberian Peninsula.

In a laudatory sermon on St. Sebastian in 1634, Vieira expressed nos-
talgia for King Sebastian as well as hope for his "return." In his sermon of
1638, the hero of the Restoration would be St. Anthony, who triumphed
against the Dutch in Bahia to defend the captaincy and, by extension, the
kingdom of Portugal.

But if Vieira was cautious and watched his words in this sermon to
honor St. Anthony, he had been even more careful in the sermon he delivered in Bahia on January 6, 1641, during the feast of the Epiphany. The

restoration of the Portuguese monarchy had already been declared a month earlier, and a war against Spain was in progress. However, news from overseas was delayed for more than a month, and Vieira's cautious sermon inadvertently condemned the revolt of the Catalans (one of several against the Spanish Crown at midcentury). Vieira also criticized the Sebastianists for preaching on St. Sebastian's return, referring to them as partisans of a "foolish chimera." Vieira even went so far as to praise Phillip IV, who governed Portugal as Phillip III, affirming that he had inherited both the crown and the blood of the late King Sebastian.

In any case, the crucial point is to analyze the ideology of restoration found in Vieira's sermons between 1630 and 1640, an ideology that would gradually turn his attention from St. Sebastian and King Sebastian to St. Anthony and King John IV, the duke of Bragança and restorer of Portuguese sovereignty.

Thus it was not just a coincidence that St. Anthony appeared in one of Vieira's first sermons as "Custodian of the Courts of Heaven." Delivered in Lisbon on September 14, 1642, the sermon was ordered by John IV, and was supposed to encourage both the nobility and the clergy to pay taxes to finance the Restoration wars against Spain. He sermonized in honor of St. Anthony, "Saint of Salt," "salt from earth, able to preserve conquered territories." Eventually St. Anthony would be acclaimed as the saint of the Portuguese Restoration, both at court and among the popular classes. Vieira, in spite of his ambiguities, became the principal architect of the saint's political side.

In this way, St. Anthony was elevated from "Recoverer of Lost Objects" to "Recoverer of Portuguese Sovereignty." St. Anthony was now lauded for his help in restoring a reconquered land. Outside the royal residence, the populace now sang a quadrille expressing this new Portuguese hero's mission:

> St. Anthony is a good saint
> Who saves father from disease;
> He must also liberate us
> From the power of the Castilians.[12]

After the Portuguese Restoration St. Anthony reemerged as an important figure in the imperial wars against the Dutch, as if foreseen by Vieira's sermon in 1638. For example, the so-called Pernambuco insurrection led by João Fernandes Vieira was deliberately started on June 13, 1645, on St. Anthony's Day. Signs of St. Anthony's divine intervention were carefully described by the Franciscan chronicler Manuel Calado in his *Valeroso Lucideno*. Friar Calado recounts the saint's apparition in Fernandes Vieira's dream and attests that the saint's advice on certain military strategies was decisive in leading the insurrectionists to victory.

In this way, St. Anthony, patron of the Portuguese Restoration, also was elected patron of the Pernambucan triumph over the Dutch, acting as restorer of the "lost autonomy." As historian Evaldo Cabral de Mello comments:

> God gave Brazil to Portugal; the Dutch heretics usurped it; St. Anthony restored it. In view of the general devotion to St. Anthony, it was necessary to recruit him, mobilizing the reluctant courage of the Luso-Brazilian population . . . St. Anthony was presumably chosen for his renown in *ante bellum* Pernambuco. His success in the so-called war of divine liberty would consolidate his preeminence in the religious manifestations of the captaincy, conferring upon him the character of military saint.[13]

Thus St. Anthony was elevated from his position as "hammer of heretics" to become the "saint of restoration" in many seventeenth-century Luso-Brazilian texts. He was the saint who "rediscovered" Portugal's sovereignty and "restored" Portuguese rule in America. It would not be long before St. Anthony's military and restorative powers were put to the test elsewhere, traveling as far as the African lands Christianized by the Portuguese. In the Congo, for example, toward the end of the seventeenth and the beginning of the eighteenth centuries, Kimpa Vita, a *bakongo* prophetess of noble origin, promoted the restoration of a decadent kingdom by proclaiming herself the reincarnation of St. Anthony. Her actions would initiate the peculiar movement of the so-called *Anthonians*.[14] Could the impact of Vieira's sermons have been felt as far away as the Congo? What is certain is that St. Anthony was transformed by the Luso-Brazilian imagination, becoming a soldier of the Restoration monarchy and its overseas conquests. Perhaps this explains the unique importance of this seraphic thaumaturge in Luso-Brazilian history.

NOTES

1. Armando de Mattos, *Santo António de Lisboa na tradição popular, subsídio etnográfico* ([Porto]: Livraria Civilização-Editora [1937]).

2. Quoted in Luiz Mott, "Santo Antônio, o divino capitão-do-mato," in *Liberdade por um fio*, ed. J. Reis and F. Gomes (São Paulo: Companhia das Letras, 1997), 127.
3. Special preachers in the Tupi culture who were believed to be able to talk with the ancestors and even to incarnate them. Basically, those Indian prophets preached about the myth of "the land without evil," a kind of paradise the Indians were forever seeking. Cf. Ronaldo Vainfas, *A heresia dos índios: catolicismo e rebeldia no Brasil Colonial* (São Paulo: Companhia das Letras, 1995).
4. Cf. Luiz Mott, "Acotundá: Raízes Setecentistas do Sincretismo Religioso Afro-brasileiro" (São Paulo: *Revista do Museu Paulista,* 1986), vol. 31, 124–47.
5. Roger Bastide, *The African Religions of Brazil: Toward a Sociology of the Interpenetration of Civilizations,* trans. Helen Sebba (Baltimore: Johns Hopkins University Press, 1978).
6. An old Moorish neighborhood.
7. Written between 1645 and 1646, it was the best chronicle on the beginning of Pernambuco's wars.
8. Muslim authorities or petty "kings" in these African lands.
9. Jacqueline Hermann, *No reino do desejado: a construção do Sebastianismo em Portugal* (São Paulo: Companhia das Letras, 1998), 230.
10. *Santo Antônio, luz do mundo* (nove sermões), ed. Clarêncio Neotti, OFM (Petrópolis: Vozes, 1997).
11. Ibid., 47–48.
12. Mott, "Santo Antônio," 121.
13. Evaldo Cabral de Mello, *Rubro veio: o imaginário da restauração pernambucana,* 2nd ed. (Rio de Janeiro: Topbooks, 1997), 311–12.
14. Louis Jadin, "Le Congo et la secte des antoniens: Restauration du Royaume sous Pedro IV et la Saint Antoine congolaise," *Bulletin de l'Institut historique Belge-Rome,* 1961.

Part 2

HOLY WOMEN, HOLY MEN

6

Francisco Losa and Gregorio López: Spiritual Friendship and Identity Formation on the New Spain Frontier[1]

JODI BILINKOFF

In 1562 a young man of twenty named Gregorio López left his native Spain for a new life in New Spain. In this he was like hundreds of such emigrants. But unlike so many others, ambitious for the adventure, the advancement, and, especially, the wealth the New World had to offer, Gregorio undertook a life he had already begun in Spain, that of a wandering hermit. Over time, tales spread of an enigmatic man of uncertain origins who underwent rigorous ascetic exercises, spent hours rapt in prayer, and was graced by God with the gifts of infused knowledge, the ability to penetrate hearts, and the company of angels. Spanish settlers and native people alike came to the holy man seeking intercessory prayer, words of advice, or a piece of his rough clothing or meager possessions as relics. Despite recurring questions about the orthodoxy of his ideas and practices, at his death in 1596 Gregorio López was regarded by many in the region around Mexico City as a saint. His cause for canonization was eventually introduced in Rome, and while ultimately unsuccessful, he gained recognition as "Venerable," a distinction the Catholic Church bestowed upon only a select few in colonial Mexico.[2]

This is an extraordinary account, to be sure, but it is not the subject of this chapter. Rather, I choose to tell another story, that of the man

115

without whom we would know virtually nothing of Gregorio López. I wish to examine the equally fascinating case of Francisco Losa, who in 1613 published *The Life That the Servant of God Gregorio López Made in Several Places in This New Spain* (*La Vida que Hizo el Siervo de Dios Gregorio López en algunos lugares de esta Nueva España*). This is, of course, a hagiographical account. But to a remarkable degree Losa interjected the story of his own life, a life intimately shared with and shaped by Gregorio López. I examine here Losa's text as simultaneously about López and about himself. Losa's narrative of friendship, role reversal, and spiritual and literary vocation, I suggest, ultimately constructs not just López but also Losa as exemplary subjects and presents them as much-needed models of male behavior in a frontier society.

On the surface there was nothing about Francisco Losa's first forty-one years to suggest anything other than the conventional life and career of a Spanish cleric. He was born in 1536 or 1537 in the town of Cea, in the province of León.[3] He immigrated to New Spain in about 1566, at approximately age thirty, having recently been ordained a priest. Within two years Archbishop Alonso de Montúfar had appointed Losa parish priest or curate (cura) at the cathedral of Mexico City; that is, he was one of those responsible for the cure of souls in the central district of the capital city. This was a fairly prestigious position, given the preponderance of Spanish elites in the parish, and it included a permanent benefice and fixed annual income. Losa was to hold this post for more than twenty years.[4]

By the late 1570s Francisco Losa had established himself as a well-respected member of New Spain's secular clergy. He earned a degree from the still-new Universidad de México, distinguishing himself in Latin letters and in canon law, especially questions of moral theology and cases of conscience *(casos de conciencia)*.[5] In 1577 Losa figured among the founding members of the Congregación de San Pedro, a confraternity for secular clerics based in Mexico City; the following year the group elected him its second leader *(abad)*.[6] He also may have served as private chaplain in a number of noble households; certainly he was acquainted with many members of Mexico's elite.[7] All in all, he was on track for a comfortable and secure, if not fabulously lucrative, career within the colonial church hierarchy. In a report to the Crown of 1575, Archbishop Pedro Moya de Contreras noted that the priest could be "somewhat arrogant or conceited" *(algo presuntuoso),* but generally praised Losa for his devoted and responsible service to the archdiocese and recommended that he be rewarded with privileges. Referring back to this period in his life in Mexico City, Losa recalled simply that he was "well known to all."[8]

Yet even in Losa's early career there were hints of the changes to come. He displayed from the start a deep and abiding commitment to charitable work among the poor and the sick, working at several hospitals in the region. By 1578 he had become almoner at the cathedral of Mexico, dispensing charity to the "shame-faced poor" (*pobres vergonzantes*) in the capital. Losa gained considerable respect from both prelates and the public at large for the conscientious way he carried out this work. In one document from the later seventeenth century, Losa is described as a "mendicant almoner" (*limosnero mendicante*), suggesting that he begged alms to give to the needy, neither an activity nor a term usually associated with members of the secular clergy.[9] This parish priest, apparently sympathetic to the idea of voluntary poverty, was also an avid reader of mystical writers: Tauler, Ruysbroeck, Catherine of Siena. Later he would express his devotion to the works of Teresa of Avila, whom he actually lived long enough to see canonized a saint.[10]

In 1578 Archbishop Moya y Contreras entrusted his almoner with a rather delicate task. A strange wandering hermit had arrived in the district around Mexico City, and while many admired his life of intense prayer and self-denial, others suspected him of holding heterodox beliefs.[11] Why did Moya choose Losa to examine Gregorio López? As we have seen, Losa, although a relatively low-ranking cleric, had received a good university education and had an aptitude for directing souls in matters of conscience, a most useful skill in the discernment of spirits. And there are indications that the prelate, already favorably disposed toward López (he would become an important devotee and protector), sent someone he knew would also be sympathetic to this lay holy man. He may have been aware of the following incident. Several months before meeting López, Losa encountered a priest who described a man

who he feared very much was a Lutheran heretic because he did not carry any [rosary] beads about him nor showed any other such signs with which good Christians showed their devotion and uprightness of heart. I asked [the priest] whether he spoke well in things touching our faith; [the cleric] answered that [the man] seemed to be well-grounded in the Catholic doctrine, that he knew all the Bible by heart, that in his behavior he was blameless. . . . I replied familiarly . . . if you should see a thief without his beads you would not therefore account him a heretic, how much less a man of so good a life, so conversant in the Holy Scripture and whose conversation seems only to be with God. . . .

The priest was so swayed by Losa's spirited and well-reasoned defense that he decided against denouncing López to the Inquisition, as he had planned.[12] Given his Erasmian-style indifference to external rituals and "signs" and his predilection for the ascetic and the mystical, Losa was certainly a "soft pitch."

Moya accordingly sent his curate to the nearby sanctuary of Nuestra Señora de los Remedios, where López was then residing, to put him to the test. This encounter would radically change the course of Losa's life. After meeting and conversing with López, Losa became convinced not only that the layman was entirely orthodox but also that he was endowed with divine graces; that he was a saint. Francisco Losa began a personal transformation that would take him from the cure of many souls in New Spain's largest parish to a life dedicated to the care, defense, and promotion of one extraordinary individual.

The first way in which Losa's new self-understanding and evolving relationship with López manifested itself involved the hermit's health. The latter suffered from a number of painful chronic ailments, exacerbated, no doubt, by a rigorous ascetic regime: denying himself food, sleeping on the ground without a blanket, wearing clothing of poor and coarse material, and the like. Soon after being examined and approved by Losa, López fell seriously ill. Losa applied both the compassion and the skills he had developed over years of charitable work toward relieving the holy man's suffering. By 1580, within two years of their first meeting, the priest had procured permission to move López to the Hospital de la Santa Cruz in the town of Oaxtepec. This institution, run by the Hospital Brothers of San Hipólito, was one of the best known and most highly regarded in the colony. López would reside there for some eight years.[13]

Losa felt compelled by duty (and pressure from his superiors) to return to Mexico City "lest I should be wanting in my office," but he returned frequently to Oaxtepec to visit López and help the hospital brothers.[14] During the 1580s Losa's personal commitment to López and his yearning to share the hermit's life of eremitic solitude and contemplative prayer deepened. Losa recalled,

> By these my often visits, I discovered every day more and more of [López's]
> great riches in virtue and spirit, whereby I became very desirous to live in his
> company. I desired of God both by means of other devout persons' prayers
> and also my own that he would let me understand his holy will. . . .[15]

The situation reached a crisis during the winter of 1588–89, when López sent news of his worsening physical condition. Losa lost no time in bringing his friend back to his own house in Mexico City. It was then that the two worked out plans for a shared life, discussing the best location for a hermitage. López "made more account of the commodiousness of the country," but Losa set out to find "some seat near the city where he might enjoy his solitariness, and I might often see him and in some manner relieve his sickness and poverty." They settled on the village of Santa Fe, two leagues from Mexico City, secured the necessary permissions, and on May 22, 1589, installed López in what would be his final residence.[16]

This still left open the question of Losa's own vocation. He had petitioned his superiors to allow him to join López and live as a hermit. But many, including Archbishop Moya y Contreras, were reluctant to lose the man who so effectively served the poor of Mexico City: "in some men's opinion, the employment which I had in Mexico was much to God's service . . . for which reason my Superiors doubted very much whether it was convenient to give me leave or not to retire myself to a solitary life."[17] Intriguingly, there is nothing in Losa's *Life* of López or other contemporary documents to indicate that anyone objected to an ordained priest living with and coming under the spiritual tutelage of a layman. Modern historians have not commented on this remarkable instance of role reversal either, a point to which I will return.

Finally, late in 1589 Losa's request was granted, a turn of events the priest understood in supernatural terms:

> At length it pleased God to dispose of this matter, as that I resolved that this
> course was convenient and my superiors condescended unto it and gave me
> license which until then was denied me. . . .[18]

It is worth noting, however, that Moya had retired in 1586, and for a variety of reasons his position remained unfilled until 1611. During this somewhat fluid period of *sede vacante* archdiocesan affairs were handled by an interim administrator, Pedro de Pravia, who was, as it turned out, a Dominican friar with an ascetic bent—and an enthusiastic supporter of Gregorio López.[19] In any case, Losa's years of waiting were now over: "So I came to dwell in Santa Fe about Christmas of the same year 1589, where I attended upon Gregory until his death. . . ."[20] The fifty-three-year-old Losa renounced his benefice, rejecting the source of his status, income, and security. Evidence of a profound conversion experience can be found right on the title page of the *Life* of López, where the author identifies himself as "Presbítero, Cura que fue en la Yglesia Catedral de Mexico," a priest who was once also a curate.

Francisco Losa and Gregorio López spent the next seven years "living in the same house, eating at the same table, and sleeping in the same chamber" until the holy man's death on July 20, 1596.[21] For the remainder of this chapter I explore this shared life and the ways in which Losa presented himself in relation to López, attending particularly to the deployment of gender roles and reversals in the construction of exemplary selves. Losa's own life, as well as his *Life* of López, were dedicated to promoting certain models of pious male behavior. While this was a traditional Christian enterprise, to be sure, I speculate that it was undertaken with special urgency in a society in which images of greedy and violent settlers and corrupt clerics dominated the cultural landscape.

Losa's single most important job with respect to López was as defender of López's orthodoxy, a task that only a priest could undertake. Put bluntly, if Losa (or some other cleric) had not given his approval, the hermit might well have found himself condemned by the Inquisition like so many of the Illuminati *(alumbrados)* in whose circles he apparently moved.[22]

When speaking as guarantor of López's orthodoxy, Losa's tone is cool, rational, sacerdotal. He represents his initial report to Archbishop Moya as having been succinct and wholly professional: "by the conferences I had with [López] I remained well satisfied touching his spirit, and judged him to be a man of solid and well grounded virtue." Losa claims that one reason he wanted to reside with López was so that he could continue to monitor his behavior and doctrinal positions.[23] Losa could also be quite aggressive in his defense of López. Losa dismisses certain friars who had disparaged the holy man's lack of formal education and clerical status as "none of the learnedest," characterizes their attacks as demonically inspired ("the common enemy used [them] for his instruments"), and acridly reminds his readers that "the hood makes not the monk."[24] I have suggested elsewhere that in portraying López, Losa highlights qualities often gendered as "female": his many illnesses and physical debilities, his meekness and humility, his indifference to worldly possessions and ambitions, his deference to clergymen.[25] This strategy not only serves to construct López as pious exemplar but also underscores Losa's own status as clerical authority and gender location as male, the dominant partner in a relationship of dependency.

Nevertheless, in almost every other regard Losa consistently and dramatically reverses the equation, stressing his own renunciation and spiritual dependence on the charismatic López in ways that gender Losa himself as "female." Losa frequently reminds his readers how his own soul has benefited from observing, conversing with, and attempting to imitate the holy man.[26] He reverently recalls how he chose López as his "master and companion for the rest of my life." And he remembers with emotion how "from the first day that I saw him . . . I presently perceived in him a certain excellence which I had not seen in any other man. This opinion increased in me even until his death. . . ."[27] This highly affective discourse of destiny is commonly found in writings by and about women who developed close relationships with their male spiritual directors. For example, the German priest John Marienwerder (d. 1417) reported that after Dorothea of Montau (d. 1394) confessed and received communion from him for the first time, "Immediately her soul was glued to her own most recent Confessor through so immense a friendship as quickly as she had ever had for any person. . . ."[28]

With Francisco Losa this effusive language reaches an apogee of sorts when he insists that

> from the first time that I visited him . . . it pleased God out of his mercy to give me such a care of Gregory that if it was necessary to do something for him, never so hard, I should not have stuck upon it. . . . [T]o say in a word, from the time that I knew him until he died in my company . . . methought I could have been content to have been his slave. . . .[29]

Indeed, he devoted himself wholeheartedly to serving the holy man. López may have addressed the priest as "Father," but Losa evinced a decidedly "maternal" (or "wifely") concern for the hermit's health and well-being. Although both Losa and López understood the latter's desire to suffer in spiritual terms, frequent expressions of anxious solicitude punctuate the biographical account. These moments also allow glimpses into their shared domestic life. Losa frets, for example, when his friend endures a terrible toothache and "would not let me send for a barber to pull it out." Only his "earnest entreaty" persuades López, who had for many years slept on the bare ground or a sheepskin, to at last cover himself with "a little thin material" or "mean coverlet."[30]

As the hermit's reputation spread, people began arriving at Santa Fe seeking advice, prayers, and thaumaturgic healing.[31] Losa consequently took it upon himself to protect López's privacy and daily routine of devotional readings and contemplation. Suppliants found that they had to first speak or send messages to López's faithful companion before they could gain permission to visit the famous man himself. Once when a certain "great Lady" whom Losa deemed insufficiently sincere came to the hermitage, he promptly "sent word unto her, that she should not come into the house." The noblewoman persisted for several hours, but Losa held firm. Only when others certified that the woman had truly resolved to amend her idle and sinful ways did he declare himself "satisfied and of the opinion that she should see [López]."[32]

And a related activity also absorbed Francisco Losa during those years at Santa Fe. Convinced as he was that Gregorio López was a genuine saint, Losa busied himself preparing his biography. By the late sixteenth century it was not unusual for confessors or other clerical promoters to take notes or begin gathering data even while their exemplary subjects were still alive.[33] In the *Life* of López, Losa reveals himself engaged in the biographical process with striking frequency and vividness.

For example, it is clear from the text that Losa carried out numerous interviews with López. During their "chats" *(pláticas)* he asked the holy man questions about his family origins, his earliest religious calling, his decision to immigrate to the New World, his preferred reading and penitential exercises, and many other topics. He also listened as López gave counsel to others. And he recorded a good deal of what he learned, sometimes exhibiting the precision and persistence of a modern-day journalist. For example, Losa remembered that he once "importune[d] him very much" to speak of his sufferings. "After many days" López finally complied, going on to "utter somewhat of that which did inwardly pass between God and him." This unexpected revelation left the biographer so "amazed" that "presently I wrote down these words which he had said, being the 23 of March in the year 1591."[34]

Information about López that Losa could not glean directly from conversations with his subject he set about compiling from other sources. He talked to priests and others who had known the hermit in his early years in New Spain. He kept correspondence that López had received or that he had solicited. He attempted to collect and corroborate the many anecdotes relating to the holy man's divine graces and miraculous healings.[35]

I suggest that the ways in which Losa presents himself in the text—as guarantor of López's orthodoxy, as caregiver, and as gatekeeper and intermediary with the outside world—are integral to this biographical enterprise. By stressing the constancy with which he monitored, attended, and observed López, and by insisting on the intimacy of their living arrangements, Losa underscores his own privileged position. He establishes himself as special spiritual friend, the man who knew Gregorio López better than anyone else. His credentials as biographer are impeccable.

As a result of this frequent and extensive authorial intervention, the *Life* of López comes to function simultaneously as autobiography and biography. Losa succeeds in constructing a text that relates his *own* story of conversion, service, and sacrifice as well as that of his subject. Fascinating in this regard are Losa's few brief references to López's feelings toward him. In sharp contrast to his own emotional outpourings, the priest portrays the holy man as utterly laconic (a virtue in the eremitic life) and rather formal and restrained in his dealings with him. López addresses his companion as "Padre Losa" and uses the honorific form "Vuestra Merced."[36] Losa recalls how responding to his frequent ministrations the holy man "always said unto me: let no man be solicitous for me, for God will have a care to provide as shall please him," and "often reprehended me for praising him."[37] After making the extraordinary statement about having been content to have been López's slave, Losa continues

> and he knew it very well and showed himself very grateful, yet I dare affirm that never anyone saw him rely or put the least hope in that which I did or could do, nor that he set his affection upon me in any excessive manner for all whatsoever I did.[38]

Losa the hagiographer makes these observations in the context of enumerating López's saintly attributes, of course, but one wonders if these words do not betray a certain disappointment by Losa the man. Nevertheless, as conversion narrative these reflections have the effect of rendering the priest's renunciation even more dramatic and selfless. The once comfortable, respected, even "somewhat arrogant" curate has become the humble servant of the Servant of God. In the Catholic culture in which Francisco Losa was raised and that he helped to perpetuate, it is precisely this willingness to forgo wealth, privilege, and even reciprocated affection that elevated his spiritual status. Losa recalled that once "as I was about to leave [López] upon some business he stayed me, saying 'keep me company.' " The priest continued, "truly the saying of Jesus Christ to his Apostles 'keep me company' had in it a great mystery. . . ."[39] Here Losa, like many hagiographers before him, depicts his exemplary subject as Christlike. Less common, however, if no less significant, is the biographer's self-identification as apostle.

After the death of López in 1596, Losa stayed on at Santa Fe for another twenty years, revealing himself to be, in the words of Antonio Rubial, a "hermit at heart" (ermitaño de corazón). He dedicated himself to preserving the memory and promoting the cult of his saintly companion. The priest continued to collect stories and written sources about López. He distributed pieces of the hermit's garments and other personal items as relics. And, of course, he composed the Life, circulating a version in manuscript by 1598. He would publish it in Mexico City in 1613.[40]

In 1616 Archbishop Juan Pérez de la Serna asked Losa to serve as chaplain at the convent of Discalced Carmelite nuns newly established in the capital. Now eighty years old, he was reluctant to leave his beloved hermitage and chosen way of life. As one of the sisters of the San José convent later recalled, Losa finally agreed, but on one condition: that the prelate allow him to take with him the bones of Gregorio López because "the two had promised one another to part neither in life nor in death."[41]

To his own surprise, Francisco Losa lived long enough to enter directly into the saintmaking process. In 1620 King Philip III, learning about the Madrid native turned New World hermit through Losa's now incredibly popular biography, ordered Pérez de la Serna to hold diocesan hearings on López's heroic virtues. On July 10, 1620, Losa offered the first and most extensive testimony in this initial step in the long canonization process.[42] This would be his last recorded public gesture of veneration, of gratitude, and of love toward the man who had completely changed his life. Francisco Losa died on August 27, 1624, at age eighty-eight. He was buried in the place he had requested in his will: in San José, beside the remains of Gregorio López.

Succeeding generations came to remember Francisco Losa with almost as much reverence as they did Gregorio López, as Losa no doubt secretly hoped. Chronicles written within a generation of Losa's death praise the priest as "most exemplary cleric," a true imitator of López in "virtue and sanctity," and a "great servant of God."[43] Mariano Cuevas, the respected Jesuit whose multivolume ecclesiastical history from the 1940s is still frequently cited, declared that Losa deserved "a most honored place in the history of the Mexican church."[44]

Cuevas discusses Losa in a section devoted to the parish clergy, and this placement may provide a key to understanding why church officials supported López and Losa and sanctioned a close friendship that inverted the expected relationship between priest and layperson. I suggest that the companions represented two sectors of colonial society that suffered from particularly bad reputations: Spanish laymen and members of the secular clergy. In his hagiographical account Losa explicitly contrasts his subject with the common run of men seeking fame and fortune in New Spain. He reminds his readers that unlike most "sons of Adam," the holy man cared nothing for material goods and status. He describes as a defining moment in López's life his witnessing of two settlers knifing one another to death in a dispute over silver in Zacatecas. This incident seals López in his conviction to live an eremitic life and provides Losa with an opportunity for moralizing reflection.[45]

Thus could Gregorio López serve as a model of pious masculinity for laymen noted for their ambition, greed, and violence. And Francisco Losa could likewise be held up as exemplary—selfless, charitable, otherworldly—in contrast to clerics often dismissed as poorly educated, venal, and corrupt. Their careers coincided with intense efforts by ecclesiastical authorities, notably Archbishop Pedro Moya y Contreras, to reform the secular clergy and bolster its power (and accordingly reduce the influence of the highly regarded mendicant orders).[46] Those responsible for recruiting young men to the care of souls in a vast new empire may well have recognized the usefulness of figures such as Francisco Losa. The priest may have dedicated his own life to serving one charismatic individual, but his *Life* of Gregorio López contributed to a much larger enterprise: the transmission and consolidation of Catholic culture in the New World.

NOTES

1. I wrote this chapter while the fortunate recipient of a Mellon Fellowship at the National Humanities Center and an American Postdoctoral Fellowship from the American Association of University Women.

2. Indispensible for the life and cult of Gregorio López is Antonio Rubial García, *La santidad controvertida: Hagiografía y conciencia criolla alrededor de los venerables no canonizados de Nueva España* (Mexico City: UNAM, 1999), 93–128.

3. Mariano Cuevas in his *Historia de la Iglesia en México* (Mexico City: Editorial Patria, 1946), II, 152, gives Losa's date of birth as 1530, but when Losa testified at diocesan hearings in 1620, he stated his age as eighty-four. Biblioteca Nacional, Madrid (BNM) MS 7819: 3v. See also Alvaro Huerga, *Historia de los Alumbrados (1570–1630)* (Madrid: FUE, 1986), III, 517.

4. Francisco Losa, *La Vida que Hizo el Siervo de Dios Gregorio Lopez, en algunas lugares de esta Nueva España . . .* (Mexico City: Juan Ruiz, 1613), BNM R/7897 29v [hereafter *Vida*]; Cuevas, *Historia de la Iglesia en México,* II, 152; Huerga, *Historia de los Alumbrados,* III, 517.

5. Losa may have also attended the Universidad de Salamanca; it is not clear whether he earned the title of *licenciado* in New or Old Spain. John Frederick Schwaller, "Los miembros fundadores de la Congregación de San Pedro, México, 1577," in *Cofradías, capellanías y obras pías en la América colonial,* ed. María Pilar Martínez López-Cano et al. (Mexico City: UNAM, 1998), 109–18; Cuevas, *Historia de la Iglesia en México,* II, 152; Huerga, *Historia de los Alumbrados,* III, 517.

6. Schwaller "Miembros." Asunción Lavrin, "La Congregación de San Pedro: Una cofradía urbana del México colonial, 1604–1730," *Historia Mexicana* 29 (1980): 562–601.

7. Francisco Guerra, in the introduction to his edition of *El Tesoro de Medicinas de Gregorio López, 1542–1596* (Madrid: Ediciones Cultura Hispánica, 1982), 20, claims that Losa served as confessor and chaplain to Don Luis de Velasco, but does not cite any evidence. But certainly the priest was very well acquainted with this important nobleman, who served as Viceroy of both New Spain and Peru. Velasco was a devotee of López's, the dedicatee of Losa's biography, and mentioned several times in the text— for example, *Vida,* 33v. Rubial, *La santidad controvertida,* 102. Losa and López also spent part of 1585 at the home of the Marqués del Valle. Agustín de la Madre de Dios, *Tesoro Escondido en el Santo Carmelo Mexicano . . .* (Mexico City: PROBURSA, 1984; orig. ca. 1648), 27.

8. Informe of 1575 cited by Huerga III: 517. For English quotations I use the translation made in Paris, 1638: *The Life of Gregory Lopes that Great Servant of God . . .* [Life]. This is available as vol. 3 in the series "English Recusant Literature, 1558–1640" (Menston: Scholar Press, 1969). I have modernized and regularized spelling and grammatical usage.

9. Losa is referred to as *limosnero mendicante* in the text panel that accompanies a dual portrait of López and Losa from the later seventeenth century. The text also mentions Losa's charitable aid to members of the Society of Jesus when they first arrived in New Spain. Losa later helped the Brothers of San Hipólito when López was staying at their hospital in Oaxtepec, and also may have been involved in a hospital near the hermitage at Santa Fe, where he held a chaplaincy. Rubial, *La santidad controvertida,* 114–16; Huerga, *Historia de los Alumbrados,* III, 528.

10. Rubial, *La santidad controvertida,* 102–3, 115; *Vida,* 117v, 122v; *Life,* 165–66. Was Losa himself a mystic *("él mismo un místico"),* as Antonio Rubial suggests in passing? *La santidad controvertida,* 98.

11. For the most detailed discussion of the doctrinal issues involved see Huerga, *Historia de los Alumbrados,* III, 509–90; also Rubial, *La santidad controvertida,* 100–5. For a fascinating interpretive essay see Alain Milhou, "Gregorio López, el Iluminismo y la Nueva Jerusalén Americana," in *Actas del IX Congreso Internacional de Historia de América* (Seville: Universidad de Sevilla, 1990), III, 55–83.

12. *Life,* 45–47; *Vida* 16r–17r; see also *Life,* 147–48. Huerga, *Historia de los Alumbrados,* III: 562–63.

13. There are a number of variant spellings of this town: Huaxtepec, Guastepec, etc. I have adopted the spelling used by Rubial. For this hospital and the hospital order and its founder, the pious layman Bernardino Alvarez, see Cheryl English Martin, "The San Hipólito Hospitals of Colonial Mexico, 1566–1702" (Ph.D. diss., Tulane University, 1976); Cuevas, *Historia de la Iglesia en México,* II: 483–87. For López's stay there, Rubial, *La santidad controvertida,* 102, 114–15; Guerra, *El Tesoro de Medicinas de Gregorio López,* 11–12.

14. *Life,* 58.

15. Ibid., 75.

16. Ibid., 71–72; *Vida* 26v–27v. López had moved from the hospital in Oaxtepec to the village of San Agustín de las Cuevas in search of *"aires frías"*; he wrote to Losa from this location.

17. *Life,* 75. Losa occasionally experienced conflicts over whether to engage in an active apostolate or to follow the contemplative life; see, for example, *Life,* 134–37.

18. *Life,* 75–76.

19. Stafford Poole in his *Pedro Moya de Contreras: Catholic Reform and Royal Power in New Spain, 1571–1591* (Berkeley: University of California Press, 1987) comments that the friar's appointment was in some ways "a strange choice, because Pravia, though capable and learned, suffered from scruples," 204. A defender of Indians against the oppressive Repartamiento system, he had declined the archbishopric of Panama three years earlier, 274, n. 2.

20. *Life,* 76; *Vida,* 29v–30v. For Losa's attendance on López at time of latter's death see *Life,* 101–5.

21. *Life,* 247; *Vida,* 107v: "comíamos a una mesa, y vivímos en una casa, y dormímos en un aposento."

22. Huerga transcribes a number of trial documents in which accused alumbrados mention Gregorio López by name; see, for example, *Historia de los Alumbrados,* III, 845–47.

23. *Life,* 53.

24. *Life,* 49–50. Rubial notes that defending López's orthodoxy became for Losa "a personal thing" *(un asunto personal), La santidad controvertida,* 101, and shows how the priest was not above forging a letter in support of López and signing another cleric's name, 106.

25. Jodi Bilinkoff, "Navigating the Waves (of Devotion): Toward a Gendered Analysis of Early Modern Catholicism," in *Attending to Early Modern Women: Crossing Boundaries,* ed. Jane Donawerth and Adele Seeff (Newark: University of Delaware Press, 2000), 161–72.

26. For example, *Life,* 64, 233–34, 248, 257–58, 276–77.

27. *Vida,* 71v–72v: "le escogí por Maestro y compañero, para lo restante de mi vida. . . ." *Life,* 203–4.

28. Dyan Elliott, "Authorizing a Life: The Collaboration of Dorothea of Montau and John Marienwerder," in *Gendered Voices: Medieval Saints and Their Interpreters,* ed. Catherine M. Mooney (Philadelphia: University of Pennsylvania Press, 1999), 168–91.

29. *Life,* 213–14. Also Jodi Bilinkoff, "Confession, Gender, Life-Writing: Some Cases (Mainly) from Spain," in *Penitence in the Age of Reformations,* ed. Katharine Jackson Lualdi and Anne T. Thayer (Aldershot, UK: Ashgate, 2000), 169–83.

30. *Life,* 202, 84. See also *Life,* 93, 212–13, 240–42.

31. On López as a healer, both thaumaturgic and herbal, see Osvaldo F. Pardo, "Contesting the Power to Heal: Angels, Demons, and Plants in Colonial Mexico," in *Spiritual Encounters: Interactions between Christianity and Native Religions in Colonial America,* ed. Nicholas Griffiths and Fernando Cervantes (Lincoln: University of Nebraska Press, 1999), 163–84. The pace of this activity picked up considerably after López's death; for use of his relics in healing, see many of the testimonies in BNM MS 7819, Rubial, *La santidad controvertida,* 116.

32. *Life,* 92–94. For their daily routine at Santa Fe, *Life,* 81–82. For other instances of Losa serving as López's *internuncio y mensajero* see *Vida,* 2r, 27v; *Life,* 93, 181, 212–13, 314. Apparently at times the two worked as a team, with López offering advice to his devotees and Losa then hearing their confessions, *Vida,* 37r–40v.

33. Bilinkoff, "Confession," Isabelle Poutrin, *Le Voile et la Plume: Autobiographie et sainteté féminine dans l'Espagne moderne* (Madrid: Casa de Velázquez, 1995), ch. 13. For a somewhat earlier period see many of the essays in *Gendered Voices.*

34. *Life,* 240–42. See also *Vida,* 1r–v, 2r–v, 4r, 8v, 9r, 116v–19v; *Life,* 101–2, 165–66.

35. For example, *Vida,* 1r–v, 4r, 8r; *Life* 111–12, 112–16ff, 140–42, 143–49. There are at least four instances in which Losa quotes from letters or cites them in their entirety: *Vida,* 4r, 199v; *Life,* 178, 272–73.

36. For example, *Vida,* 35r, 90r.

37. *Life,* 212, 199.

38. *Life,* 214. Losa also may be attempting to deflect suspicion of overly "familiar" friendship or erotic attachment between himself and López, or even worse, accusations of sodomy. For a contemporary case from the viceroyalty of Peru see Geoffrey Spurling, "Honor, Sexuality, and the Colonial Church: The Sins of Dr. González, Cathedral Canon," in *The Faces of Honor: Sex, Shame, and Violence in Colonial Latin America,* ed. Lyman L. Johnson and Sonya Lipsett-Rivera (Albuquerque: University of New Mexico Press, 1998), 45–67.

39. *Life,* 100. It is not clear exactly which scriptural text Losa is paraphrasing here. In another intriguing passage (*Life,* 87), Losa mentions that López regarded John the Baptist as his special patron saint, an identification that is not surprising given his chosen solitary life in "the wilderness." But if Gregorio López is John the Baptist, who does that make Francisco Losa?

40. Rubial, *La santidad controvertida,* 106–7. For example, *Vida,* 22r; *Life,* 122, 220–22. Huerga, *Historia de los Alumbrados,* III, 517–18.

41. Mariana de la Encarnación, "Historia del Convento [de San José] de las carmelitas descalzas de la ciudad de México desde su fundación" (orig. 1641), transcribed in Manuel Ramos Medina, *Místicas y descalzas: Fundaciones femeninas carmelitas en la Nueva España* (Mexico City: Condumex, 1997), 357–58: "no apartarse en vida ni en muerte." See also the chronicle of Agustín de la Madre de Dios, *Tesoro Escondido en el Santo Carmelo Mexicano,* 27–29.

42. "Neither did I think I should outlive him so much as to be able to write of him," *Life,* 76–77. BNM MS 7819 3v–111v.

43. Antonio Vázquez de Espinosa, *Compendio y descripción de las Indias Occidentales* (orig. 1629), transcribed by Charles Upson Clark (Washington, D.C.: Smithsonian Institution, 1948), 149: "tambien le imitó el padre Francisco de Loza sacerdote en virtud, y santidad. . . ." Alonso Remón, the Mercedarian friar who brought out the edition from which the 1638 English translation was made describes the author as "Father Francisco Losa, a great servant of God, who had been curate of the Cathedral of Mexico and left all to accompany and converse with holy Gregory and to cherish and tend him (as he did until his death)," *Life,* 4–5.

44. Cuevas, *Historia de la Iglesia en México,* II, 152.

45. *Life,* 207; *Vida,* 5r–v. In 1630 another hagiographer proclaimed that to a land so plagued by greed and ambition God sent López as "an antidote" *(antídoto y reparo destas enfermidades),* cited in Rubial, *La santidad controvertida,* 111–12. Two of López's contemporaries were similarly held up as models for their renunciation of wealth and status. For Bernardino Alvarez (1514–84), the soldier turned hospitaler, see Martin, "The San Hipólito Hospitals of Colonial Mexico"; Rubial, *La santidad controvertida,* 114–15; Cuevas, *Historia de la Iglesia en México,* II, 483–87. For Fernando de Córdoba y Bocanegra (1565–89), a nobleman who gave up his inheritance to follow López into "the wilderness," see Vázquez de Espinosa, *Compendio y descripción de las Indias Occidentales,* 149; Rubial, *La santidad controvertida,* 106, 110–13; Cuevas, *Historia de la Iglesia en México,* II, 489. Biographers in the later seventeenth and eighteenth centuries often treated López together with Alvarez or Bocanegra or both, Rubial, *La santidad controvertida,* 110–16.

46. For the generally sorry state of the secular clergy, efforts at reform, and tensions between seculars and regulars, see Cuevas, *Historia de la Iglesia en México,* II, 130–33, 142–45; Poole, *Pedro Moya de Contreras: Catholic Reform and Royal Power in New Spain,* esp. ch. 9–10; John Frederick Schwaller, *The Church and Clergy in Sixteenth-Century Mexico* (Albuquerque: University of New Mexico Press, 1987), ch. 3. There was at least one other contemporary secular priest lauded for his virtues: Juan González, a canon of the cathedral of Mexico who renounced his position for a life of contemplative prayer and to teach Christian doctrine to Indians, Cuevas, *Historia de la Iglesia en México,* II, 133–38.

7

In the Shadow of the Cloister: Representations of Female Holiness in New France

DOMINIQUE DESLANDRES

Every time Christianity encounters a new frontier, it needs martyrs and saints to legitimize the spread of its doctrine.[1] Thus, as in early Christian times, the "athletes of Christ" marked the early days of New France through the ascetic and mystical exploits that would lead to their celebration as saints. The best-known were the Jesuit martyrs, but they were not alone; through their various activities, women, too, were involved in what came to be called the "mystical epic" of the colonization of Canada.

Discovered by Frenchman Jacques Cartier in 1534, New France was initially confined to the St. Lawrence Valley, with colonial economic exploitation and settlement really only starting after the Treaty of Vervins (1598). Quebec City, the heart of the colony, founded in 1608, remained a simple fur trading post for many years. Eventually, the French settled along the banks of the St. Lawrence River, despite raids by the Iroquois Five Nations against them and their Amerindian allies. The settlers were quickly drawn into Amerindian conflicts, taking sides against the Iroquois. In 1615 and 1625, Recollect and then Jesuit priests started missions for the nomadic people around Quebec City—referred to as Algonquins by modern anthropologists—who traded fur with the settlers. The missionaries soon discovered the existence, farther west and south of Quebec City, of semisedentary peoples whom they felt were the most promising prospects for conversion to Christianity: the Hurons of the Iroquoian family, who constituted the central axis of the fur trade in the west. From 1632 to the erection of the diocese of Quebec in 1658, the Jesuits' religious monopoly in New France was almost total. However, terrible epidemics quickly devasted the Amerindian peoples, who lacked immunity to European diseases. These epidemics decimated Amerindian populations and jeopardized the lives of missionaries, who were often denounced by the natives as "sorcerers" intent on killing them all. From the arrival of religious women in New France in 1639 until the conclusion of the Great Peace of Montreal in 1701, the situation was difficult for the French and their allies alike due to epidemics, warfare, the risks of the fur trade, low immigration, and the instability of the missions.[2]

In this settlement of a New France in America, the role of women was crucial, especially that of saintly women. But how did these women perceive themselves? How were they viewed by their fellow settlers? What traces of their lives did they intend to leave behind for posterity? What traits did their witnesses seek to imprint on their readers' consciousness? These questions have led me to reconsider the relationship between female holiness and the society that feeds it and is fed by it—a relationship that, as we will see, is one part power and one part seduction. As part of my general research into the representations of female holiness in New France—holiness as evidenced by traces left within the cloister and as an intended object of remembrance—I would like to examine more closely the various images constructed by religious women in New France. I highlight the projects they pursued, the various models of sanctity to which they referred, and the different ways they achieved sainthood, including their involvement in the creation of the colony's sacred history.[3]

SAINTLY WOMEN IN NEW FRANCE: HOLY, ACTIVE, AND COLONIAL

The women I will discuss here did not come to Canada to have children, as one would expect in a new settlement.[4] Their ultimate aim was to achieve their own salvation by contributing to the missions of their male counterparts. Their involvement was original in that it combined the spiritual nature of a quest for holiness with the very material tasks of structuring a colonial society. These women, from 1639 on, established a system of religious and social welfare, first in Quebec, then in Trois-Rivières and Montreal. All along the St. Lawrence River, they established a variety of institutions, such as teaching convents, hospitals, and *reclusoirs* (hermits' cells) that provided New France's nascent society with the essential services of education, medicine, poor relief, and spiritual solidarity.[5] All these projects, often extraordinary for the time, frequently motivated by very personal aspirations, were accomplished in a special context, a context that can easily be described as an atmosphere of sanctity. This atmosphere nurtured these women's ardent and secret desires to achieve sainthood and, in a roundabout way, caused them to present themselves as saints. It led others to recognize their holiness and to support their actions in the world.

The Ursuline Marie Guyart de l'Incarnation (1599–1672) left everything, even her son, to become a missionary among the "Savages" and a spiritual leader for Quebec's small settler community. With the help of two other sisters from her religious order, she founded the first teaching convent in North America. At the same time, three Hospitalière nuns established a hospital, the Hôtel-Dieu.[6] All these women showed a similar degree of dedication and independence from their families, and all of them ultimately received support from their kin and friends. Their male counterparts clearly viewed them as great agents of conversion.

Marie de l'Incarnation's friend Madame de la Peltrie (1603–72) entered into a *mariage blanc,* a spiritual marriage, to use her personal fortune to found pious institutions in this "barbarian" country: thus she lived a devout life and died like a saint. In Quebec, the Hospitalière nun Catherine de St.-Augustin (1632–68), deemed a living saint by her contemporaries, battled all her life in the secrecy of the cloister against the demons that invaded the colony. In the settlement that was to become Montreal, a place considered in the seventeenth century to be one of the most dangerous in the world, Jeanne Mance (1606–73), a *dévote,* decided to found a holy city and erect the Hôtel-Dieu in Montreal, to save bodies as well as souls. Her friend the teacher Marguerite Bourgeoys (1620–1700) explored new ways of educating young girls in a Christian way, while their protégée Jeanne Le Ber (1662–1774), a recluse, followed an extraordinary path to sanctity, as I will discuss below. These well-known matrons of New France's history books are regarded as the "mothers" of the colony. But what lies behind their hagiographies? They opted for action and managed to gain support for their projects as well as acceptance and admiration. They were select women, women who chose. They cleared their very own paths to power and succeeded in winning over their fellow settlers.

SELECT WOMEN, SPECIAL PROJECTS

Before considering the goals of these women, let us first review some biographical information that will help us better understand their actions in New France. Marie Guyart de l'Incarnation was born in 1599, in Tours, France, to a family of silk manufacturers.[7] Married to Claude Martin in 1617 and widowed two years later, she raised her only son, Claude, while running her brother-in-law's carting business for more than six years until she decided to retreat from society. In 1631 she entered the Ursuline convent in Tours, leaving her son in her sister's care, and pronounced her vows after two years of novitiate. By then she had formed the great project of converting souls, and with the help of a whole network of supporters ranging from close relatives to the queen mother of France, she succeeded in being sent to Canada.[8] On this journey she was accompanied by Marie de Savonnières de La Troche (1616–52), known in religion as Marie de Saint Joseph, and Cécile Richer (1609–87), known as Cécile de Ste. Croix. Marie Guyart died in Quebec in 1672 after a long life of ecstatic visions and down-to-earth missionary work as an educator of girls. In 1639 she founded the first Ursuline convent in America with the intention of converting Amerindian girls to Christianity, thus becoming the first female missionary outside Europe.

Marie Guyart's friend Marie Madeleine Chauvigny de la Peltrie was born to a noble family in Alençon, France, in 1603. The lay founder of Quebec's Ursuline convent, she died in that city in 1671. Widowed at twenty-two years of age, she decided to devote her fortune to the conversion of the Canadian "Savages," a project bitterly opposed by many in her family. To appease her father's anger and gain control of her fortune, she entered into a marriage of convenience with a *dévot*, Jean de Bernières. Then she met Marie de l'Incarnation in Tours and, in 1639, made the crossing to Canada with her and two other Ursuline nuns. In Quebec the four of them established a convent. Four years after her arrival, she briefly accompanied Jeanne Mance and Paul de Maisonneuve to help found the community of Ville-Marie on the island of Montreal, returning to the Ursulines some eighteen months later.[9] She resumed her financial support of the convent, continued her labor of devotion, and died "in the odor of sanctity."[10]

Quebec's Hospitalières order was founded by two women often forgotten by history. The first is Marie de Vignerot Combalet (1604–75), duchess of Aiguillon, niece of Cardinal de Richelieu, a *dévote* involved in many charities and close to St. Vincent de Paul. The second is the Carmelite Madeleine de St. Joseph, first prioress of the Paris Carmel. Her zeal for the missions of New France was such that she convinced her friend the duchess of Aiguillon to contribute to the "dilatation" (expansion) of Christianity by endowing Quebec's Hôtel-Dieu. These two women then recruited three Hospitalière nuns from Dieppe: Marie Guenet de St. Ignace (1610–46), superior and founder of the Hôtel-Dieu, arrived in Quebec in 1639 with two other nuns, Anne Le Cointre de St. Bernard (1611–79) and Marie Forestier de St. Bonaventure (1612–98). The latter became the hospital's second superior, running it from 1645 to 1683. All three intended to save souls while nursing bodies, and considered themselves apostles to the Amerindians; this vocation is often stated in the *Annales* of the order. The generous care they provided both to the settlers and to the Amerindian populations during the many terrible epidemics they endured contributed to their aura of sanctity.[11]

One of the most famous Hospitalières was Marie Catherine de Simon de Longpré, known in religion as Catherine de St. Augustin, who was born in St.-Sauveur-le-Vicomte, in Normandy, France, in 1632, and died in Quebec in 1668. In 1644, at age twelve, she entered the Hospitalières of Bayeux. In 1648, at sixteen, still too young to take her final vows, she defied her family and left for Quebec. Twenty years later, highly esteemed by her peers, she was about to be nominated as hospital superior when she died. It was only after her death that her secret mystic life was revealed in the biography written by her Jesuit confessor Paul Ragueneau. In her diary she wrote of her saintly visions and the supernatural help she received in her continuous battle against demons.[12]

Jeanne Mance was born to a bourgeois family in Langres, France, in 1606. After raising her eleven brothers and sisters from 1626 to 1640, she discovered her vocation for the Christianization of Canada when one of her cousins, the Jesuit Jean Dolbeau, left for Quebec. Very soon she became acquainted with a network of *dévots* from all levels of the Parisian society, including the queen herself, Anne of Austria. She became a member of the Société Notre Dame de Montréal, created by Jerôme de La Dauversière to establish a holy city called Ville Marie on the island of Montreal. In 1659, with the assistance of *dévote* Angélique Faure de Bullion and the Hospitalières of La Flèche, and despite continuous Iroquois attacks on Montreal, she succeeded in founding the city's Hôtel-Dieu, which she administered until her death. She was, along with the governor, Paul de Maisonneuve, one of the pillars of the settlement of Ville-Marie, later called Montreal. She died in 1673 with a "reputation of sanctity."[13]

Jeanne Mance's friend Marguerite Bourgeoys was born to a bourgeois family in Troyes, France, in 1620. She died in Montreal in 1700, having founded the Congrégation Notre-Dame de Montréal. In 1640 she entered the lay and external congregation attached to Congrégation Notre-Dame, founded by Alix Leclerc and Pierre Fourier for the education of girls. Paul de Maisonneuve accepted her plan for a noncloistered community of teaching nuns in Ville-Marie. Founded in 1653, this institution lasted into the 1990s. Marguerite Bourgeoys also helped in the settlement of *les filles du roy,* those virtuous orphan girls endowed by the king and sent to New France to find a husband and start a family. Along with Jeanne Mance, Bourgeoys was lionized as a "mother" of Ville-Marie.[14]

Jeanne Le Ber was among the first native-born Montrealers. Born in 1662, she died in 1714, as a recluse linked to the convent of the Congrégation Notre-Dame, which she helped to finance. Through her mother, she was related to the famous Lemoine family of sea captains and governors. Jeanne's godfather was Paul de Maisonneuve, and her godmother, Jeanne Mance, and Jeanne Le Ber was raised in the spirit of these first "Montrealists." Cultivating many ties with Jeanne Mance's Hôtel-Dieu and Marguerite Bourgeoy's congregation, she studied with the Ursuline sisters of Quebec, who taught her, among other things, the art of embroidery, which she would later use to adorn most of Montreal's altars. After returning to Montreal in 1677, she received marriage proposals from noblemen and officers—the "most distinguished men of the colony"— but turned them all down. In 1685 she withdrew into the solitude of a room in her family home. Eight years later, using the money she inherited from her mother, and with her father's consent and endless support, she financed the construction of a *reclusoir* adjacent to the convent of the Congrégation Notre-Dame. The three-story building comprised a sacristy-parlor on the first level, a room on the second, and a workshop on the third. In 1695 she made her solemn entry into the *reclusoir,* where she lived, prayed, and worked until her death.[15]

All of these women were true to projects that reflected a very particular quest for sanctity, a holiness that was not necessarily of the same nature as that of men.

MODELS OF SANCTITY

The holy women of New France adhered to a model of sanctity imposed by theologians and hagiographers; they adhered to it but also modulated and inflected it in very personal ways. This traditional model has been described in the following terms: the future saint was born into a Catholic family; showed a love for religious life at a very young age; joined an order; and, following an often spectacular conversion, entered the "way of holiness." Then the saint heroically practiced all the expected virtues, and in return, God gave her supernatural gifts such as that of prophecy or of miraclemaking. According to the hagiographic model, the saint's death was exemplary and edifying, and her funeral often provoked a collective frenzy. The saint's reputation for holiness, already well established during her life, continued to spread after her death, and her miracles were fervently recorded until she was finally canonized.[16]

These narratives may reveal the gender biases of the authors' traditional culture, which viewed male saints as being more "active" and the females as more "passive." As medievalist Caroline Bynum has put it, holy men were admired for what they said and did, and holy women, for what they were.[17] In the beginning of the seventeenth century, however, things were changing, especially in France and Italy, where female contemplation intermingled with action. Biographers as well as autobiographers were looking for new Teresas of Avila—that is, women of virtue who were both mystical and active and were involved in the dealings of the "real world."[18] These changes can also be observed in the context of New France, whose historical sources present various types of female holiness. In these sources we find a very active cloistered Ursuline nun, the multitalented Marie Guyart de l'Incarnation, climbing the walls of her newly erected convent and advising the building's architect and masons while constantly conversing with God. We also discover a "quieter" Ursuline nun, Marie de

Saint Joseph (1616–52), whose fate corresponds exactly to the medieval model of female sainthood.[19] Among the laywomen regarded as saints we find active founders such as Madame de la Peltrie, who lived in many different convents, or Jeanne Mance, who resisted the very idea of entering a convent while remaining the quintessential *dévote,* or Marguerite Bourgeoys, who finally yielded to pressure and accepted the cloistering of her congregation, or even Jeanne Le Ber, who found a radical "middle way" by secluding herself. All these women shared highly spiritual motivations, but followed extraordinarily varied paths, breaking with traditional saintly models. This variety reflects the profusion of female experiences of holiness recorded in the same period in Europe, especially in France, where nuns and widows—and sometimes married, pious women—were involved in projects as diverse as education, medical and social care, secret benevolent associations, and the promotion of devotions and prayers. Listing all these "holy experiences" would take up too much space; in France, these female enterprises include lay mystic Antoinette Réveillade converting Cesar de Bus, Jeanne de Chantal founding the Visitadine Order, Louise de Marillac collaborating with Vincent de Paul on pious works, barmaid Marie des Vallée inspiring Jean Eudes' mission in Normandy, Marie Rousseau directing Jean-Jacques Olier, and Madame Guyon doing the same for Fénelon, not to mention the educational and charitable work of the Ursulines—especially that of Anne de Xaintonge in Dijonais—and of the Hospitalières.

The eager responses that greeted Jesuit superior Paul Le Jeune's appeal for female help in his New France mission indicate that women of his time did not consider the cloister to be an obstacle to missionary zeal, activity, and holiness.[20] In the early days of the colony, the Jesuits realized that they needed the help of women. Le Jeune was convinced that a hospital was a necessary asset for the conversion of the Amerindians; in 1636 he wrote: "the charity [of hospital nuns] would do more for the conversion of the Savages than all our expeditions and words."[21] He was also certain of the necessity of female teachers for educating young Amerindian girls as well as the daughters of the settlers. In 1637 he received offers of help from numerous female communities, such as the Carmelites of Aix-en-Provence, the Annonciades célestes of Paris, the Benedictine nuns of Montmartre, the Visitadine nuns, as well as the Hospitalières and the Ursulines, whose missionary ardor would take concrete form in 1639 with the establishment of Quebec's Hôtel Dieu and Ursuline convent. These various reactions, as well as Le Jeune's comments, show that French society was ready to see women "lose the fear associated with the weakness of their Sex, cross so many seas and live among the savages" and thus find their way to sanctification.[22]

And so the religious women of New France lost their fear indeed. Empowered by the example of the primitive church, they found their way to New World missions. For example, because the Virgin Mary was a traveler, a teacher, one "who had shared all the fruits of the primitive church with the apostles," the sisters of Marguerite Bourgeoys felt entitled to refuse cloistering and to share the fruits of evangelization equally with men.[23] Similarly, the Ursulines who came to Canada felt they were as much apostles in the New World as were the Jesuits.[24] And the lay founders, the Hospitalières of Quebec and Montreal, bore the same apostolic and somewhat egalitarian spirit.[25]

Furthermore, these holy women of New France not only wanted to be apostles, they also modeled themselves on the lives of the saints and hoped that, like the saints, they might achieve miraculous results. These women had the will, the profound desire, to be saints;[26] they cherished the opportunity to contribute to the holiness unfolding before their very eyes. They wanted to offer themselves "in a holocaust for the son of God" while proselytizing among the "pagans." Many even hoped to be beaten to death or have their throats cut; in short, they aspired to die violently for Jesus Christ,[27] and even though they felt undeserving, they thought that in so doing they would receive the palm of martyrdom. They were literally obsessed by these bloody feats; they could not stop describing at length the martyrdoms of the Canadian Jesuits and, above all, the miraculous sequels to these events, of which they were often the first to benefit. Many of them later experienced visions, prophecies, and the direct intervention of dead Jesuit martyrs such as Antoine Daniel, Jean de Brébeuf, or Isaac Jogues, all of whom met heroic deaths while missionizing in Huronia.[28] Thus the holy women of New France shared with the holy men "this spirit that urges the servants of the Gospel over land and sea and that makes living martyrs of them before they are consumed by fire and sword. The inconceivable trials they underwent were greater miracles than the resurrection of the dead."[29]

SMALLER BUT HEROIC VIRTUES LIVED, TAUGHT, AND REVEALED

Since martyrdom was almost impossible for women in the security of the cloister, one common path to sanctity was literally to take on the role of the Iroquois. Women inflicted upon themselves mortifications *(macérations)* as ferocious as the blows dealt by "savage" enemies of the French; they also displayed to a heroic degree the "smaller virtues" of poverty, obedience, and chastity, as well as courage and patience in the face of hardship, especially during sickness and agony. All of them offered themselves as sacrifices, and all of them tried to maintain a reasoned discourse on the practice of sanctity.[30] And from the mass of maxims, rules, advice, and examples that the holy women followed and compelled their "students" to follow, a veritable "how-to" book of holiness can be re-created.

These rules can help us to define certain aspects of the true personalities of the women who followed them. Repetitive prescriptions and rules serve to combat common failings. By examining these failings, we may learn something of the nature of the woman who tried to fight them, or more precisely, we may better understand how she perceived herself. Let us take the example of Marie de l'Incarnation, who in 1648 told her son how she made a vow to follow a whole set of "maxims" to fight what she considered to be her most terrible shortcomings; should we understand that she considered herself too quick to justify herself (first maxim), to complain (second maxim), and to boast (third maxim); that she was conscious of her temptation to yield to envy (fourth maxim), to antipathy (fifth maxim), to impatience (sixth maxim), and to sullenness (seventh maxim); that she found herself to be neither nice nor humble (eighth maxim), too quick to take offense, and restless (ninth maxim); that she considered that she withstood with difficulty the pains of the body and of the spirit, the humiliations and mortifications wrought by God and people (tenth maxim); that she admitted indulging "certain appetites, inclinations, and natural penchants" (eleventh maxim) and disobeying "divine movements and inspirations" as well as her spiritual adviser (twelfth maxim)?[31] The additional vows the Ursuline took herself—among others, St. Teresa of Avila's vow of perfection—and the ones she advised her son and niece to take, are indicative of her self-perception, or at least of the models of holiness that inspired her.

Similarly, we can probe the Ursulines' *épistémè* by examining the series of exemplary lives they read, studied, or wrote and define the model favored by holy nuns. Let us consider, for example, the *Année bénédictine ou les Vies des saints de l'Ordre de saint Benoît pour tous les jours de l'année,* by Jacqueline de Blémur,[32] or Anne de Beauvais' *Vie,* or the life of Mère Marguerite de St.-Xavier, which captivated Marie de l'Incarnation. She herself related the lives of two nuns and one laywoman, all of whom she considered to be, if not saintly, at least exemplary women.[33] After her own death, Marie de l'Incarnation became the subject of many narratives relating her virtues.[34] We can easily repeat the same exercise with the Hospitalières of Quebec and of Montreal or with the nuns of the Notre Dame congregation, upon whom Marguerite Bourgeoys imposed "the rules of divine wisdom,"[35] advising her fellow sisters to be suspicious of "the rule of human prudence."

The imitation of saintly models by the religious women of New France seems to have had two effects. First, in imitating the virtues of established saints, these colonial women received a transfusion of holiness; identification was so complete that the boundaries between the self and the venerated model melted away.[36] Second, this religious mimetism served as a guarantee of legitimacy, both in the eyes of the community and in those of the women themselves.

THE CASE OF MARIE DE L'INCARNATION

Through the imitation of saints, holy women and men followed the path of their Lord, the *Imitatio Christi,* trying to share his sufferings. And many were the missionaries of New France who explained their mission and vocation in mystical terms. The vocabulary and symbolism used were common to both sexes and all religious orders, but Marie de l'Incarnation's expression of this mysticism was truly exemplary. God was wholeness, the missionary was emptiness. God infinitely magnified all that the true Christian sought to obtain in this life and in the afterlife.

> My soul is to love, and love is to my soul; and I dare to say it, all goods are common and there is no distinction between his and mine. Even if the soul sees by a soft look that her beloved belongs to her, and her to him, she enjoys being his slave. And though she is enriched by his goods, she wants everything for him and nothing for her: she wants to be nothing and him to be everything, and in this she finds her fulfilment. She loves nothing more than to be destitute, all empty, and to watch with kindness the plenitude of her beloved. How lovable is this occupation![37]

All the missionary narratives testify to it: God is the great performer of missionary work. He acts according to His own good will and pleasure; all missionaries are convinced that "to convert a soul depends on the Almighty";[38] and Marie de l'Incarnation characteristically states that "what the creature cannot do by herself, here God accomplishes it in an unthinkable way."[39] By inhabiting the missionaries, God chose them, he made them act, he protected them and gave them confidence; he made them stronger, assisted them, guided them, and above all, he delegated his power. And as an anonymous missionary wrote: "no one would believe the efficiency of grace and the powerful reassurance God gives to his servants, in the midst of the most horrible tempest and despair."[40] For God was obviously endowed with a power that the missionaries ontologically lacked; this power helped them in their mission and legitimated their action.[41] Since the missionaries were divine proxies, they seemed to be able, almost at will, to release this power when they invoked it for the needs of their cause.[42]

Since the missionaries were sent by God, they considered themselves apostles like those of the primitive church, who were their great models of perfection,[43] apostles who shared God's powers simply because they were vested by God. Besides, the task in New France was matched with the assignment and the delegation of powers: Christianization seemed in fact to demand miraculous gifts.[44] And in this seventeenth-century wonder-making atmosphere, did the missionaries not display the same disposition for languages, eloquence and adaptability, courage and martyrdom, even thaumaturgy and miracleworking, that were possessed by the first apostles? This was true of the holy women of New France: think only of the extraordinary linguistic capacities of a Marie de l'Incarnation, of the strength of a Marguerite Bourgeoys, a Jeanne Mance or a Jeanne Le Ber, of the miracles performed by Catherine de St.-Augustin.

Furthermore, God acted omnipotently through the agents He chose, and in so doing, He gave a legitimacy to the missionaries' actions.[45] In other words, the missionary said: "It is not me, it is God who acts or who talks through me." This rhetoric was at the time incredibly persuasive, since it constituted a mandate everyone had to obey, for fear not only of being damned but also of being responsible for the damnation of the divinely elected. And this rhetoric, common to both sexes, would prove to be extremely powerful in helping women's social and religious promotion.

For it is God who prompted the missionary to act "for His greater glory." It is God who inspired in Marie de l'Incarnation this "extreme desire of the apostolic life; notwithstanding her weakness, it seems that what God was pouring into her heart was able to convert all of those who did not know Him and did not love Him."[46] And it was this unshakable confidence, this sublime unreasoning, this divine madness, that incited Marie de l'Incarnation to commit an act that remains difficult to understand: the abandonment of her still young son to enter the Ursuline convent of Tours and eventually become the first female missionary to leave France.[47] In this system of thought, God was the active principle: the believers had to conform to the divine dictate, to lose themselves, and in so doing find themselves; in "abandoning oneself" one found one's "center" and reached the "bottom of one's soul"; through this deep understanding, one defined and constructed oneself.

FABRICATION OF ONE'S OWN SAINTLY IMAGE

Biographies and autobiographies play a crucial role in forming religious images.[48] We must remember that hagiographical literature was read daily by would-be saints, who seem to have modeled their own behavior on that of their famous predecessors. This was obviously the case of the female saints of New France—and of colonial Latin America, as Kathleen Ann Myers points out[49]—but again, as we will see, they went farther in the fabrication of their own saintly image. In the process of determining sanctity, no one was neutral, neither the future saint nor the society that was ready to recognize her as a saint.

All the women under study deliberately chose the path of sanctity. With a great many protestations of humility, each of them demonstrated in the end that God had elected her. Each presented herself as the least of the least, a "miserable worm." But God's ways were inscrutable: each of these saintly women would find evidence of divine favor both obvious and incomprehensible.[50] This notion of blessed humility, which I call "reverse humility," is a recurrent theme in hagiographical literature, and was used by all male hagiographers in New France. What is more surprising, however, is to find this theme expressed by the saintly women themselves.[51] Many are the descriptions of visions, ecstasies, intimate dialogues with God, supernatural gifts, and prophecies that the holy women confided to their readers and followers: not only did they show that they were selected by God, but also they insisted on being considered as living proof of celestial intervention.[52] In a way, while writing about herself, the holy woman became her own hagiographer.

All the references that women made to their own mortifications suggested divine election. Their physical and psychological capacity to withstand suffering, visibly inscribed on their bodies, was associated with miracles that distinguished them in the eyes of God, they hoped, as well as in the eyes of their contemporaries.[53] Thanks to their relationship with the sacred, which was for them and their kin obvious, proven, and acknowledged, the holy women of New France had the authority to give what may be called "lessons in sanctity."[54]

The parlors of New France can be considered "doors left ajar" through which information could flow in and out. For example, it was almost compulsory for every newcomer to New France to visit Marie de l'Incarnation, for she could inform them about the natives' languages and customs as well as on the necessity of adopting good Christian behavior.[55] Marie de l'Incarnation was not alone, for the Hospitalières (through their work with the sick), Marguerite Bourgeoys, and sometimes even Jeanne Le Ber—against her will—received visitors who came to their parlors for spiritual guidance. Evidence of these visits can be found in the nuns' personal papers or in the texts written about them. Some women even became "directors of conscience" in their parlors or in the intimacy of a correspondence or a spiritual testament,[56] while others opened new and extraordinary paths of sanctity for other women.

AN EXTRAORDINARY PATH TO SANCTITY: THE CASE OF JEANNE LE BER

This leads to the case of Jeanne Le Ber, who, through her exemplary life, forged a very original path, a third way, for those who aspired to sanctity.[57] In fact, Jeanne Le Ber refused the two usual routes offered to women: getting married or becoming a nun; she found a distinctive way to express her religious vocation, which was very shocking at first, but in the end was accepted by everyone in New France. Thus the woman deemed to be "the colony's best catch" (le plus beau parti de la colonie), the richest and most beautiful heiress in New France,[58] resisted the idea of marriage or of entering a nunnery, and voluntarily imprisoned herself, despite all opposition. Through her vow of total solitude she expressed a most extreme affirmation of the self. Was it revolution, renunciation, or enunciation?

Jeanne Le Ber never relinquished her self-control. On the contrary, she used it in a very surprising way, one that is somewhat repellant for those of us who condemn anorexia and masochism but that fits the seventeenth-century standard of female holiness.[59] She showed an extraordinary control over her body, submitting it to a drastic discipline, as well as an ability to manage her finances very carefully and independently. "Self-assurance," "resistance," "control"—these terms help us understand her terrible choice and shed light on the projects of other saintly women.

Jeanne Le Ber was a woman who chose and who knew how to impose her choice on the people around her. Like other women examined in this study, she had an extraordinary capacity of choosing her destiny at a time when the social, legal, and political structures restricted women's possibilities. For this she was not burned; instead, her choice was acknowledged and respected. Once walled-in, Jeanne Le Ber could communicate with the external world through a small window in her sacristy door. A young cousin of hers, Anne Barrois, was given the task of delivering her meals and all the things she needed. Jeanne was charismatic but also very practical. Despite her isolation, she continued to handle business and legal arrangements.[60]

Paradoxically, by shutting herself in, she freed herself from all controls other than those she chose to impose on herself. It is difficult today to explain the incredible freedom this decision afforded her. In abandoning herself to total solitude, Jeanne Le Ber found herself; in giving up the ordinary ways of womanhood, she gave herself the chance to reach her "center" and acquire extraordinary power. First, she withdrew into a sphere of silence,[61] a kind of fortress shielding her not only from the words of those who surrounded her but also from society's prohibitions and customs. What power is given to the one who doesn't answer! Then she withdrew into her father's house, became a sort of ghost kindly haunting the place, but remained informed of everything that went on in the colony. What power is given to the one who is invisible! Finally, she withdrew into the *reclusoir* built according to her instructions, where she adopted a strict monastic lifestyle, but never took the formal vows of a nun. Silent, invisible, powerful, totally in the image of her God, she nevertheless made herself an imposing presence; people sought her out for advice and assistance. From the heart of her prison, she was thought to perform miracles, to act on the life of the whole colony.[62]

After her death, the body of Jeanne Le Ber "was exposed for two days in the congregation's chapel to satisfy the devotion of the people, who came to touch her body with their rosaries." She was then exposed to the fervor of the whole parish of Montreal before being solemnly buried; her funeral was attended by the clergy and a huge crowd of people. Her biographer reports that many who prayed to her obtained physical and spiritual graces. At least three people claimed to have been healed thanks to her intervention: a French lady, a *sauvagesse* (an Amerindian woman), and a nun of the Congrégation Notre-Dame. The first two saw their scrofula disappear, which is interesting because the ability to cure this skin disease was generally regarded as a gift bestowed by God exclusively on the French king.

A HISTORY IN THE MAKING

All the holy women of New France expressed the same sense of being part of history in the making. Certain they had been selected by God, they felt the need to act in exemplary ways for the sake of posterity. They recognized that they were writing the sacred history of the colony, a history of which they were an integral part. Thus, the three first Hospitalières,

> encouraging each other with heroic examples, regarding themselves as exiles for the glory of God, they endured [the difficult labors] agreeably, thinking that they were opening the way of perfection for a great number of virgins who would dedicate themselves to God in this new colony. They viewed themselves as models for those who would follow them. Thus, they didn't endure all these trials for themselves alone, they didn't spare themselves either, being very hard on themselves, adding continuous mortifications to the pains they had in their hospital functions, refusing any kind of relief and suffering with joy the absence of all the most necessary things, having compassion only for the others and proving it at every occasion through extraordinary charity.[63]

In addition to being part of the colony's sacred history, these religious women were convinced of being surrounded by other holy individuals. Marie Guyart de l'Incarnation, for example, called the Jesuits "saints" and rejoiced in seeing them live in horrible but godly poverty *(dans un dénuement épouventable).*[64] She never hesitated to use the adjectival or substantive form of the word "saint" to designate not only her Jesuit colleagues[65] but also some of her fellow nuns, such as Marie de St. Joseph, and even certain lay women, such as Madame de la Peltrie, who, in her judgment, was "running swiftly along the path to holiness."[66] As for Marie de St. Joseph, Marie de l'Incarnation said: "She lived and died a saint. I invoke her every day, as do many others, with devotion and fruitfully: in a word, here her memory is blessed."[67] Like the other holy women of the colony, the Ursuline hunted for holiness, looking for it everywhere around her, both in France and New France.[68] She was prepared to find it among country folk as well as the Amerindians who, once converted, became exemplary Christians.[69] And if humility prevented Marie and her peers from proclaiming themselves saints, it did not prevent them from reporting the Amerindians' exalted opinion of them.[70]

There was thus a certain ambience in which the would-be saints of the early seventeenth century developed.[71] Some were convinced that the very air in New France was propitious for the men and women searching for "holy perfection" in a "purified life." This explains why the people around these saints so attentively recorded their words and deeds, collected their remains, and promoted their cults. Most orders put great care into preserving the bodies of their dead saintly women, and even shared them with other religious orders—male and female—of the colony and of France as a gesture of solidarity.[72] One of the most striking examples is the transfer of the body of the Ursuline Marie de St. Joseph, deceased in the "odor of sanctity." The whole convent gathered around the coffin to verify the state of the body: it was "consumed" and transformed into a paste as white as milk, and did not give off any unpleasant smell; rather, a fragrance of iris impregnated the hands of those who touched the remains. All of the nuns present "were filled with such great joy and sweetness that words failed to express their feelings."[73] The Ursulines carefully preserved the white paste, even sending some of it to convents in France.[74] This is how Marie de St. Joseph's memory remained "always precious" and in the "odor of benediction" in the hearts of the Ursulines; the miracles she was said to have accomplished confirmed their conviction of having a saint in their ranks. Still, Marie de l'Incarnation remained very prudent, writing,

> I am not thinking of sending these remains as the relics of a saint; since whatever consideration we have of her virtue, only God knows for sure if she is a saint, only the Church can declare her such. My aim was only to send them, in order that they be preserved like the precious objects we inherit from loved ones. For my part, I invoke her every day and her remembrance is a blessing.[75]

This practice was not unique to the Ursulines. Remembrance of exemplary women through the collection of their relics was a well-established custom in New France. The bodies of all saintly women would be carefully preserved and often shared with other religious orders. A popular cult would spring up around these women, but care was taken not to draw too much attention to them; the nuns did not wish to interfere with Rome's omnipotent power to name saints.

All the women described here were the subjects of biographies intended to serve their causes for canonization. The duty of memory imposed itself very quickly, sometimes while the holy woman was still alive. This explains why their contemporaries so carefully gathered all the traces they left behind. Thus the Ursuline Françoise de Saint Bernard refused to destroy the personal papers that Marie de l'Incarnation had entrusted to her care; Catherine de St. Augustin's diary was entrusted to her biographer; and Marguerite Bourgeoys' will was carefully preserved. These heroines' words were avidly noted,[76] always for edification: "For it is good," Étienne Montgolfier, Jeanne Le Ber's second biographer, wrote characteristically at the beginning of the eighteenth century, "that selected souls be exposed to the faithful's piety . . . that sinners find continuous censure of their lives and the halfhearted an incentive against their baseness. . . . It is important to show everyone that rare souls bring all virtues to the point of heroism."[77] And when Marguerite Bourgeoys died, bishop François de Laval stated: "She was edifying during her life; she must serve now as an example. She was simple and humble and God gave her many graces . . . we didn't fail to remember her and we will continue to do so, we believe that she will soon enjoy the happiness of the Saints and that, being close to Our Lord, she will be of enormous assistance to your community."[78] So the edification of the people motivated the writing of these biographies, but also the literal edification or construction of history, a history written in the great book of Christian achievements. For the holy women of New France were also the ones who made, recounted, and legitimized history.

As we have seen, the religious women of New France received a celestial guarantee for their actions, actions they devised, expected, and imposed on the rest of the world. And if the settlers of New France applauded the projects and exploits of these saintly women, it was because they needed them, practically and spiritually. Most settlers asked that a hospital or convent run by nuns be established in their communities.[79] They also cherished their holy women, living or dead, because in this dangerous time and place, in this society on the margins, they needed these very special individuals who enjoyed a privileged relationship with the sacred and who could fulfill, through their extraordinary powers, the functions of protection, healing, guidance, and legitimization.

NOTES

1. Donald Weinstein and R. M. Bell, *Saints and Society: The Two Worlds of Western Christendom, 1000–1700* (Chicago: University of Chicago Press, 1982), 161–62.

2. On this see Louise Dechêne, *Habitants and Merchants in Seventeenth-Century Montreal,* trans. L. Vardi (Montreal: McGill-Queens University Press, 1992); Denys Delâge, *Bitter Feast: Amerindians and Europeans in Northeast North America, 1600–64* (Vancouver: UBC Press, 1993); William J. Eccles, *France in America* (Markham: Fitzhenry & Whiteside, 1990); Jacques Mathieu, *La Nouvelle France: les Français en Amérique du nord, XVIe–XVIIIe siècle* (Quebec: Presses de l'Université Laval, 1991); Bruce G. Trigger, *The Children of Aataentsic. A History of the Huron People to 1660* (Montreal: McGill-Queen's University Press, 1976); Marcel Trudel, *Histoire de la Nouvelle France,* vol. 3, *La seigneurie des Cent Associés, 1627–1663,* pt. 1, *Les événements* (Montreal: Fides, 1979).

3. See Marie de l'Incarnation, *Correspondance,* ed. G. M. Oury (Solesmes: Abbaye de Saint-Pierre, 1971) [hereafter *MI*]. This volume also contains the necrologies used here. For Marie de l'Incarnation's two autobiographies see Marie de l'Incarnation, *Écrits spirituels et historiques,* ed. Dom Albert Jamet, 2 vols. (Quebec, reprint from Ursulines de Québec, 1985). See also Marguerite Bourgeoys, *Écrits autographes,* ed. Hélène Bernier (Montreal: Fides, 1958); and *Les écrits de Mère Bourgeoys: autobiographie et testament spirituel (1697–1698),* ed. S. S. Damase de Rome (Montreal: Congregation Notre-Dame, 1964) [hereafter *EMB*].

   Claude Martin, *Vie de la Vénérable Mère Marie de l'Incarnation* (Paris, 1681), ed. Jean Lonsagne and Guy-Marie Oury (Solesmes: Abbaye de Saint Pierre, 1981); François Xavier de Charlevoix, *La vie de la Mère Marie de l'Incarnation* (Paris: Antoine Claude Briasson, 1724); Paul Ragueneau, *La vie de la Mère Catherine de Saint Augustin,* 1671 (Quebec: facsimile reprint, archevêché de Québec, 1923); Étienne Montgolfier, *La vie de la vénérable sœur Jeanne Le Ber,* 1779, original manuscript at Archives de Saint Sulpice in Paris; François Vachon de Belmont, "Éloge de quelques personnes mortes en odeur de sainteté à Montréal, en Canada, divisé en trois parties," *Rapport de l'archiviste de la Province de Québec,* 1929–1930, 144–66 [hereafter *RAPQ*]; Charles Glandelet, *La vie de la sœur Marguerite Bourgeoys,* (Montréal, [1715]), ed. Hélène Tremblay (Montreal: C.N.D., 1993); Michel François Ransonnet, *La vie de la Sœur Marguerite Bourgeoys* (Liège: Barnabé, 1728).

   Marie Morin, *Histoire simple et véritable* [annals of the *Hôtel-Dieu de Montréal*], ed. Ghislaine Legendre (Montreal: Presses de l'Université de Montréal, 1979); Jeanne-Françoise Juchereau de Saint Ignace et Marie-Andrée Régnard Duplessis de Saint Hélène, *Les annales de l'Hôtel Dieu de Québec, 1636–1716* (Quebec: facsimile reprint, Hôtel-Dieu de Québec, 1984); "Le Vieux récit ou Les annales du premier monastère des Religieuses Ursulines," manuscript, vol. 1 (1612–38), 1–194.

   Reuben G. Thwaites, *The Jesuit Relations and Allied Documents,* 73 vols. (Cleveland: Burrows, 1891–1901). Lucien Campeau's edition corrects and completes Thwaites' edition; see his *Monumenta*

Novae Franciae, 8 vols. to date (Quebec-Rome: Bellarmin-Institutum Historicum Societatis Iesu, 1967–) [hereafter *MNF*]; François Dollier de Casson, *Histoire du Montréal 1640–1672* [1672], ed. Marcel Trudel and Marie Baboyant (Montreal: Hurtubise, 1992).

4. On the women of New France see Allan Greer, *The People of New France* (Toronto: University of Toronto Press, 1997), 60–75.

5. For more on this subject see Dominique Deslandres, "Les femmes missionnaires de Nouvelle-France" in *La religion de ma mère: les femmes et la transmission de la foi,* ed. J. Delumeau (Paris: Le Cerf, 1992), 74–84. François Rousseau, *L'idée missionnaire aux 16ᵉ et 17ᵉ siècles. Les doctrines, les méthodes, les concepts d'organisation* (Paris: Spes, 1930); Jean Delumeau, *Un chemin d'histoire. Chrétienté et christianisation* (Paris: Fayard, 1981); and Marc Venard, *Réforme protestante, réforme catholique dans la province d'Avignon, XVIe siècle* (Paris: Cerf, 1993). For the *ancien régime* see Elisja Schulte van Kessel, "Virgins and Mothers between Heaven and Earth" in *A History of Women,* vol. 3, *Renaissance and Enlightenment Paradoxes,* ed. Natalie Z. Davis and Arlette Farge (Cambridge, Mass.: Harvard University Press 1991), 132–66; Mary E. Wiesner, *Women and Gender in Early Modern Europe,* 2nd ed. (Cambridge, Eng.: Cambridge University Press, 2000), 213–63. For religious women in New France see Elizabeth Rapley, *The Dévotes: Women and Church in Seventeenth-Century France* (Montreal: McGill-Queen's University Press, 1990); Leslie Choquette, " 'Ces Amazones du Grand Dieu': Women and Mission in the Seventeenth-Century Canada," *French Historical Studies* 17 (1992): 628–55; Allan Greer, "Colonial Saints: Gender, Race, and Hagiography in New France," *William and Mary Quarterly,* 3rd series, LVII, n. 2 (April 2000): 323–48, as well as the works referred to n. 6–13.

6. In the seventeenth century the Hôtel Dieu was not only a place to receive medical care, it also functioned as a hospice for the poor, the elderly, and sometimes the deviant. See Jean-Pierre Gutton, *La société et les pauvres. l'exemple de la généralité de Lyon, 1534–1789* (Paris: Les Belles Lettres, 1971); and Michel Foucault, *Madness and Civilization: A History of Insanity in the Age of Reason,* trans. Richard Howard (New York: New American Library, 1965).

7. *MI;* Marie de l'Incarnation, *Écrits spirituels et historiques;* Martin, *Vie de la Vénérable Mère Marie de l'Incarnation;* see also Henri Bremond, *Histoire littéraire du sentiment religieux en France,* vol. 6, *La conquête mystique* (Paris: Bloud et Gay, 1923), 1–226; G.-M. Oury, *Marie de l'Incarnation* (Quebec/Solesmes: Presses de l'Université Laval/Abbaye St. Pierre, 1971); Dominique Deslandres, "Marie de l'Incarnation et la femme amérindienne," *Recherches amérindiennes au Québec* 13 (1982): 277–85; Dominique Deslandres, "L'éducation des Amérindiennes d'après la correspondance de Marie Guyart de l'Incarnation," *Studies in Religion/Sciences religieuses* 16 (1987): 91–119; Dominique Deslandres, "Le rayonnement des Ursulines en Nouvelle-France," in *Les religieuses dans le cloître et dans le monde* (St.-Etienne: Publications de l'Université de St.-Etienne, 1994), 885–99; Dominique Deslandres, "Qu'est-ce qui faisait courir Marie Guyart? Essai d'ethnohistoire d'une mystique d'après sa correspondance," *Laval théologique et philosophique* 53 (June 1997): 285–300; Dominique Deslandres, " 'Le Diable a beau faire . . . ,' Marie de l'Incarnation, Satan et l'Autre," *Théologiques* 5 (1997): 23–41. Maria-Paul del Rosario Adriazola, *La connaissance spirituelle chez Marie de l'Incarnation, la Thérèse du Nouveau Monde* (Quebec-Paris: Anne Sigier-Le Cerf, 1989); Jean Comby, *L'itinéraire mystique d'une femme, Marie de l'Incarnation, ursuline* (Montreal-Paris: Bellarmin-Le Cerf, 1993); Natalie Z. Davis, *Women on the Margins: Three Seventeenth-Century Lives* (Cambridge, Mass.: Harvard University Press 1995), 63–139; Anya Mali, *Mystic in the New World: Marie de l'Incarnation (1599–1672)* (Leiden: Brill, 1996); Marie-Florine Bruneau, *Women Mystics Confront the Modern World: Marie de l'Incarnation (1599–1672) and Madame Guyon (1648–1717)* (Albany: SUNY Press, 1998), 33–122.

8. Françoise Deroy-Pineau and Paul Bernard, "Projet mystique, réseaux sociaux et mobilisation des ressources: le passage en Nouvelle-France de Marie de l'Incarnation en 1639," *Archives de sciences sociales des religions* 113 (2001): 61–91; Guy-Marie Oury, "La correspondance de Marie de l'Incarnation d'après le registre des bienfaiteurs des Ursulines de Québec," *Église et théologie* III (1972): 5–44.

9. In following Mance and Maisonneuve, Madame de La Peltrie left the Ursulines without financial resources; happily for them, she changed her mind, came back to Quebec, and resumed her aid to the convent.

10. Marie-Emmanuelle Chabot, "Chauvigny de la Peltrie, Marie-Madeleine de," *Dictionary of Canadian Biography,* 14 vols. to date (Toronto: University of Toronto Press, 1966–), 1: 207–8 [hereafter *DCB*]; Françoise Deroy-Pineau, *Madeleine de la Peltrie, amazone du Nouveau Monde* (Montreal: Bellarmin, 1992). On spiritual marriages see Dyan Elliott, *Spiritual Marriage: Sexual Abstinence in Medieval Wedlock* (Princeton, N.J.: Princeton University Press, 1993).

11. Each year the authors of the Jesuit Relations devoted a chapter to the Hôtel-Dieu de Quebec and its activities. Albert Jamet, introduction to Juchereau, *Les annales de l'Hôtel-Dieu de Québec,* xv, 57–60, and passim; Ste. Jeanne de Chantal Martin, "Guenet, Marie," *DCB,* 1: 347–49; Jean-Guy Pelletier, "Forestier, Marie," *DCB,* 1: 310; Lucien Campeau, "Le Cointre, Anne," in *MNF* 4: 775; François

Rousseau, "Hôpital et société en Nouvelle France: L'Hôtel-Dieu de Québec à la fin du 17ᵉ siècle," *Revue d'histoire de l'Amérique française,* 31 (1997): 29–47; Rousseau, *La croix et le scalpel: Histoire des Augustines et de l'Hôtel-Dieu de Québec, 1639–1892* (Quebec: Septentrion, 1989), vol. 1; Cécile Lacharme, "Charité et rédemption: vision du pauvre et vision de soi chez les Hospitalières de l'Hôtel-Dieu de Québec et de Montréal, 1636–1675" (M.A. thesis, Université de Montréal/Université Lumières Lyon-II, 1997).

12. Ragueneau, *La vie de la Mère Catherine de Saint Augustin.* See also Guy-Marie Oury, *L'itinéraire mystique de Catherine de Saint Augustin* (Solesmes: Abbaye de Solesmes, 1985).

13. Juchereau, *Annales de l'Hôtel Dieu de Québec,* 108; see also Morin, *Histoire simple et veritable;* François Dollier de Casson, *Histoire du Montréal, 1642–1672;* Guy-M. Oury, *Jeanne Mance et le rêve de M. de la Dauversière* (Tours: C.L.D., 1983); Françoise Deroy-Pineau, *Jeanne Mance. De Langres à Montreal, la passion de soigner* (Montreal: Bellarmin, 1995); Marie-Claire Daveluy, *La Société de Notre-Dame de Montréal 1639–1663* (Montreal: Fidès, 1965); this book contains a facsimile of *Les véritables Motifs des Messieurs et Dames de la Société de Notre-Dame de Montréal* (Paris, 1643).

14. Vachon de Belmont, "Éloge de quelques personnes mortes en odeur de sainteté," 167–89; see also Patricia Simpson, *Marguerite Bourgeoys and Montreal, 1640–1665* (Montreal: McGill-Queen's University Press, 1998); Estelle Sabart, "La sainteté féminine par les valeurs mariales: le cas de Marguerite Bourgeoys," (M.A. thesis, Université de Savoie, 1999).

15. Vachon de Belmont, "Éloge de quelques personnes mortes en odeur de sainteté," 144–66; see also Marie-Paul Dion, "La recluse de Montréal, Jeanne Le Ber," *Église et théologie* 22 (1991): 33–65; Françoise Deroy-Pineau, *Jeanne le Ber: La recluse au cœur des combats* (Montreal: Bellarmin, 2000). On the medieval tradition of the anchorites see Ann K. Warren, *Anchorites and Their Patrons in Medieval England* (Berkeley: University of California Press, 1986).

16. Jean-Michel Salmann, *Naples et ses saints à l'âge baroque (1540–1750)* (Paris: P.U.F., 1994), 236. See also Hippolyte Delehaye, *Cinq leçons sur la méthode hagiographique* (Brussels: Société des Bollandistes, 1934); André Vauchez, *La sainteté en Occident aux derniers siècles du Moyen Âge d'après les procès de canonisation et les documents hagiographiques* (Rome: École française de Rome, 1981); Vauchez, "L'influence des modèles hagiographiques sur les représentations de la sainteté dans les procès de canonisation (XIIIe–XVe siècles)" in *Hagiographie, cultures et sociétés, IVᵉ–XIIᵉ siècles* (Paris: Études Augustiniennes, 1981), 585–96; Jean-Claude Schmitt, "La fabrication des saints," *Annales E.S.C.* (March–April 1984): 286.

17. Carolyn W. Bynum, *Holy Feast and Holy Fast: The Religious Significance of Food to Medieval Women* (Berkeley: University of California Press, 1987), 24–25, as quoted in Greer, "Colonial Saints," 323–48.

18. Christian Renoux, *Sainteté et mystique féminines à l'âge baroque. Naissance et évolution d'un modèle en France et en Italie,* 3 vols. (Ph.D. diss., Université de Paris-I, 1995), 2: 632–46 and passim; see also François Le Brun, "À corps perdu. Les biographies spirituelles féminines du XVIIe siècle," *Le temps de la réflexion* 7 (1986): 389–408; Antonio Rubial García, *La santidad controvertida: Hagiografía y conciencia criolla alrededor de los venerables no canonizados de Nueva España* (Mexico City: UNAM, 1999), 73–77, 165–201; Kathleen Ann Myers, "Saints or Sinners? Life Writings and Colonial Latin American Women," paper delivered to the Colonial Saints Conference, Toronto, May 2000.

19. *MI,* 436–66, "Récit de la vie, des vertus, et de la mort de la Mère Marie de Saint-Joseph" (Spring 1652).

20. Paul Le Jeune (1591–1664) was the superior of the Jesuit mission in Quebec from 1632 to 1639, in Trois-Rivières from 1639 to 1649, and procurator of the Canadian mission in Paris from 1649 to 1662. He is the first writer of the famous *Jesuit Relations. MNF* 3: 530–32.

21. *MNF* 3: 56 (Le Jeune, 1636) and *MNF* 2: 562–63 (Le Jeune, 1636).

22. *MNF* 2: 562–63 (Le Jeune, 1634); see also Deslandres, "Les femmes missionnaires de Nouvelle-France," 74–76; Simpson, *Marguerite Bourgeoys,* 47–50, 67–68; Rapley, *The Dévotes,* 100–6; and Ragueneau, *La vie de la Mère Catherine de Saint Augustin,* 18–19.

23. For her biographer, Glandelet, Marguerite Bourgeoys was sure to follow the same path as the Virgin Mary: "She who succeeded her Son in the conduct of the community of the first Christians, from her son's death to the descent of the Holy Spirit." Glandelet, *La vie de la sœur Marguerite Bourgeoys,* 20. Bourgeoys, *Écrits,* 78, 80, 82, 284; E. Montgolfier, *La vie de la vénérable Sœur Marguerite Bourgeoys dite du Saint Sacrement* (Ville-Marie, W. Gray [1780] 1818), 199.

24. For example, "we are all here in the same design," wrote Marie Guyart, *MI,* 88, letter to one of her brothers, September 1, 1639; see also *MI,* 734–35, letter to Angélique de la Conception, August 19, 1664; Glandelet, *La vie de la sœur Marguerite Bourgeoys,* 20.

25. The duchesse d'Aiguillon specified that the Hôtel Dieu of Quebec was founded "for the Savages, in order to contribute to their conversion and redemption." Juchereau, *Les annales de l'Hôtel Dieu de Québec,* xx, 11–12, 52, 73; Morin, *Histoire simple et véritable,* 26–27 and passim.

26. For example, *MI,* 227, 228, 376.

27. *MI,* 68; letters to her son, September 1, 1643, 184; October 3, 1645, 270; September 7, 1648, 344; August 30, 1650, 395; October 26, 1653, 515; September 16, 1661, 658; and July 30, 1669, 837. Letters to F. de St-Bernard, September 1653, 506 and to P. Poncet, October 25, 1670, 909.

28. For example, *MI,* letter to the Ursuline Community of Tours, 1649, 364–66; letters to her son, 1649, 379–80 and 1650, 396–99; letter to Gabrielle de l'Annonciation, 1649, 387–88. Ragueneau, *La vie de la Mère Catherine de Saint Augustin,* 113–15, 119–24; Juchereau, *Les annales de l'Hôtel Dieu de Québec,* 72–73, 148, 151–52, 239. See also for the French context, Jacques Le Brun, "Mutations de la notion de martyre au XVIIe siècle d'après les biographies spirituelles féminines," in *Sainteté et martyre dans les religions du Livre,* ed. Jacques Marx (Brussels: Editions de l'Université de Bruxelles, 1989), 77–90.

29. *MI,* letter to her son, October 22, 1649, 376.

30. *MI,* letter to her sister (1644), 236; letters to her son, (1651), 414, and (1653), 515. See G.-M. Oury's appendices in *MI,* 1010–30. See also the edifying deaths in *MI,* 284, 287, 584, 621. Bourgeoys, *Écrits,* 139–40.

31. *MI,* letter to her son, September 7, 1648, 342. This vow was taken in 1645. See also *MI,* letters to her son, October 25, 1670, 898–99; October 8, 1671, 932.

32. *MI,* letter to her son, October 21, 1669, 868. *MI,* letters to C. de St.-Joseph, October 1, 1669, 853, and September 12, 1670, 883. For Mother de St.-Xavier's life, written by Jean Marie de Vernon, Paris, 1665, see *MI,* letter to the Mother Superior of Dijon, August 9, 1668, 805–6.

33. See Marie de l'Incarnation's life of Mother de St.-Joseph (*MI,* letter to the Ursuline community of Tours, spring 1652, 436–73); letters to R. de St.-François, September 18, 1652, 490–91, September 15, 1668, 818, and 737; Marie de l'Incarnation's life of Mother Anne Bataille de St.-Laurent (*MI,* letter to the Ursuline communities of France, September 1, 1669, 843–47); and Marie de l'Incarnation's life of Madame de la Peltrie (*MI,* letter to P. Poncet, October 25, 1670, 904–14). She also gives her opinion on the life of Catherine de St.-Augustin (*MI,* 813–14 and 887).

34. *MI,* 1010–36, appendices (1672).

35. Bourgeoys, *Écrits,* 138–44 and on the interior rule, 144–50.

36. The Virgin Mary's model was especially important for Marguerite Bourgeoys. Bourgeoys, *Écrits,* 19, 20, 77, 78, 80, 82, 107, 125. See also Sabart, "La sainteté féminine par les valeurs mariales: le cas de Marguerite Bourgeoys," 28–44. Mary was seen as protector, "as the remora fish which stops the great boat," since she shielded sinners against divine wrath. Bourgeoys, *Écrits,* 94. Regarding the Virgin Mary and St. Joseph as patron saints for Marie de l'Incarnation see *MI,* 236, 343, 478, 634. Recent saints also could be taken as models; for example, Francesco di Paola was a legend in Marie de l'Incarnation's family, *MI,* 661.

37. *MI,* letter to Dom Raymond de S. Bernard, 1635, 59. See also *MI,* letter to the same, December 16, 1635, 56, and *MNF* 3: 122 (abstract of letters, 1635); *MNF* 3: 124 (abstract of letter, 1635); and *MNF* 3: 140 (Garnier, 1636).

38. *MNF* 3: 207 (Le Jeune, 1636). See also *MNF* 3: 113 (Brébeuf, 1635) 3: 126 (abstract of letters, 1635); 3: 195, 199, 201, 204 (Le Jeune, 1636); 3: 309, 321–22 (Brébeuf, 1636).

39. *MI,* letter to her son, 1643, 185. See also *MI,* letter to Dom Raymond de S. Bernard, December 16, 1635, 56.

40. *MNF* 3: 120–23 (abstract of letters, 1635); see also 3: 113 (Brébeuf, 1635); 3: 309 (Brébeuf, 1636); 3: 190, 198–99, 288 (Le Jeune, 1636).

41. *MI,* letter to her son, October 23, 1649, 385.

42. "God helps," "God's stroke," and "omnipotent God" are recurrent formulas in the missionary narratives, but ones with deep significance; they are much more than mere figures of speech. For example, *MNF* 3: 46 (Paul Le Jeune, 1635); and *MNF* 3: 204, 241 (Le Jeune, 1636); *MI,* letter to Claude de Ste.-Agnès, Supérieure des Ursulines de Dijon, 14 September 1645, 249. See also in *MNF* 3: 21, 46 (Le Jeune to Cardinal de Richelieu, 1635); 3: 85, 10 (Brébeuf, 1635), 8; (Perrault, 1634–35), 119; (Ch. Garnier, 1636), 153; (Le Jeune, 1636), 198, 204, 271, 289, 304; (Brébeuf, 1636), 307, 321.

43. See, for example, *MI,* 201, 207, 279, 365, 380, etc., in *MNF* 3: 124 (Extrait de lettre, 1635); (Brébeuf, 1635), 119; (Extrait de lettre, 1635), 127; (Garnier, 1636), 140; (Le Jeune, 1636), 243, 266, 341, 344, 346, 403. (Le Jeune, 1637), 564; (Lemercier), 1637, *MNF* 3: 683, 781.

44. Jean de Brébeuf was convinced of it; for example, *MNF* 3: 321 (Brébeuf, 1636).

45. *MI,* letter to her son, September 14–27, 1641, 260–61, where Marie de l'Incarnation enthusiastically commented on this "heavenly favor" that enacted conversions through a zealous neophyte.

46. *MI,* letter to R. de St.-Bernard, 1635, 26. Marquise de Combalet, quoted by Le Jeune, 1636, *MNF* 3: 194. See, for example: *MNF* 3: 89 (Brébeuf, 1635); 3: 120 (abstract of letters, 1635); 3: 242 (Le Jeune, 1636); 3: 307 (Brébeuf, 1636).

47. "We have to do it this way," Marie de l'Incarnation explained to her son, "and obey God without reasoning because He doesn't want reasoning in the execution of his absolute will" (*MI,* letter to her son, 1669, 837). This abandonment has been much discussed by modern literary scholars, historians, and psychoanalysts (see, e.g., M.-F. Bruneau, "Le sacrifice maternel comme alibi à la production littéraire chez Marie de l'Incarnation," *Études littéraires,* 27 [1994]: 67–73; Jean-Noël Vuarnet, *L'aigle-mère* [Paris, Flammarion, 1997]; Jacques Maître, *Anorexies religieuses, anorexie mentale* [Paris, Le Cerf, 2000]). Her son Claude Martin (1619–96) was the favorite correspondent of his mother, and also her biographer. See

his *La vie de la vénérable Marie de l'Incarnation* (1677; reprint, Jean Lonsagne and Guy-Marie Oury, eds.: Solesmes, Abbaye de Saint-Pierre, 1981).

48. Concerning other contexts see Isabelle Poutrin, "Souvenirs d'enfance. L'apprentissage de la sainteté dans l'Espagne moderne," *Mélanges de la Casa Velazquez*, 23 (1987): 331–54; Peter Burke, "How to Be a Counter-Reformation Saint," in *Religion and Society in Early Modern Europe 1500–1800*, ed. Kaspar von Greyerz (London: G. Allen & Unwin, 1984), 45–55; Jodi Bilinkoff, "Confessors, Penitents, and the Construction of Identities in Early Modern Avila," in *Culture and Identity in Early Modern Europe (1500–1800): Essays in Honor of Natalie Zemon Davis*, ed. Barbara B. Diefendorf and Carla Hesse (Ann Arbor: University of Michigan Press, 1993), 83–100.

49. See Myers, "Saints or Sinners? Life Writings and Colonial Latin American Women." This was also the case in Europe: Thomas F. Mayer and D. R. Woolf, eds., *The Rhetorics of Life-Writing in Early Modern Europe: Forms of Biography from Cassandra Fedele to Louis XIV* (Ann Arbor: University of Michigan Press, 1989); Isabelle Poutrin, *Le voile et la plume: autobiographie et sainteté féminine dans l'Espagne moderne* (Madrid: Casa de Velázquez, 1995).

50. *MI*, letter to her son, October 26, 1653, 516; see also *MI*, 10, 68, 141, 219, 344, 376, 396, 433, 533, 536–37, 594, 896; Juchereau, *Les Annales de l'Hôtel-Dieu de Québec*, 11 and passim.

51. Marie de l'Incarnation, *Autobiographie*, in *Écrits spirituels et historiques*, 2: 68; Bourgeoys, *Écrits*. On this theme see Marie-Florine Bruneau's case study, "Le projet autobiographique: Guyon à l'orée de la modernité," *Papers on French Seventeenth-Century Literature*, 10 (1983): 60.

52. See, for example, Bourgeoys, *Écrits*, 185.

53. Marie de l'Incarnation, *Autobiographie*, 71, 96–97, 101–2, 108–9, 114, 131, 145, 204–5, 246–47; Bourgeoys, *Écrits*, 97, 138; *MI*, 813–14, 887; *EMB*, 73. Cf. Vauchez, *La sainteté en Occident*, 224–27; Louis Félix Boisset, "Souffrir: un chemin," in *L'itinéraire mystique d'une femme, Marie de l'Incarnation*, ed. J. Comby (Paris: Le Cerf, 1993), 135–65; Louis Cognet, *Crépuscule des mystiques* (Paris: Desclée, 1991), 23, 25; Robert Bultot, "Bonté des créatures et mépris du monde," *Revue de sciences philosophiques et théologiques*, 62 (1978): 363–94.

54. For example, *MI*, 240, 299, 368–69, 404, 431, 500, 503, 561, 567, 588, 596, 609, 816; Marie de l'Incarnation, *Autobiographie*, 114, 291; Bourgeoys, *Écrits*, 97, 138.

55. See Deslandres, "Le rayonnement des Ursulines en Nouvelle-France," 885–99.

56. For example, Marie de l'Incarnation wrote extensively to various spiritual followers. Deslandres, "Qu'est-ce qui faisait courir Marie Guyart?," 294–95. See also Deroy-Pineau, *Jeanne Le Ber*, 104; Simpson, *Marguerite Bourgeoys*, 181.

57. For a good recent synthesis on Jeanne Le Ber see Deroy-Pineau, *Jeanne le Ber*. See also Leo-Paul Desrosiers, "Le milieu où naît Jeanne Le Ber," *Revue d'histoire de l'Amérique française*, 16 (1962–63): 155–77.

58. *RAPQ*, 147. Jeanne's mother was Jeanne Le Moine, of the famous Le Moine-D'Iberville family.

59. Bynum, *Holy Feast and Holy Fast*, 219–44; Henry Chadwick, "The Ascetic Ideal in the History of the Church," in *Monks, Hermits, and the Ascetic Tradition*, ed. William J. Sheils (London: Basil Blackwell, 1985), 2–3. Maître, *Anorexies religieuses*, 37–46.

60. Deroy Pineau, *Jeanne Le Ber*, 117, 120–21; Desrosiers, "Le milieu," 155–77.

61. *RAPQ*, 151–56.

62. *RAPQ*, 154, 159–62.

63. Juchereau, *Les annales de l'Hôtel-Dieu de Québec*, 12. Bourgeoys, *Écrits*, 122.

64. *MI*, letter to her son, September 1, 1643, 185. See also letter to her niece, October 20, 1668, 831.

65. *MI*, 64, 338, 403, 406, 533, 497, 613, 616.

66. On Marie de St.-Joseph: *MI*, letter to an Ursuline of Tours, October 24, 1652, 497; and letter to F. de St.-Bernard, September 1653, 505. On Mme. de La Peltrie: letter to P. Poncet, October 6, 1667, 784; and letter to C. de St.-Joseph, October 1, 1669, 853.

67. *MI*, letter to an Ursuline of Tours, October 24, 1652, 497.

68. *MI*, letter to Ursulines of Tours, summer 1670, 876, where she praised an Ursuline nun she considered a saint.

69. *MI*, letter to her son, 1654, 533. See also, for example, *MNF* 4: 283 (Le Jeune, 1640). Le Jeune wrote about Paul Aniskouaskousit's holy life and death and wished to keep his body as a relic.

70. Thus the "savages" called the Ursulines "the holy girls." *MI*, letter to her son, September 24, 1654, 544. See also *MI*, to a nun of Tours, 1660, 639–40 and *MI*, letter to M-G. Rolland, October 10, 1648, 353.

71. *MI*, 639–40.

72. See Dominique Deslandres, "Signes de Dieu et légitimation de la présence française au Canada: le 'trafic' des reliques ou la construction d'une histoire," *Les Signes de Dieu aux XVIe et XVIIe siècles*, ed. G. Demerson and B. Dompnier (Clermont Ferrand: Ass. des Publ. de la Faculté de Letters de Clermont-II, 1993), 145–60.

73. This transfer of coffins occurred either on November 3, 1661 (according to Claude Martin) or during the spring of 1662 (according to *Annales des Ursulines de Québec*). *MI,* letter to Gabrielle de L'Annonciation, 1663, 721–22. The deceased Ursuline was Marie de St.-Joseph.
74. *MI,* letter to Renée de Saint-François, 737–38.
75. *MI,* letter to Gabrielle de L'Annonciation, 1663, 722.
76. *MI,* letter to her son, October 26, 1653, 516. For example, see *Les annales du premier monastère des Religieuses Ursulines;* Ragueneau, *La vie de la Mère Catherine de Saint Augustin,* 13; Glandelet, *La vie de la sœur Marguerite Bourgeoys;* Martin, *Vie de la Vénérable Mère Marie de l'Incarnation;* Juchereau, *Les annales de l'Hôtel-Dieu de Québec;* Morin, *Histoire simple et véritable.*
77. Montgolfier, quoted by Deroy-Pineau, 154. See also, for Catherine de St.-Augustin, Ragueneau, *La vie de la Mère Catherine de Saint Augustin,* 6.
78. Letter from Monseigneur de Laval, first bishop of Quebec to the Congregation Notre-Dame at the moment of Marguerite Bourgeoys' death, January 1700 in Glandelet, *La vie de la sœur Marguerite Bourgeoys,* 152.
79. Even at the height of Iroquois attacks, the settlers simply refused to let the nuns go back to France (*MI,* letter to her son, 1651, 422; letter to Angélique de la Conception, 1664, 735; Juchereau, *Annales de l'Hôtel-Dieu de Québec,* 91–92).

8

Isaac Jogues:
From Martyrdom to Sainthood

PAUL PERRON

Isaac Jogues was one of eight Jesuit missionaries, beatified in 1925 and canonized in 1930, who lost their lives during the Iroquois-Huron wars of 1642–49. Accounts of their execution, along with their biographies, are related in print for the first time in *Jesuit Relations,* published for the most part by Octave Cramoisy, from 1632 to 1673.[1] Each death, beginning with René Goupil's, is narrated by the Jesuit in charge of the mission in Huronia or Quebec, in the *Relation* that covers the year in which it occurs. Yet the account of Isaac Jogues' capture, torture, hiding, release, and escape to France, followed by his return to Quebec 1½ years later, and finally his capture and assassination by the Iroquois in October 1646, is the most interesting by far, from the point of view of its composition, and its relation to the rest of the narrative enfolding it. Jogues' narrative, a founding text, is the most intricate and fascinating of all, since it is constructed in several stages, and it spans several *Relations.*[2] It is also dialogical to the extreme, as it has a number of different narrators as well as narratees, who cite and constantly refer to one another, and it incorporates and integrates numerous sources, both written and oral, in constructing the persona of Jogues. Indeed, even before Jogues says "I" in his own narrative, he emerges as the complex intersection of the directly and indirectly reported and transcribed voices of all the speaking and writing subjects of New France (both Christian and non-Christian) and the mother country inscribed in his narrative. Polyglotic, the subject "I" speaks and says by and through the polyphonic "we."

The introduction to the *Relation* of 1642, dated October 4 and written by Barthélemy Vimont, the superior of the mission of Quebec, and chapter 11 of the same *Relation,* composed by Paul Le Jeune,[3] provide the first mentions of Isaac Jogues' captivity among the Iroquois. Vimont simply notes that, if he is still alive, the priest is a prisoner of the enemy, along with two other French servants and twenty-three Christian Huron captives. However, Le Jeune's short narrative of the missionary's capture is preceded by a long description of the Iroquois wars against the Algonquins, and the subsequent campaign against the French. Le Jeune quotes another missionary, Jacques Buteux, who was told about the cruelty of the Iroquois by one of two Algonquin women captured with Jogues, but who subsequently escaped from their clutches. Most of the tale is directly narrated by Buteux, who adopts the perspective and point of view of the captured woman (indirect discourse). On occasion, however, the actual witness is allowed to speak on her own, but only for a brief moment, by addressing the missionary directly. She shifts the scene into the present tense as though it were actually unraveling before Buteux, or any other listener/reader. She begins her story at the moment she is about to go to bed, with a premonitory statement in the present: "We are done for, the Iroquois are killing us."[4] The narrator-missionary immediately appropriates her scene, displaces the witness by speaking in her stead, substituting in the evaluative mode his voice, his vision, for hers, in the past tense: "I do not know what instinct pushed her to pronounce these words." He shifts once more into the present: "be that as it may, at the same time she says this, these armed tigers enter the cabin, seizing some of the inhabitants by the hair, others by the waist."[5] The narrator describes the massacre, always in the present, as though observing it firsthand. He becomes the center of focalization, the eyewitness, investing the text with his missionary sentiments and beliefs. Though he substitutes his voice for hers, he does not assume total responsibility for the narrative, leaving it with the woman who lived the event and saw it with her own eyes, and therefore can be considered a reliable witness.[6]

The Iroquois are described as an undifferentiated mass, appearing suddenly in the night and, much like the plagues of old, bringing death and destruction to the French, their Christian allies, and all of their enemies. Like the demons of Christian lore, these agents of fire cook and torture their victims, even devour them. Moreover, these instruments of hell attack and destroy the social unit of Christianity par excellence, the family. A further motif is developed, that of the passive flock, which in turn evokes the pastor to come: "Their supper being cooked, these wolves devoured their prey, one attacks a thigh, another a breast. Some suck the marrow from the bones, others split open a head to extract the brain." The inhumanity of the other is stressed when the narrator states, "In short, they eat men with such appetite and with more joy than hunters eat wild boar or deer."[7] The Iroquois are subsequently characterized as "wolves," as devouring children, and when the aggressors bring their captives to the village they are depicted in diabolical terms: "Some Demons awaited the prisoners . . . Entering this hell . . . Like Demons with the souls of the damned . . . dance in the midst of these Demons . . . these tigers . . . these Demons . . . *Homo homini lupus;* man becomes a wolf for a man when he is governed by Demons . . . the fury of these lions."[8]

Immediately after announcing that man is a wolf for man, without naming the main protagonist, Jérôme Lalemant refers directly to the tale he is about to narrate. "Alas! Is it truly possible that the Father and the Frenchmen, about whom I shall soon speak, has been treated this way by these Barbarians, who captured and recently took them to their country."[9] This constitutes the minimal narrative of the priest's capture, and it is followed by four paragraphs describing the activities of the enemy in the spring, before once again turning to the events leading to the battle and describing those that follow in the past tense. Chapter 12 of the *Relation* of 1643, again edited by Barthélemy Vimont, covers the Iroquois wars during that period. When the Iroquois returned to the St. Lawrence Valley they had with them three or four Huron taken prisoner the previous year with Isaac Jogues and the French. Two of them escaped, met with Jean de Brébeuf in Trois-Rivières, and let him know that the captives were still alive. Again we have embedded narratives, where the Huron relate to Brébeuf, who relates to Vimont, who relates to Filleau. . . . The *Relation* of 1644, covering what occurred in Huronia from June 1642 to June 1643, was recomposed by Jérôme Lalemant and sent to Quebec. It includes another abbreviated account of Jogues' capture and treatment by the Iroquois narrated by Lalemant, who learned of it from one of the Huron Christian captives who, in turn, had escaped from the Iroquois.

The *Relation* of 1645 mentions only that Fathers Isaac Jogues and François Bressani, when they returned to New France, embraced as friends: "those who had torn their bodies to pieces, ripped out their nails and cut off their fingers, in a word, those who had treated them as tigers would."[10] A peace treaty is reached among the French, their allies, and the Iroquois that will hold for a year. The *Relation* of 1646 signed by Jérôme Lalemant begins by referring to the treaty in question and is followed by an account of the deaths of Fathers Anne de Nouë and Enemond Masse. Both of these deaths are placed under the sign of martyrdom, though the former died in an accident of nature, and the latter of natural causes. In the next chapter, titled "Of the Mission of the Martyrs began in the Land of the Iroquois," Lalemant again evokes all the deaths of the French missionaries in terms of martyrdom: "When I speak of a Mission among the Iroquois, it seems to me that I speak of a dream, but nevertheless it is true, and we are right in giving it the name of the Martyrs; for in addition to the cruelty with which these Barbarians treated some persons impassioned for the salvation of souls, in addition to the sorrows and fatigues that those destined for this Mission are bound to incur, we can say in truth that it has already been turned crimson by the blood of a Martyr."[11] During the period from 1642 to 1649 of the French-Huron-Iroquois wars, the motif of martyrdom permeates the discourse of conversion, with the Iroquois assuming the role of Satan, the sworn enemy of the true church. In fact, at this time the mission attained the state when conversion was considered possible if, and only if, the missionaries were persecuted and executed for their faith by the hellhounds of Satan. "It is credible (if this endeavor succeeds) that the plans we have against Satan's empire for the salvation of these people will only bear fruit if they are soaked with the blood of some other martyrs."[12]

The *Relation* of 1647, composed by Jérôme Lalemant and sent from Quebec to Paris on October 20, 1647, is much different from the previous ones dealing with Isaac Jogues and Jean de La Lande. It begins with a brief mention of their deaths in the dedication to Étienne Charlet, the provincial of the Jesuit order and, for the most part, it will expand on the elementary narrative program of the life and death of these two missionaries. However, contrary to all the earlier segments concerning them both, a specific end, a teleological finality of martyrdom, organizes and gives meaning to all the events of their lives. Yet, much like the previous *Relations*, this is a composite and complex text in which Lalemant, as editor, integrates, melds, and weaves together various written as well as a large number of verbal narratives that are, at first blush, difficult to disentangle. The fourth chapter opens abruptly with a micronarrative nine lines long, about Jogues' origins in Orleans, his arrival in New France, his six years in Huronia, and his death, that recapitulates, or mirrors, in an extremely condensed form, the story that is about to unravel. However, before focusing on the main topic, the narrator makes a series of comments of a metatextual nature regarding the origins of the tale he is about to relate, and the reliability of all the information contained therein: "What was said about his [Jogues'] labors in the earlier *Relations* came for the most part from a few Indians, who were fellow sufferers. But what I am about to write came from his own pen and from his own mouth. I had to use the authority as his Superior, and gentle persuasion in more intimate conversations to discover what the low self-esteem he had of himself was kept hidden under a profound silence."[13] Here Lalemant grounds truth in the visual and the corporeal experience of the person who lived the event, Jogues, who becomes the ultimate guarantor of what is described. In so doing the narrator depreciates the witnessing and oral reporting of the indigenous people who only saw what happened to the missionary, spoke about it, but could not write about it. From this perspective, to *say* is to have *seen* and *experienced* for oneself. Yet, in Lalemant's narrative, the fact that Jogues assumes the roles of embedded narrator, actant, and scriptor, guarantees the truth of what occurred. Lalemant and Jogues tend to become one and the same, since they share the same presuppositions about the potential of language not only to reconstitute the event but also about its ultimate meaning in terms of a shared and unquestioned eschatology. This melding of voices is borne out when the focus of the narrative abruptly shifts from Lalemant to Jogues himself: "Let us hear him speak on this subject, and on the outcome of his journey. Obedience having proposed to me and not ordered me to go down to Quebec, I offered wholeheartedly to do so. . . ."[14] The shifting of the focus from Lalemant to Jogues will be relayed by other European witnesses, who *saw* and fixed in *writing* what they *perceived*. Here, seeing is the differential trait of knowing and, contrary to the voice of native informants, writing founds events as having occurred, as truth.

The five following chapters, which give the most complete and final account of the life and death of Isaac Jogues, can be considered as the founding narrative of his martyrdom that not only led to his canonization but also to that of the seven other missionaries. It became the model of the genre in the *Relations,* and the form of its content and expression generated the accounts of the seven others who lost their lives during this troubled and violent period in the history of the mission. It is, in fact, composed, that is, put together and structured by Lalemant, and is considered as the ultimate rewriting of all events of Jogues' existence deemed significant in the establishment of his hagiography. Although the oral witnessing of native informants is said to be unreliable, Lalemant's narrative, established from other written accounts, in the main, covers the same ground as theirs. In these chapters we are dealing with embedded narratives at the level of enunciation where the primary enunciator, Lalemant, conjoins not only the role of scriptor/witness but also, from time to time, of actor, since he both tells the story and, at various moments, intervenes as an actual character in the tale. He, in turn, is relayed by Jogues, who also has the role of enunciator and primary actor, which he shares with other enunciator/ actors who knew the victim and gave evidence of the degree of their knowledge through their writings.

All of these enunciators, who must be defined by and through intersubjective relations of communication (real or virtual), confirm their narrative competence—founded on a certain number of presuppositions or variable rules, belonging to the cultural and social codes, the ideologies, defining them as Europeans—by the simple performance, or act, of narrating. Such conventions, beliefs, and institutions constitute the symbolic network of culture[15] that is both shared by individuals and assigns them a specific place[16] in the symbolic order and hierarchy. Each enunciator and enunciatee is defined by a common base of theoretical knowledge (writing, measure, time, etc.), a passion—actual or by proxy—to convert the heathen, physical, mental, and moral power, and a duty to impose the true faith. These modalities, which constitute their competence, are organized in ordered series, with obligation or duty (to God's dictates) commanding, in sequence, the will, knowledge, and power of all the actants concerned. What differentiates each narrating trustworthy actor is the degree and intensity of the modalities that motivate his competence, but not their order. It is also presupposed that all of these modalities enabling narrative to come into being in the form of writing and reading, have been sanctioned by a large number of social and religious institutions of obvious European origins. Each and every enunciator and enunciatee has in turn been destined by the Sender, God, and simply carries out his order to write, read, believe, and live for the true Receiver, God, Who has mandated him or her to undertake this divine project.

Moreover, this *Relation,* like all the others, is organized in terms of descriptions, scenes, dialogues, where personae interact physically, emotionally, intellectually, and spiritually. The discursive construct Jogues, the main subject (S1), is depicted by Lalemant, progressively and in stages, as the prototypical and exemplary missionary who will attain God's will through suffering, sacrifice, and dying for the faith. At the most elementary level of analysis, S1, who has been mandated by God, and whose competence has been sanctioned by the social, cultural, intellectual, and religious institutions (presupposed), will undertake a journey, or quest, into the unknown. He will undergo a series of qualifying tests, reported and evaluated by a series of representatives of the temporal and spiritual orders, before being legislated into the eternity of sainthood by the final sanctioning body of the church. In turn, each test in the series can be considered as the transformation of one state *(s1)* of S1 into another state *(s2),* and the entire sequence, making up the narrative, can be transcribed as: $s1(S1)$ tr. $s2(S1)$ tr. $s3(S1)$ tr . . . $sn(S1)$, where *sn* represents the end point. It should be noted, however, that the transforming agent, or catalyst, necessary to bring S1 to the penultimate end point of martyrdom and to the end point of canonization is none other than the collective antisubject (S2), the Iroquois.

The originality of Lalemant's narrative, though, must be attributed to the textualization of the episodes, to the rhythm and intensity of their staging, to the complex interplay and changes in focalization, to the enunciative strategies set in place, to the impact created by the overlay of recurring characters and events. For the reader or scriptor of the *Relation* of 1647, the name Jogues is not an empty signifier, nor is it a simple potential, waiting to signify through the creation of a temporalized actional intrigue. The signifier, Jogues, has an anaphoric function that sets in motion, in the reader, a *memoria,* a temporal arc (past-present-future), reaching at one and the same time back to all the intratextual and intertextual references to his prior deeds and actions in all the *Relations,* and forward, projecting his inevitable future, in death and martyrdom. The signifier, Jogues, evokes a body that has previously been tortured and mutilated, a body in action, an acting body, a body being acted on. It is by and through the description of the body in action that the hero's physical, moral, and spiritual qualities are revealed. Yet the complete story of his life and death must be told and iterated a final time, in large part by himself, before being frozen in timeless legend.

In narrating his own capture, Jogues organizes events for the most part by using the pluperfect tense, which, as I noted, is the time of historical discourse that maintains a temporal distance between the time of narration and the time of the event. The first sequence of torture, related in the pluperfect, is framed by two sequences of ministration, narrated both in the present and past tenses: ". . . I call one of the Iroquois guards . . . he approaches, and having seized me he put me with those that are called the miserable of this world. . . . This good young man confessed immediately. Having given him absolution, I approach the Huron, I instruct and baptize them. . . ." "I was also seeking my share, I visit all the captives, I baptize those who were not yet baptized, I encourage these poor wretches to suffer. . . . I learned during this visit that we were twenty-two captives."[17] This shifting in and out of historical time into the present imposes another temporal rhythm on the reader—that of distancing and presentifying the events made flesh as they are conjured up in the act of reading. The historically temporalized action of the body is folded into the timelessness of the gesture of ritual. Yet, the violence with which his captors torment him is described in the pluperfect:

> They fell upon me with an enraged fury. They beat me with their fists, with sticks and with their weapons, flinging me to the ground half-dead. As I was beginning to breath those who had not struck me, approaching, tore off the nails of my fingers with their teeth. And then biting one after the other the ends of my two forefingers stripped of their nails, causing me extreme pain, crushing them and grinding them as if between two stones, until splinters and small bones emerged.[18]

Although the racked body is described in the past, the images unravel both with violence and uncommon slowness, as the use of the gerundive: "flinging," "approaching," "biting," "causing," "crushing," and "grinding" stretch out the tormented and mutilated body in time, creating in the reader, through intensified durativity, reactions of attraction and repulsion, identification and horror. His mutilated, festering, and suffering body in movement is depicted in all its horror during the thirteen-day trip from the place of capture to the Iroquois village: ". . . hunger, the burning heat, threats and the hatred of these Leopards, the pain of our wounds, which were not bandaged and were rotting to the extent that they produced worms, caused us, in truth, great suffering."[19] Eight days into this trip the party meets up with another band of Iroquois on the warpath, and the captives are made to run the gauntlet. Blows hail down on them, and Jogues falls once more to the ground and passes out near death:

> They wanted to bring me back alive to their country, they gather me in their arms, and carry me covered in blood to this stage. Having regained my senses, they make me come down. They cast a thousand insults at me, they make me the sport and object of their reviling. They begin to beat me again, raining down on my head, and on my neck and on my entire body a hail of blows with their sticks. It would be too long for me to write down the full extent of my suffering. They burned one of my fingers, they crushed another with their teeth and they continued to press and twist with the rage of Demons those that were already torn. They tore at my wounds again and again with their nails and whenever my strength failed me they applied fire to my hands and my thighs.[20]

The manipulated and punished body is once more depicted graphically as it is caught up in a whirligig of changes of tenses from the pluperfect to the present, to the pluperfect and to the imperfect. Not only does this shifting in and out position the reader before what is happening, but it creates rhythm and tension in the description. The assailed, sensitized, passive body is projected out of the horror of the historical into the abhorrence of the vivid, timeless now ("they gather me," "carry me covered in blood," "make me come down," "they cast," "they make me their plaything"). The racked body is seized, struck, and dismembered by violent, sudden gestures in the pluperfect, which reduces the moment to a single point in time, inscribing it in a causal chain, maintaining ambiguity between temporality and causality, calling for a development, an unraveling, an end of tribulation[21] ("they burned," "they crushed"). Finally, the tortured body, subjected to the throes of lasting, recurring, and agonizing suffering, is enfolded in the imperfect tense, stretching and reiterating the activity over time, imposing a tempo of haunting and excruciating duration, iteration, and tension ("they begin to beat me again," "they continued to press and twist," "they tore at my wounds again and again," "whenever I lost . . . they applied"), that not only engages the intellectual attention of the reader but actually provokes intense feelings of identification, empathy, torment, and repulsion. Indeed, if through and by Jogues' experience, the flesh is made word, by his narrative the word is made flesh for the reader, who, in turn, experiences Jogues's travails in the depths of her or his own body.

The tortures continue, and Jogues gives isolated examples of scenes that include other individual protagonists, but also dialogue between them. They go on to the village, and the missionary lives a real Calvary along the way as he bears his cross, describing events that occurred as either singular, durative, or iterative. The captives meet up with another party in the wilderness before being paraded from one village to another and tortured again and again. They are once more made to run the gauntlet and flagellated, then exposed on a platform. The priest is further mutilated, then stretched out and tied to the stake, all the while offering up his sufferings to the Lord. These tortures, and variations of them, are repeated in two other villages, each spanning a three-day period. Jogues is sentenced to death with some Huron captives and preparing for the end: "My soul is very pleased on hearing these words; but God himself was not, he wished to prolong my martyrdom. These Barbarians changed their minds and said the Frenchmen had to be kept alive."[22] He witnesses Goupil's assassination, then the narrative switches back to Lalemant: "This young man or this holy martyr, having been slain in this way, the Father returns to his cabin; one of his captors holds a hand to his chest to feel whether fear did not make his heart beat."[23] It should be noted that the description of the body is never a completed portrait so that, in the end, the reader cannot have in mind an actual image of the man Jogues. The description isolates, focuses on, and redepicts parts of the body that are amputated, bludgeoned, burned, scratched, cut, torn out. The more gruesome detail it goes into, the more the totality is dissolved and diffused, and though the parts bear a metonymic relation with the whole, they do not evoke an individualized physical portrait but rather function indexically, since they conjure up heroic moral and spiritual strength under the adversity of suffering and persecution.

Jogues spends the year captive in the Iroquois village, has dreams and visions like the patriarchs of old, and his life is in constant danger. Once an angry warrior enters the priest's hut and strikes him over the head twice with a bludgeon, leaving him half dead.[24] Lalemant narrates Jogues's flight to freedom, after Jogues learns that the Iroquois were awaiting his return to the village to kill him. In doing so, he comments on the composition of his work and its intratextual links with other *Relations:* "This news was the occasion for his deliverance, of which, having sufficiently mentioned in the *Relations* of 1642 and 1643 in chapter 14, I will only relate here a few particulars that were either barely, or not touched on at all."[25] In his escape from his captors, his body is once more mutilated, but this time by a guard dog, and his wounds are treated before he boards a ship for England, where, on arrival, he is robbed of his cassock and hat and makes his way to France. The rest of Jogues's adventure, as he heads to meet his fate, is told at an extremely accelerated pace, compared with his capture and torture at the hands of the Iroquois, which comprise the major portion of the narrative and cover a much briefer period of time. This structural amplitude of variations, 282 lines for several hours dealing with his capture and first torture, compared with 9 lines for his 1½-year stay in France, is accompanied by an acceleration of the rhythm of the tale as it winds to a conclusion. The end is marked by an increasing number of summaries and ellipses, contrary to the beginning—the capture, torture, and constant threat of death at the hands of the Iroquois, which is marked by long, drawn-out scenes.

In the tale of Jogues, the Iroquois are reduced to a horrifying presence, and they are never described corporeally. Indeed, as I remarked, for the narrators and narratees they are an ominous, demonic, disincarnate, evil presence, reduced to the violent, inhuman gestures they carry out on their enemies' bodies. They are the menacing, absent signifieds in the intersubjective communication between Christians and potential Christians that can appear at any moment and wreak havoc on the colony and the missions. Yet they are always there, and felt in the hearts, souls, and in the very bodies of the individuals who fear them. Of all of the sign systems making up interpersonal relations in this text, the body is at once the most omnipresent, the most complex, and the most expressive semiotic system, since it generates and incorporates all others. As such the body in action, the tormented, mutilated, and sacrificed body, is at the origin of all the experience of the senses and of the mind, and is the most outspoken advocate of the true faith. When Jogues is waiting for a boat to escape from the Dutch settlement, a young man came up to him, took him aside, and "threw himself at his feet, taking up his hands to kiss them, and crying out: 'Martyr, Martyr of Jesus Christ.' He interrogated him and found out he was Lutheran. He could not help him as he did not know his language, he was Polish."[26] When he was in Paris, the "Queen having heard of his sufferings, says out loud: 'Romances are feigned, but here is a genuine combination of great adventures.' She wished to see him, her eyes were touched with compassion at the sight of the cruelty of the Iroquois."[27] The tortured and scarred body, the incarnation of the flesh made word, is the most eloquent and convincing of all languages, since it actualizes in its expressive materiality to the ultimate degree the believers' values that inform their semantic universe. Marked and mutilated by the hereditary temporal representatives of the negative values that threaten the very existence of the missions and the Huron nation, the disfigured body, through semiosis, constitutes an ultimate semiotic system that articulates the material and spiritual values of human experience. As such, the torn and tortured body moves and provokes emotional responses from all actual and potential believers and consolidates their shared semantic universes and value systems.

In the second part of chapter VIII, dealing with the sequel to Jogues's death, Lalemant evaluates and interprets the events that occurred over the missionary's lifetime. Contrary to the other segments of the Jogues narrative (especially those relating to his capture and torture that are overwritten and amplified in successive *Relations,* so that what occurred once is narrated on numerous occasions—repetition and iteration creating an effect of intensity, horror, and truth), this segment fills in some minor gaps in the narrative but also serves to give a final orientation and reading to the text. Once more, Jogues is evoked as a martyr by all those who come into contact with him, or hear of him. Public opinion, or the doxa, is unanimous about the ultimate meaning of the life and death of the missionary, and Lalemant articulates their voices in the final segment of his hagiography. He begins by stating that all the missionaries in New France, the collective "*we*," continue to speak as one: "We have honoured this death as the death of a Martyr, and though we were in different places, several of our Fathers, without knowing anything about the others because of the distance, could not reconcile themselves to celebrate for him the Mass of the Dead. . . ."[28] The secular clergy and religious orders also voice this same opinion and: "honoured this death, feeling rather more inclined to invoke the Father than to pray for his soul."[29] This is reechoed as a logically constructed argument by: "Several learned men, and this idea is more than reasonable that he is truly a martyr before God. . . . This death is the death of a martyr before the Angels. . . . We are persecuted for our doctrine that is none other than Jesus Christ's, according to them we depopulate their lands, and it is for this doctrine that they killed the Father, and consequently we can consider him as a martyr before God."[30]

The tale closes with an injunction and an invitation to the reader to reexamine, with the narrator, over his entire lifetime Jogues's moral and spiritual qualities: "Let us say a few words about the virtues of our Martyr."[31] This can be considered as the final ethopeia or argument that integrates the reader in the eulogy, through the use of the possessive pronoun "our," convincing her or him that we are, in fact, dealing with an indisputable case of martyrdom. This section, analeptic in nature, sweeps back over his early years, organizing all the events of his life in terms of the end that is there transforming everything. This apologia is tautological and simply states that already in France young Jogues was what he will become, since he demonstrated *there* all the qualities that he will reveal *here*, in New France. Most of the sequences, related in the imperfect, are durative and iterative, and they simply reiterate the implied fundamental proposition that we can state as follows: "What he repeatedly did, before and after his capture and death, prepared him for martyrdom. Therefore he is a martyr." The amplitude of all of these iterative analepses, both internal and external, bring a repeated temporal consistency that subordinates the *past* to the *now* of enunciation, to the description of Jogues's moral and spiritual portrait. "He was endowed with . . . he approved in his early years those who chastised him . . . he spent a large part of the day before the holy Sacrament . . . he was naturally apprehensive . . . although he was of a hasty and quick temper . . . more than a hundred times over they said to him."[32] The other analepses, which are singulative, since they relate one time what occurred once, are vivid illustrations of these qualities that all martyrs must possess and demonstrate.

Lalemant also constructs his conclusion in the ironic mode since, on the one hand, Jogues is systematically presented as interpreting at one level all that he does, thinks, feels, and believes, while, on the contrary, everyone who comes into contact with him is said to have a different opinion. The parallelism of these two iterated points of view constitute a limited number of semantic series (or isotopies) that give and ensure enormous cohesion and give great impact to this final plea. He has a low opinion of himself (he considers himself unworthy of all that befalls him, and lets those about him know this), whereas everyone who comes into contact with him holds and voices a contrary point of view: "He was endowed with a rare humility . . . To show him however little esteem for that which he had endured for Jesus Christ . . . When the Queen desired to see him he could not persuade himself that she truly desired it . . . He was tormented when she asked to see his hands that were all torn."[33] Cruelty/forgiveness; hate/love make up another series of isotopies: "Never in the midst of his suffering, or during the greatest cruelties of these treacherous people, did he feel any loathing for them; he considered them with the eye of compassion a mother holds for a child of hers. . . ."[34] Purity/sin; cowardliness/courage are two other series: "One cannot express the care he took to kept his heart pure . . . made him say that he was only a coward, and yet the Superiors who knew him, depended on him as firmly as a rock";[35] along with, eating/abstinence and humility/arrogance: "I already remarked that he would rather content himself with a little water and corn flour . . . than eat meat that he knew was sacrificed to the Devil. . . . Although he was of a hasty and quick temper, he nevertheless knew so well to submit when Christian humility and charity required it."[36] Child/adult is the final pair: "The Father who was with him during the last year of his life in Montreal did recognize that God was preparing him for Heaven. Having given him the sentiments of a child, he examined all the folds and recesses of his conscience, from the first use of his reason to then, revealing them with the humility and candor of a child."[37] Here the child is literally and figuratively father of the man predestined, and prepared for his final end.[38]

A singular, exemplary incident encapsulates the interplay between the seemingly contradictory constitutive isotopies of Jogues' moral and spiritual portrait. During his captivity, an Iroquois who had fallen ill dreamed that to be healed a dance and other ceremonies had to be held with the missionary present, his prayer book in hand. Some Iroquois came and told the missionary that he held the key to the recovery of the suffering warrior. He, in turn, "rebukes the vanity of their dreams" and refuses to come with them. Other messengers are sent, and when he continues to rebuff them they decide to carry him off against his will: "But as he was agile and very deft and very little burdened with flesh, he evades them and takes to his heels. They pursue him with all their might. They find that he had the legs of a stag, and that if he had wished to escape he could have done so, since he outstripped the best runners of the country." And Lalemant continues, giving unequivocal meaning to the scene: "In fact charity alone kept him among the Iroquois, for he preferred the salvation of the captives to his life and liberty. In conclusion, he returned to the village resolving to die rather than in any way to associate with their superstitions. Our Lord desired that they spoke no more of this with him."[39] This scene shows and demonstrates to one and all that Jogues is not what he is perceived to be for his tormentors, but that he is what he appears to be for the narrator, all those who knew him, and the reader, a heroic and exemplary figure who, in living out his role predestined and motivated by God, willingly abnegates his own will and intelligence, his tendencies and flesh, placing them entirely in the service of the Lord. Lalemant brings closure to the composition of the life and death of the martyr by framing Jogues' decision to abandon willingly the Iroquois in 1643 with the help of the Dutch settlers of Fort Orange (later Albany, New York) with an anticipatory vision he had of his own fate. He would not have escaped "if he had not seen that his life was over and that he could no longer help these poor Barbarians. If he did not know he would return and find them once more he could never have abandoned them: but our Lord prolonged his life so that he could once again present it as a burnt-offering in the land where he had already began his sacrifice."[40] The signification of Jogues' desire to flee from the dangers he faced during his captivity is recuperated by the fate he met at the hands of the Iroquois three years later. The last image left the reader is that of the convergence of all the events witnessed and experienced into the grand adventure of martyrdom, the written testimonial of which will call out and beckon the other seven martyrs to be inscribed with him in the pantheon of Canadian sainthood.

NOTES

1. Published as a series of annual volumes between 1632 and 1673, *Jesuit Relations* form the textual basis of this study. Rather than relying on any modern translations, I have made use of a facsimile edition of the original seventeenth-century Jesuit Relations: *Relations des Jésuites*, 6 vols. (Montreal: Éditions du Jour, 1972) [hereafter *RJ*]. Passages quoted in this article are my own English translations.
2. *RJ*, 3 (1642): 45–52; *RJ*, 3 (1643): 61–69; *RJ*, 3 (1644): 71–74; *RJ*, 4 (1647): 17–42.
3. Paul Le Jeune, missionary at Quebec, Sillery, Tadoussac, Trois Rivières, and Montreal from 1639 to 1649 and superior of the Canadian Jesuit missions between 1632 and 1639, was the first compiler of

Jesuit Relations. See Léon Pouliot, "Le Jeune, Paul," in *Dictionary of Canadian Biography,* 14 vols. to date (Toronto: University of Toronto Press, 1966–), 1: 453–58.

4. *RJ,* 3 (1642): 45.

5. Ibid., 46.

6. The narrator's change of verb tense is significant. For the most part the tale is narrated in the past, hence maintaining a temporal distance between the time of the event and the time of the narration, which, as Émile Benveniste demonstrated, *Problèmes de linguistique générale* (Paris: Gallimard, 1967) is the time of the historical enunciation and the historical narrative.

7. *RJ,* 3 (1642): 46.

8. *RJ,* 3 (1642): 47–48.

9. *RJ,* 3 (1642): 48.

10. *RJ,* 3 (1645): 2.

11. *RJ,* 3 (1646): 6.

12. Ibid., 14. This is Guy Laflèche's thesis in *Le Martyre d'Isaac Jogues par Jérôme Lalemant.* Laval: Les Éditions du Singulier, 1989, to which I fully subscribe.

13. *RJ,* 4 (1647): 17. See Guy Laflèche, *Les Saints Martyrs Canadiens,* vols. 1 and 2 (Laval: Les Éditions du Singulier, 1988 and 1989).

14. *RJ,* 4 (1647): 17–18.

15. See Clifford Geertz, as cited in Paul Ricoeur, *Time and Narrative,* 2 vols. (Chicago: University of Chicago Press, 1984), 1: 57–58.

16. See Paul Perron and Gilles Thérien, "Ethno-historical Discourse: Jean de Brébeuf's *Jesuit Relation* of 1635," *The American Journal of Semiotics* 7, nos. ½ (1990): 61–64.

17. *RJ,* 4 (1647): 19–20.

18. Ibid., 19.

19. Ibid., 20.

20. Ibid.

21. See Roland Barthes, "L'Écriture du roman," in *Le Degré zéro de l'écriture* (Paris: Gonthier, 1964), 29–38, where he establishes a link between historical discourse and the novel through the use of the past tense that is not meant to express time but instead a causality, an inevitability between events as they unfold.

22. Ibid., 24.

23. Ibid., 26.

24. Ibid., 32.

25. Ibid., 33.

26. *RJ,* 4 (1647): 34.

27. Ibid., 36–37.

28. *RJ,* 4 (1647): 38.

29. Ibid.

30. Ibid., 38–39.

31. Ibid., 39.

32. Ibid., 38–41.

33. Ibid., 39–40.

34. Ibid., 41.

35. Ibid., 40.

36. Ibid., 41

37. Ibid., 40.

38. The narrator continues the Christic analogy, stating: "This made the Father believe that the Kingdom of Heaven belonged to him and that he was not distant from it" (Ibid., 40).

39. Ibid., 41.

40. Ibid., 42.

9

Martyred by the Saints: Quaker Executions in Seventeenth-Century Massachusetts

CARLA GARDINA PESTANA

In October 1659, two men and a woman walked through the streets of Boston to their deaths. An armed guard of a hundred men accompanied them. A crowd of curious onlookers watched the condemned persons and the unprecedented display of military might. All gathered at the place of execution. The three embraced. The matronly woman stood with a halter around her neck as her two younger companions were killed in turn. The soldiers then moved to release her. The woman, who seemed stunned that she was not to die along with her martyred friends, refused to leave the platform. She had to be pulled down and carried back to prison. Later she would be transported out of the colony. Less than one year later, this aspiring martyr, Mary Dyer, would join her companions. Brought back to the place of execution on May 21, 1660, Dyer, too, would suffer death. All three were Quakers, executed by the authorities in Massachusetts Bay Colony as part of a vigorous but ultimately unsuccessful effort to rid the colony of these dangerous heretics.[1]

The martyrdoms of Mary Dyer, William Robinson, and Marmaduke Stevenson as well as that of a fourth person, William Leddra, killed in 1661, are unique in Anglo-American history: nowhere else in the English-controlled colonies of the Atlantic world did Protestants die for their faith.[2] In contrast to the sainted martyrs of New France, the killers of these four Quaker missionaries were not Indian peoples resisting conversion to an alien faith but fellow Englishmen. Nor did the executions occur across the great confessional divide of seventeenth-century Europe, that between Protestant and Catholic. Both the Quakers and those who executed them were Protestants, at least in name. The divide in this case was between the reformed Protestantism upheld by the Massachusetts Bay Colony and the non-Calvinist faith of the most prominent of the new sects that had arisen in England during the civil wars of the previous decade. Dying for their faith outside the Roman Catholic tradition, these martyrs had no future as saints in the traditional sense of an individual canonized by the church for their sanctified life. In keeping with the Protestant rejection of such Roman Catholic traditions and with its promotion of the priesthood of all believers, those who put the Quakers to death called themselves "saints." By this they meant they had been chosen by God, elected for a rare and treasured salvation that set them apart from the misguided and ultimately damned believers in Quakerism or, for that matter, Catholicism. The saints of New England thus made martyrs of the Quaker witnesses in a strange case of New World martyrdom exacted on English Protestants by English Protestants. It was a struggle that cannot be fully understood in the same terms as the martyrdoms of Catholic priests tortured and killed by Native Americans. Both Quaker and Catholic New World martyrdoms drew upon the traditions that were basic to both faiths and reveal some instructive similarities despite their obvious differences.

For all their discontinuities with the typical New World martyr, these Quaker witnesses participated in the long-standing Christian tradition of martyrdom. They drew upon many beliefs that similarly motivated martyrs who embraced other versions of the Christian faith.[3] In their own writings and in the writings of their coreligionists who eulogized them, the four witnesses emerge as believers who willingly accepted death as a necessary defense of the truth. Depictions have them dying with the appropriate demeanor of the martyr. The three who walked to the place of execution in 1659 embraced joyously, transported by love for each other and for their God. Fortitude and calm in the face of torture and death offered signs of the veracity of their faith and the strength of their conviction in it. Although in many respects the new Quaker movement rejected older religious beliefs and practices—leading some to conclude that they were not even Christian—they acted upon widely shared understandings of the proper death for a godly person set upon for his or her faith. The creation of a Quaker hagiographic tradition and a literature of suffering were central to the developing identity of the sect.

Quakerism emerged during the upheaval of the English revolution. Although it would eventually coalesce into a sect with a shared doctrine and a loose organizational structure, in the first years Quakerism amounted to a movement of like-minded people who responded in a similar way to the dislocation in English religious and political life. They shared a conviction that clergymen, organized churches, and carefully hammered-out doctrinal positions were inessential and even dangerous to spirituality. Instead they thought each person should follow an inward light or seed, which would guide actions and reveal truth. Anyone could learn to follow this light, and doing so was essential to salvation. Eager to get this message out, Quakers preached to anyone who would listen and challenged the established churches and ordained ministers they encountered as spiritually dangerous and misleading. A fundamentally democratic movement, Quakerism encouraged all those convinced of its message to become witnesses for the truth. As one appalled critic pointed out, "sometimes girls are vocal in their covenant, while leading men are silent."[4] Their message perfectly suited to the period of civil wars, regicide, and interregnum, the Quaker witnesses attracted many converts between about 1647, when the first "convincements" occurred, and 1655, when the first witnesses set sail for the colonies. Between 1655 and 1661 they visited Barbados, Jamaica, Bermuda, Maryland, Virginia, and every colony in New England. With no centralized organization to dispatch the witnesses on missionary visits, each traveled as moved by the spirit. This spontaneous outpouring of transatlantic Quaker missionary activity was remarkably comprehensive despite being uncoordinated.

When the Quakers came to Massachusetts Bay, they confronted another religious movement with a mission to change the world. The largest New England colony had been founded almost three decades earlier by men who were critical of the Church of England. They saw the church then established in England as insufficiently reformed and warned that it was drifting back toward the hated Roman Catholics on matters of liturgy and doctrine. Unable to reform the church after decades of effort and unhappy about the direction of change within England, disillusioned members of the godly community choose to immigrate to the New World, where they would be free to create the society and the churches they thought best. In Massachusetts Bay they gathered congregational churches made up only of the godly, known as the "elect," the "saints," or the "visible saints." They limited participation in the government to male church members, to ensure the godliness of the state. The government did not tolerate dissent, which it understood as sinful rebellion. Like the Quakers who emerged subsequently, the godly saints who embraced the New England way were part of the impulse within English society to reform religion and thereby transform society. Since the Bay colonists had left England in the 1630s, civil wars, regicide, and the disestablishment of the Church of England had dramatically altered the political and religious landscape. As a result, the Quakers, although they arose from a similar impulse, differed dramatically from the "puritan" reformers of an earlier era, and they frightened the more conservative defenders of New England orthodoxy.

Massachusetts Bay Colony authorities watched the rise of Quakerism and the general increase in religious liberty in England with horror. They feared that their colony might become infected by any one of a number of radical religious sects, and they vigilantly guarded against the possibility through the 1640s and early 1650s. When Quakers first arrived in Boston in 1655, the government threw them in prison, then shipped them away at the earliest opportunity. Immediately thereafter it passed the first in a series of laws intended to protect the colony against the Quaker threat. If they needed any encouragement the authorities could note that their own harsh response to the sect had a parallel in a backlash against Quakers that began in England in 1656. Quaker witness James Nayler, having re-created Christ's entry into Jerusalem by entering Bristol on an ass in the company of women signing "Hosanna," had been tried by Parliament for blasphemy and ordered to undergo a series of brutal punishments. Even in relatively tolerant England, the tide turned on the Quakers.[5] Far from requiring encouragement, the Bay Colony dedicated its resources to combating Quakerism, and its determination was cited in England to encourage the anti-Quaker backlash there.[6] In Massachusetts by October 1658, the authorities had despaired of ridding the colony of Quaker witnesses. When fines levied on ship's masters who brought witnesses into the colony closed off that avenue, dozens of Quakers traveled overland from Rhode Island to witness in the colony. A new law allowing for banishment on pain of death resulted, an act that its authors characterized as self-defense.[7]

This latest penalty would, it was hoped, "make them shie in coming amongst us."[8] But it had the opposite effect. Quakers came specifically to defy the new law. As one of those martyred in 1659, William Robinson, declared in a letter to other Quakers: "oh! If I never See your faces more in the outward man, the will of God be done, for I am given freely up, my Life to Lay downe at this Towne of Boston, or theire BLOODY LAWES TO BREAKE."[9] A few months later he would be dead, and the bloody laws still stood.

Even before the Boston deaths, Quakers began producing a body of literature that documented the afflictions endured by the faithful in the colonies.[10] This literature aimed at two purposes: to document the proper suffering of individual Quakers persecuted for promoting the truth, and to castigate those responsible for these grave injustices. At times the prophetic, judgmental component of these writings supplanted the presentation of appropriate suffering. Then the tracts focused on the sinfulness of the perpetrators so completely that the reader easily lost sight of the individual sufferer. Shaped by the expansive, millenialistic qualities of the movement in this period, these writings—like the witnesses whose toils they recounted—sought to convert others before the end of time. This early literature of sufferings was part of a polemical battle with New England over the nature of the true faith and the appropriateness of New England's response to Quakerism. A 1659 harangue by Quaker leader George Fox suggested the tenor of these attacks as well as the style of many witnesses' confrontations with the unconvinced. "Nothing will quench your rage but the blood of the innocent, and burning, and banishing, and spoiling of goods, and making havock of them, and putting to death, taking away life; nothing will satisfie you devourers, it seems but life."[11] Repeatedly Quakers made the point that New Englanders, who came to America to escape religious persecution by the bishops of the Church of England, persecuted Quakers in turn. As George Fox queried, "who would have looked for such fruits from New England, who themselves were once under suffering and banishment?"[12] The early suffering literature pursued multiple agendas, only one of which was the documentation of suffering for the true faith.

The suffering itself was central to the early Quaker self-understanding, a fact that made the new sect similar to other Christian faiths even as the Quakers denied the parallels. According to Quaker historian J. Canby

Jones, Quakers embraced two spiritual weapons (and their only weapons were spiritual): love and suffering. For the Quakers, the light within bestowed the power to participate in "heroic acts of corporate witness," including to suffer willingly for their faith.[13] Brad S. Gregory finds that love and suffering are intertwined in martyr accounts in various traditions, and it is therefore not unique to the Quakers to frame it in this way.[14] Counter-Reformation Catholicism developed the ideal of heroic suffering, and martyr accounts helped to disseminate that ideal to the European (and American) Catholic community. The Quakers and other radical English Protestants asserted their complete rejection of the Roman Catholic tradition of saints, and they did not read church hagiographies. *Flos Sanctorum* (or *The Lives of the Saints*) was not published in English after the 1630s, and it was never published in England itself, but only in English editions on the Continent. De Vorgaine's *The Golden Legend*, another account of saints' lives, appeared in London only until the Protestant Reformation arrived there, the last edition produced in 1527.[15] Without access to these Catholic inspirational sources—and with little apparent consciousness that they participated in any such tradition—the Quakers' ideas about how to suffer properly nonetheless included many of the standard conventions of Catholic hagiography.[16]

With the 1659 executions in Boston, the image of suffering martyrs reached full flower. Just before his death, William Robinson wrote a letter to his fellow Quakers, "the Lord's People," in which he eagerly anticipated his martyrdom. "I shall enter with my Beloved into Eternal Peace and Rest, wherein I am swallowed up: with the Life of it I am filled, and in it I shall depart my Everlasting Joy in my Heart, and Praises in my Mouth, Singing Hallelujah unto the Lord."[17] Mary Dyer similarly embraced death. When ordered to prison to await her hanging, she replied, "Yea, and joyfully I go." En route she informed her escort, the marshal of the court, that he could "let her go alone, for she would go to the Prison without him." The marshal reportedly replied, "I believe you Mris [Mistress] Dyar, but I must do what I am Commanded."[18] Willingness to die for one's faith being one sign of a martyr, Quaker acceptance of persecution pointed toward martyrdom.

The joyousness of the occasion provided a major theme of the martyr writings. Peter Peirson, who provided Quakers in England with an account of the 1659 executions, observed that "they walked along in pure retired

Chearfulness to the Place of Execution, triumphing in the strength of the Lamb, over all the wrath of man, and fury of the Beast, in the pure retired Heavenly Dominion of the Invisible God."[19] Dyer informed the Massachusetts authorities that she anticipated "I shall eternally rest (with the faithful and true Witnesse of God), everlasting Joy and Peace . . . with Him is my Reward, with whome to live is my Joy, and to dye is my Gain."[20] William Leddra, the last of the four to die, anticipated the end in the same frame of mind. He wrote to his friends shortly before his execution, after a year in prison in chains: "I have waited as a Dove at the window of the Ark, and have stood still in that Watch, which the Master of the House did at his coming (without whom I could do nothing) reward with the fulness of his Love, wherein my heart did rejoyce."[21] A rejoicing heart under such dismal circumstances offered a further indication that those who died did so as martyrs.

They did not falter at the moment of death, another indication that God was truly with them. To prove this point and to offer an inspiration to others, sympathetic observers recorded the last words of each condemned witness. William Robinson said, as the executioner prepared to turn him off the ladder, "I Suffer for Christ, in whom I live, and for whom I die."[22] Marmaduke Stevenson declared, "This Day shall we be at Rest with the Lord."[23] When Mary Dyer died in 1660, the moments before her death were taken up with an exchange with the crowd about her beliefs and her attitudes toward the colony's leaders. Despite this potentially distracting repartee, Quakers declared that she ended her life hitting the correct note. When taunted that she claimed to have been in paradise, she replied, " 'yea, I have been in Paradise several dayes.' And more she spake of her Eternal Happiness, that's out of mind. And so sweetly and chearfully in the Lord she finished her Testimony, and dyed a faithful Martyr of Jesus Christ."[24] A year later William Leddra said from the ladder, "Know, that this day I am willing to offer up my Life for the Witness of Jesus." The man who recorded his words, himself neither a Quaker nor a resident of the Bay Colony, found Leddra's performance extremely affecting: "I am not of his Opinion," Thomas Wilkie confided in a letter to a friend, "but yet truly me thought the Lord did mightily appear in the man."[25] Dying well was a persuasive gesture, one that, as David Hall has observed, had the power to invert the meaning of an execution.[26] Leddra then went on to say, "Lord Jesus, receive my spirit," as had Christ, and in his turn, the early Christian martyr Stephen before him.[27]

That Leddra and his companions "blessedly departed with Praises in their mouths"[28] offered an important clue to the veracity of their conversion. The way in which the condemned met their death was thought to indicate first and foremost the state of their souls. Those who faltered were suspected of having a false conviction of their own godliness. In the face of death, a person who professed to be among the converted bolstered the truth of this claim in how he acted in his last moments. Signs of doubt or fear indicated hypocrisy and a lack of true faith. This was true of those who died at home in bed, surrounded by loved ones. The same standard held for those who confronted death publicly. The spectacle of a public death appealed in part because it offered an opportunity to gauge the sincerity of the faith of the condemned. For a person condemned on account of her faith, the mandate to die well was all the more forceful. Both the state of the individual soul and the justice of the cause in which she died were tested when she met a martyr's death.[29]

Quaker martyrs, though they certainly knew the importance of dying well from the many public executions and discussions of deathbed repentance that permeated English religious culture, went beyond these basic points to participate in other aspects of the martyr tradition. One of these was the erotic language associated with the death of a martyr. Martyrs like Robinson described their spiritual state in ecstatic terms. "The Streams of my Father's Love runs daily through me from the Holy Fountain of Life, to the Seed throughout the whole Creation; I am overcome with Love, for it is my Life, and length of my Days; it's my glory, and my daily Strength: I am swallowed up with Love, in Love I live, and with it I am overcome."[30] This erotic rhapsody on love in Robinson's writings was consistent with the way in which martyrdom was traditionally portrayed. As Daniel Boyarin has written of the birth of the martyr tradition, "they died with joy, with a conviction not only that their deaths were necessary, but that they were the highest of spiritual experiences. Another way of saying this would be to spotlight the eroticism of these texts. They are all about love, about dying for God. What was new in martyrology was the eroticization of death for God, in the representation of martyrdom as the consummation of love."[31] Stevenson and Robinson, both of whom wrote letters just before their executions, participated in this mystical tradition. They ruminated on love and reveled in the passion that upheld them as they approached death.

At times, prospective Quaker martyrs seemed more focused on union with other believers than on union with Christ. William Robinson wrote to three leading Quakers a few months before his death, "I am broken in pieces with the Remembrance of you, who are as A seal upon my Breast, feel me oh! Feel me in your own lives, given up for the service of the lord for the Seed, to which the God of heaven hath regard to: my Life is sacrifyced up, and laid downe in the Will of God: for the Redemption of the Seed."[32] On the eve of his death, he sought union with other believers: "feel me when [love] runs from the Fountain into your Vessel, when it issues gently, like new Wine, into your Bosoms; when the Strength and power of it you feel, when you are overcome with the Strength of Love (which is God) then feel me present in the Fountain of Love. . . . Feel me wrapt up with you in the pure Love."[33] Marmaduke Stephenson expressed similar feelings. Just before his execution he wrote: "My love and life runs out to you all who are chosen of God and faithful, for you are dear unto me, the Lord knows it, and are as seals upon my breast, your lambs of my Fathers Fold, and sheep of his Pasture, the remembrance of you is pretious to me my dearly beloved ones."[34] Later, in a long, rapturous passage, he added, "I am filled with love when I think upon you, and broken into tears for the remembrance of you."[35] While the focus of their emotions may seem to veer off of God to rest upon their fellow Quakers, this distinction between other believers and God was not one that the early Quakers would have understood. Believing that each of them contained something of Christ within—often rendered as a seed or a light—these early Quaker witnesses communed with each other and with the deity simultaneously in long, erotic passages that seemed to slip back and forth between God and the faithful as the object of their desire. This slippage involved no such thing as far as they were concerned (one of the many aspects of Quakerism that horrified the movement's New England opponents), since God and the entire community of the faithful were united in love.

George Bishop, a Bristol Quaker who collected accounts of the martyrs and published an extended relation of the confrontation in New England, vigorously promoted the idea that the four witnesses died as martyrs. His description of the execution day that ended with the death of two men and the release of Mary Dyer emphasized that the three went to their deaths cheerfully. Using classic Christian symbolism of union with Christ as a marriage, he likened the atmosphere to that of a wedding day. "So being come to the place of Execution, Hand in Hand, all three of them, as to a Wedding Day, with great cheerfulness of Heart; and having taken leave of each other, with the dear Embraces of one anothers Love in the Love of the Lord."[36] When Dyer was finally killed the following spring, Bishop asserted that she met her death "even Out of the Body in the Joy of the Lord."[37] In describing the deaths of her two companions on the earlier occasion, he carefully presented the key moment: "Your Exec“tioner put W. Robinson to Death, and after him M. Stevenson, who died, both of them, full of the Joy of the Lord, and steadfast in him, and have received a Crown of Life." Bishop insisted upon this point, adding: "Sealing their Testimony with their Blood, (which was the most that could be done), their Countenances not changing."[38]

Much of Bishop's tract responded to New England efforts to discredit the martyrs. The passage above about "their Countenances not changing" continued: "(though the Priests thought to have found it Otherwise, and had some of them spoken to this purpose, that they should see whether they would change countenance, when they had a Halter about their necks)."[39] "The Priests"—as Quakers contemptuously styled the ordained ministers of any church—had an interest in proving that the Quakers died badly, hesitating at the moment of death. For the ministers of New England, most prominently Boston minister John Norton, the Quakers were not martyrs but deluded or evil heretics, bent not on spreading but on destroying the true faith. As much as Bishop wanted to document that the condemned witnesses died serenely, "the Priests" sought to demonstrate the opposite. The question of how Bishop's coreligionists greeted their demise was highly politicized. According to Bishop, Stevenson and Robinson "remained as fresh (in a manner) even after they were dead, as they were before (as was observed by some)."[40] While a countenance that remained serene even at the moment of death offered evidence of true faith, a body that remained fresh indicated sanctity. In those Christian churches that identified and venerated saints, an uncorrupted body, a body that remained fresh, was one sign of sainthood.[41] Bishop, assuming he was even aware of the significance to Catholics of an uncorrupted body, seems to have hesitated to draw that conclusion, committing himself to the idea only "in a manner." Despite this hesitation, Bishop's *New*

England Judged, Not by Man's, but by the Spirit of the Lord fought to win acceptance in the pantheon of Christian martyrs for Marmaduke Stevenson, William Robinson, Mary Dyer, and William Leddra.

English men and women had two sources for information about martyrs readily available in the seventeenth century: the Bible and the great English Protestant martyrology, *Actes and Monuments,* by John Foxe. They did not look to Catholic sources, such as *The Golden Legend* or *Flos Sanctorum,* and they would have objected had anyone suggested that they do so. Foxe's martyrology, popularly known as Foxe's Book of Martyrs, dealt with early Christian martyrs and those from the recent English past. Interested in commemorating the Marian martyrs of his own day, he embedded their stories into a history that promoted a Protestant perspective on what constituted legitimate martyrdom. He championed the national English church in its formative and difficult days. His book was widely available in seventeenth-century England, distributed to every parish church along with the Book of Common Prayer and the Bible.[42] Occasionally Quakers made explicit reference to Foxe. Edward Wharton, one local Quaker convert who witnessed the executions, made mention of the archpersecutor Bishop Edmund Bonner, a direct reference to the English events popularized in the *Actes and Monuments.*[43] But Foxe, despite his widespread popularity in England, was an odd choice as a model for the Quakers. Because they were Anglicans, Foxe's martyrs offered dubious models for those who opposed the Anglican hierarchy. Non-Anglicans, including Quakers, struggled with the applicability of Foxe's hagiography to their own experiences and its veracity as sacred history. References to Foxe's martyrs in the early Quaker writings were therefore relatively rare. Quakers who wrote about the martyrs typically dealt with the Church of England less as a spiritual home to other martyrs and more for the church's role in persecuting future New Englanders prior to their migration to America. They evinced greater awareness of the recent history of persecution by the Church of England and pointedly tied that history to the events in Boston.[44] Use of Foxe's martyrs as a parallel to the executions in Boston rose over time, with later commentators more likely to use the example of the Marian martyrs when discussing the Quakers than contemporaries had been.[45]

Biblical sources were less problematic, and Quakers used them freely. English Protestants focused their attentions on Scripture, and especially the more radical among them claimed to be clearing away years of Catholic and Anglican invention that obscured biblical truths. In one early attempt by English Protestants to sweep away "papist" corruptions, John Marbeck published his own *Lyves of Holy Sainctes* (1574), which offered an early "biographical dictionary of the Bible" to counter the classic Catholic sources.[46] The first Quakers, by virtue of their prior training in other Protestant churches and their immersion in the biblicist culture of mid-seventeenth-century England, were fully versed in the Bible. Traveling to Boston to witness the executions of Stevenson and Robinson, Alice Cowland hoped to prepare the corpses of the martyrs as Christ's had been prepared. She brought a "Linnen wherein to wrap the dead Bodies of them who were to suffer."[47] John Southwick, a convert to Quakerism in Massachusetts, likened the persecution of witnesses to the martyrdom of Christ and the apostles.[48] Early Quaker leader George Fox saw the biblical drama of Herod condemning Christ replayed in the sentences in Boston: "Did not you the Herods of New-England, Whip and Banish, and after HANG four Servants of Christ when he was manifested in his people in New England, Herod-like?"[49] To George Bishop, the New Englanders played the role of the Jews rather than that of Herod.[50] This equation of the Quaker witnesses with Christ would recur repeatedly in later accounts of the martyrs. It was also a standard trope of Christian martyrdom in the Catholic tradition, not to mention in Christian devotional literature more generally.[51] An eighteenth-century Friend thought the martyrs demonstrated that the Quakers suffered as Daniel had in biblical times.[52] Others adopted the mantle of Christ's suffering for their lesser punishments. After a whipping, Horred Gardiner knelt, echoed Christ's dying words, "The Lord forgive you for you know not what you do."[53] John Knott has recently pointed out how such references "magnified" the achievement of contemporaries by placing them on a level with the early Christians. The early Quakers thought of themselves as reenacting Scripture, and suffering as martyrs was essential to that reenactment. Whereas their opponents sought to return to the forms of the early church, the Quakers believed that they were in a sense a part of the original Christian community. The continuity that they emphasized among themselves, the first Christians, and indeed Christ Himself made their views among the most radical being floated in the English religious milieu at the time.[54]

The claim that Quakers died as saintly martyrs enraged the Massachusetts Bay Colony authorities. They asserted that the Quakers were killed as disturbers of the peace and not for their religious views. This tactic had a venerable English tradition, having been used for the first time against English Catholics in the sixteenth century.[55] But the Bay Colony's anti-Quaker polemics made clear that their peace was disturbed by men and women with beliefs they viewed as heretical and dangerous. Official sources, including a tract written by minister John Norton at the government's request, a broadside published by order of the court, and a manuscript justification circulated to all the towns in the colony, explained the government's policy toward Quakers.[56] These justifications attack the idea that the condemned died as martyrs. Norton asserted "that these persons canonize themselves as saints of the most high is a strong delusion." Norton's use of the term "canonize" attempted to associate the Quakers with the hated Roman Catholics, an equation that had been made to the sect's detriment earlier, although without reference to martyrdoms, sainthood, or canonization.[57] Norton further pointed out that not suffering but rather the veracity of the cause for which the suffering was endured made the martyr. By this criterion, in his mind at least, the Quakers did not qualify.[58] The Bay Colony authorities depicted the executed men and woman as suicides, who had the freedom to stay away but refused to use it to save themselves. George Bishop found the claim that the Quakers were suicides, not martyrs, especially infuriating: "This shift will not serve you before the Judge of all, who is drawing near to Judgement, and will render to you according to your deeds, before whom you are naked and bare, and who sees your Hearts."[59] Contradicting the official position that Quakers were not killed for their heresy, a great deal of ink was spilled by Norton and others to demonstrate that the missionaries' beliefs were blasphemous and dangerous.[60] Many colonial observers understood that the authorities went after the Quakers to suppress erroneous belief. As one supporter of the official policy put it:

> Blessed be God, the Government and Churches both, did bear witness against them, and their loathsome and pernicious Doctrine: for which they were Banished out of this Jurisdiction, not to return without Licence, upon pain of Death. The Reason of that Law was, because God's People here, could not Worship the true and living God, as He hath appointed us in our publick

Assemblies, without being disturbed by them: And other weighty Reasons; as the Dangerousness of their Opinions, &c. Some of them presumed to Return, to the loss of their Lives, for breaking the Law, which was made for our Peace and Safety.[61]

Norton himself called out to one Quaker preaching from the ladder with a noose around his neck to be quiet or else he would die with a lie in his mouth.[62] Quakers combated efforts to dismiss the four executed missionaries as suicides or heretics and instead maintained the claim to martyr status.

Suffering for their faith became a key component of the Quakers' group identity, not just in New England but throughout the Atlantic world as well. As one New England observer put it, with some amazement, "They seemed to suffer patiently, and take a kind of pleasure in it." Another remarked, rather ambiguously, "Quakers are more in Sufferings."[63] Enduring affliction became so central to the Quaker movement that the Quakers were often accused of overemphasizing it. Quaker pamphleteers felt compelled to defend the sect as early as 1670 on this point. Christopher Holder declared that they did not find justification for their faith in their suffering, but rather in Christ.[64] Occasionally punished with fines and imprisonment or, in the case of James Nayler, more severe sanctions prior to the restoration of the Stuart monarchy (1660) and of the Church of England (1661), afterward the sect became a persecuted minority. Fines, seizure of goods for failure to pay tithes or fines, and imprisonment were the most common punishments in restoration England. To document the persecution and to give Quakers a sense that their small-scale, local struggles were part of a larger drama, the sect began to collect reports of all sufferings endured by Friends. The resulting compilation, published by Joseph Besse as *Collection of the Sufferings of the People called Quakers,* enumerated every seized cow and every day's imprisonment.[65] Besse also recounted in detail the treatment of Quaker missionaries, especially in New England, where persecution had reached unprecedented heights. *Sufferings of the People called Quakers* reprinted long passages from earlier accounts of the martyrs, but Besse occasionally departed from this approach to provide commentary of his own. If anything, his exegesis located the dead Quakers even more firmly within a tradition of Christian suffering and redemptive death. To do so supported larger efforts to earn Quakers social acceptance within Britain even as it fostered the conception of Friends as true Christians.

Besse explained the meaning of the deaths in Boston. "Thus Mary Dyer departed this life, a constant and faithful Martyr of Christ, having been twice led to Death, which the first Time she expected with an entire Resignation of Mind to the Will of God, and now suffered with Christian Fortitude, being raised above the Fear of Death, through a blessed Hope, and Glorious Assurance of Eternal Life and Immortality."[66] Besse's gloss presented Dyer as the classic martyr: constant and faithful, resigned, serene in the face of death, even willing to stare death in the face twice. She enjoyed a martyr's reward. Eternal life and immortality were the hope of all believers, and the Quaker martyr could attain nothing more than that. Besse offered a similar commentary on the death of the last martyr, William Leddra. "Thus dies William Leddra, whom we leave resting in Peace from his Labours, and reaping the Fruits of his Meekness, Patience, and other Christian Virtues, which was conspicuous in the Course of his Life, and enabled him to meet Death with Intrepidity."[67] In the deaths of Dyer, Leddra, and the others, the Quakers beheld the ultimate sacrifice for the faith. Besse's detailed enumeration of seemingly endless cases of minor persecution threatened to submerge the account of the four martyrs with the sheer number of such incidents. But placing these widely varied examples of suffering within the same narrative also served to elevate the more prosaic struggles of the Yorkshire Friend who lost a cow.

The martyrs served as potent symbols for the sect once this early heroic era had passed. As Hugh Barbour and William Frost argued, the prestige of the martyrs was one of the movement's strengths as it set about consolidating the gains of the early period of expansion.[68] When Isaac Pemberton advocated religious liberty during the American Revolution by citing the four Quakers killed in Boston more than a century earlier, he demonstrated that the memory of the martyrs still carried great symbolic weight. Robert Treat Paine, who heard his tirade and may have felt implicated in his ancestors' part in the affair, complained that Pemberton "bellowed loud on New England Persecution and Hanging of Quakers etc."[69] Anyone who demonstrated intolerance of Quakerism might be castigated for complicity in the martyrdoms. The wife of a Presbyterian preacher at Talentire in 1678 or 1679 who favored punishment of Quaker witnesses was said to prove "that she only wanted power to follow the example, and imitate the barbarity of her brethren in New England."[70] According to Cotton Mather, who abhorred what the sect had done to the reputation of his beloved New England, Quakers fell back on the executions when they were beaten on every other point.[71] Mather was correct that the martyrs were centrally important to the Quakers, although he appreciated their usefulness in scoring debating points rather than their contribution as sectarian hagiography. Members of the Society of Friends reported the importance of the martyrs' tale in their own conversion to or thinking about the sect.[72] Even non-Quakers were captivated by their heroic example. John Winthrop Jr. expressed "tender respect" for them, according to Rhode Island Quaker William Coddington.[73] Boston became a site of pilgrimage, especially among Friends in America.[74]

That the authorities had denied the martyrs liberty of conscience received increased attention over time. In underscoring the need for religious freedom, Quaker polemicists began to move away from an aggressive defense of the faith for which the martyrs died.[75] Instead they increasingly emphasized the witnesses' inoffensive demeanor, a revision that, while it deemphasized the religious polemic, also drew on the imagery of the martyr—content to die because her faith was true. Martyrdom for a true faith rested uneasily alongside a liberal emphasis on each believer enjoying the freedom to pursue his or her version of the truth. A poem written in 1677 captures the shift in emphasis:

> Those that in conscience cannot wrong a worm,
> Are fin'd and whip'd, because they can't conform;
> And time hath been which ne'er shall be forgot,
> God's servants have been hanged, none knows for what,
> Except for serving of their blessed Lord,
> For quaking and for trembling at his word.
> Let these black days, like the fifth of November,
> Be writ in red, for ages to remember.[76]

The reference to the anti-Catholic Guy Fawkes' Day (the fifth of November) hinted at the limits of toleration in the Anglo-Atlantic world in 1677, but the overriding aim was the inclusion of Quakers in the community of those whose conscience was protected. After the Quakers came out for liberty of conscience and dropped the missionary activism of their first decades, martyrs who died for religious freedom began to replace martyrs who lost their lives for aggressive proselytizing in favor of their own faith. This shift was especially visible in the polemical writings intent upon chastising the Massachusetts authorities, which were legion.[77]

The Quakers constructed their hagiographies with two purposes in mind: to promote the idea that the four witnesses died in defense of their faith, and to attack the Massachusetts Bay Colony for its intolerance. The two purposes were interrelated, not the least because the identity of the condemned as "witnesses of Christ" placed the authorities who had them killed in the wrong. After the battles were long past, once a degree of relativism about religious truth had taken hold, intolerance emerged as the major point at issue. At the time that the first hagiographies were being constructed, however, the two purposes worked very much in tandem. Joan Brooksop's 1662 tirade captured the intimate relationship between the rightness of the witnesses and the offensive nature of the response to them. In "A Lamentation for New England" she avowed, "Oh how doth my Soul pity you, that ever ye should be so ignorant of your own Salvation, to turn the truth of our God into a ly, and put his Servants to death, when he sent them among you to warn you of the Wrath to come."[78] By killing Quakers, the colonial authorities destroyed a gift from God, according to Brooksop. Intolerance, in this view, was somewhat beside the point. They had acted against God by slaying his messengers—that was the main problem.

The Quaker writings about the executions served both polemical and hagiographic ends, and they did so in ways that distinguished them from other colonial martyr accounts. All hagiographies arguably include a component of persuasion, as they promote the idea that the deceased earned a martyr's laurels. The accounts thus served to persuade a mainly European audience that martyrdom had in fact occurred. Most American martyrs died at the hands of Native Americans. Accounts of these deaths were intended for an audience that did not include the perpetrators themselves. Those accounts attended to the motives of the killers only insofar as was necessary to prove that they acted in hatred of the faith of those who died. This criterion was essential to the canonization that hagiographers sought for their subjects. Beyond demonstrating this hatred, the accounts of Catholic martyrs in America pay little attention to the perpetrators but rather focus on the spiritual state of the victim. The audience for the Quaker martyrologies, however, included the very men responsible for the killings. The Quaker accounts therefore attacked the responsible parties, naming names and demanding justice.[79] Chastising the persecutor and calling for repentance were major features of all these tracts, giving them an element that was lacking in other colonial martyrologies.

Although the Quakers and their oppressors were all part of the same community of discourse, able to participate in pamphlet exchanges about the meaning of the deaths in Boston, they were divided in fundamental ways. Quakers rejected the Bay Colony's belief that salvation was limited to a handful of elect, arguing instead that it was available to all comers. The Quakers' missionary zeal arose from the dual conviction that all could be saved (if they would only open themselves to the light or seed within) and that time was short. These beliefs made them aggressive proselytizers. At the same time, their theology of the light, their insistence that Scripture was only one source of divine inspiration, and their hostility to an established ministry made them dangerous radicals in the eyes of the Massachusetts establishment. The colony's commitment to defending orthodoxy had been well established prior to the arrival of the Quaker witnesses, and the vehemence of the colony's response to them was predictable. Although the executions might seem to outsiders to represent a case of English Protestants killing their fellow English Protestants, the gulf that divided the Bay Colony establishment from those they hung was wide. So wide was it that the necessity of killing Quakers seemed, as the authorities declared, self-evident. As they complained in the prologue to their published justification, which they thought they should not even have to bother to publish; "The justice of our proceedings, supported by the authority of this Court, the lawes of this countrje, & the lawes of God, may rather perswade us to expect incouragement & comendation from all prudent & pious men, then convince us of any necessity to apologize for the same."[80] Other colonists echoed this confidence in the correctness of their position. Diarist John Hull remarked of the executions, "And well they deserved it."[81] Given their sense of the justice of their cause, the authorities would be stunned over the coming years to find their region becoming infamous for executing Quakers. As it would turn out, William Coddington was correct when he observed that New England would have "small cause to boast such murders."[82]

The four martyrs themselves sometimes got lost in this polemic, but this cannot be attributed to the controversial nature of the literature alone. Singling out four martyrs from all the suffering believers contradicted the Quakers' democratizing impulses. Every one of the faithful, as the martyrs-to-be reminded their coreligionists, partook of the love, the light, the seed that bound them together and to God. No one could be extraordinary in this schema. No opportunity for the heroic suffering of a select few (who—as Catholic saints—would then serve as intercessors for the rest of humanity) existed in this program. This difference helps to explain why the published litanies of suffering cataloged executed witnesses alongside those who endured fines, seizures, and whipping. All suffering was part of the same experience, the lamb's war that the convinced fought on behalf of the truth. To elevate the suffering of one over that of others violated this ethos. The listing of punishments on the title page of a 1660 anti-New England pamphlet—"22 have been banished upon pain of Death. 03 have been Martyred. 03 have had their Right-Ears cut. 01 hath been burned in the hand with the letter H. 31 have received 650 stripes. 01 was beat while his body was like a jelly"—was intended to underscore the brutality of the persecutors. It also worked against privileging any one affliction over the others.[83] Suffering for the seed was the goal. As Mary Dyer stated prior to her death: "It's not mine own Life I seek, (for I chuse rather to suffer with the people of God, than to enjoy the Pleasures of Egypt) but the Life of the Seed, which I know the Lord hath blessed."[84] To privilege Dyer's accomplishment, or that of any of the martyred men, was in a sense to miss the point of the Quaker martyrs, who died to bring a universal and chiliastic faith to the world. Their martyrdom was a form of witness, like their preaching, and it was successful to the extent that it succeeded in the goal of converting others. Beyond that, it had no purpose and needed no special treatment.

For the Quakers, martyrdom would never lead to the vaunted status of the canonized saint. By dying as they did, the martyrs garnered no special accolades. They may have served as uplifting examples, but they were not exemplars in the way that a Catholic martyr could be. Their reward was the same as that of any of the faithful when they died. Although the Quakers cultivated the reputations of their martyrs, they rejected the spiritual hierarchy that made other martyrs candidates for sainthood. They also rejected the exclusionary vision of their New England adversaries, who posited that only a few were saved. For the Quakers, all could be saved, all those who were saved would suffer, and all who died in the faith could expect the same reward in heaven. Quakers may have been martyrs, but they died at the hands of self-professed saints who rejected their universal vision.

NOTES

1. For contemporary accounts see Edward Burrough, *Declaration of the Sad and Great Persecution* (London, 1660), 22–30; Marmaduke Stephenson [and William Robinson], *A Call from Death to Life* (London, 1660); George Bishop, *New England Judged, Not by Man's, but by the Spirit of the Lord* (London, 1661). Many short notices of these events appeared in contemporary accounts; see, for instance [John Josselyn], *Chronological Observations of America* (London, 1674), reprinted in *Collections of the Massachusetts Historical Society*, 3rd ser., 3 (1883): 389. Histories of the early Quakers include Hugh J. Barbour, *The Quakers in Puritan New England*, Yale Publications in Religion 7 (New Haven, Conn.: Yale University Press, 1964), and Barry Reay, *The Quakers and the English Revolution* (London: Temple Smith, 1985). On the executions in particular, see Rufus M. Jones, *The Quakers in the American Colonies* (New York: W. W. Norton, 1966), 79–86, Carla Gardina Pestana, *Quakers and Baptists in Colonial Massachusetts* (Cambridge: Cambridge University Press, 1991), 32–36, and "The City upon a Hill under Siege: The Puritan Perception of the Quaker Threat to Massachusetts Bay, 1656–1661," *New England Quarterly* 56 (1983): 323–53. The armed guard ordered by the court was one hundred men, although many Quaker sources put the number at two hundred; see *The Records of the Governor and Company of the Massachusetts Bay,* ed. Nathaniel B. Shurtleff, 5 vols in 6 (Boston, 1854), 383.
2. French Protestants were killed in Florida in 1565 by Spanish Catholics in an effort to root out heresy (and rival claimants) from the Americas; see David J. Weber, *The Spanish Frontier in North America* (New Haven, Conn.: Yale University Press, 1992), 61–63.
3. See Judith Perkins, *The Suffering Self: Pain and Narrative Representation in the Early Christian Era* (New York: Routledge, 1995).
4. Francis Higginson, *Irreligion of the Northern Quakers* (London, 1653), reprinted in *Early Quaker Writings, 1650–1700,* ed. Hugh Barbour and Arthur O. Robinson (Grand Rapids, Mich., 1973), 70.
5. Leo Damrosch, *The Sorrows of the Quaker Jesus: James Nayler and the Puritan Crackdown on the Free Spirit* (Cambridge, Mass.: Harvard University Press, 1996). Christopher Hill, *The World Turned Upside Down* (London, 1972), 249–50, sees the Nayler incident as a turning point in the English Revolution.
6. An account of the treatment accorded Quakers in Massachusetts was published in London just as the Nayler case was in the news; *Mercurius Politicus* 34 (December 18–24, 1656): 7450, 7451, 7466 (mispaginated).
7. The laws against Quakers can be found in *Records of the Governor and Company of the Massachusetts Bay in New England,* VI, part i, 277–78, 308–14, 321, 345–47. John Norton, *Heart of New England Rent* (Cambridge, 1659), 54, made the claim of self-defense. T. Canby Jones, "The Bible: Its Authority and Dynamic in George Fox and Contemporary Quakerism," *Quaker Religious Thought* 4 (1962): 20.
8. Anonymous letter, printed in Frederick B. Tolles, ed., "A Quaker's Curse—Humphrey Norton to John Endicott, 1658," *The Huntington Library Quarterly* 14 (1951): 420.
9. William Robinson's Letter to George Whitehead, George Fox, and George Rofe, July 12, 1659, *Collections of the Massachusetts Historical Society,* ser. 4, vol. 9 (1872): 154.
10. On the general trend see Richard T. Vann, "Friends Sufferings—Collected and Recollected," *Quaker History* 61 (1972): 24–35. For early New England examples see Francis Howgill, *Popish Inquisition newly erected in New-England* (London, 1659); Humphrey Norton, *New England Ensigne* (London, 1659); *New England a Degenerate Plant Who having forgot their former Sufferings, and lost their ancient tenderness, are now become famous among the nations in bringing forth the fruits of cruelty* (London, 1659).
11. George Fox, *The Secret works of a Cruel People made Manifest* (London, 1659), 15.
12. Fox, *The Secret works of a Cruel People,* 16. Also see *Cain against Abel* (London, 1675), 4, 30.
13. Jones, "The Bible: Its Authority and Dynamic," 20. Brad S. Gregory, *Salvation at Stake: Christian Martyrdom in Early Modern Europe* (Cambridge, Mass.: Harvard University Press, 1999), 61. On the centrality of sufferings to Quaker identity see Richard L. Greaves, "The 'Great Persecution' Reconsidered: The Irish Quakers and the Ethic of Suffering," in *Protestant Identities: Religion, Society, and Self-Fashioning in Post-Reformation England,* ed. Muriel C. McClendon, Joseph P. Ward, and Michael MacDonald (Stanford, Calif.: Stanford University Press, 200), 212–13.
14. Brad S. Gregory, *Salvation at Stake: Christian Martyrdom in Early Modern Europe.*
15. Alfonso de Villegas' *Flos Sanctorum* appeared in English translation in Douai (1609, 1614, 1615, 1624), St. Omer (1621, 1623, 1634, 1638), and Rouen (1628, 1636). *The Golden Legend* was published in London ten times between 1483 and 1527. See *The English Short-Title Catalogue (1475–1640),* comp. A. W. Pollard and G. R. Redgrave; and *The English Short-Title Catalogue (1640–1700),* comp. Donald G. Wing.
16. My argument shares common elements with works by Margo Todd and Charles Hambrick-Stowe, which have shown how English "Puritans" participated in European intellectual and pietistic traditions of long standing. See Todd, *Christian Humanism and the Puritan Social Order* (Cambridge, 1987); and Hambrick-Stowe, *The Practice of Piety: Puritan Devotional Disciplines in Seventeenth-Century New England* (Chapel Hill, N.C., 1982).

17. "Copy of W. R. his Letter to the Lord's People," October 23, 1658, in Stephenson, *A Call from Death to Life,* 29.

18. "A brief Relation of the Bloody Sentence of Death" in Edward Burrough, *A Declaration of the Sad and Great Persecution* (London, 1660), 23. The same story also appears in Stephenson, *A Call from Death to Life,* 26.

19. Account of Peter Peirson, printed in Burrough, *A Declaration of the Sad and Great Persecution,* 24.

20. Account of Peter Peirson, 26.

21. William Leddra, letter from Boston Goal, March 13, 1661, printed in William Robinson, *Several Epistles given Forth* (London, 1669), 10.

22. Account of Peter Peirson, 24.

23. Ibid.

24. Ibid., 30.

25. Thomas Wilkie to Mr. George Lad, March 26, 1661, printed in Bishop, *New England Judged* (1661), 197.

26. David D. Hall, *Worlds of Wonder, Days of Judgment: Popular Religious Belief in Early New England* (New York: Alfred A. Knopf, 1989), 188–89.

27. George Bishop, *New England Judged: The Second Part* (London, 1667), 26. For Stephen see *The Acts of the Apostles,* 6:59. John R. Knott takes this dying speech as evidence of the Quakers' reliance on John Foxe's *The Actes and Monuments of these Latter Perillous Dayes* (London, 1563). But, of course, the source may well have been the Bible, unmediated by Foxe. See *Discourses of Martyrdom in English Literature, 1563–1694* (New York: Cambridge University Press, 1993), 221.

28. Account of Peter Peirson, 24.

29. The expectation for a martyr's death is described in Warren W. Wooden, *John Foxe* (Boston: Twayne, 1983), 44. For a "good death" more generally see Ralph Houlbrooke, *Death, Religion, and the Family in England, 1480–1750* (Oxford: Clarendon Press, 1998), ch. 7.

30. "Copy of W. R. his Letter to the Lord's People," October 23, 1658, in Stephenson, *A Call from Death to Life,* 28–29. "The Seed" in this passage refers to "the Seed of redemption, which is Christ"; also known as "the Measure, the Light, and, rarely [in the writings of George Fox], that of God in every man." See Jones, "The Bible: Its Authority and Dynamic," 19.

31. Daniel Boyarin, *Dying for God: Martyrdom and the Making of Christianity and Judaism* (Stanford, Calif.: Stanford University Press, 1999), 107.

32. William Robinson's Letter to George Whitehead, George Fox, and George Rofe, 12 July 1659, *Collections of the Massachusetts Historical Society,* ser. 4, vol. 9 (1872): 154.

33. "Copy of W. R. his Letter to the Lord's People," October 23, 1658, in Stephenson, *A Call from Death to Life,* 28–29.

34. "Copy of M.S. Letter to the Lords People," n.d., in Stephenson, *A Call from Death to Life,* 26.

35. Ibid., 27.

36. Bishop, *New England Judged,* (1661), 93. See Song of Solomon for this passage.

37. Bishop, *New England Judged* (1661), 110.

38. Ibid., p. 83

39. Ibid.

40. Ibid.

41. On Roman Catholic saints and uncorrupted bodies see Donald Weinstein and Rudolph M. Bell, *Saints & Society: The Two Worlds of Western Christendom, 100–1700* (Chicago: University of Chicago Press, 1982), 50; Caroline Walker Bynum, *The Resurrection of the Body in Western Christianity, 200–1336* (New York: Columbia University Press, 1995). Russian Orthodox adherence to these ideas is discussed in Eve Levin, "From Corpses to Cult in Early Modern Russia," unpublished paper.

42. Foxe, *The Actes and Monuments.* William M. Lamont, *Godly Rule: Politics and Religion, 1603–1660* (London: Macmillan, 1969), 24–25, 78–79.

43. George Bishop, *New England Judged: The Second Part* (London, 1667), 24. Also see reference in Edward Burrough, *Declaration of the Sad and Great Persecution* (London, 1660), 29.

44. For Bishop referring to Anglican persecution of the New Englanders see *New England Judged,* 139; for George Fox using the Church of England in the same way see *Secret Works of a Cruel People,* 16, quoted above.

45. See for instance, William Coddington, *A Demonstration of True Love* (London, 1674), and John Whiting, *Truth and Innocency Defended against Falsehood and Envy* (London, 1702), 77. Barbour, *Quakers in Puritan England,* 4–5, discusses the Quakers' use of Foxe, citing a 1653 example of Margaret Fell, who used it to get George Fox released from prison.

46. John Marbeck, *The Lyves of Holy Sainctes, Prophets, Patriarches, and Others in Holy Scripture* ([London], 1574); quotation from R. A. Leaver, *The Work of John Marbeck* ([Oxford], 1978), 72.

47. Bishop, *New England Judged* (1661), 189.

48. Joseph Besse, *A Collection of the Sufferings of the People Called Quakers,* 3 vols., (London, 1733, 1738), II: 210.

49. George Fox, *Something in Answer to a Law Lately made* (London, 1679), 9. Also see George Fox "Paper to Magistrates," misdated 1657, in *The Swarthmore Documents in America,* ed. Henry J. Cadbury (London: Friends' Historical Society, 1940), 42–46. In *Cain against Abel* (London? 1675), Fox used a different biblical image, casting New England as the murderous brother of Genesis.

50. Bishop, *New England Judged: The Second Part,* 29.

51. For the Quaker reference, see Thomas Maule, *An Abstract of a Letter to Cotton Mather* ([New York], 1701), 6. The devotional classic that made this connection was Thomas à Kempis, *Imitatio Christi* (1424), or "The Imitation of Christ."

52. John Richardson, *An Account of the Life of . . . John Richardson* (Philadelphia, 1783), 23–24.

53. Humphrey Norton, *New England's Ensigne* (London, 1659), 72.

54. Knott, *Discourses of Martyrdom in English Literature,* 34, 236. On this latter point see also the discussion in Nigel Smith, *Perfection Proclaimed: Language and Literature in English Radical Religion, 1640–1660* (Oxford: Clarendon Press: 1989), 25. Henry J. Cadbury explores how the Quaker movement saw itself as paralleling that of the early Christians in *Quakerism and Early Christianity,* Swarthmore Lecture 1957 (London: George Allen & Unwin, 1957). The relationship that Quakers saw between their own and biblical times differed radically from the views of their opponents; see a helpful discussion in Theodore Dwight Bozeman, *To Live Ancient Lives: The Primitivist Dimension in Puritanism* (Chapel Hill: University of North Carolina Press, 1988), app. 3, "Separatists and Quakers," 364–68.

For a most helpful discussion of all these issues see Melvin B. Endy Jr., "Puritanism, Spiritualism, and Quakerism: An Historiographical Essay," in *The World of William Penn,* ed. Richard S. Dunn and Mary Maples Dunn (Philadelphia: University of Pennsylvania Press, 1986), 281–301.

55. Gregory, *Salvation at Stake,* 328; Helen C. White, *Tudor Books of Saints and Martyrs* (Madison: University of Wisconsin Press, 1963), 144, notes that it was widely accepted at the time that "if heresy disturbs the peace of the commonwealth, the severity of the magistrates is justified."

56. John Norton, *The Heart of New England Rent* (Cambridge, 1659; revised ed., London, 1660). For the arguments discussed in this paragraph see esp. 73, 74–75, 94, 95, 82 (mispaginated), 66. For the order to Norton to produce the tract see *Records of the Governor and Company of the Massachusetts Bay,* ed. Shurtleff, 4, part i, 348. The broadside and manuscript are in Shurtleff, 384–90.

57. Norton, *Heart of New England Rent,* 52–53. For a discussion of other references see Pestana, "The Puritan Perception of the Quaker Threat to Massachusetts Bay, 1656–1661," 338–40.

58. John Norton, *An Appendix* [*to the Heart of New England Rent*] (London, 1660), 93.

59. Bishop, *New England Judged* (1661), 119.

60. The first two-thirds of Norton's *Heart of New England Rent* is dedicated to proving this point.

61. *Memoirs of Roger Clap, 1630* (Boston, 1731); reprint ed., 1844; 2nd ed., 1854, Collections of the Dorchester Antiquarian and Historical Society.

62. Bishop, *New England Judged,* 93.

63. John Hull, "Some Observable Passages of Providence toward the Country," printed as "John Hull's Diary of Public Occurrences" in *Transactions and Collections of the American Antiquarian Society* III (1857): 182. "The Autobiographical Memorandum of John Brock," American Antiquarian Society, *Proceedings* 53 (1943): 105.

64. Christopher Holder [and John Rous], The *Faith and Testimony of the Martyrs and Suffering Servants of Christ Jesus persecuted in New England vindicated, against the lyes and Slanders cast on them by Nathaniel Morton* (London, 1670), 6.

65. Besse, *A Collection of the Sufferings of the People Called Quakers.*

66. Besse, *A Collection of the Sufferings of the People Called Quakers,* II, 207.

67. Ibid., 219–20.

68. Hugh Barbour and J. William Frost, *The Quakers,* Denominations in America, vol. 3 (New York: Greenwood Press, 1988), 96.

69. Quoted in Thomas J. Curry, *The First Freedoms: Church and State in America to the Passing of the First Amendment* (New York, Oxford University Press, 1986), 131.

70. James Dickinson, "A Journal of the Life and Travels of James Dickinson," in *The Friends Library,* ed. William Evans and Thomas Evans, vol. 12 (Philadelphia, 1848), 371.

71. Cotton Mather, *Little Flocks Guarded against Grievous Wolves* (Boston, 1691), 100.

72. John Richardson, *An Account of the Life of . . . John Richardson* (Philadelphia, 1783), 23–24, 25. John Gratton, "Journal of the Life of John Gratton," in *The Friends Library,* ed. William Evans and Thomas Evans, vol. 9 (Philadelphia, 1845), 296–97, 299. Also see "Memoirs of the Life and Convincement of Benjamin Bangs" in *The Friends Library,* ed. William Evans and Thomas Evans, vol. 4 (Philadelphia, 1840), 215.

73. William Coddington to John Winthrop Jr., June 29, 1672, *Collections of the Massachusetts Historical Society,* ser. 4, VII (1865), 287.

74. For one instance among many see *The Diary of Caleb Cresson* (Philadelphia, 1877), 69, 70–71.

75. Carla Gardina Pestana, "The Quaker Executions as Myth and History," *Journal of American History* 80 (1993): 441–69.

76. George Joy, *Innocency's Complaint against Tyrannical Court Faction in New England* [Boston, 1677].

77. For a discussion of some of the literature see Pestana, "Quaker Executions as Myth and History."

78. Jone Brooksop, *An Invitation of love unto the Seed of God Throughout the World* (London [1662]), 14.

79. See, for example, the contemporary works cited in n. 1 above.

80. *Records of the Governor and Company of the Massachusetts Bay,* ed. Shurtleff, 4, part i, 384.

81. Hull, "Some Observable Passages," 189.

82. Coddington, *Demonstration of True Love,* 8.

83. Burrough, *A Declaration of the Sad and Great Persecution.*

84. Account of Peter Peirson, 26.

10

St. Palafox: Metaphorical Images of Disputed Sainthood

ANTONIO RUBIAL GARCÍA

> To invent is to draw out something that has not been seen before and has not been imitated in another.
> —Sebastián de Cobarruvias, *Tesoro de la lengua castellana* (Madrid, 1611)

Before the Enlightenment, in the languages derived from Latin, the word "invent" possessed a meaning that related to showing, teaching, and making known. Narratives—historical, pictorial, and literary—were all understood to be "inventions"; the word was even used to describe religious events. The "invention of the Cross," for example, referred to the finding of this relic by St. Helena, the mother of Emperor Constantine. Therefore, to "invent" was not to fabricate falsehood, as it is for us, but to recount reality.

Invention, nevertheless, must follow certain canons and make use of various resources, in accordance with the guidelines of the queen of the liberal arts: rhetoric. To become valuable and to legitimize its veracity, a good invention should use the multiple resources of demonstrative nature: praising of virtues, condemnation of vices, elaboration, *exempla,* proofs, digression, and citation of authorities, such as the Bible or Christian or Greco-Latin authors. Such appeals are directed at fulfilling three basic objectives: to teach moral behavior *(docere),* to entertain *(delectare),* and to arouse feelings of repudiation or admiration *(movere).* These objectives were as valuable for literature and history as they were for genre painting, whose narrative function favors strong connections to rhetoric.

In contrast to what occurs in reality, the criteria of veracity used in such disciplines gave much less importance to what actually happened, and instead placed greater emphasis on the moral teaching that the fact brought with it. That is to say, the truth did not have as much to do with what *was* as it did with what *should be.* In the final instance its value was determined by the extent to which it could serve as a guide for journeying through the world on the path toward eternal salvation.

This technique was especially valuable in the creation of portraits or texts of a biographical nature, and even more so when dealing with important figures associated with the church. (It also was used extensively by the nobility and the state.) In the narration of the life or the presentation of the image of its most outstanding members, the saints, the church felt the necessity of emphasizing the exemplary aspects of their religious and moral behavior.

New Spain, included in Western canons since the sixteenth century, found it necessary from 1700 onward to *invent* (that is to say, to make known) the lives and images of men and women of outstanding sanctity. This need became more urgent during the eighteenth century, given that Rome did not officially authorize the veneration of any of these people by the faithful of the church.

One of these figures was Juan de Palafox, bishop of Puebla, a man of outstanding political achievement between 1640 and 1649. Among other positions, he held those of king's inspector, interim archbishop of Mexico, and viceroy. His disputes with the religious orders, especially the Society of Jesus, were a central feature of his career in New Spain, and they colored his political and religious image, in Europe as much as in America, for more than a century following his death. The bishop's defense of the rights of the king over those of the church, together with the stubborn opposition of the Jesuits, transformed Palafox's image into a political flag. In fact, his beatification process (initiated between 1665 and 1690) was strongly connected with the fight between Jansenists and Jesuits early in the eighteenth century. It also was linked to the battle that pitted enlightened royalists against papal authority in the eighteenth century.

Although the Palafoxian cause developed mostly in Europe, New Spain—and especially the city of Puebla—were intimately involved. Here Palafox would be converted not only into the most complete model of episcopal sanctity, but also into a glorious and heroic figure. Pueblans challenging the religious primacy of Mexico City, the viceregal capital, took special pride in their bishop-hero and expressed their local patriotism in popular narratives and legends about Palafox. These stories range from the apocryphal tale that tells how Bishop Palafox ordered an honorific epitaph to be inscribed in the tomb of Catalina de Erauzo (the Monja-Alférez, who died in 1650), and how he even attempted to bring her bones to the city of Puebla.[1] The apocryphal news (the prelate left New Spain in 1649) illustrates one of the most useful Baroque techniques employed to give credibility to what is narrated: the endorsement of an authority. This process of mythification appears also in the numerous popular legends recorded by Brother Francisco de Ajofrín, who associated Palafox with miraculous deeds, such as the elimination of mosquitoes from a certain area, or the protection from storms and lightning for an altar he placed in Cholula.[2] Pueblans followed the bishop's process of beatification with great interest, and its successes became the occasion for ostentatious festivities that sometimes ended in brawls.

Palafox's presence in the collective unconscious of Mexico, especially in Puebla, may lead us to expect a rich and extensive hagiography. But in fact the hagiography is extremely limited as compared with that devoted to other important Pueblan saints, such as Sister María de Jesús Tomellín. The only substantial biography of Bishop Palafox known to be written before 1900 was composed and published in Madrid in 1666, immediately after the opening of the beatification process, by his friend Antonio González de Rosende.[3] The work, which presented Palafox as a hero against the Jesuits, was adapted by various learned authors in New Spain during the eighteenth century: Diego Antonio Bermúdez de Castro related his life in his *Teatro Angelopolitano* of 1746, and Cardinal Francisco Antonio de Lorenzana included a biography of him in his edition of *Concilios provinciales mexicanos*. Nevertheless, the impact of such texts must have been quite small.

What, then, was the medium by which Bishop Palafox became so popular during the eighteenth century? Undoubtedly the most efficient propaganda medium, apart from sermons, was the iconography that emerged at the time of his beatification process. As a consequence we are left with abundant examples of engravings, pictures, and canvases. These images take a variety of forms.

The most common form of portraiture of the Pueblan bishop was traditional in its representation of religious figures: he is standing, surrounded by symbols of his post (miters, crosiers, and crosses) and with pens, inkwells, and books, signs of his enormous literary production, both theological and juridical. The first portrait of which we are aware is that by the painter Diego de Borgraf. Among the innumerable portraits of this type, almost all are of medium size, for they were made to be hung in sacristies and chapter halls. We also find oval portraits of small size, which only show the bishop's torso. From their size, they appear to be devotional objects made at a moment hopeful of imminent beatification.

The multiplication of portraits of the bishop began, in fact, when Palafox was still living. In an edict of 1653, the Tribunal of the Holy Office prohibited the circulation of his portraits because people made offerings of candles to them and gathered them at shrines in their homes, along with those of canonized saints.[4] The Inquisition, which ordered them to be confiscated, collected nearly six thousand of them in Mexico alone.[5] During his lifetime, the bishop had attacked the tribunal for corruption, a circumstance that helps to explain the Inquisition's persecution of Palafox's memory.[6] In spite of this prohibition, the cult continued. Another edict, of 1675, again denounced people who invoked Palafox in their time of need, "placing some of his portraits by the sick" and circulating "a brief compendium about his life which refers to several miracles and does not have the statement of objection that Holy Father Urban VIII ordered."[7] In 1691 yet another edict banned portraits of the bishop, which were now appearing beside those of Catarina de San Juan, the converted Hindu slave turned holy lay sister who had recently died:[8]

> While some documents confirmed the confiscation of portraits, several others requested permission to keep the prohibited images. In a 1674 letter, Pueblan painter Juan Rubí de Marimount asked to paint a copy of a portrait of Palafox owned by Bachiller Francisco Lorente. The latter had a license from the Inquisition to keep his portrait despite the general ban. . . . Although they initially approved Rubi's request, the inquisitors rescinded his license in 1680 after becoming frustrated by the volume of similar petitions.[9]

There is no doubt that this extended use of the Palafoxian image was the result of successful propaganda by the secular clergy against the regulars. The latter had reproached Palafox for secularizing (i.e., turning over to the secular clergy) the regular parish churches in 1641.

Such veneration remained alive even at the close of the eighteenth century. Beristain recounts that "there is hardly a cloister, palace, or hut where you do not find one or more portraits of the *venerable señor,* who is known and worshiped by this epithet."[10]

In the eighteenth century another kind of image appears. At this time, depictions of the bishop begin to show him surrounded by emblems and allegorical figures. The source of inspiration was an engraving made in Madrid in 1665 and published in the *Vida* by Antonio González Rosende. In explicating the drawing, the author associates Palafox with glory and renown. The drawing includes symbols that represent his work as a writer, the triumph over enemies, the defense of episcopal authority, and the perfect equilibrium that Palafox achieved between virtue and power. In the drawing, moral instruction leads to a meditation on the brevity of life and the necessity to practice asceticism and Christian devotion to save oneself.

Rosende's model served to exalt the figure of Palafox in engravings as much as in large-size paintings. An example of the former is a drawing by Vicente Espejo commissioned by the Carmelites. Its many copies served to collect alms for the bishop's beatification process. Palafox is depicted along with episcopal emblems (crosier, cross, and miter) and military symbols (drums, bugles, and flags), and beneath is a heart wrought with a crucifix. Many copies of this drawing were seized by the Inquisition in one of its numerous campaigns against the spread of Palafox's image.[11]

Even so, the allegorical schema spread most widely during the eighteenth century through large paintings. We know of at least three examples of these, all of which are associated with the Carmelites. (See figure 10-1 for one version of this image.) In these three oil paintings, six female figures and one male figure are gathered together with traditional emblems. In the lower part of the painting, four women represent Faith (with a miter and the Eucharist), Fortitude (associated with the virtue of constancy and victory, represented by a packsaddle and an olive branch next to a crown of laurels), Wisdom (with a book and a star on her brow), and Prudence (who holds a mirror on which is tangled an asp). The life and works of the prelate are alluded to in cartouches and phylacteries. In the extreme upper left there is a woman, representing the soul, emitting a stream of light from her breast, in which are images of the Holy Spirit and Sts. John the Evangelist and John the Baptist. This is a clear allusion to

Figure 10-1

Miguel Cabrera, *Allegories of the Virtues of Palafox,* 1765. Museo de Arte Colonial, Morelia, Mexico. Courtesy of the Instituto Michoachan de Cultura.

the third John: Juan Palafox. Below her, a temple and a masculine figure crowned with the miter symbolize the institutional church and the cathedral of Puebla to which the prelate put the finishing touches. A St. Teresa of Avila in the upper right of the painting completes the emblems and refers to the relations between the Carmelite order and the man portrayed. Beside the saint's mouth is a cartouche with Isaiah's phrase (57:21) "My Spirit is with you." In the lower portion of the painting the open book "the epistle of St. Teresa of Avila commented on by Palafox" completes the Carmelite allusions in these paintings.[12]

This same emblematic, Carmelite, construction can be found in an enormous canvas in the transept chapel of the church of Carmen in Puebla (figure 10-2). In it, Palafox uses his hand to divert water from a fountain to the mouths of various sheep at his feet. He is watched by saints (and by

Figure 10-2

Anonymous, *Juan de Palafox on Mount Carmel with Friars and Nuns*, oil painting, eighteenth century. Convento del Carmen, Puebla, Mexico. Courtesy government of Mexico, Conaculta.

the prophet Elijah) as well as by distinguished Carmelites of his own family (among them his mother Ana de Casanate, named in religion Sor Ana de la Madre de Dios, and her three brothers and two sisters) who move about in a paradise of trees, flowers, and birds. St. John of the Cross and St. Teresa, sitting on a small hill, write in books and give out phylacteries alluding to Palafox's works and sufferings. In the upper right of the painting, volume VII of the bishop's works is placed above a palm tree, making allusion to his commentaries on the works of St. Teresa of Avila. In the upper left of the painting, volume VI, the mystic book of Palafox, *Varón de deseos* (*Man of Desires*), appears above another palm tree. At the bottom of the canvas, the biblical text from Ecclesiasticus 15:3 imparts meaning to the entire composition: "She [the law] will give him . . . the water of wisdom to drink."

The abundance of Palafoxian works associated with the Carmelites is not unwarranted: they were the most faithful promoters of his cause for beatification between 1760 and 1768, perhaps because the prelate's life was closely associated with their order. Palafox himself had commented on and published an epistolary of St. Teresa; she and St. John of the Cross played important roles in his conversion; and his mother, two aunts, and three uncles joined this religious order. Moreover, the Carmelites were his only support in the face of Jesuit persecution; they suffered the same fate as he for being his spies, messengers, and agents. For all these reasons, and because of the great love it had for Palafox, the Carmelite order revered him, and placed him in the company of their most notable bishops. An example of this Carmelite devotion to Palafox may be seen in the painting of the Virgin of Carmen in the temple of Soledad in Puebla. In this work, the prelate resembles a donor beneath the image, and he is located on a second plane, behind St. John of the Cross and St. Teresa.

A third group of representations transformed the figure of Palafox into a metaphor and placed him in paintings with a historical theme. The first examples of this type of representation also date back to the middle of the seventeenth century, when the bishop was still living. His chamber painter, Pedro García Ferrer, painted him as a shepherd leaning on his staff in the Nativity scene that decorated the altar of the kings of the Pueblan cathedral. The representation not only alludes to the bishop's role as shepherd of his flock; it also recalls Palafox's work titled *El pastor de Nochebuena* (*The Christmas Eve Shepherd*).[13]

The painting by García Ferrer is part of a long tradition born in the Renaissance. At that time it was common in paintings on a biblical theme for patrons and painters to be portrayed as characters in the scene. In the eighteenth century, however, Palafox appeared in ways that departed from the conventions of Western art. His face was superimposed onto historical figures related to the lives of various saints.

An example of this approach may be found in a painting in the series dedicated to the life of St. John of God by the artists Berrueco and Talavera for a clinic run by the hospital brothers in Atlixco (figure 10-3). Here, Palafox takes the place of the bishop of Tuy, Brother Sebastián Ramírez de Fuenleal. He places on St. John the habit later to be worn by the order the latter founded. The selection of Palafox's face to represent Bishop Fuenleal was not made at random. Before being bishop of Tuy (between 1528 and 1535), Brother Sebastián had held the position of bishop of Santo Domingo and president of the second *audiencia* of New Spain, in which he distinguished himself through acts in support of indigenous peoples. The parallels with Juan de Palafox are obvious: both were Spaniards with political and ecclesiastical offices in the Indies; both had been defend-

Figure 10-3

Luis Berrueco, *The Life of St. John of God,* oil painting, eighteenth century. Palafox appears as the seated bishop of Tuy. Church of San Juan de Dios, Atlixco, Puebla, Mexico.

ers of the poor and promoters of works for their benefit; and finally, both had occupied an episcopal see upon their return to Spain.

On other occasions, the episcopal allusions were closer in time to Palafox. In the sanctuary of San Miguel del Milagro, an anonymous painting from the end of the seventeenth century represents Diego Lázaro, an Indian to whom the archangel Michael appeared. Diego Lázaro is depicted as a water-carrier who brings the water of salvation before an episcopal figure who has Palafox's face. In fact, according to the narrative of the miracle by the Jesuit Francisco de Florencia, the bishop who witnessed the miracle was Gutierre Bernardo de Quiróz, a predecessor of Palafox in the Pueblan see. Perhaps the outstanding role that Palafox played in the spread of this cult can explain this iconographic license.

Palafox received the same treatment in another anonymous painting that belongs to a series on the life of St. Nicholas of Tolentino (figure 10-4). Since a legend written in the lower part says that it was commissioned by Brother Miguel de Jáuregui, prior of Puebla, the work must have been kept in the convent of St. Augustine in Puebla. Today, however, it is found in the Augustinian convent of Atlixco. The oil painting is divided into two parallel scenes that refer to a miracle by the prodigious saint,

Figure 10-4

Anonymous, *Miracle of St. Nicholas of Tolentino,* oil painting, eighteenth century. Palafox appears as a bishop receiving sacred relics. Eighteenth century. Convent of San Agustín, Atlixco, Puebla, Mexico. Courtesy of the government of Mexico, Conaculta.

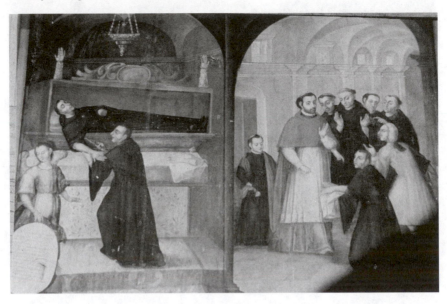

whom Pueblans also swore was their patron against lightning in 1753. The first scene tells the anecdote of the German friar who cut off the arms of St. Nicholas' corpse to take them back to his native land as relics. According to the quotation painted in oil, despite the fact that Nicholas had been dead for forty years, the mutilated limbs gushed blood, a powerful remedy against fatal accidents. It is curious that the metal reliquary that would later hold the arms appears above the tomb. Beholding such a miracle, the devout thief was obliged to notify the prior of the convent. From then on, so the legend goes, the arms have sweated and bled, announcing famines, wars, and plagues. At the beginning of the fourteenth century, numerous bishops of Tolentino attested to this miracle and celebrated it with great solemnity, affirming that the saint's blood would protect and defend the church. In 1656 Pope Alexander VI ordered an inquiry to make public the cult of these relics. In 1700, several decades before the Atlixco picture was painted, Bishop Mazerata authorized the cult as a result of a miracle that occurred just prior to the War of the Spanish Succession.[14] These episcopal endorsements are shown in the right-hand panel of the painting, in which a monk presents the miraculous, sacred relics before one of the

Tolentino bishops, whose face possesses Palafox's features. The strangest thing about this painting is that it was preserved by a religious order, though that fact is not incomprehensible. In spite of the fact that the bishop had secularized three parochial churches of this order during his administration, many Augustinians were drawn in the eighteenth century to the anti-Jesuit cause, so much so that several of their most distinguished members were accused of Jansenism.

But how does one explain Palafox's presence in a painting with clear Jesuit roots, such as the one by Cristóbal de Talavera in 1730 (figure 10-5)? The oil painting is currently in the university museum in Puebla, although it must have belonged to the College of Jesuits. It represents Father Baltasar Alvarez, the Jesuit confessor of St. Teresa, who appears teaching the spiritual exercises of St. Ignatius to four prototypical figures: a knight, a Jesuit priest, a soldier, and a bishop. The bishop, in contrast to the others, is not a stereotype but Palafox himself, toward whom the Jesuit has shown special deference by putting his hand on his lap. Were there perhaps Jesuits in Puebla who sympathized with the Palafoxian cause? Or was the painting an attempt to ease the tensions between the partisans and the opponents of the society, tensions that had as one of their points of conflict the very figure of Bishop Palafox? A few years later, in 1753, María Narváez appeared before the tribunal of the Inquisition in Mexico City to denounce two Jesuit priests: "She testified that while her brother lay dying, the pair refused to hear his confession until Palafox's engraved portrait was removed from the wall above his bed."[15]

Up to this point, representations of Palafox did not directly allude to any aspirations to sanctity, since the Holy Congregation of Rites had not yet approved the cult. Nevertheless, there are at least two paintings in which Palafox's face is used to represent canonized saints. One of these, a work by José de Ibarra depicting various people adoring the Eucharist, is in the cathedral in Puebla (figure 10-6). One of these, San Pedro de Osma, bishop of Osma from 1101 to 1109, is shown with Palafox's face. Palafox occupied the same episcopal see as did San Pedro, though five hundred years later. However, there is another difference between them: Palafox died in this see and is buried in it, while San Pedro went on to become archbishop of Toledo. Was there perhaps a feeling that the deserving Palafox ought to have been similarly promoted rather than ending his days a minor bishop presiding over the village of Osma?

Figure 10-5

Cristóbal de Talavera, *Father Baltasar Alvarez*, 1730. This oil painting depicts the Jesuit confessor to St. Teresa of Avila teaching seated figures, one of which, a bishop, displays Palafox's facial features. Universidad Autónoma de Puebla.

Figure 10-6

José de Ibarra, *Adoration of the Eucharist,* oil painting, eighteenth century. One of the figures adoring the Eucharist, the medieval bishop San Pedro de Osma, has the face of Palafox. Cathedral of Puebla. Courtesy of the government of Mexico, Conaculta.

Another oil painting that portrays Palafox as a saint was by an anonymous artist and is kept in the sanctuary of the Virgin of the Light, which is also in Puebla. Palafox is represented as St. Ambrose in the series of the four church doctors. Comparing Palafox to the other bishop with the same see must not have seemed overly serious. However, likening him to one of the great doctors of the Latin church (also a bishop, but of Milan) must have bordered on heresy, notwithstanding Palafox's impressive theological production.

By the eighteenth century, the bishop of Puebla had, to New Spain's benefit, become the prototype of a Counter-Reformation bishop: charitable, reforming, virtuous. Yet, at the same time, he was also the model for Bourbon-era bishops: defenders of the monarchy's privileges over the church, indisputable leaders of the secular clergy, and promoters of the secularization of the regular parish churches in the mid-1700s. In an enormous painting in the sacristy of the cathedral of Puebla, Palafox is shown as one of the three key figures in the history of these and of the cathedral (figure 10-7). Beneath the protective cloak of the Immaculate Virgin are Bishop Domingo Pantaleón Álvarez Abreu and his chapter, patrons of the construction of the building. Next to them are Brother Julián Garcés,

Figure 10-7

José Joaquin Magón, *Patrocinio de la Inmaculada Concepción,* oil painting, 1750. This tableau commemorating the construction of the Cathedral of Puebla shows Juan de Palafox next to the Virgin. Cathedral of Puebla. Courtesy of the government of Mexico, Conaculta.

founder of the see, and Juan de Palafox, who completed the cathedral. The scene was painted in 1750 to commemorate Bishop Pantaleón Alvarez Abreu's edifice.

In addition to demonstrating the extraordinary growth in the veneration of the Aragonese bishop in Puebla, these paintings are proof of the enormous interest, among all elements of society, from the masses to the intellectual elite, in the success of the beatification process. The promoters and consumers of such images also contributed to the abundant alms that were collected in the cities of Spanish America, including Lima and Buenos Aires, for the beatification process. A sculpture of Palafox in the church of San José de Chiapas (where bishop Francisco Fabian y Fuero created a Palafox sanctuary in the second half of the eighteenth century) is evidence that his prompt beatification seemed imminent, as only canonized saints could be represented in sculpture. His image printed in several university dissertations (in a place traditionally occupied by canonized saints) shows the same confidence of success.[16]

Yet it never came to pass. Paradoxically, the dissolution of the Society of Jesus in 1773 weakened the cause of Palafox's beatification, as it made Pope Clement XIV anxious to avoid any further affronts to the sur-viving pro-Jesuit faction in the College of Cardinals.[17] After that date, Palafoxian iconography declined in New Spain, as did the reputation of the Aragonese bishop. Nevertheless, his image, exalted through rhetoric and paintings, had been the object of a process of invention without par-allel in the history of American colonial saintmaking.

NOTES

1. *Última y tercera relación en que se hace verdadera del resto de la vida de la Monja Alférez, sus memorables virtudes y ejemplar muerte en los reinos de Nueva España* (México: Imprenta de Hipólito de Rivera, 1653) in Rima de Vallbona, ed., *Vida y sucesos de la Monja Alférez* (Tempe: Arizona State University, 1992), Appendix 5, 174.

2. Francisco de Ajofrín, *Diario de viaje,* 2 v. (México: Instituto Cultural Hispano Mexicano, 1964), v. II, 15, and 202.

3. Antonio González Rosende, *Vida y virtudes del Illmo. y Exmmo. señor Ivan de Palafox y Mendoza* (Madrid: Julián Paredes, 1666); Antonio Rubial, "Las sutilezas de la gracia. El Palafox jansenista de la Europa ilustrada" en *Homenaje a Don Juan Antonio Ortega y Medina* (México: Instituto de Investigaciones Históricas, UNAM, 1983). Gregorio Bartolomé, *Jaque Mate al obispo virrey. Siglo medio de sátiras y líbelos contra don Juan de Palafox y Mendoza* (México: Fondo de Cultura Económica, 1991). Cristina de la Cruz Arteaga, *Una mitra sobre dos mundos. La del venerable Juan de Palafox y Mendoza, obispo de Puebla de los Angeles y de Osma* (Sevilla: Artes Gráficas Salesianas, 1985), 409.

4. Archivo General de la Nación, México [hereafter AGN], ramo Inquisición, sección Edictos, vol. III, folio 11; Gregorio M. Guijo, *Diario, 1648–1664.* 2 vols. (México: Porrua 1952), 1: 220; Genaro García, *Documentos inéditos y muy raros para la Historia de México,* 36 vols. (México: C. Bouret, 1905–11), 7: 157, letter from the viceroy duke of Albuquerque.

5. De la Cruz Arteaga, *Una mitra sobre dos mundos,* 409.

6. During Palafox's visit with the viceregal authorities, the inquisitors, including Juan Mañozca, launched a campaign to ruin his reputation. This included offensive satire and serious accusations of atheism. The inquisitors imposed harsh punishments (including excommunication) on many of his sympathizers in Puebla for considering their prelate to be a saint. Among his sympathizers were several nuns. José Toribio Medina, *Historia de la Inquisición en México* (México: Ediciones Fuente Cultural, 1952), 228, letter of Juan de Palafox, August 10, 1647.

7. AGN, Inquisición, v. 640, exp. 3, sheet 10r–10v, transcription by Juan García de Palacios, 1675.

8. AGN, Inquisición, sección edictos, vol. I, doc. 14.

9. Kelly Donahue-Wallace, "Prints and Printmakers in Viceregal Mexico City, 1600–1800" (Ph.D. diss., University of New Mexico, 2000), 285.

10. Mariano Beristain y Souza, *Biblioteca Hispanoamericana Septentriona,* 3 vols. (México: Universidad Nacional Autónoma de México, Instituto de Estudios y Documentos Históricos, 1980–81), 2: 432.

11. AGN, Inquisición, vol. 641, exp. 4, box 152, file folder 4.

12. Jaime Cuadriello et al., *Juegos de ingenio y agudeza* (México: Museo Nacional de Arte/CNCA, 1994), 248ff.

13. Mariano Fernández de Echeverría y Veytia, *Historia de la fundación de la ciudad de la Puebla de los Angeles en la Nueva España, su descripción y presente estado,* 2nd ed., 2 vols., ed. Efrain Castro Morales (Puebla: Ediciones Altiplano, 1962–1963), 2: 106.

14. Fray José Gil Ramírez, *Portentos milagrosos y devota novena del taumaturgo eremita . . . san Nicolás Tolentino,* ed. Teodosio Cruz Aedo (Guadalajara, 1839).

15. Donahue-Wallace, *Prints and Printmakers in Viceregal Mexico City,* 285.

16. Two examples of published dissertations bearing a portrait of Palafox on the title page can be found in the AGN: a medical dissertation by Joseph García Sarrieta and a theology dissertation by Joseph Mari Gil y Camino.

17. See Antonio Rubial García, *La santidad controvertida: Hagiografía y conciencia criolla alrededor de los venerables no canonizados de Nueva España* (Mexico City: UNAM, 1999), 230–37.

Part 3

THE USES OF THE SACRED

11

Writing a Relic: The Uses of Hagiography in New France

JULIA BOSS

During a 1998 visit to the Jesuit archives in St.-Jérôme, Quebec, I had a chance to see some of the community's great treasures. The archivist led me into the inner sanctum of rare book and document storage, and stopped in front of a tall, locked metal cabinet. On the wall above us hung a painting of the Jesuits' North American martyrs: in return for grisly deaths in the seventeenth-century mission field, their twentieth-century portraitist had rewarded them with postures of saintly devotion and a bed of billowing clouds, from which they now gazed down beatifically. The cabinet doors swung back to reveal a large silver-plated reliquary housing bone fragments from three of the martyred missionaries. On a shelf beside the reliquary was a red morocco box, and inside the box lay a bound manuscript, reverentially wrapped in dark blue velvet. That manuscript contained the central text in the hagiography of the Jesuit martyrs: "Memoires touchant la Mort et les Vertus des Pères Isaac Jogues, Anne de Noüe, Anthoine Daniel, Jean de Brébeuf, Gabriel Lallemant, Charles Garnier, Noël Chabanel et Un seculier René Goupil." It is also known as the "Manuscript of 1652."[1]

In modern collections, manuscripts and relics are often intermingled. In the Jesuit archives, contact relics—a piece of fabric that touched the martyrs' bones, a small packet of earth from the tomb of the beatified Mohawk woman Kateri Tekakwitha—are classified alongside the manuscripts that celebrate venerated persons' holy lives and miracles. Secular archives preserve similar objects. The Amherst College Library, for example, offers a lock of Noah Webster's hair along with his family papers. Yale's Beinecke Library recently devoted a special exhibition (called "Things") to the strange objects that had found their way into the university's libraries, everything from "Ezra Stiles's baptismal cap and dress (1727)" to "a piece of Napoleon's carriage."[2] Few historians are immune to the emotional response triggered by the objects, or manuscripts, that our subjects held in their hands: they make the past present. As historians living in an era of online sources and microfilm, we yet cling to a blind faith that the "originals" will lead us to some higher truth, and we may regard scholars just back from the archives with a curious reverence once reserved for pilgrims returning from Jerusalem. Encountering the "lives" of Jesuit martyrs in the pages of the closely guarded "Manuscript of 1652" is different from reading the "life" of Ursuline Marie de St.-Joseph in a leather-bound volume of the *Lettres de la Vénérable Mère Marie de l'Incarnation* (printed in Paris in 1681), which is in turn unlike reading on microfiche a copy of Paul Ragueneau's 1671 *Vie de la Mère Catherine de Saint-Augustin*.

These are familiar observations; perhaps, in a sense, too familiar. I have begun this chapter at the archivist's cabinet to suggest that even as scholars have become more aware of their own responses to the documents and objects they lightly call "relics," and more comfortable with metaphorical uses of Catholic categories, an underlying historical Catholic materialism has been neglected. Rather than treat the Manuscript of 1652 as a surviving "relic" of a distant Catholic past, this chapter will instead consider the relationships that Catholics of seventeenth-century New France themselves constructed between manuscript and relic. How did they connect hagiography and veneration, text and object, narrative content and print or manuscript context? How did they use these texts and objects to make sense of a new environment, and to define their relationship to the Catholic world they had left behind them in Europe? The juxtaposition of manuscript and relic in the archivist's cabinet at St.-Jérôme recalls a widespread medieval practice. Hagiographic manuscripts were not kept in a monastery's library, but in its treasury, close to the valued relics they authenticated.[3]

Hagiography is as old as the church itself. From brief lists of martyr-saints read in the early church to the full-scale "lives" produced in the Middle Ages, the genre developed for purposes of "edification" and "emulation":

to encourage devotion to the saints, and to set examples of Christian virtue and sacrifice before the faithful. Because saints were expected to demonstrate virtue to a heroic degree, sacred biographies or "lives" devoted many pages to illustrating their subjects' piety, modesty, charity, and the like. While laypersons might be cautioned against imitating saints' more extreme behaviors (severe fasting or other bodily mortifications), the heroically virtuous life of a Catholic Reformation figure such as Teresa of Avila could inspire an ordinary reader to emulate her virtues on a more modest scale. In New France, as elsewhere in the early modern Catholic world, saints' lives served these edifying purposes. Missionaries drew from them stories to tell converts; Quebec's second bishop included "saints' lives" on his list of books that every family should own; and early religious communities in Quebec and Montreal stocked their libraries with hagiographic narratives (the Jesuits, of course, had a life of St. Ignatius, while the early Ursuline library was well supplied with lives of exemplary religious women and men).[4] To read model lives helped sustain a sense of vocation and reinforced a shared ideal of behavior.

Beyond the immediate purposes of edification and emulation, the lives of venerables also could serve a variety of social uses that were essential to the articulation of Catholic community. For the Catholic religious in North America, lives of venerables were uniquely suited to the work of maintaining links strained by geographical distance. As in France, religious orders and lay congregations systematically distributed within their ranks lives of exemplary members.[5] The collective reading of these and other hagiographic narratives made possible an "imagined community" of French Catholicism.[6] On both sides of the Atlantic, according to the same schedule, the religious gathered in their refectories to read the same hagiographic texts, participating in a ritual of simultaneity that denied spatial barriers, and temporarily obscured awareness that New France's "hours" were linked to a sunrise that took place long after Europe's.

The exchange of hagiographic narratives also played a role in the definition of Catholic community. The gift or loan of a "life" could reinforce a relationship between giver and recipient. Such gifts connected New France's religious to European supporters of their mission, who figured as donors and even as subjects of these books: the Ursulines of Quebec, and Jeanne Mance of Montreal, owned lives of French mission patron Monsieur de Renty; the Parisian printer Sébastien Cramoisy (who also produced the well-known Jesuit Relations) gave the Jesuits a volume of saints' lives; and the Ursulines also received as gifts many of their lives of holy persons.[7] Hagiographic narratives were exchanged as New Year's gifts, and saints' lives were given as school prizes.[8] In a world where books were scarce, the loan or gift of a life might be a sign of special favor by the giver, or a recognition of special merit in the recipient. In a letter of 1668, for example, Marie de l'Incarnation thanked the superior of the Dijon Ursulines for a life of "the venerable Mother [Marguerite] de saint François Xavier," and explained that she had been lending it to "persons of the highest piety" in Quebec.[9] The book had helped the Ursuline nun to distinguish "the pious" in Quebec—those worthy of reading the life—and to link those worthy colonists to the book's donors in France.

Saints' lives traveled the networks of exchange that linked New France's colonists to the world of European Catholicism: money, books, rosaries, "little devotions," and relics flowed out of France; in return, donors received the assurance that the missionaries' converts would act as "mediators with God" on their behalf.[10] The outflow of hagiographic narratives and relics reinforced a spatial understanding of the Catholic Church in which Europe's "holiness" might be transmitted, piece by piece, to American soil. Relics of early Christian martyrs and medieval saints were sent to found American altars (Canon Law prescribed that every altar must contain a saint's relics). The Ursulines rejoiced when Marie de l'Incarnation's son Claude Martin sent to them "a particle of the True Cross encased in crystal, hermetically sealed," and the entire population of Quebec turned out to celebrate the arrival of the complete bodies of Sts. Flavian and Felicité in 1666.[11] Like the transfer of these relics to New France, the westward movement of saints' lives simultaneously reinforced European centrality and sustained ties between center and distant periphery.[12]

Within a few decades of their arrival in New France, missionaries began to claim that holiness also existed on the church's North American "frontier." That is, they began to write hagiography and to adapt the historical details of life in New France to the conventions of what was, by the middle of the seventeenth century, a highly standardized genre. Following the death of an exemplary "servant of God," acquaintances composed narrative accounts of the holy person's life and virtues, recalling evidence of special divine favor such as visions or miraculous healings.[13] They also described the subject's holy death, be it a peaceful occasion for sacraments, or, as for several of New France's "servants of God," the result of painful tortures. If demonstrations of heroic virtue were substantial, favors from God sufficiently numerous and miraculous, and the deceased's "reputation for sanctity" enduring, Rome might eventually pursue the canonization process officially required to declare someone a saint. Canonization could not take place for several decades, and could not take place at all without a widespread reputation for sanctity; hence such accounts were often reproduced for circulation, to build *fama*. As the Jesuit Jacques Buteux laments on the first page of the Manuscript of 1652, saints' most heroic deeds—"such as miracles"—were often hidden by their equally heroic modesty.[14] The responsibility for uncovering the venerable's deeds and "secret writings" thus fell to those who had survived. The project of canonization was inescapably a project of publication.[15]

Like readers of saints' lives, those who wrote hagiography in New France were engaged in the work of community definition. Seventeenth-century French Catholic authors, wherever they lived, hoped to add French names to a canon of saints dominated by Italians and Spaniards, and the many new religious orders sought canonization for their founders and members. But the quest for inclusion was intensified among missionaries seeking recognition for their efforts. Writing lives of fellow colonist-missionaries helped New France's authors define the relationship of their colony to the European metropole.[16] By celebrating uniquely American sufferings and exploits, they could publicize their subjects' "heroic virtue." Yet New France's hagiographers were no less eager to demonstrate to European readers that their subjects, despite their exile in the North American wilderness, had not been "barbarized" by the experience but still remained firmly in the world of European Catholicism.

New France's religious wrote many texts in the hagiographic mode, circulating obituary notices, elegies, and "lives" to readers in New France, France, and Rome. They produced such elaborate composite manuscripts as the "Elegies of some persons deceased in odor of sanctity at Montreal," sent by Montreal's Sulpicians to their counterparts in Paris, and included sections devoted to the recluse Jeanne Le Ber, to community founder Marguerite Bourgeoys, and to "a virtuous Iroquois woman."[17] Occasionally the genre was adapted for Indians who had converted to Catholicism: for the "virtuous Iroquois woman" in the Sulpicians' text, or for Catherine Tekakwitha, who was the subject of two distinct life narratives, one of them eventually printed in the *Lettres édifiantes et curieuses.*[18] More typically the subjects were French missionaries: throughout the 1640s the lives and sufferings of Jesuit missionaries were prominently featured in the annual series of *Jesuit Relations.* The *Relation* for 1652 also offered readers a life of Marie de St.-Joseph, the first Ursuline to die on North American soil; the editor proposed that it would "wrong the public to lock up this treasure in the houses of the Ursulines alone."[19]

1652

In the hagiography of New France, 1652 is an important date. In that year, not long after the destruction of the Jesuits' Huron mission, Quebec superior Paul Ragueneau directed a scribe to produce a manuscript celebrating the missionaries who had died (often quite violently) in the decade before. The result was the "Manuscript of 1652" now held in the Jesuit archives. The manuscript is introduced by a title page; title and part titles are decorated with ornate capitals; texts are copied in a neat scribal hand. As the formal title "Mémoires" suggests, this is a composite text, drawing together narrative fragments from many sources. In the document's three-hundred-odd pages, twenty-four separate items are grouped according to eight biographical subjects: there are narratives describing the virtuous lives of New France's missionaries, and their deaths at the hands of "enemies of the faith"; there are spiritual writings by Brébeuf and Jogues; a letter written by Jogues during his Iroquois captivity; a doctor's description of the badly dislocated shoulder that Brébeuf endured, without complaint, for two full years.[20] Much of the manuscript's contents had previously been published in *Jesuit Relations.* (Ragueneau's scribe worked from those printed versions, not from older manuscripts: at the head of several chapters appear notices that material has been copied from ["*descript de*"] the relevant *Relation.*) Ragueneau corrected the transcription, and he and his assistant Joseph-Antoine Poncet added signed attestations to each item.[21]

From external evidence, it seems clear that Ragueneau, together with the bishop of Rouen (who claimed jurisdiction over New France), hoped to initiate canonization proceedings for the Jesuit martyrs.[22] Thus the text is eager to demonstrate that the martyrs died "in hatred of the faith" (the absolute requirement for canonization of a martyr), and to buttress this central claim with abundant supporting evidence of holiness. Notwithstanding an "exotic" North American setting and torture scenes vividly described, the texts in the Manuscript of 1652 conform closely to the conventions of the European genre. In the circular logic of hagiography, New France's authors defended the saintliness of their subjects by invoking the virtues of older saints from whose lives the new venerables had themselves derived inspiration.[23] Thus was the Jesuit missionary Anne de Noüe compared to St. Isidore and St. Marcel "among the poor and the wretched," while Jean de Brébeuf was depicted accepting his missionary charter from St. Paul. New France's authors also brought a Catholic explanatory framework to their descriptions of the martyrs' deaths: when the Iroquois pour boiling water over Brébeuf and Gabriel Lalemant, the Manuscript account notes three separate acts of pouring, "in derision of holy baptism." Anne de Noüe, meanwhile, dies with his body "in the posture of a St. Francis Xavier, arms crossed, eyes open and turned toward heaven."[24]

New France's hagiographers recognized that colonial martyrs could best achieve (an ultimately European) canonization if their sufferings crowned such European accomplishments as an unwavering performance of the Jesuit rule and a special devotion to the holy sacrament or the Virgin Mary. Thus in the Manuscript's life of Brébeuf we see reported not only his visions of the cross, which are interpreted as a prediction of his martyrdom, but also his charity toward neighbors, his poverty, and the ecstatic character of his prayer life.[25] Anne de Noüe's chroniclers praised him as "very exact in the observation of his three vows," and noted with admiration that he retained no possessions save some spiritual writings and a few "instruments of mortification." Observers made much of the fact that Antoine Daniel was killed while saying Mass, and they celebrated Charles Garnier's exemplary devotion to the Virgin Mary.[26] A colonial venerable, apparently, had to demonstrate mastery of European virtues before he could be rewarded for his overseas heroics.

A similar orientation toward Europe may be discerned in the "Account of the life, virtues, and death of Mother Marie de Saint-Joseph" that Marie de l'Incarnation sent to the Ursulines of Tours in the spring of 1652.[27] The account was to serve as the obituary notice by which the superior of an Ursuline convent customarily informed other communities of a member's death. These notices circulated in print and manuscript among the Ursuline houses; by participating in the circulation of *lettres nécrologiques,* independently founded houses asserted their membership in the coalescing network of houses conforming to the "rule" of Paris.[28] The "life" of Marie de St.-Joseph is longer than most obituary letters, but its division into short segments suggests that Marie de l'Incarnation expected it nonetheless to be read aloud in the order's refectories.

Like the Manuscript of 1652, Marie de l'Incarnation's life of Marie de St.-Joseph celebrates its subject's conformity to established models of sanctity. Lives of female saints typically describe an early vocation and a gradual growth in virtue and piety. In this account Marie shows an early inclination toward charity (secretly giving away her meals to the poor) and a firm commitment to modesty and sexual purity. The author includes a lengthy catalog of her subject's virtues: attachment to the Ursuline Rule; dedication to prayer; love of suffering and poverty; humility, obedience, and purity. The first half of the narrative chronicles Marie's life in France, where she demonstrates her virtue by renouncing food, the vanities of aristocratic life, marriage, and the comforts of family. In the story's second half, set in North America, self-imposed suffering is no longer required. New France is presented as a purer alternative to France, where the temptation to vanity is reduced, and the opportunity for imitating Christ's suffering is greatly increased.

When she died, Marie de St.-Joseph left behind a body invaded by gangrene. Nevertheless, when her corpse was exhumed for translation a decade later, it reportedly retained a miraculously preserved heart and brain:

> Her heart, which had sustained so many holy transports for her Spouse, and her brain, the instrument for so many holy thoughts, were still intact. All her bones were in place, each in its natural position. The entire body was without any foul odor.

Indeed, after washing the bones for reburial in a new coffin, the sisters found that their hands "exuded a fragrance like irises."[29]

By the seventeenth century, it had become a hagiographic commonplace that a holy woman's corpse should remain intact and should exude not the stench of corruption but a sweet fragrance termed "the odor of sanctity."[30] The heart was ranked highest in the early modern anatomical hierarchy; it was understood to be the seat of the soul and might stand metaphorically for the entire person.[31] But the survival of this particular heart merits special attention. The hagiographic narrative stresses that during her lifetime, Marie de St.-Joseph had felt that she "carried in her heart all the French and all the 'savages,' " and she had explicitly offered her own sufferings in expiation for the nascent church in New France.[32] Her death, moreover, took place at a time when the French Catholic Church in North America was particularly concerned over issues of fragmentation and disintegration: What was their relationship to the European Catholic Church they had left behind? Would the French colony be wiped out by some disaster? How should they define the relationship between the French colonial church and Indian converts, who even when Christian never escaped the label *sauvage*? The miraculous incorruptibility of Marie de St.-Joseph's heart might seem to promise a similar preservation for the church in New France.

As an intercessor, Marie de St.-Joseph would seem especially concerned with protecting the vulnerable from New France's special dangers: she rescued one man from an icy river, and recalled from captivity a girl named Anne Baillagon, who after nine years with the Iroquois "so liked the *Sauvages'* customs that she [had] decided to spend the rest of her life with them." The sexual implications of Marie's own bodily integrity are underscored by the story of Anne's rescue:

> Living among Pagans during her long captivity it was impossible that [Anne] would not have committed many sins against the sanctity of Christianity. She had nonetheless always maintained a very great purity; and it was believed that this Mother had been made her Angel to conserve her in this integrity.[33]

Marie de St.-Joseph's body presents an interesting paradox. It was representative of the church in New France, yet detached and preserved intact from the New World around it. The powerful symbolism of Marie de St.-Joseph's relics draws, in part, on the powerful anthropomorphic resonance of "cloister" and "virginity."[34] The corpse never left the Ursuline cloister, an inviolate "European" architectural structure transplanted to American soil. Moreover, Marie de l'Incarnation seems to have resisted requests to disperse the departed sister's bones, even though the division of bodies was not unusual in seventeenth-century French culture. She contemplated sending to France some of the "white paste" that clung to the corpse's bones, but reconsidered an impulse to send bones to a relative in France, worrying that these precious items might be lost en route.[35] Less risky was to send a small box of bones to the hospital sisters of Quebec, in an exchange that signified the union of these two New World houses.

When Marie was reburied, it was not in North American soil, but in the vault beneath the Ursuline monastery. From this location, as the house's superior explained, "if one day by some reversal of fortune we had to return to France, we could easily retrieve it." And in that cloistered location, Claude Martin later hoped, the relics would be safe from the "alarms of the Iroquois."[36] Although New France was the setting for Marie's sufferings, she sustained no tangible connection with the land or landscape of New France: indeed, it is this quality of separation that made her relics valuable to colonial Catholicism.

HEAVEN AND EARTH

Circulated in manuscript among the Ursulines, or reprinted in the Jesuit Relations, the life of Marie de St.-Joseph helped to reinforce a primarily "spatial" sense of Catholic community, a sense of the Catholic Church that could extend outward from Europe to include new regions, without falling victim to bodily corruption. Scholars of early American history have become quite familiar with the idea of spatially organized discursive communities within which colonists came to define themselves in relation to their countries of origin, and in their relationship to each other. Several of these studies have placed particular emphasis on the role of print technology, especially the activities of colonial presses, in this process of self-definition.[37] In contrast to the English colonies, which were perhaps more abundantly provided with printing presses than England itself, New France had no press of its own until the 1760s.[38] In the realm of print, French colonists continued to participate in a textual world they understood as French. Even books authored by colonists were reimported in printed form.

Reading the same hagiographic books as their French counterparts may have encouraged New France's inhabitants to sustain a more broadly defined "imagined community" that readily embraced inhabitants on both sides of the Atlantic. Geographic limitations on access to print, and institutional restrictions on content and distribution, kept New France's religious closely linked to metropolitan culture, and did much to forestall the development of a French colonial version of the American "republic of letters." But the strength of the hagiographic community organized in earthly space depended less on technologies of reproduction, or patterns of distribution, than on its relationship to heavenly space and time. Like other inhabitants of European colonies in North America, New France's Catholics found that the texts and practices that drew them closest together were historical and commemorative in character. But while Anglo Americans united around remembering King Philip's War, French colonists focused on the lives of saints and, as time wore on, holy persons of colonial production.[39] In the commemorative practice of hagiography, the book was valued not only as a collection of pious words but also as a sacred meeting place, a site where Catholics on earth might gain direct access to the heavenly communion of saints.[40]

Early modern Catholics saw frequent evidence of interaction between the parallel worlds of heaven and earth, spirit and matter. Most obviously and officially, at the moment of consecration in the Eucharist, God was believed to intervene directly to transform earthly bread and wine into the body and blood of Christ. The window between mundane and celestial worlds also could open without priestly assistance: religious and laypersons saw visions of the saints or the Virgin Mary, or they heard inner voices directing their actions. When a holy person died, the fortunate few present at the deathbed might experience with him or her a glimpse of the heavenly reward beyond. Saints in heaven maintained an ongoing relationship with believers on earth, and used their proximity to God to intercede on behalf of earthly counterparts. Those on earth sustained a firm belief in the importance of direct physical connection to the heavenly community of saints, whether by means of "corporeal relics" (entire bodies, bones, oils, and unguents distilled from holy flesh), or "contact relics" (objects used by the saint, or brought into contact with the venerated body after death). The Council of Trent had drawn a clear distinction between saints who "reigning together with Christ, offer their prayers to God for people," and Christ, "our sole redeemer and savior." Theologians were careful to distinguish between the worship *(latria)* owed to God alone and the veneration *(dulia)* appropriate to the bodies of saints and "other sacred memorials," and they argued over the precise significance of saints' relics.[41] In popular practice, however, physical proximity to a saint's relic was understood to mean greater access to that holy person's intercessory power before God: relics were sites where matter and spirit came together.[42]

The perceived close relationship between book object and departed subject may, in fact, explain the importance of hagiography in Catholic community formation. Objects with physical presence, reciprocally exchanged among the members of a community, hagiographic books also linked earthly readers to heavenly protection. New France's missionaries, in a quite literal sense, included departed subjects as participants in their imagined hagiographic community. Yes, when the Ursulines of Paris sent their obituary letters to Quebec, or when the Paris Ursulines printed and distributed Quebec's *lettres nécrologiques* among their European houses, New France's Ursulines were reassured of an ongoing connection to their European origins.[43] Yes, receiving the life of Marguerite de St.-François Xavier connected Marie de l'Incarnation to Ursulines in France, and lending it to "persons of the highest piety" in Quebec cemented relationships among elite Catholic colonists in North America. However, Marie de l'Incarnation also reminded the book's donor, "We regard [Marguerite] here as one of our protectors, now that she is in Heaven and in a condition to protect us."[44]

New France's religious hoped that the saints whose lives they read would join with them in their missionary labors, and they hoped that their own departed subjects would intercede between heaven and European readers—especially to inspire vocations and donations. A fine example comes from the life of the Hospitaler Mother Catherine de Saint Augustin, whose father opposed her wish to go to Canada. Her hagiographer writes:

> [T]his good Gentleman, falling sick from grief & melancholy . . . asked to see a Relation newly arrived from Canada, which spoke of the death of the Jesuit Father Isaac Jogues, massacred by the Iroquois. . . . This father prostrate with sadness, was seized suddenly with . . . a sleep undoubtedly mysterious; during which he was inspired and directed strongly to permit our Catherine to make this great voyage.[45]

The "massacred" venerable Jogues, through the medium of the printed relation, could intercede to foster a bond between God and his "good Gentleman" reader—and, no less significantly—foster a bond between the reader in France and the church in North America.

BODY AND BOOK

When we speak of the written page as the place where author, subject, and reader meet, we are usually in the realm of theory. But the Manuscript of 1652 was produced by a culture that envisioned this meeting in quite literal terms. The manuscript might be considered a "holy place," originally built in 1652 with the expectation that future visitors would add their own *ex votos* to the original structure. I would like now to turn back to this manuscript, and specifically to a consideration of "authority." When we talk about the formation of textual communities, we often emphasize the capacity of writing to detach itself from persons; here, the direction is reversed. The move from the printed Relations to the Manuscript of 1652 is characterized by a process of *repersonalization:* where the printed Relations bury authors and characters alike under generic references to "one of ours" or "a Huron Christian of good repute," the manuscript identifies actors and witnesses by name. Where the printed Relations subsume the works of multiple authors under the general authority of the superior, the manuscript reintroduces those same authors and describes their relation to the subjects. The attestations stress the eyes of the witnesses, the eyes and ears of the attestor who has neither seen nor heard anything contrary to the truths contained in the document before him. This dimension of corporeality in witnessing—and the assertion of identity between text and writer, word and flesh—may be found in other documents from New France and, indeed, throughout the seventeenth-century Catholic world. In some cases it is expressed metaphorically: the *donné* (servant) Christophe Regnault wrote that he would "sign with his blood" his own account of the deaths of Brébeuf and Lalemant.[46] Elsewhere we see the image reified: descriptions of vows signed, or written entirely, in the blood of the devout are almost commonplace in seventeenth-century hagiography.[47] Although the Manuscript of 1652 is written in a more ordinary ink, it shares this emphasis on corporeal presence: we see a constant reiteration of the physical connection between the written text and the persons of witnesses. The Manuscript of 1652, in this sense, conveys an "authority" that was not present in the printed *Relations* from which many of the texts were copied— nor, for that matter, in the oral accounts that Huron Christians brought back from the sites of the martyrs' sufferings.

The manuscript's attestations defend the text against future emendations that might corrupt the truth—the bodily integrity?—of the original. But the structure of the manuscript implies an understanding of authority that also extends forward in time: the Manuscript of 1652 is incomplete. In its three hundred pages, at irregular intervals, there appear five blank sections. The blanks are unquestionably integral to the manuscript:

they bear the scribe's original ruled margins, and they are included in the contemporary pagination.[48] There is no apparent bibliographical explanation: although it is conceivable that the manuscript would have been copied in pieces, and that the occasional blank might fall at the end of a gathering, some of the blank sections fall within gatherings, and each is exactly three pages long.[49] In a colony where paper was scarce, from which some Jesuits sent to Rome final vow statements written on bark, this would be a lot of paper to waste without a purpose.[50]

The blanks do, however, have a purpose, for hagiography is an inherently additive genre. A holy person's supporters often appended accounts of recent miracles to later editions of printed lives.[51] Pierre Cholenec's manuscript life of Catherine Tekakwitha concludes with a chronological list of miracles tacked onto the original narrative. Several of New France's missionaries followed the European precedent of keeping "miracle books" in which to record (as they occurred) wonders wrought at pilgrimage sites through saints' intercession.[52] In the Manuscript of 1652, the previously printed life of Antoine Daniel has been augmented with a narrative of Daniel's appearance in a vision.[53] But most of the manuscript's lives lack the substantial evidence of miracles that could transform a venerable into a saint. And so blank pages follow the lives of martyrs otherwise perceived as strong candidates for sainthood.[54]

The manuscript thus exhibits a "cocreative" potential characteristic of New France's scribal culture—embracing future reader-authors in the process of its production.[55] This cocreative character is especially common in the dictionaries, grammars, and prayer-books produced for work with indigenous people. Unlike the Manuscript of 1652, the pedagogical materials tend to be anonymous, undated, and devoid of scribal flourishes. But one finds in those works a quality of anticipation, an invitation for addition, directly relevant to our present subject. Surviving dictionaries have blanks after French words for Algonkian or Huron equivalents not yet discovered; some authors left blank pages at the end of each letter of the alphabet for new vocabulary entries; a manuscript copy of an Illinois-language prayer book incorporates blank leaves to allow for additional prayers.[56] The blanks in the Manuscript of 1652 reveal its compilers' recognition that hagiography, like lexicography, was a collective project: only with the additions of later authors would the work become complete. The potentially cocreative manuscript acknowledges that the temporal dimension of Catholic community extends forward to future reader as well as backward to author-witness—and leaves physical room for those future comers to this place of holiness.

A "miracle book" was typically kept at the shrine where a saint's relics were housed, to record the moments when pilgrims gained miraculous access to the saint's intercessory power. But a shrine presupposed the presence of relics. And in the case of the Jesuit martyrs, the need for relics was not easily met: their bodies were anything but intact. Several of the venerated missionaries had been victims of Iroquois ritual torture that including flaying and burning of flesh. Several of the manuscript's narratives relate fruitless efforts to retrieve a martyr's body, or mourn "the loss of such a dear treasure" to New France's rivers and forests. Before transporting the bodies of Brébeuf and Lalemant from Huronia to Quebec City, servants of the French missionaries had rendered the corpses further, boiling away remaining flesh and dividing the dried bones into separate silk bags.[57] Back in Quebec, the pattern of dispersal continued. Those charged with retrieving the martyrs' remains gave some of the bones to Madame de la Peltrie (founder of the Ursulines), and Marie de l'Incarnation hoped these might be sent *en cachette* to Claude Martin in France.[58] A catalog of relics ultimately preserved by the Jesuits is distressingly partial: the skull of Brébeuf "except for the lower jaw," femurs and two vertebrae of Gabriel Lalemant, a fibula ("incomplete") of Charles Garnier, nothing at all for Antoine Daniel, Noël Chabanel, Isaac Jogues, or René Goupil.[59]

The Jesuit martyrs' history is one of fragmentation: the horror of bodies dismembered, and even the subsequent joy of miracles, which inevitably involved recourse to some fragmentary relic. In a typical example (after unsuccessful efforts with "the Relics of several saints"), Marie Regnouard of Beauport was able to exorcise a demon from her servant Barbe Hallay with "a rib of the departed Reverend Father Jean de Brébeuf that Reverend Father Ragueneau had the charity to give me on his return from the Hurons."[60] The bodies were irretrievably fragmented, but as unrecovered bones and rendered flesh were left to blend into New France's earth, French Catholics saw potential for a fusion of martyr body and mission landscape. Missionary successors would eagerly affirm this identification in later references to the transformative influence of the martyrs' blood.[61] Even Barbe Hallay's resistance to imported relics might testify to the specific identification of person and place. Yet there was no single central shrine containing relics of all the Jesuit martyrs. In its absence, might the Manuscript of 1652 have become the site of a remembering not only metaphorical but physical? Might the manuscript have served as both hagiography and shrine, both authentication and relic?

As I have suggested above, not only the *witness* of a life, but also the *subject,* were believed to be accessible through the medium of the written word. Understood most basically, the narrative of a martyr's life and death offered an occasion for contemplative devotion: like an image (or, for a composite manuscript, an altarpiece), the saint's life was a starting point for prayer.[62] But the potential for access went beyond mere devotion. If contemporaries expected the Manuscript of 1652 to offer virtually un-mediated access to the truth, they also cherished a belief in what Alain Boureau has called the "propagation of the sacred": the potential for the sacred to migrate from contents to container.[63] Simple physical contact with a saint's "life" might precipitate a miracle. In this use of hagiography, the intercession of the saint might be achieved through the medium of a book much as through a relic. Such a "propagation of the sacred" might transpire with any saint's life, printed or manuscript. But printed hagio-graphies were not, it seems, the ideal medium for the "propagation of the sacred." New France's Catholics often accorded a higher status to printed objects that had been in the possession of holy persons than they did to printed books describing those persons. Physical connection to the "relic" was, in many cases, more valuable than the intellectual rapport that united the book's subject to the book's possessor. Books previously owned by martyrs were sought as contact relics. Thus Catherine de St.-Augustin found "a very special assistance" when she prayed before an image that "had been witness to all that [Father Bressani] had suffered."[64] Thus the manuscript writings of departed venerables were among the most valued of relics. After Pierre Chaumonot's death in 1693, his writings were guarded by "persons of quality" (while other admirers demanded his hair and teeth); the writings of Marie de l'Incarnation and of Marguerite Bourgeoys were likewise treasured as relics.[65]

And, to take this line of interpretation farther still, a manuscript nar-rative, having moved in a direct line of transmission from body to witness to scribe to attestor to reader, maintained a surprisingly, and even mirac-ulously, close physical connection to its subject. To give a sense of how lit-erally this could be understood, we might consider a truly striking French account from La Flèche in 1644. In the narrative, a deceased Hospitaler appeared to members of her convent bearing an edifying message from heaven. The witnesses to this apparition prepared and signed a document attesting the miraculous event (a document, in other words, not unlike the Manuscript of 1652). That document then itself undertook a series of miraculous apparitions—appearing under tables, transporting itself from a locked chest to an altar, where it was later found in adoration before the holy sacrament—until, the account concludes, "It was finally resolved that we would read [the document] aloud every month in community, and it would be kept fast in the treasury, and since then we have no longer seen these transportations." The manuscript imitated its subject's miraculous appearances, until the Hospitalers recognized it as a "treasure." They stored this "embodiment" of the departed sister in their *trésor,* and agreed to a regular reading of its contents that could bring her, and her message, back into the surviving community.[66]

The French document's insistence that it be stored in the convent's treasury—like the juxtaposition of reliquary and manuscript in the archivist's cabinet at St.-Jérôme—recalls the traditional pairing of hagiography and relic. In a typical case of hagiography and veneration (such as that of Marie de St.-Joseph), the hagiographic text served a purpose secondary to the relics, valued because it authenticated and publicized miraculous relics.[67] For the Manuscript of 1652, the relation between body and book is altered. The story of the search compensates for the bones lost irretrievably to water and fire. In a dramatic shift of meaning, the Manuscript of 1652, rather than *authenticating* the community's relics, actually *takes the place of* those relics. While a printed narrative could accomplish the crucial work of publicizing a venerable's deeds, a manuscript made possible a one-to-one substitution: vulnerable, unique body transformed into vulnerable, unique manuscript, which would henceforth be guarded in the Jesuits' Quebec archives.

After collecting the remains of Gabriel Lalemant and Jean de Brébeuf from the site of their martyrdom, Christophe Regnault laid out the bodies on pieces of bark and spent the next two hours in contemplation of these objects "pitiful to see." He was "considering" the corpses to verify that "what the *savages* had told us of their martyrdom and death was true." Here are the terms in which he "read" Brébeuf's body, seeking correspondence between testimony and flesh:

I saw and touched the great many large blisters that he had in various parts of his body, from the boiling water that these barbarians had poured over him in derision of holy baptism. I saw and touched the wound from a belt of bark full of pitch and resin that had grilled all his body. . . . I saw and touched his two lips that had been cut off because he spoke always of God as they made him suffer. I saw and touched all the places on his body that had received more than two hundred blows with clubs. I saw and touched the top of his scalped head. I saw and touched the opening that these barbarians had made to rip out his heart.[68]

Before his own return from the Huron country, Joseph Poncet prepared for himself a reliquary. In a "little copper box" he placed

. . . a small piece of paper on which I had written in my own blood . . . the names of our Fathers martyred in America, and a short Prayer in which I asked Our Lord for a violent death in his service, and the grace to shed all my blood for the same cause.

When Poncet was himself later captured and feared that he, too, would meet death at the hands of Hurons and Iroquois, he "saw constantly before my eyes the sentence of my death written in my own blood, so that I could not revoke it."[69]

Regnault's silent dialogue with the corpse of Jean de Brébeuf and Poncet's contemplation of his "reliquary": both images underscore the centrality of the physical object in the commemorative community-formation practices of Catholic New France. Hagiography and veneration offered support to earthly relationships because each text or relic concentrated within itself the potential for a powerful personal connection between individual Christian and individual saint. Regnault's repeated phrase "I saw and I touched . . . I saw and I touched" is a statement of witnessing, but also of communion. While Regnault was reading Brébeuf's relics, Poncet was reading his own blood-soaked tribute to the Jesuit martyrs, a textual relic that bound him irrevocably to the persons and sufferings of the Jesuit martyrs. And the Manuscript of 1652, where Poncet's hand attested the narrative of Brébeuf's death, occupied a similar position between "text" and "relic." In early modern Catholicism, lines between the cultural categories of hagiography and veneration were never clearly drawn. There may, however, be something particularly "American" about this relationship of body and book. France's North American colonists had only limited access to European relics, shrines, and books; in consequence, they may have been more susceptible to a strain of belief in which a book could become the physical site of saintly holiness.[70] The blank pages in the Manuscript of 1652 imply a remarkably concrete understanding of "reader response": they provide an opportunity to record the miraculous results of an encounter with the "word made flesh" in a new land.

NOTES

1. "Memoires touchant la mort" [hereafter *MS. 1652*], Archives de la Société de Jésus, Canada français [hereafter ASJCF], St.-Jérôme, Quebec, CSM no. 210. See also *Rapport de l'archiviste de la province de Québec* (1924–25): 3–93. Translations from this and other French sources are my own.

2. Joseph W. Reed, *Things: Objects in the Yale Collections,* Exhibition at Beinecke Rare Book and Manuscript Library, April 21–July 8, 1995 (New Haven, Conn.: Yale University, 1995). Jill Lepore describes her discovery of Noah Webster's hair in "Historians Who Love Too Much: Reflections on Microhistory and Biography," *Journal of American History* 88 (June 2001): 129–44.

3. Alain Boureau, "Franciscan Piety and Voracity: Uses and Strategems in the Hagiographic Pamphlet," in *The Culture of Print: Power and the Uses of Print in Early Modern Europe,* ed. Roger Chartier, trans. Lydia G. Cochrane (Cambridge, Eng.: Polity Press, 1989), 21; Francis Wormald, "Some Illustrated Manuscripts of the Lives of the Saints," *Bulletin of the John Rylands Library of Manchester* 35:1 (1952), 248–66.

4. The Jesuit collection included Louis de Cressolles, *Anthologia sacra seu de selectis piorum hominum virtutibus, animique ornamentis* (Paris: Sébastien Cramoisy, 1632–38), cited in *The First Canadian Library: The Library of the Jesuit College of New France* (Ottawa: National Library of Canada, 1972), 22–23, and [Bouhours], *La vie de Saint Ignace,* 2nd ed. (Paris: Sébastien Mabre-Cramoisy, 1680), cited in Pariseau, *La Bibliothèque du Collège de Québec* (Graduate School of Library Sciences, McGill University, Occasional Papers, 1972), 15. Seventeenth-century "lives" in the Ursuline collection include Jean-Baptiste Saint-Jure, *La Vie de Monsieur de Renty,* 2nd ed. (Paris, 1652), a copy which may have been part of a 1652 gift from the author of "all his books" (Registre des Bienfaiteurs, Archives des Soeurs Ursulines de Québec [hereafter AUQ]); [Soeur Marie-Dorothée Desbarres], *La Vie de la Vénérable Mère Anne Seraphine Boulier* (Dijon, 1689), copy annotated "Des Ursulines de Quebec 1695"; Jean Maillard, *La Vie de la Mère Marie Bon, de l'Incarnation, Religieuse Ursuline de Saint Marcellin, en Dauphiné* (Paris, 1686), copy annotated "Noviciat . . . A Quebec 1686"; François Losa, *La Vie du bienheureux Grégoire Lopez* (Paris, 1686), copy annotated "Aux Ursnes De Kebec"; Marguerite du St-Sacrament, *Conduite chrétienne et religieuse . . . Avec un Abregé de sa Vie* (Lyon, 1687), copy annotated "Aux Ursulines de Quebec 1691." Sébastien Rasle, *Suite de la Vie de R. P. Pierre Joseph Marie Chaumonot, de la Compagnie de Jésus* (New York: À la presse Cramoisy de Jean-Marie Shea, 1858), 21; Antonio Drolet, *Les bibliothèques canadiennes, 1604–1960* (Ottawa: Le cercle du livre de France, 1965), 23; Jean de la Croix de Saint Vallier's recommendation of "la vie des Saints" appears in *Mandements, lettres pastorales et circulaires des Évêques de Québec,* ed. H. Tètus and C.-O. Gagnon (Québec, 1987), vol. 1, 333.

5. Albrecht Burkhardt, "Reconnaissance et dévotion: les vies de saints et leur lectures au début du XVIIe siècle à travers les procès de canonisation," *Revue d'histoire moderne et contemporaine* 43: 2 (1996): 216, 222; Jacques Le Brun, "Rêves de religieuses: Le désir, la mort et le temps," *Revue des Sciences Humaines* 211: 3 (1988): 27.

6. Using the term as defined by Benedict Anderson in *Imagined Communities: Reflections on the Origin and Spread of Nationalism* (London: Verso, 1983).

7. Drolet, *Les bibliothèques canadiennes,* 29, citing "la vie de Mr. de Renty" in Mance's inventory. Regarding Gaston de Renty as a patron of New France's missions see Louis Châtellier, *Europe of the Devout: The Catholic Reformation and the Formation of a New Society* (New York: Cambridge University Press, 1989). For Cramoisy's gift see *The First Canadian Library,* 22–23. The Ursulines' collection of "lives" included titles received in 1687 from a Monsieur Josse (possibly the printer Louis Josse, who did work for the Paris Ursulines): R. P. de Vernon, *La Vie de Saint Louis* (1662); R. P. Jean-Marie, *La Vie de la Ven. Mere Marguerite de S. Xavier, Ursuline de Dijon* (1670) (Registre des Bienfaiteurs, AUQ), and other probable gifts, such as a copy of *La Vie de S. Madeleine de Pazzi* (1669), annotated "aux Ursulines de Québec 1687, Marie le Roux-Bourdon 1673."

8. Paul Ragueneau inscribed *"pour estrennes"* in a copy of *Jesuit Relations* for 1636, which he gave to the prioress of the Carmelites of Bourges. For other books as New Year's gifts see *Le Journal des Jésuites*

publié d'après le manuscrit original conservé aux archives du Séminaire de Québec [1871], ed. C. H. Laverdière and H. R. Casgrain, 3rd ed. (Montreal: Les Editions François-Xavier, 1973); on New Year's as an occasion for book exchanges see Natalie Zemon Davis, "Beyond the Market: Books as Gifts in Sixteenth-Century France," *Transactions of the Royal Historical Society,* 5th series, 33 (1983): 83.

9. Marie de l'Incarnation, August 9, 1668, in *Correspondance,* ed. Guy Oury (Solesmes, France: Abbaye Sainte-Pierre, 1971), 805.

10. Marie de l'Incarnation, letter to the Ursulines of Tours, spring 1652, *Correspondance,* 451.

11. "Liste de Saints Relliques qui sont dans le Monastère de Sainte Ursulle de Quebec" (1700), Archives de l'Archidiocèse de Québec, AAQ 12 A, Régistre des insinuations ecclésiastiques, vol. A, 750–54. Marie de l'Incarnation describes the procession for Sts. Flavian and Felicité in a letter to Claude Martin, October 16, 1666, *Correspondance,* 767. Regarding relics in New France, especially their role in reinforcing Catholic community, see Dominique Deslandres, "Des Reliques comme vecteur d'acculturation au XVIIe siècle," *Western Society for French History Proceedings* 20 (1993): 93–103.

12. The distribution of Roman relics to distant outposts of Christendom in the late antique period served a similar purpose of reinforcing solidarity. See Peter Brown, *The Cult of the Saints: Its Rise and Function in Latin Christianity* (Chicago: University of Chicago Press, 1981), 94–96. Peter Moogk notes French colonists' need for the reassuring presence of familiar religious institutions in "Reluctant Exiles: Emigrants from France in Canada before 1760," *William and Mary Quarterly,* 3d ser., 46 (1989): 463–505, esp. 473.

13. The Catholic Church makes a formal distinction between "servant of God"—a term acceptably applied to any exemplary person—and "venerable," "blessed," or "saint"—terms that correspond to stages in the canonization process and thus to particular forms of devotion. Thomas F. Macken, *The Canonisation of Saints* (Dublin: M. H. Gill, 1910), 3–4. I use these terms interchangeably in general references to the circulation of hagiographic narratives.

14. Buteux, "Narré de la prise du Père Isaac Jogues," *MS. 1652,* 1.

15. For an analogous Mexican Franciscan collection, see Serge Gruzinski and Jean-Michel Sallmann, "Une source d'ethnohistoire: les vies de 'vénérables' dans l'Italie méridionale et le Mexique baroque," *Mélanges de l'Ecole française de Rome: Moyen Age–Temps Modernes* 88: 2 (1976): 793. Regarding the workings of the canonization process see Pierre Delooz, "Towards a sociological study of canonized sainthood in the Catholic Church," in *Saints and their Cults: Studies in Religious Sociology, Folklore and History,* ed. Stephen Wilson (New York: Cambridge University Press, 1983), 189–216, esp. 189–201; Thomas F. Macken, *The Canonisation of Saints* (Dublin: M. H. Gill, 1910), and Burkhart, "Reconnaissance et dévotion," 217. Regarding qualifications for sainthood, and the dominance of martyr-saints in the seventeenth century see Donald Weinstein and Rudolph M. Bell, *Saints and Society: The Two Worlds of Western Christendom, 1000–1700* (Chicago: University of Chicago Press, 1982), esp. "Who Was a Saint?," 141–165.

16. The colonial hagiographic project thus serves as an especially strong example of the center-periphery negotiation that Peter Burke suggests typically characterized canonization processes in this period. See Burke, "How to Be a Counter-Reformation Saint," in *Religion and Society in Early Modern Europe 1500–1800,* ed. Kaspar von Greyerz (London: George Allen & Unwin, 1984), 45–55.

17. François Vachon de Belmont, "Eloges de quelques personnes mortes en odeur de sainteté à Montréal," Manuscrits du Séminaire de Saint-Sulpice (Paris), no. 553, printed in *Rapport de l'archiviste de la province de Québec* (1929–30): 144–89.

18. Allan Greer, "Savage/Saint: The Lives of Kateri Tekakwitha," in *Habitants et Marchands: Twenty Years Later,* ed. Sylvie Dépatie et al. (Montreal: McGill-Queen's University Press, 1997), 138–57.

19. *The Jesuit Relations and Allied Documents: Travels and Explorations of the Jesuit Missionaries in New France, 1610–1791,* ed. Reuben Gold Thwaites (Cleveland: Burrows Brothers, 1896–1901) [hereafter *JR*], 38: 68–69. My translation. Allan Greer offers a very useful introduction to New France's hagiography in "Colonial Saints: Gender, Race, and Hagiography in New France," *William and Mary Quarterly,* 3d series, 57 (April 2000): 323–48.

20. For a description of the manuscript see Lucien Campeau, *Monumenta Novæ Franciæ,* Historica Societatis Iesu, Missiones Occidentales (Rome and Quebec, 1967–) [hereafter *MNF*], IV, 43. Christophe Regnault titled his narrative of the martyrdom "Recit veritable du Martyre Et de la Bienheureuse mort, du Pere Jean de Brebœuf & du Pere Gabriel L'Alemant En la Nouuelle france, dans le pays des hurons par les Iroquois, Ennemis de la Foy." National Archives of Canada [hereafter NAC] MG 18 E 10 (published in *MNF* VII, no. 100).

21. Ragueneau corrects spellings of Huron names (*MS. 1652,* 194) as well as scribal errors, replacing "timitatis" with "timiditatis" (p. 91), or "charité" with "chasteté" (p. 254). The attestations are dated either August or December, 1652.

22. Ragueneau noted in 1653 that the archbishop of Rouen "has given another order,—one for making an Inquiry regarding the lives and blessed deaths of our Fathers." *JR* 38: 189.

23. See Gruzinski and Sallmann, "Une source d'ethnohistoire," 794–95; Burkhardt, "Reconnaissance et dévotion," 218.

24. *MS. 1652,* 144, 206, 173, 136–37.

25. *MS. 1652,* 164–65, 172–75.

26. *MS. 1652:* Brébeuf, 142; Anne de Noüe, 138–39; Antoine Daniel ("Il tomba prononceant le St. nom de Jesus"), 160; Garnier's special devotion to the Virgin Mary, 251.

27. Marie de l'Incarnation, *Correspondance,* 436–73.

28. "Liste des monastères des ursulines ou nostre congregation de paris envoye les lettres circulaires des Religieuses defuntes" (1658), AUQ.

29. Marie de l'Incarnation describes the translation of the body to its new coffin in a 1663 letter to Mère Gabrielle de l'Annonciation (de la Troche), *Correspondance,* 721–23.

30. Carolyn Walker Bynum, "Bodily Miracles and the Resurrection of the Body in the High Middle Ages," in *Belief in History: Innovative Approaches to European and American Religion,* ed. Thomas Kselman (Notre Dame, Ind.: University of Notre Dame Press, 1991), 68–106; Carlos M. N. Eire, *From Madrid to Purgatory: The Art and Craft of Dying in Sixteenth-Century Spain* (Cambridge: Cambridge University Press, 1995), esp. 425–45.

31. Scott Manning Stevens, "Sacred Heart and Secular Brain," in *The Body in Parts,* ed. David Hillman and Carla Mazzio (New York: Routledge, 1997), 263–82.

32. Marie de l'Incarnation, *Correspondance,* 452.

33. Marie de l'Incarnation, *Correspondance,* 466. On hagiography's close association with sexual purity and bodily integrity see Bynum, "Bodily Miracles," 79.

34. My understanding of this resonance builds on Robert Blair St. George's analysis of house-body analogies in New England, particularly New Englanders' beliefs regarding personal spiritual integrity in the face of demonic attack. See his *Conversing by Signs: Poetics of Implication in Colonial New England Culture* (Chapel Hill: University of North Carolina Press, 1998), esp. 181–88.

35. Marie de l'Incarnation, *Correspondance,* 722, and letter to Mère Renée de St.-François, Ursuline of Tours, August 19, 1664, *Correspondance,* 738. See also Elizabeth A. R. Brown, "Death and the Human Body in the Later Middle Ages: The Legislation of Boniface VIII on the Division of the Corpse," *Viator* 12 (1981): 221–70, esp. 264–65.

36. Marie de l'Incarnation, *Correspondance,* 722; letter from Claude Martin to the superior of the Quebec Ursulines, 1670s, Centre Marie de l'Incarnation/AUQ.

37. Benedict Anderson, *Imagined Communities;* Michael Warner, *The Letters of the Republic: Publication and the Public Sphere in Eighteenth-Century America* (Cambridge, Mass.: Harvard University Press, 1998); Armstrong and Tennenhouse, *The Imaginary Puritan: Literature, Intellectual Labor, and the Origins of Personal Life* (Berkeley: University of California Press, 1992), 196–216. Less print-focused is David Cressy, *Coming Over: Migration and Communication between England and New England in the Seventeenth Century* (Cambridge: Cambridge University Press, 1987).

38. Warner, *Letters of the Republic,* 31; Marie Tremaine, *A Bibliography of Canadian Imprints, 1751–1800* (Toronto: University of Toronto Press, 1952). The proliferation of printing presses in the English colonies was uneven; New France's experience in many ways resembles the "history of absences and censorship" that David D. Hall has described for the early Chesapeake. See "The Chesapeake in the Seventeenth Century" in his *Cultures of Print: Essays in the History of the Book* (Amherst: University of Massachusetts Press, 1996), 97–150.

39. On collective memory in early America see Jill Lepore, *The Name of War: King Philip's War and the Origins of American Identity* (New York: Alfred A. Knopf, 1998), and David Waldstreicher, *In the Midst of Perpetual Fetes: The Making of American Nationalism, 1776–1820* (Chapel Hill: University of North Carolina Press for IEAHC, 1997). Regarding the temporal dimension in reciprocal exchanges see Annette B. Weiner, "Reproduction, a Replacement for Reciprocity," *American Ethnologist* 7 (1980): 71–85; in hagiography see Michel de Certeau, *L'écriture de l'histoire* (Gallimard, 1975), chap. 7, "Une variante: l'édification hagio-graphique," 274–88.

40. Peter Brown describes the saint's tomb as a site of temporal compression, where memory of the deceased and hope for the future resurrection of the saints were experienced in the present. Brown, *Cult of the Saints,* 76. I propose that the hagiographic book offered a similar occasion for compression.

41. *Decrees of the Ecumenical Councils,* ed. Norman P. Tanner (Washington, D.C.: Georgetown University Press, 1990), vol. 2, 774–75.

42. On images or relics perceived as "signs that indicated the presence of the saint" see Edward Muir, "The Virgin on the Street Corner: The Place of the Sacred in Italian Cities," in *Religion and Culture in the Renaissance and Reformation,* ed. Steven Ozment (Kirksville, Mo.: Sixteenth-Century Journal Publishers, 1989), 30.

43. An early example is Marie de l'Incarnation's 1669 obituary of Sister St.-Laurent, AUQ, 1/1/1.3.

44. "On la regarde ici comme l'une de ses protectrices, à présent qu'elle est dans le Ciel, et en état de la protéger." Marie de l'Incarnation, *Correspondance,* 805. Peter Brown argues that during the liturgical reading of a saint's life or "passio," the Christians of late antiquity believed the saint to be actually present, and experienced sweet smells and miraculous healings. *Cult of the Saints,* 82.

45. Paul Ragueneau, *La vie de la mère Catherine de Saint Augustin, religieuse hospitalière de la miséricorde* (Paris, 1671), 42.

46. Regnault, "Recit veritable," *MNF* VII, 491.

47. See, for example, John Baptist St.-Jure, *The Holy Life of Monr. de Renty, a Late Nobleman of France, And sometimes Councellor to King Lewis the 13th* (London: John Crook, 1658), 233.

48. The page numbers were in place by December 1652; in an attestation of that date Ragueneau refers to preceding text by page number. *MS. 1652,* 272.

49. For a description of the piece system see Lucien Febvre and Henri-Jean Martin, *The Coming of the Book: The Impact of Printing 1450–1800,* trans. David Gerard, ed. Geoffrey Nowell-Smith and David Wootton (London: NLB, 1976), 21. The "pieces" theory can be sustained for some sections of the Manuscript of 1652. The group of texts devoted to Garnier, for example, is contained on pages 241–72 (a thirty-two-page unit, the last three blank). The section for Chabanel fills pages 273–88 (the last three blank). But the material on Brébeuf begins on pages 169–215 (the last three of these pages, immediately following the "vie" of Brébeuf, are blank). The text then resumes on page 216, a verso. The material on Anne de Noüe fills pages 119–56 (thirty-eight pages, not a logical unit of gatherings for a quarto-format manuscript).

50. For requests for paper see, for example, "Lettre de la Reverende Mere Superieure des Religieuses Hospitalieres de Kebec en la Nouvelle France" in *Jesuit Relation* for 1665–66 (*JR* 50: 160–63); *Jesuit Relation* for 1666–67 (*JR* 51: 114–15); *Jesuit Relation* for 1667–68 (*JR* 52: 108–9).

51. See Boureau, "Franciscan Piety and Voracity," 47, regarding a 1648 reprint of a life of St. Reine, and Burkhardt, "Reconnaissance et dévotion," 218.

52. Pierre Cholenec, "La vie de Catherine Tegakoüita, première Vierge Irokoise," NAC MG 17 6–3 (vol. 2). On the last page of the manuscript, Cholenec amends the scribe's copy in his own hand: "J'ajoute que Mr. Remy a donné des attestations iuridiques, signées de sa main, de . . . guérisons miraculeuses." These miraculous healings are reported in "Certificat de Mr Remy, curé de la Chine, des miracles faits en sa paroisse par l'intercession de la B. Cath. Tegakwita," ASJCF No. 344.1; for another "miracle book," Thomas Morel, "Miracles arriues en LEglise De Ste Anne du petit Cap Coste de Beaupray En Canada," Archives du Séminaire de Québec [hereafter ASQ], Paroisses diverses, No. 72.

53. *MS. 1652,* 166–68.

54. Miracles were almost always necessary to achieve canonization (although martyrs were treated more leniently in this respect). Delooz, "Towards a Sociological Study of Canonized Sainthood," 201; Macken, *Canonisation of Saints,* 45–46.

55. Regarding "cocreativity"—manuscript's conventional openness to emendation and augmentation— see Arthur Marotti, *Manuscript, Print, and the English Renaissance Lyric* (Ithaca, N.Y.: Cornell University Press, 1995), 135–37. Harold Love, citing Walter Ong, likewise suggests that because manuscript was closer to the give-and-take process of conversation, readers felt more free to "intervene." *Scribal Publication in Seventeenth-Century England* (Oxford: Clarendon Press, 1993), 142.

56. Anonymous Abenaki-French dictionary, NAC MG 18 C 8, 1–3; Antoine Silvy, "Dictionnaire Montagnais," NAC MG 18 C10; L'Abbé Jerome Sasseville, *Notes on the Two Jesuit Manuscripts Belonging to the Estate of the Late John Neilson* (New York, 1887), 12–15; *Facsimile of Père Marquette's Illinois Prayer Book* [attributed to Claude Allouez] (Quebec: Quebec Literary and Historical Society, 1905), 72–93, 177–85 blank. Sasseville, *Notes,* 8–9.

57. Regnault, "Recit veritable," *MNF* VII, 492.

58. Marie de l'Incarnation, *Correspondance,* 379.

59. Regarding "la perte d'un sy cher trésor," *MS. 1652,* 30; for relics of Daniel, *MS. 1652,* 167. The list of relics appears in *Apothéose des Bienheureux Martyrs Canadiens de la Compagnie de Jésus* (Québec: L'Action Sociale, 1926), 145.

60. ASJCF CSM no. 247, "Récit du soulagement d'une possedée par l'entremise des reliques du R. P. Jean de Brébeuf."

61. Cholenec's life of Kateri Tekakwitha suggests that the blood of Isaac Jogues, the first Jesuit to preach to the Iroquois, had been "the seed of Christianity in this unbelieving land" [la semence du christianisme dans cette terre infidèle]. "Lettre du père Cholenec . . . au père Augustin le Blanc," (1715), in *Lettres Edifiantes et Curieuses, Ecrites des Missions Etrangères* (Lyon, 1819), vol. 4, 28.

62. Maureen Ahern compares a colonial Mexican martyrology to a Baroque altarpiece in "Visual and Verbal Sites: The Construction of Jesuit Martyrdom in Northwest New Spain in Andrés Pérez de Ribas' *Historia de los Triumphos de nuestra Santa Fee* (1645)," *Colonial Latin American Review* 8:1 (1999): 7–33.

63. Boureau, "Franciscan Piety and Voracity," 15–16, describing the reading of saints' lives as a magical prac-
    tice in which one is "more 'touched' or 'struck' by the truth than 'instructed' by it." See also Burkhardt,
    "Reconaissance et dévotion," 226–27.

64. Ragueneau, *La vie de la mère Catherine de Saint Augustin,* 340.

65. Rasle, *Suite de la Vie de Chaumonot,* 33–34; obituary letter for Chaumonot, ASQ, Lettres R, no. 4.
    Regarding Marie de l'Incarnation, see Guy Oury's introduction to her *Correspondance,* xvii. On Marguerite
    Bourgeoys' writings (written in the late seventeenth century but dispersed in the early nineteenth
    century), Sister Ste.-Henriette, *Histoire de la Congrégation de Notre-Dame* (Montreal: Congrégation
    de Notre-Dame, 1941). This phenomenon also was seen in Europe and Mexico: a note in the hand of
    Antonio de Colellis was used to preserve his disciples from sickness. Gruzinski and Sallmann, "Une
    source d'ethnohistoire," 808.

66. Annales de Moulins 1740. Archives des Religieuses Hospitaliàres de St.-Joseph, Montreal.

67. The traditional hierarchical relationship of manuscript to relic is implicitly recognized in the Fourth
    Lateran Council's ruling against the sale of relics and its related order that prelates "should not in future
    allow those who come to their churches, in order to venerate, to be deceived by lying stories or false
    documents." *Decrees of the Ecumenical Councils,* ed. Tanner, vol. 1, 263.

68. Regnault, "Recit veritable," *MNF* VII, 491–92.

69. *JR* 40: 121–23. For a different reading of Poncet's vow see Deslandres, "Des Reliques comme vecteur
    d'acculturation au XVIIe siècle," 100.

70. A similar development may be seen in New England, where totemic uses of books (especially Bibles) also
    were known. See David Cressy, "Books as Totems in Seventeenth-Century England and New England,"
    The Journal of Library History 21:1 (1986): 92–106.

12

Iroquois Virgin: The Story of Catherine Tekakwitha in New France and New Spain

ALLAN GREER

*L*a gracia triunfante en la vida de Catharina Tegakovita, india iroquesa was published in Mexico City in 1724.[1] The bulk of the book consists of a long hagiographic text translated from the French and recounting the life, death, and postmortem "glories" of Catherine Tekakwitha, an Iroquois of the Mohawk tribe born in 1656 in what is now northern New York. Sometime enemies of the French, the Mohawks admitted Jesuit missionaries to their midst in the 1660s and 1670s, with the result that many converted to Christianity and moved to a mission settlement near Montreal. Tekakwitha, a sickly and reclusive teenage girl, was among them, embarking on her trek northward only after suffering persecution at the hands of her "pagan" fellow villagers. Once installed in the Jesuit-sponsored mission of Kahnawake, she joined a group of young women who had renounced sex and marriage in favor of a life of religious perfection. Tekakwitha's "penances" (fasting, self-flagellation, sleep deprivation, etc.) were particularly severe, her dreams and visions exceptionally illuminating. She died in 1680 at age twenty-four and, beginning almost immediately after her death, she became the object of a cult among Native and French-Canadian Catholics. The book catalogs her virtues, dramatizes her trials and tribulations as a Christian among pagans, dwells on her edifying death, and reports on the postmortem apparitions and miraculous cures indicative of saintly status. Although she was never canonized, Tekakwitha's life narrative bears all the marks of a classic hagiographic text.[2]

Originally composed by Pierre Cholenec, a Jesuit missionary at Montreal, the life of Tekakwitha was published in Paris in 1717, then taken to New Spain, where another Jesuit, Juan de Urtassum, translated it into Spanish seven years later. This was an unusual instance of a text circulating through the Catholic Atlantic world from the northern empire of France, via Europe, to the southern empire of Spain. Presumably, Mexican readers were quite unfamiliar with North America in the early eighteenth century, and Urtassum's well-intentioned attempt to provide some geographical orientation could not have helped matters. He locates the "Provincia de los Iroqueses" on the borders on New Mexico, just east of the land of the Apaches. The Iroquois, Urtassum continues, were never "conquered" by the French (of course the French empire was not built on conquest, but on a hegemonic alliance system); "so brave and jealous of their liberty," they resembled the Araucanians of faraway Chile.[3] Thus the life story of Catherine Tekakwitha/Catharina Tegakovita came to the attention of colonial Mexico as an exotic tale from an unknown land. Yet at the same time, hers also was the story of an *India* and of the power of God's grace to effect perfection even within this portion of humanity. Viewed from that perspective, it addressed perennial issues about the spiritual potential of natives, issues that were then very much to the fore in the capital of New Spain.

The occasion of this venture into an intercolonial commerce in hagiography was a debate raging within ruling circles of Mexico City over the establishment of a convent for Indian nuns. A former viceroy, the marqués de Valero, had donated forty thousand pesos to establish a Franciscan convent to be called Corpus Christi and to be reserved for upper-class Indian women. Billed as a measure to encourage *cacique* fathers to attend to the education of their daughters, the viceroy's project horrified many within the capital's creole elite. Opposition to Corpus Christi only found an outlet in the spring of 1723, after Valero had returned to Spain. By that time, workers were just finishing construction of the convent at a choice location across from the Alameda, a fashionable park at the western edge of Mexico City, and the first contingent of eighteen Indian nuns had already been selected. At that point the monastic foundation came before the *audiencia* of New Spain and the local *cabildo* (city council) for approval.

These bodies had authority over religious foundations, mainly to ensure that sound financial arrangements were in place so new establishments would not drain resources from the local economy. After extensive debates and inquiries, the *audiencia* turned back the application, while the *cabildo* gave its very reluctant approval, suggesting that the "sumptuous building" might better be used as a school to teach Indian girls how to earn an honest living.[4] The ex-viceroy, now presiding over the Council of Indies in Seville, still had his way, however. He secured a royal edict overruling the *audiencia* and, amid great pageantry, Corpus Christi opened its doors to Indian nuns in 1724.[5]

The convent was torn by strife through the greater part of its eighteenth-century history as native nuns struggled to escape the tutelage of Spanish sisters, but following these disputes would take us far from the *gracia triunfante,* an artifact of the controversies of 1723–24. The life of Tekakwitha was translated into Spanish, as the book's preface states quite clearly, to refute the arguments of the anti-Corpus Christi forces. These arguments had little to do with the economic considerations that theoretically justified *cabildo* and *audiencia* interference on the subject. The local authorities did register concern that the marqués de Valero's endowment might not be sufficient and that the nunnery would strain the charitable resources of local residents, but it was quite evident that their opposition stemmed from a conviction that Indian women were unsuitable material for the nun's vocation.[6] Accordingly, the hagiographic counterblast was all about proving that natives could indeed qualify for the religious life. Attached to the translated biography of Catherine Tekakwitha was a series of appendices, including brief profiles of pious *indias* from Mexico, as well as a learned "punto apologetico" by Dr. D. Juan Ignacio de Castorena y Ursua, "Vicar-General of the Natural Inhabitants of this Archdiocese," defending the spiritual capacity of native women. The bulk of the book consists of a saint's life, but this is clearly hagiography deployed with a polemical purpose. In the European tradition, sacred biography often was used as a weapon to settle questions of power and influence; thus the *Gracia triunfante* fits into a well-established subgenre of the political pamphlet in the form of a sacred biography.[7]

Drawing on the documents generated by the *audiencia* inquiry, as well as on the more terse records of the *cabildo* inquiry on Corpus Christi and the "punto apologetico" attached to the *gracia triunfante,* it is possible to reconstruct the basic contours of the debate. The *audiencia* materials are particularly interesting. In the course of hearings over three months, the *audiencia* consulted three Jesuits, two Franciscans, three nuns, and three convent chaplains. Most of these expert witnesses were chosen because of their experience ministering to natives in the vicinity of the capital, and each was asked for his views on the spiritual and moral capabilities of Indians. Most lined up squarely on one side or the other of the question whether native women could become nuns. Surprisingly, in view of their "liberal" reputation, it was the three Jesuits who took the hardest anti-Indian line (though it was also a Jesuit who translated the pro-Corpus Christi life of Tekakwitha into Spanish). This chapter will begin with an examination of the public debate on Corpus Christi before opening the puzzling question of how and why a work of hagiography should come into play as a polemical instrument.

To some degree, discussions took the form of a recapitulation of centuries-old European discourses on the nature of generic "savages" and their qualifications as fully human subjects. In the Las Casas tradition, Father Andres Xavier Garcia told the *audiencia* that natives were honest, humble, immune to covetousness and ambition.[8] He and other partisans of Corpus Christi insisted that talent and intelligence could be found among Indians just as it could among Europeans. Witnesses on the other side sometimes followed what might be called a Sepúlveda line, insisting on their instability and limited understanding. The Jesuit Alexandro Romano took a position seemingly drawn straight from pre-Christian Greek views on wild barbarians. Before the Conquest, he declared, Indians lived in the mountains; even after being "reduced," they retain "their natural opposition to society and civil existence" and are thus disinclined to live in a community.[9] This is indeed an eccentric take on Aztec civilization, but it led Romano to the inevitable conclusion that natives remained unfit for the collective existence of a monastic régime. Other witnesses in the anti-Corpus Christi camp dwelled on the legal status of Indians, "who are not even admitted as lay brothers to religious orders, and who are exempted, because of their frailties, their uncouth rustic ways and their limited abilities, from certain ecclesiastical regulations to which everyone else is subject."[10]

Although discussions about the nature and capabilities of the generic Indian-as-minor are by no means absent from the Corpus Christi dispute, they were not a central theme. This was a debate about gender as well as race. The main focus was on *indias,* not Indians, and it was their qualifications for a specific, and profoundly gendered role, that of nun, that exercised the priests and officials of Mexico City. Could an *india* become a nun? Each of the terms of that contested equation carried a load of connotations in New Spain, and the struggles of 1724 revolved around the question of whether the two could be in any degree compatible.

Native women were "better" than native men, most parties to the debate agreed; they were more modest, sober, and devout, more hard working and amenable to direction than their brothers and husbands. Humility, a prime requisite of religious perfection, was their characteristic virtue. Yet, according to their detractors, the *indias* lacked one other, indispensable virtue: constancy. As would-be nuns they could not be relied on to keep their vows. Presumably the vows of poverty and obedience posed no difficulty to humble native women; rather it was the vow of chastity that was at issue. There was a specific and unmistakably sexual undertone to the allegation of "inconstancy," one that frequently surfaced in explicit form: Indian women could not be relied on to remain chaste and celibate.

Accordingly, the *audiencia* hearings on the Corpus Christi convent tended to take the form of an inquest into the sexuality of colonized women. *Indias,* Alexandro Romano observed, have difficulty keeping even their marriage vows. How could they be expected to observe the much more demanding requirements of the religious estate, for as nuns they would need the strength to master "all the passions" and "mortify their disorderly appetites"?[11] Some other witnesses commented more discreetly on native women's deficiencies in the area of "vows" and "constancy," but the theme of chastity/sexuality was clearly central to the entire inquiry.

It was also the sole preoccupation of the court's investigation of three *indias caciques* of questionable character supposedly destined for Corpus Christi. Two of these women had married, and one, Luisa de Rivero, was discovered to be running a petticoat shop *(puesta de enaguas)* on the main square of the city, in company with a Spanish man she *claimed* to have married![12] When the mother superior-elect of Corpus Christi was eventually given an opportunity to respond to these "discoveries," she pointed out that the three women had all long since given up their plans to enter the religious life and so there was no scandal, simply the normal process of selection that brought only the truly dedicated postulants into a religious order while others dropped by the wayside.[13] Thus, without uncovering any irregularity in recruitment, the *audiencia* officials had managed, through this part of the investigation, to cast doubt on the sexual propriety of the Corpus Christi enterprise.

When Spanish men spoke of native women as though they were incapable of chastity, they were not so much "arguing a point" as revealing an ontological premise. In the colonizers' discursive universe, the term "Indian woman" implied sexual impurity. Perhaps this association was confirmed by lived reality in a racially stratified society where white men often enjoyed power over the bodies of women of the subaltern races. Psychological forces set in motion by the earliest sexual experiences of colonial childhood would likely have tended to reinforce this image. To the extent that Spanish babies were cared for by *india* nursemaids,[14] then all the intimate bodily contact inseparable from childcare and constitutive of infant sexuality may well have played a part in shaping the erotic desires of the creole elite. Would Spanish babies then grow up to be Spanish men and women who viewed native women with desire overlaid with guilt and anxiety?[15] Quite likely they would, though the point needs to be confirmed by empirical research.

In any case, the association of Indian women with the taint of sexuality was not constituted solely in the realm of individual personality formation. That connection was also manifest in the discursive practices of colonialism. "White" New Spain saw itself as the product of historical processes of discovery, conquest, and colonization, all of which tended to be understood through sexual metaphors. In what Anne McClintock calls "the erotics of imperial conquest," the Spaniards (and Europeans more generally) were depicted entering, possessing, and ravishing a feminized America.[16] Texts and visual images frequently used women's bodies as "the boundary markers of empire." The New World's women, like its other treasures and allurements, were there to be taken by the men from Europe, and so even if an individual *india* led a life of blameless chastity, she would still be ascribed a species identity suggestive of sexual availability.[17]

As object of erotic desire, the native woman also represented the dangers of breakdown and assimilation that haunted the psychology of colonialism. Contrary impulses racked New Spain (and other colonial societies), for the urge to possess and enjoy appeared to lead toward an eradication of the fundamental distinction between colonizer and colonized. This threat of hybridity loomed everywhere, as Spaniards acquired new tastes in food from native cooks, as Nahuatl vocabulary entered their language, etc., and in this context, the sexuality and procreative fertility of Indian women served as a metonym for the assimilative power of the conquered; it implied the emergence of a "bastard race" that would leave no trace of the Spaniards' identity.

Such fears of submergence, together with the contending forces of desire and repulsion, are characteristic features of the psychology of colonialism, but they seem to have been particularly intense in New Spain, as compared, for example, to New France. Central Mexico was home to a substantial native population, far more numerous, even after the demographic disasters associated with the Conquest, than the Indians the French encountered in Canada; the weight of numbers alone were suggestive of a powerful capacity to assimilate. Moreover, the general Spanish approach to New World colonization, reliant as it was on coerced native labor—whether conscripted for temporary labor service or recruited through the workings of a nominally free, racially organized labor market—fostered close contact between Spaniard and Indian. Attempts were made to maintain physical boundaries between the "republic of the Indians" and the "republic of the Spaniards," but these experiments in apartheid were doomed to failure in Mexico City. The voracious hunger of Spanish residents for domestic servants, and cheap labor of all sorts, though satisfied to some extent in the early seventeenth century by African slaves, tended to draw thousands of natives toward the heart of the European city, right into the very homes of the Spanish conquerors.[18] Within the urban Spanish "republic," the Indian presence was both a necessity and a menace. Economically, culturally, and sexually, the European impulse to embrace the Indian contended with fears of engulfment and a consequent determination to ensure subordination and maintain boundaries.

The drive to preserve distinctions in spite of the intimate relations of exploitation underlay a wide range of practices and symbolic gestures, many of them similar in a general way to manifestations of racism and protoracism observable in almost any colonial situation: the tendency to assign a diminished personal identity to members of the colonized races, the stigmatizing of mixed-race people, measures to discipline the colonized and provide privileges to the colonizers. Among the special features of Spanish colonialism in the early modern period was the heavy reliance on the law, with racial differences formally instituted in the language of

limpieza de sangre (purity of blood) adapted from Iberian legislation originally designed to discriminate against Jews and Moors. In the American
setting, state and church deployed the concept of "pure [Spanish] blood"
to exclude nonwhites from positions and practices that conferred status.
Thus "Indians" so designated (and, of course, we know that in real life
there was considerable indeterminacy and slippage in racial designations)
could not, for example, wear shoes, carry weapons, ride horses, or—most
significant for present purposes—enter the clergy or the religious orders.[19]

In this colonial society, dedicated to the impossible goal of exploiting
natives while avoiding contaminating contact with them, purity anxieties
tended to have a particular racial-sexual focus. To be more specific, concern centered on women's bodies. While Spanish men themselves were the
most active agents of miscegenation, they chose to regard white women's
fertility as the key to preserving the conquerors' racial integrity. Mexican
fathers were particularly vigilant in policing the honor of their daughters,
and husbands guarded the fidelity of their wives with unusual determination.[20] The image of native women as sexually tainted therefore found its
counterpart in the ideal of sexual purity among Spanish women. The
opposition of purity and impurity in matters of race ("blood") tended to
merge with a parallel opposition of pure and impure female sexuality.

This topic brings us back to the subject of nuns, the fundamental category, along with *indias,* in the Corpus Christi controversy of 1723–24. In
light of the foregoing discussion, nuns seem notable as women with a
unique claim to perfect purity on both racial and sexual grounds. The oath
of chastity was central to ceremonies by which one entered a religious
order and, prior to taking the oaths, every postulant in New Spain had to
produce a certificate of *limpieza de sangre,* guaranteeing that her blood was
untainted by Jewish, Muslim, or Indian ancestry.[21] Thus, whatever other
social, religious, and personal purposes convents may have served for the
people of the capital, nuns had an important symbolic role for "white"
Mexico City as the embodiment of reserved female sexuality.

Nuns were often referred to in the language of the time as "virgins,"
and great weight was attached to that term. In point of biological fact,
they were not all virgins—widowed women sometimes entered religious
orders—but they were assigned a species identity that connected them to
ancient Christian traditions venerating undefiled female bodies. Of course,
male clerics also were supposed to be celibate, but sexual abstinence was

simply one virtue among many they were expected to cultivate; for nuns it was a defining feature of their identity. From the fourth century, "Dedicated women came to be thought of as harboring a deposit of values that were prized by their male spokesmen, as peculiarly precious to the Christian community."[22] Because the prayers of virginal "brides of Christ" were thought to have special potency, medieval cities valued convents for the protective powers that radiated from them.

It is true that there was more to a nun's life than prayer alone. Many women's orders founded during the Counter-Reformation dedicated themselves to worldly service in fields such as education and medical relief. Ursulines and hospital nuns first came to New France in response to a call for women who would take an active part in converting the Indians, and they were supported by colonists' donations and government grants primarily because of their efforts to succor the sick and indigent and to educate French and native girls. But any such practical orientation was less apparent in New Spain; indeed, the female orders of colonial Mexico City were all strictly contemplative. A guide to the city published in 1697 referred to the twelve local nunneries as so many "choruses of angels in their purity": "Happy city, where the prayers of prudent Virgins, brides of Jesus, in the different convents, form well-ordered armies of angels, and choirs that are terrifying in the eyes of Hell, lovely in the eyes of Heaven."[23] Outwardly, the convents of Mexico were centers of prayer and islands of purity, and they enjoyed public support mainly on that basis.

Viewed from the inside, of course, convents were something quite different. Of the thousand or so Spanish women who enjoyed official status in the convents of Mexico City in the late seventeenth century, many—Sor Juana Inés de la Cruz being the most famous example—found intellectual or artistic fulfillment in the cloistered life, fulfillment that would have been almost impossible in the married state. Other nuns pursued religious perfection through a personal regime of extreme asceticism, while still others, especially in the more lax establishments, enjoyed considerable comfort and ease.[24] Colonial convents were hierarchical institutions, with nuns from wealthy families enjoying privileges unavailable to their more humble sisters. Attending to the drudge work was a substantial corps of servants, *indias,* and mixed-race women who cooked, cleaned, and washed. Disqualified by "purity of blood" barriers (as well as by poverty) from taking the veil, these women, in many cases, saw their role as one of serving God through serving a sister, and in many respects they did partake of the monastic life. Some, noted in the pages of the *Gracia triunfante* and the *audiencia* inquest, spent an entire lifetime within the cloister, observing simple vows of chastity, poverty, and obedience. Thus the city's convents were not lily-white institutions, but rather multiracial communities mirroring, in important ways, the society beyond their walls. And yet, in the dominant colonial view, a true nun was of untarnished Spanish extraction and the public personality of every convent derived from the race of the conqueror.

Just as the term *india* carried connotations of polluting sexuality, so the word "nun" indicated racial and sexual purity.[25] Like Indian women, though in a contrary sense, the female religious orders of New Spain, with their white consecrated "virgins," served a symbolic purpose as "boundary markers of empire." How then could an Indian woman be a nun? There was a sense of ontological incompatibility, with racialized sexuality at the core, driving and sustaining opposition to the establishment of Corpus Christi convent in 1724. To overcome that opposition and create a space for a religious house for *indias,* the churchmen and secular leaders who championed the marqués de Valero's project had to open a breach in the insurmountable barrier of "purity" that separated native women from the sphere of the religious virgins.

The campaign in favor of Corpus Christi was fought with various ideological and political weapons, including the ultimately decisive royal decree sent from Spain, but insofar as supporters had recourse to the printed word in their attempt to win adherents in Mexico, they relied on another *deus ex machina* in the form of a holy biography from faraway Canada. Of all the literary genres available, why deploy hagiography as the main vehicle of political debate? And why select the life of a northern Iroquois woman when the annals of Mexico and the rest of Spanish America offered several profiles, much closer to home, of Indian women of exemplary piety?

The *Gracia triunfante,* as noted earlier, was not entirely given over to hagiography. Tacked on as an appendix was Juan Ignacio de Castorena y Ursua's reasoned theological argument in favor of the establishment of a convent for *indias.* The main thrust of his *punto apologetico* was reflected in the title of the book: divine grace could triumph over all obstacles, selecting individuals, even from among the unpromising materials of Indian society, and equipping them for a life of perfection. Though the dominant tone of his text was austere and rational, Castorena did indulge in some revealing metaphorical excursions.

> Can any good be derived from the Indies? No one can be in doubt of the gold, silver, pearls, and fruits, or of the talents of virtue, management, nobility, and letters of those residing there, unless some second Anaxagoras should arise to say that snow is black. They only make difficulties regarding the religiosity of the Indian women; though they might concede to them a natural inclination to other virtues, such as humility, poverty, indifference to the things of the world, obedience, and mortification, yet they dispute [their ability to observe] the vows of purity and enclosure.[26]

In this passage, Castorena draws on traditional tropes associating native women with the mineral riches and other natural bounty of the New World, but he gives them a novel spin. Instead of emphasizing *india* sexuality and procreative fertility, the author points to native virtue as the treasure that American women offer. And if vows of purity and clausura seem to present obstacles, it must be remembered that chastity is a gift of God, unattainable by individuals of any nation in the absence of divine grace.

In addition to philosophical arguments and reconfigured colonialist metaphors, the *Gracia triunfante* also presents empirical "proof," in a chapter profiling five devout Mexican *indias,* most of the text paraphrased from the pages of Carlos de Sigüena y Góngora's *Paraíso Occidental* (1683),[27] that Indian women are indeed capable of attaining the heights of spiritual achievement. Attentive to the basic issue in the Corpus Christi controversy, the author makes a point of insisting on the *continencia* of all five, and on their "virginal purity," comparable to that of Catherine Tekakwitha. But, however admirable their lives may have been, their life stories remain sketchy, fragmentary, and, in two cases out of five, literally anonymous. One girl from Michoachan is cured of a paralyzing illness when she promises to dedicate her virginity to Jesus. She resists parental pressure to marry and later enters a convent, taking simple (i.e., unofficial) vows of chastity and clausura. The longest section of the chapter is devoted to Petronila de la Concepcion, a native girl who came from her home near Mexico City to serve the nuns of the convent of Jesus Maria. Once, when praying before an image of Ecce Homo, the Lord reached out from the picture and placed his hand over her heart. Taking simple vows to imitate the nuns in their devotions and austerities, she was rewarded with further visions. The Virgin Mary appeared to her during the flood of 1629 and gave her assurances that neither the convent nor the city would be destroyed. Illumination on this order made hers a more spectacular life than that of Catherine Tekakwitha, who never experienced anything quite so miraculous during her lifetime.

In the truncated biography of Petronila there is virtually no information on the first ten years of her life: nothing on her family, nothing on the native milieu in which she was reared, nothing on her experiences when she was expelled from the convent due to illness (except that she prayed fervently to be cured so that she could return to the nuns). In this account, she simply materializes out of the shadowy suburban world of hispanicized Indians who catered to the needs of New Spain's elite. For the chroniclers of the convent of Jesus Maria, Petronila and others like her belonged to an inferior caste that formed an integral part of colonial society. She was the familiar other, a convent servant with circumscribed autonomy and attenuated personal identity. Her family and ethnic background were unimportant and/or unknown; it sufficed to say that she was an Indian. Jesus touched her heart in an extraordinary gesture of affinity for the humble of this world, but who was this woman so honored?

Catherine Tekakwitha was not the intimate other, but the exotic other; not only in the remote setting of Mexico, but even in the eyes of the French Jesuit who served as her confessor and later as her biographer. The Iroquois were, as the Spanish translator of her life noted, never conquered. Even those who converted to Catholicism and moved to live in the confines of Montreal maintained their autonomy as junior allies, rather than subjects, of the king of France.[28] They did not pay tribute, nor did they owe labor service and they almost never worked for colonists, even as paid servants. Though affected by European culture in multiple ways, Tekakwitha's people remained visibly Iroquois in costume, language, and economic organization. She herself probably knew not a word of the French language, and consequently the Jesuit missionaries had to learn Mohawk to communicate with her and with the other converts. There were close connections between the French settlers and the natives of New France at a number of points related to trade, war, and diplomacy, but the two societies were not fully integrated. Consequently, Indians appeared still as strangers to the colonists, not as a subordinated caste within the colonial social system. They were not unfamiliar strangers, to be sure, especially not to Jesuits such as Father Cholenec, who lived among them and spoke their language, but they had nothing to do with the people who cleaned one's boots and cut one's firewood.

This sense of cultural distance may have made it easier for the French Jesuits to regard Tekakwitha as a full subject, an actor in a spiritual drama, rather than a servant with a diminished personal identity. It is true that the Jesuits of New France recorded dozens of brief profiles of exemplary converts that were every bit as fragmentary and anonymous as the passages from *Paraiso Occidental* devoted to Petronila de la Concepcion and the other, nameless, Christian *indias.*[29] Eventually, however, they produced a substantial work of "sacred biography" that, in Spanish translation, occupied 144 pages in *La gracia triunfante* (compared to 36 pages for all five exemplary Mexican lives). Coverage of the phases of Tekakwitha's life is uneven, but there are no blank spaces: her ancestry, birth, and childhood among the "pagan" Mohawks are recounted, as well as her conversion, baptism, and flight to Montreal. Her vow of perpetual virginity and her heroic penitential practices naturally receive disproportionate attention, but following the treatment of this subject comes a long, concluding chapter on her edifying death and on the apparitions and miracles that signaled her "glorification." Whereas other texts, both Spanish and French, celebrating pious natives consist of vignettes emblematic of holiness, this one conveys a sense of biographical completeness: it tells the "whole story" of a full person.

To Catholic readers of the period, the story of Catherine Tekakwitha would be all the more compelling because of the way it conformed so closely to established hagiographic templates. The early chapters with their dramatized account of "pagan tyranny" among the Mohawks and the persecution of the neophyte Christian are closely modeled on tales of early Christian martyrdom; moreover, the theme of movement between the evil "wilderness" and the sanctified "city" is also a classic trope.[30] When Tekakwitha later enters her period of "glorification," her ascetic practices are described in terms drawn from the lives of the women saints of the late Middle Ages. The greatest of these, Catherine of Siena, was her name saint, and some elements in her biography correspond precisely to details from the life of that fourteenth-century saint. (For example, both Catherines explained their severe penances as atonement for having allowed an older sister to dress them in alluring finery when they were young.[31]) In the realm of hagiography, a discourse of archetypes,[32] originality is no virtue; rather, hagiographers were inclined to adjust their accounts to conform to genre models. Thus, whereas the original French life of Tekakwitha describes her face after death as wearing a serene expression, Juan de Urtassum felt the need to insert a sentence into the Spanish translation about a sweet odor emanating from her corpse, an added touch indicative of saintly status.[33]

A vow of chastity, sworn one year before Tekakwitha's death, constitutes a central turning point in the narrative. According to Father Cholenec's 1717 text, the young woman went to the mission chapel, and there the priest administered a solemn vow by which she dedicated her virginity, in perpetuity, to Jesus and Mary. Such a vow, performed publicly and under the auspices of the church, would have distinguished Tekakwitha's case from that of dozens of Canadian and Mexican *indias* who swore "simple vows," undertaking privately and personally to avoid sex and marriage; and it was the solemn vow that enabled Cholenec to present her to the world as "the First Iroquois Virgin." Catherine's crowning "achievement" lay in the way the colonial church recognized and framed her personal dedication. (In fact, there is strong evidence to suggest that Tekakwitha never did take the solemn vow. She desired it ardently but, according to another French Jesuit well acquainted with the case, her confessor, Pierre Cholenec, refused permission; she was, after all, only an Indian, and he had heard rumors about past sexual misconduct! After her death, doubts melted away, and it was agreed that she "deserved the merit of her intention," so Cholenec provided her retrospectively with a solemn vow.[34] The process of adjusting the raw data of Catherine's life to fit the conventional patterns of hagiographic narrative began well before Juan de Urtassum's translation.)

Why, we asked, did a saintly story from a distant colony come to be the main weapon for combating opposition to Corpus Christi? Clearly this unique case of a native woman consecrating her virginity in the highest, most formal way possible strengthened the claim that Indians could indeed observe the nun's vow of chastity. But this exemplary case could have been evoked in a single brief paragraph if it was simply a matter of adducing evidence to score points in a debate. Why translate and publish the entire book-length story of Tekakwitha's life? I would suggest that the text in its integrity, and in its material form as a volume of sacred biography, possessed a peculiar power to command the assent of Catholic readers.

The mission here was something more than "winning an argument." Proponents of the Corpus Christi project had to reengineer the fundamentally sexualized image of native women and create a space for nuns who were also Indians. To link the category *india* with the signs and emblems of Christian saintliness and purity required a special kind of book, one whose quasisacred format served to guarantee its authority.[35]

NOTES

1. Michael W. Mathes, ed., *La gracia triunfante en la vida de Catharina Tegakovita, india iroquesa, y en las de otras, Assi de su Nacion, como de esta Nueva-España* [Mexico: Joseph Bernardo de Hogal, 1724] (Madrid: Ediciones Jose Porrua Turanzas, 1994).

2. "Lettre du Père Cholenec . . . au Père Augustin LeBlanc . . . le 27 aout 1715," *Lettres édifiantes et curieuses écrites des missions étrangères,* 30 vols. (Paris: N. Leclerc, 1708–71), vol. 12 (1717): 119–211.

3. *La gracia triunfante,* 3–4. "Tan brava, y zelosa de su libertad." (This and subsequent quotations translated by the author.)

4. Archivo historico de la Ciudad de Mexico [hereafter AHCM], Fundaciones, vol. 2262, May 24, 1723.

5. On the history of Corpus Christi, see Asunción Lavrin, "Indian Brides of Christ: Creating New Spaces for Indigenous Women in New Spain," *Mexican Studies/Estudios Mexicanos* 15 (Summer 1999): 225–60. Other secondary works dealing with the convent and the conflicts surrounding its establishment are: José Maria Marroqui, *La Ciudad de Mexico,* 3 vols. (Mexico City: La Europa, 1900), 1: 189–91; P. Mariano Cuevas, *Historia de la Iglesia en Mexico,* 4 vols. (Mexico City: Ediciones Cervantes 1942), 4: 189–90; José Ignacio Rubio Mane, *El Virreinato,* 4 vols. (Mexico City: Instituto de Investigaciones Historicas 1955–63), 4: 215–20; Josefina Muriel, *Las Indias Caciques de Corpus Christi* (Mexico: UNAM, 1963); Ann Miriam Gallagher, "The Indian Nuns of Mexico City's *Monasterio* of Corpus Christi, 1724–1821," in *Latin American Women: Historical Perspectives,* ed. Asunción Lavrin (Westport, Conn.: Greenwood Press 1978), 152–53; Maria Justina Sarabia Viejo, "La Concepcion y Corpus Christi, Raza y Vida conventual Feminenia en Mexico, Siglo XVIII," in *Manifestaciones Religiosas en el Mundo Colonial Americano,* ed. Clara Garcia Ayluardo and Manuel Ramos Medin (Mexico City: Condumex 1994), vol. 2: 16–19; Maria Concepcion Amerlinck de Corsi and Manuel Ramos Medina, *Conventos de Monjas: Fundaciones en el México virreinal* (Mexico City: Grupo Condumex 1995), 122–27; Josefina Muriel, "Las indias cacicas en la época virreinal," *Arqueologia Mexicana* 5, no. 29 (1998): 56–63.

6. For documents generated by the *audiencia* inquiry see Archivo general de la nacion [hereafter AGN], historia, vol. 109, expediente 2, fols. 8–55. The more terse records of the *cabildo* debates are in AHCM, Actas de Cabildo, May 24–25, 1723.

7. Alain Boureau, "Franciscan Piety and Voracity: Uses and Stratagems in the Hagiographic Pamphlet," *The Culture of Print: Power and the Misuse of Print in Early Modern Europe,* ed. Roger Chartier, trans. Lydia G. Cochrane (Princeton, N.J.: Princeton University Press 1989), 15–58.

8. AGN, historia, vol. 109, expediente 2, fol. 36v, Andres Xavier García, May 20, 1723. Cf. Bartholomé de las Casas, *A Short Account of the Destruction of the Indies.* ed. and trans. Nigel Griffin (London: Penguin 1992); Juan de Palafox y Mendoza, *Virtudes de indios* (Madrid: Imprenta de Tomas Minuesa de los Rios, 1893); Mario Cesareo, *Cruzados, Martires y Beatos: Emplazamientos del cuerpo colonial* (West Lafayette, Ind.: Purdue University Press, 1995), 95–97.

9. Ibid., fol. 32–32v, Alexandro Romano, May 20, 1723. On the classical origins of this view see Anthony Pagden, *The Fall of Natural Man: The American Indian and the Origins of Comparative Ethnology* (Cambridge: Cambridge University Press, 1982), 21.

10. Ibid, fol. 53, conclusions of oydor fiscal, Dr. Pedro Malo de Villavucencio, November 4, 1723.

11. Ibid., fol. 33–33v.

12. Ibid., fol. 41v, affidavits dated June 16, 1723.

13. Ibid., fol. 43v–44, testimony of Me. Petra de San Francisco, October 23, 1723.

14. Serge Gruzinski, *Histoire de Mexico* (Paris: Fayard 1996), 265, 298; Antonio Rubial García, *La Plaza, el palacio y el convento* (Mexico City: Sello Bermejo, 1998), 103.

15. Anne Stoler, *Race and the Education of Desire: Foucault's History of Sexuality and the Colonial Order of Things* (Durham, N.C.: Duke University Press, 1995); Gilberto Freyre, *The Masters and the Slaves: A Study in the Development of Brazilian Civilization* (New York: Alfred A. Knopf, 1956), 278–79.

16. Anne McClintock, *Imperial Leather: Race, Gender, and Sexuality in the Colonial Contest* (New York: Routledge, 1995), 21–25.

17. Louis Montrose, "The Work of Gender in the Discourse of Discovery," in *New World Encounters,* ed. Stephen Greenblatt (Berkeley: University of California Press, 1993), 177–217; Peter Mason, *Infelicities: Representations of the Exotic* (Baltimore: Johns Hopkins University Press, 1998), 61–63.

18. Gruzinski, *Histoire de Mexico,* 297–99; Rubial García, *La plaza,* 29–36.

19. On the rules regulating race in general see Rubial García, *La plaza,* 29–36; Gruzinski, *Histoire de Mexico,* passim.

 On the status of natives in connection specifically with the church and the religious orders see Robert Ricard, *The Spiritual Conquest of Mexico: An Essay on the Apostolate and the Evangelizing Methods of the Mendicant Orders in New Spain: 1523–1572,* trans. L. B. Simpson (Berkeley: University of California Press, 1966); Francisco Morales, *Ethnic and Social Background of the Franciscan Friars in Seventeenth-Century Mexico* (Washington, D.C.: Academy of American Franciscan History, 1973); Stafford Poole, "The Declining Image of the Indian among Churchmen in Sixteenth-Century New Spain," in *Indian-Religious Relations in Colonial Spanish America,* ed. Susan E. Ramirez (Syracuse, N.Y.: Syracuse University Press, 1989), 11–19; Stafford Poole, "Church Law on the Ordination of Indians and Castas in New Spain," *Hispanic American Historical Review 61* (November 1981): 637–50.

20. Ann Twinam, "Honor, Sexuality, and Illegitimacy in Colonial Spanish America," in *Sexuality and Marriage in Colonial Latin America,* ed. Asunción Lavrin (Lincoln: University of Nebraska Press, 1989), 118–49; Ramon A. Gutiérrez, *When Jesus Came, the Corn Mothers Went Away: Marriage, Sexuality, and Power in New Mexico, 1500–1846* (Stanford, Calif.: Stanford University Press, 1991), 207–40.

21. Ascunción Lavrin, "Women in Convents: Their Economic and Social Role in Colonial Mexico," in *Liberating Women's History: Theoretical and Critical Essays,* ed. Bernice A. Carroll (Urbana: University of Illinois Press, 1976), 257.

22. Peter Brown, *The Body and Society: Men, Women, and Sexual Renunciation in Early Christianity* (New York: Columbia University Press, 1988), 263.

23. Fray Agustín de Vetancurt, "Tratado de la ciudad de Mexico," in *La Ciudad de México en el siglo XVIII (1690–1780): Tres crónicas,* ed. Antonio Rubial García (Mexico City: Cien de México, 1990), 126, 122.

24. Asunción Lavrin, "Unlike Sor Juana? The Model Nun in the Religious Literature of Colonial Mexico," in *Feminist Perspectives on Sor Juana Inés de la Cruz,* ed. Stephanie Merrim (Detroit: Wayne State University Press, 1991), 61–85; Rubial García, *La plaza,* 158–59.

25. The classic anthropological study of this general topic is Mary Douglas, *Purity and Danger: An Analysis of the Concepts of Pollution and Taboo* (London: Routledge & Kegan Paul, 1966).

26. *Gracia triunfante,* unpaginated appendix.

27. *Gracia triunfante,* 209–45. Cf. Carlos de Sigüena y Góngora, *Paraíso Occidental* (Mexico City: Juan de Rivera, 1683, Cien, 1995), libro tercero, cap. xiv–xv.

28. On the Christian Indian communities of New France see Louise Dechêne, *Habitants et marchands de Montréal au XVIIe siècle* (Paris: Plon, 1974), 22–42; James Axtell, *The Invasion Within: The Contest of Cultures in Colonial North America* (New York: Oxford University Press, 1985), 43–70; David Blanchard, ". . . To the Other side of the Sky: Catholicism at Kahnawake, 1667–1700," *Anthropologica* 24 (1982): 77–102; Bruce G. Trigger, *Natives and Newcomers: Canada's 'Heroic Age' Reconsidered* (Kingston, Ont.: Queen's University Press 1985), 286–96; Denys Delâge, "Les Iroquois chrétiens des 'réductions,' 1667–1770: II-Rapports avec la Ligue iroquoise, les Britanniques et les autres nations autochtones," *Recherches amérindiennes au Québec* 21 (1991): 39–50; Gretchen Green, "A New People in an Age of War: The Kahnawake Iroquois, 1667–1760" (Ph.D. diss., College of William and Mary, 1991); Jan Grabowski, "The Common Ground: Settled Natives and French in Montréal, 1667–1760" (Ph.D. diss., Université de Montréal, 1993); Marc Jetten, *Enclaves amérindiennes: les 'réductions' du Canada 1637–1701* (Quebec: Septentrion, 1994).

29. Allan Greer, "Colonial Saints: Gender, Race, and Hagiography in New France," *William and Mary Quarterly* 3rd Series 57 (April 2000): 323–48.

30. Allan Greer, "Savage/Saint: The Lives of Kateri Tekakwitha," in *Habitants et marchands, vingt ans après. Lectures de l'histoire des XVIIe et XVIIIe siècles canadiens,* ed. Sylvie Dépatie et al. (Montreal: McGill-Queen's University Press, 1998), 138–59; Michel de Certeau, "A Variant: Hagio-Graphical Edification," in his *The Writing of History,* trans. Tom Conley (New York: Columbia University Press, 1988), 269–83.

31. Greer, "Savage/Saint," 148–49.

32. Richard Kieckhefer, "Imitators of Christ: Sainthood in the Christian Tradition," in *Sainthood: Its Manifestations in World Religions,* ed. Richard Kieckhefer and George D. Bond (Berkeley: University of California Press, 1988), 1–42.

33. *Gracia triunfante,* 134.

34. Claude Chauchetière, "La Vie de la B. Catherine Tegakouita, dite à présent La Saincte Sauvagesse," Archives de la société de Jésus, province du Canada français, manuscript 343, p. 126; Greer, "Savage/Saint," 148.

35. See Alain Boureau's highly suggestive study "Franciscan Piety and Voracity."

13

"Redeemer of America": Rosa de Lima (1586–1617), the Dynamics of Identity, and Canonization[1]

KATHLEEN ANN MYERS

Here is a Rose, new flower of a new world, that from the Pacific Ocean of the Indies exudes peace, springtime, and joy. Could it be that it exudes sanctity as well?

—Leonard Hansen, "Dedicatoria," *Vida admirable de Santa Rosa*

On April 29, 1671, bells rang throughout Lima, Peru, to announce the arrival of the papal bull from Clement X that proclaimed America's first saint, Rosa de Santa María. A criolla woman who was born less than a century after Columbus's voyages to America had been elevated to the highest ranks of the Roman Catholic Church. A contemporary Dominican chronicler, Juan de Meléndez, describes the celebration that followed in Lima.[2] Religious brotherhoods dedicated to Rosa displayed their floats, churches brimmed over with flowers and candles for the event, and Limeños of all classes and races poured into the streets to follow the procession. Even the highest-ranking state officials, the viceroy and vicereine, attended the Mass in Rosa's honor and received the official Roman hagiography and portrait of the saint. Meléndez goes on to report that when a miraculous voice spoke to the assembled crowd, witnesses interpreted the event as yet another sign that Lima had indeed received God's favor.

Rosa de Santa María (1586–1617) had been a popular figure for Limeños for more than half a century, with mass veneration beginning almost at the moment of the mystic's death at age thirty-one. Throngs of people fought to catch a glimpse of Rosa in her open casket at the Church of Santo Domingo, where this lay holy woman associated with the Dominican order had so often been seen in the past praying for Lima's inhabitants. Chronicles of the period record that the viceroy summoned the civil guard to control crowds that were clipping pieces of her clothing to keep as holy relics.[3] Soon Limeños were adorning their houses with portraits of Rosa to honor her and to invoke her protection. They also began to form religious brotherhoods and to found the Dominican Convent of Santa Catalina, whose establishment Rosa had prophesied.[4]

Ecclesiastical officials in Lima responded immediately to this popular devotion by taking testimony from witnesses as to Rosa's life and miracles. This first local "diocesan process" (proceso arzobispal) aimed at documenting Rosa's saintly qualities for canonization took two years to complete (1617–19). By 1625, however, the attitude of the church seems to have changed: the Inquisition in Lima had confiscated her writings, and some of her lay followers were prosecuted ("processed") by this same office. These actions reflected growing concern about the rise of local lay religious movements. In the meantime, Rosa's cause had crossed the Atlantic: the king of Spain supported her case (1624), and Rome initiated a second official "apostolic process" (proceso apostólico) to gather further testimony about her life (1630–32). But her cause came to a halt once again when Pope Urban VIII's new requirements for sanctity tabled the discussion for nearly twenty years. By the middle of the seventeenth century, a dramatic exception to the new rules allowed the case to be resumed against the backdrop of a series of hagiographic biographies whose intent was to promote the Peruvian woman. Her case now moved quickly, and Rosa was canonized in exceptionally rapid order (1656–71). Soon, Catholics throughout the Spanish Empire invoked the saint's protection, and young girls emulated Rosa's life of prayer and penance as depicted in sacred biographies.

Until recently, critics never questioned why a young woman noted for her extreme penitential practices became an American and European heroine, exalted equally by king and pope, Spaniards and Limeños, Dominican clergy and young girls. The more than four hundred works published about her before the twentieth century simply recount the hagiographic elements of Rosa's life that had been established in the seventeenth century. But that uniformity has been shaken since then with the publication of primary texts that cast Rosa's life in a new light. Domingo Angulo published several of Rosa's letters (1917); Bruno Cayetano and Luis Millones published significant portions of the canonization testimony (1992, 1993); and Luis Getino rediscovered and published Rosa's iconolexic collages about her spiritual life (1937). Significantly, Getino argues that Rosa's intellectual ingenuity matched that of St. Teresa.[5] More recently, with the emergence of new cultural histories and the study of *mentalités,* critics have begun to examine the broader contexts of Rosa's life: the role of the Counter-Reformation, the extirpation of idolatrous practices in Peru, and the development of a criollo identity. Scholars such as Luis Galve, Frank Graziano, Teodoro Martínez Hampe, Fernando Iwasaki, Luis Millones, and Ramón Mujica Pinilla ask why Rosa de Lima was America's first saint. Although their arguments differ, all agree that she became a valuable symbol of identity for Lima during a time of dramatic changes both in the city and the church.[6] A recent study of the politics, dogma, and iconography involved suggests that Rosa was in the right place at the right time and that her image could be molded to fit the changing needs of the faithful.[7]

Building on the work by Galve, Iwasaki, and Mujica Pinilla, in particular, I propose to reformulate the question of why Rosa was the first New World saint and pose some additional questions. What role was played by the changing church standards for sainthood? Why did some clerics promote hagiographies about Rosa's life, while others limited access to the spiritual writings and public works of Rosa and her friends? What was omitted in the process of representing Rosa as an official saint? Responding to these questions may further our understanding of the process of defining official sanctity, which affected individual spiritual practices and popular culture; it also may shed light on attempts to control lay spirituality and to regulate the role of women within the church. Before these questions can be addressed directly, a brief biographical account is in order.

THE HOLY PORTRAIT OF AMERICA'S ROSA

By the time of Rosa's birth in 1586, Lima, named by conquistadors as the "City of the Kings" and founded by Francisco Pizarro fewer than fifty years earlier, was a place of extreme contrasts and rapid growth. Innovations in silver production and the establishment of Spanish institutions had created a densely populated and racially mixed city of both splendor and squalor; moreover, Lima was vulnerable to the dangers of earthquakes and pirates, as well as the deep political and religious rifts that ran through the entire Viceroyalty of Peru. Struggles over Indian labor, native rebellions, civil wars, factions within religious orders, and unrest due to the extirpation movement of native religions in the Andes characterized the civil and ecclesiastical politics of the period. The opulence of city architecture and the wealth of the criollo elite stood in stark contrast to the increasing numbers of American-born vagabonds, displaced indigenous peoples, and African slaves.[8]

In this cauldron of social and economic unrest, religious fervor and asceticism flourished. With the arrival of the new archbishop, Toribio de Mogrovejo, in 1581, the Peruvian church took new initiatives, setting up a printing press to publish catechisms and devotional works and establishing a council, the Concilio Limense (1582), to centralize the process of evangelization. Men and women flocked to religious houses, giving their lives to the church. By 1614 at least 10 percent of the estimated 25,454 inhabitants were members of religious orders. A significant number of these men and women would subsequently receive special recognition from the church.[9] Besides Rosa, three Limeños from the early seventeenth century would later be canonized by Rome, not to mention a substantial list of aspirants whose cases were to receive serious consideration.[10]

In this city, which was filling with both riches and ascetic saints, Rosa lived, died, and was later proclaimed a saint. Most of the information about her life comes from the two canonization processes (1617–19, 1630–32) and hagiographic stories of her heroic Christian behavior.[11] Briefly, Rosa, one of eleven children, was born Isabel Flores de Oliva to María de Oliva and Don Gaspar de Flores. Divine favor reportedly blessed the infant when a servant saw the baby's face transformed into a rose, a symbol of a European flower transplanted to the New World. From that day forward the child was called Rosa. At age five the girl heard the life story of the popular Italian saint, Catherine of Siena (1347–1380) and soon began to imitate her ascetic practices. One source states that Rosa soon memorized the complete life story of Catherine.[12] Like the Italian holy woman, Rosa built a hut in her backyard for prayer and penitential practices.

Rosa's parents were criollos of modest means. Although her father had received a post as an armsmaker (arcabuquero) for the king, at times he worked at several modest occupations, including that of dyer. Rosa's mother and sisters supplemented the family's income by sewing and running a home school for girls learning needlework. During her adolescent years, Rosa moved to the Andean mountain town of Quives, where her father worked for a period as overseer of an *obraje* (textile factory employing conscripted Indian labor).[13] Biographers say little about these years, but they do mention Rosa's compassion for indigenous laborers and her confirmation by the bishop and future saint Toribio de Mogrovejo.

By the time of her return to Lima, Rosa, like her exemplar Catherine of Siena, had received the spiritual gift of mystic marriage to Christ. She then chose a lifestyle that was appropriate to her spirituality, that of a lay holy woman, and became known only by her religious name of Rosa de Santa María. Not surprisingly, this choice set her in conflict, both with her mother, who wanted her to marry, and with her confessor, who wanted her to enter a convent. Biographers report that Rosa undermined her mother's efforts to present suitors for marriage by putting hot chili peppers in her eyes, and her confessor's efforts to make her a nun by freezing in place when on her way to the Convent of Santa Clara.[14] Later, Rosa became a tertiary—first informally associated with the Franciscan order (c. 1603–1606/7), and then the Dominican order (c. 1606/7), like her model Catherine. She took simple religious vows, which required chastity, poverty, and obedience but did not require perpetual enclosure.

During this time Rosa followed a rigorous schedule of work, prayer, and penance. The proceedings for her canonization state that she generally worked ten hours a day, prayed twelve hours, and slept two.[15] Much of her workday consisted of sewing for her mother. To keep awake at night and pray, Rosa was given to hanging herself by her hair. Other severe penances included wearing a crown of thorns (later, of metal) and sleeping on a bed that was designed to cause suffering. Her first biographer, Pedro Loayza, elaborates:

> From a tender age she slept upon beds made for penitents. The first one that she had was made of three wide planks . . . the one that served as the headboard had a hole into which she inserted her head, in this way was her body broken in or yoked like a burro. . . . This saintly woman also made another bed out of seven sticks, latticed in the form of a grill, out of some cattle horns, which she placed on a board, and between the joints she placed many sharp ceramic shards. . . . She slept upon this bed for fifteen or sixteen years.

Rosa's most famous biographer, Leonard Hansen, depicts her self-mortification in yet more detail. She walked barefoot in the garden with a heavy cross on her shoulders, suffered painful illnesses, and whipped herself as atonement for the sins of the world:

> In addition to these [penances] filled with compassion in times of public calamities, she endeavored to imitate her Teacher [Catherine of Siena] with acts of penitence . . . she would wound her body, sometimes for the troubles afflicting the entire Holy Mother Church, other times for the anguish and dangers suffered by her homeland, mercilessly making of herself a bloody sacrifice. . . .

Rosa's fasts were equally rigorous. Again like Catherine of Siena, she tried to subsist by eating nothing but the Communion host, though she added a New World element to the regimen: Indian servants helped with her special diets and mortifications. The belief was that fasting and penances helped to purify the person and redeem humankind.

Rosa's spiritual practice included active prayer for souls and for the city of Lima. Biographers report that she was graced with divine gifts such as intercessional powers, mystical union with Christ, and prophecy. According to Counter-Reformation doctrine and popular belief, such powers were the physical manifestations and outgrowths of Rosa's chosen status before God. She spent hours in solitary prayer beseeching God's intervention to cure a variety of community ills, ranging from natural disasters to suffering souls in purgatory. As the intermediary for miracles, Rosa tamed both earthquakes and disease-carrying mosquitoes as God responded to her appeals to save her native city from destruction.

By 1613, Rosa took up residence with a neighboring family, the Gonzalo de la Mazas, whose home was a haven for pious local laypeople. There Rosa developed her spiritual gifts as she advised Jesuits and Dominican friars, visited prominent women, established a circle of religious followers, and taught her patron's two daughters. She also formed prayer groups when the city was in danger. Hagiographers credit her group's intercessory powers with saving Lima in 1615 from the Dutch Protestant pirate Janis van Speilberg. Although she was active in the local community, as a woman Rosa was prohibited from carrying her evangelism beyond the city to the Andean foothills, where Native Americans lived. As one confessor noted, Rosa lamented these limitations: " 'Oh, I wish I were a man, just so I could participate in the conversion of souls,' and to this end she exhorted all the preachers she knew to convert many souls and go out and reduce to God and order all the idolaters of this land. And she urged that they make this the primary goal of their studies." A visible yet at times reclusive figure within Lima, Rosa became popularly known as one of its protectors during her own lifetime.

Even though Rosa was recognized for her spiritual gifts and compassion, she was nonetheless scrutinized by the Inquisition. In 1614 Rosa was examined informally by several members of the Inquisition, but the consensus was that Rosa was following an orthodox path. Within three years of her examination and after years of extreme fasts and penances, Rosa was dead. In his testimony, Gonzalo de la Maza reports: "The health and constitution of the said blessed Rosa was by then so wasted by so many ailments and pains that she could not produce anything of note at her labors nor help her parents in the way that she had done during the course of her life."[16] Upon her death, a number of her closest followers reportedly experienced flights of spirit *(arrobamientos)*, several of which are transcribed in the canonization processes as a sure sign of Rosa's holiness.[17] In the years following her death, Catholics in places as far away as Antwerp and Sicily were interviewed as witnesses to Rosa's miraculous intercessions.[18]

The first stage in the Rosa's canonization process began immediately upon her death and was initiated by at least three sections of Limeño society: city officials, the archbishop of Lima, and the Dominican order.[19] For two years, from 1617 to 1619, an official council took testimony from witnesses close to Rosa, including some seventy-five family members; members of her religious circle; and various clergymen, mostly Dominican friars and Jesuits.[20] More than half the witnesses were male religious. Included in this canonization file is a short biography written by her Dominican confessor, Pedro de Loayza.[21] During these years, popular veneration of Rosa grew so rapidly that the Dominicans decided to exhume Rosa's body and move her tomb to a more visible place in the church of Santo Domingo (1619). A second Dominican confessor, Luis de Bilbao, delivered a panegyric sermon to celebrate the occasion.

Given this evidence of Rosa's spiritual stature among the laity and the Dominicans, the suspension of her cult in Lima five years later comes as a surprise. A reason for the suspension may rest with the Dominicans themselves, who were experiencing a schism in their order, occasioned in part by a dispute over the choice of a candidate to promote as a Dominican saint.[22] Not only was the cult suspended, but also the censor of the Inquisition, Luis de Bilbao—one of Rosa's own confessors—demanded, in compliance with the inquisitor general's orders in 1622, that Rosa's works and personal effects be turned over to his office.[23] The Inquisition also examined many of Rosa's followers for evidence of the heretical practice of Illuminism *(alumbradismo)*.[24] Her lay spiritual guide, Juan del Castillo, and her close companion, María Luisa Melgarejo, had their writings censured, and a handful of lay holy women were publicly processed by the Inquisition. Ironically, while Limeños were debating the spiritual practices of Rosa and her group, officials in Spain began to promote her case. Phillip IV sent the 1617 *proceso* to the Council of the Indies, which then forwarded it to the Spanish ambassador in Rome (1624). The king was so enthusiastic about Rosa's sanctity that he soon named her patron of his armed forces, even though she was not yet a saint.

Although the case stagnated for several years, by 1630 the Holy See in Rome had opened an official inquiry into canonization.[25] Now out of the hands of Limeños, local Dominicans, and the Crown, the case was solely under the jurisdiction of the highest ecclesiastical office. In this *proceso apostólico* officials interviewed a larger and broader cross-section of society: of the 147 witnesses, about half were women, and many were ordinary citizens. Spurred perhaps by the immense popular devotion to Rosa, the church increasingly shifted its focus from associating Rosa with the Dominican order to making her a symbol for the city of Lima. The complete apostolic document for Rosa's canonization was presented to the Vatican's Sacred Congregation of Holy Rites in 1634.

But Rosa's case came to another halt because of Urban VIII's reforms. Responding to Protestant attacks on Catholic veneration of the saints, the pope added new rules to the Council of Trent's stated criteria for sanctity. The new rules encouraged more historical documentation about a candidate's life and required that fifty years elapse between the death of a candidate and consideration of the individual's case for sanctity. Rosa had died only seventeen years earlier.

In 1656 a new pope, Alexander VII, made an exception to the fifty-year rule, and heavy lobbying by the Dominicans in Rome and the Spanish Crown helped to reactivate Rosa's candidacy. A rapid succession of events ensued. A year later Philip IV sent his ambassador to Rome, again to promote the case. The influential English Dominican Leonard Hansen was asked in 1664 to write a biography of Rosa. His four-hundred-page Latin text, *Vita mirabilis mors pretiosa venerabilis Sororis Rosa de S. Maria,* became the most successful hagiography of her life. Written by someone who never knew her, the account, which drew on the two *procesos,* none-theless offers a compelling portrait of Rosa as the Catherine of Siena of the New World. Although initially written for a Roman audience, the biog-raphy was quickly translated into several languages and widely dissemi-nated, hence becoming a valuable tool for promoting Rosa's cause.[26] In spite of several competing biographies, Hansen's work became the classic life of Rosa for the next few centuries. In addition to the commission of Leonard's hagiography, the Dominican Gonzalez de Acuña was sent to Rome to oversee Rosa's case (1661), and the queen of Spain, Mariana of Austria, sent a petition to Rome on Rosa's behalf (1665). Reports of local miracles and celebrations in Lima and miraculous apparitions of Rosa in Europe further pressured Rome. In 1668 Rosa de Santa María was beat-ified; in 1669 Clement IX declared Rosa patron of Lima and Peru; in 1670 Pope Clement X extended this title to patron of America and the Philippines; and in 1671 Rosa became a saint.

During the next century, dozens of hagiographic representations of Rosa emerged in paintings and texts.[27] Popular images of the saint include Rosa holding the city of Lima in her hand; appearing as a double for the beloved Virgen del Rosario; carrying an anchor to symbolize her faith; and practicing severe mortification.[28] Rosa became a symbol for a Catholic America and a reason for celebration. As part of the festivities held in Lima upon Rosa's canonization, for example, a poetry contest *(certamen)* was held.[29] More traditional religious works, such as prayer books, novenas, and sermons based on the saint's life and prayers, also were published extensively in Lima and Mexico. In increasingly grandiloquent, symbolic language, criollos and Spaniards alike turned Rosa into a religious and political icon. For the latter, she often represented a new type of conquis-tador, while for the former, the saint proved America's parity with the Old World.[30] For both, Rosa was a powerful symbol of America's triumphant Roman Catholic Christianity. The Spanish count Oviedo y Herrera, previously posted to Peru, wrote a lengthy epic poem (1711) portraying the saint as being integral to the conquest and evangelization of America.[31] In a license to publish a sermon preached to celebrate Rosa's beatification, the censor for the Inquisition represents Rosa as converting the American "jungle"; her "virtuous fragrances . . . have converted into a paradise of holy delights the previously barbarous jungle of our South America."[32] Whereas Rosa's model, Catherine of Siena, had labored among Christians to reform and further Dominican causes, Rosa, her devotees insisted, had sought to convert pagans to Christianity. Through her, Rome itself was to be brought to an acceptance of America's essential role in the history of the universal Catholic Church. Rosa became the symbol for a New World that had been saved, evidence that the idolatrous practices of natives had been conquered and Catholicism firmly implanted. The Dominican chronicler Juan Meléndez once again captures the common sentiment as he calls her "our heroic *criolla*," the "redeemer" of the New World, in a world in which there are "two spheres," Lima and Rome.[33]

HAGIOGRAPHY AND RESCRIPTING A LIFE STORY

An examination of the canonization process and hagiographies suggests that ideology and practice with regard to sainthood changed in the Counter-Reformation church of the seventeenth century. The early church's original definition of saint as any holy person became more complex as church bureaucracy and centralization grew.[34] By Rosa's time, Rome orchestrated all canonization processes in its struggle to balance popular veneration of local holy people with the new requirements for official recognition of a saint. As a result, there was a long hiatus from 1629 to 1658, when no new saints were added to Catholic altars.[35] Besides demonstrating doctrinal purity and the theological virtues of faith, hope, and charity, a Counter-Reformation saint had to demonstrate heroic virtue in the faithful imitation of Christ through asceticism, contemplation, and active service to Christianity. As the renunciation of worldly passions and possessions, asceticism strengthened the individual in stamping out vices and following Christ in suffering for the sins of others. Contemplation and prayer also drew a person closer to God, by developing the art of spiritual dialogue and the readiness to receive divine messages. A saint might then witness divine grace working through her in the form of such miracles as healings, prophecies, and intercessions, as well as corporeal, imaginary, and intellectual visions.[36] Unlike saints from earlier periods, however, Counter-Reformation saints needed only a few miracles to prove their sanctity, while proof of heroic virtue carried far more weight. Such heroic lifestyle had to reflect post-Tridentine guidelines that advocated subordination to the guidance of ecclesiastical hierarchy and observance of the sacraments, in particular confession and communion.

These official requirements for sainthood influenced the *procesos* and the hagiographies about Rosa's life. All texts accentuate Rosa's ascetic, prayerful, and heroic life. The hagiographies also seek to inspire emulation in readers. The standard questions asked of most witnesses in the processes of 1617–19 and 1630–32 elicited critical biographical information as well as evidence of Rosa's moral qualities and the special merits she received through divine action. A second set of questions from the 1630s documented miraculous intercessions.[37] Closely following the structure and information of the two *procesos,* hagiographies delineate the life of Rosa according to ideals of heroic virtue and God's grace; individual aspects of her life story are far less important than proving her conformity within the community of saints. Following a two-part organization, the hagiographies generally recount the chronological life and death of the subject and then examine the virtues. (A variation was to narrate the life, the virtues, and then the death of the subject.) The life narrative sets forth examples of moral behavior, prayer and penance, observance of the sacraments and dogma, and evidence of God's hand working directly in the subject's life. Leonard Hansen's popular hagiography of Rosa clearly demonstrates his awareness of these guidelines for the representation of sanctity: the preliminary pages explain his historical method and emphasize his close observation of the guidelines established by the Congregation of Holy Rites, "This history was not taken from apocryphal accounts lacking weight and authority, but rather from the proceedings that by order of the Holy See were held in Lima, in order to list her in the catalog of the saints."[38] Serving as proof of sanctity (before 1671) and exemplary models for the faithful, hagiographical narratives of Rosa were the church's public representation of a holy life according to post-Tridentine rules.

The question arises, however, as to whether material was omitted in the process of establishing Rosa's conformity with the criteria for sanctity. Probably there were not-so-holy elements in Rosa's life—or, at least, elements that the church did not want to promote publicly. Two topics recur in the *procesos* and hagiographies that are polemical yet carefully controlled for meaning: the fact that Rosa had been questioned informally by several members of Lima's Inquisition, and the fact that she wrote about her spiritual life. Although Hansen presents the interrogation as proof of her orthodoxy, and her poetry and prayers as spontaneous compositions for God,[39] the historical record of events between 1622 and 1625 indicates that Rosa's group threatened goals the church had set in Lima and that she may have been an accomplished mystic writer. Like Teresa of Avila, Luis de León, John of the Cross, and Ignatius of Loyola in sixteenth-century Spain, it appears that Rosa was the subject of Inquisitorial scrutiny and that her spiritual writings and public teachings were censored because the orthodoxy of her beliefs and behavior was suspect. At the time, the political and ecclesiastical climate in Spain was such that this censorship was generally overturned, and subsequent hagiographies silenced or reinterpreted the Inquisitorial interventions in the lives of saints. In Rosa's case, her 1614 examination by the Inquisition ultimately served to help build a saintly portrait of her.

The first *proceso* records the 1614 examination of Rosa as a dialogue among the lay doctor employed by the Holy Office in Lima, Juan del Castillo; her confessor, the inquisitor Fray Juan de Lorenzana; and Rosa, with her mother observing the encounter.[40] When Castillo asked Rosa about her "interior impulses," including her prayers, visions, and penances, she responded by speaking of her spiritual practice and supernatural encounters with the divine. He continued the exploration of her spirit by asking if she had experienced authentic mystic union with the divine *(oración de unión),* characterized by the highest level of visionary activity ("intellectual visions"), or whether she had brought these supernatural occurrences on herself, perhaps by fasting too severely. More important, Castillo and Lorenzana wanted to differentiate her spiritual practices from the those of the *alumbrados* and thus define them as orthodox. Castillo based his inquiry on Teresa's mysticism, which he had studied for his own book of commentaries on the Spanish saint's writings. The verdict was that Rosa was privy to the highest form of religious experience, thus making her a bona fide mystic.[41]

In quoting passages from this dialogue with the Inquisitors, most biographers describe the process as a rustic talking to learned men about divine mysteries. Hansen places the examination in the context of the popular dialogue genre—which focused on drawing out an essential truth—and presents the place, interlocutors, and theme of the dialogue. He argues that the examination provided proof of her sanctity,[42] because Castillo was a well-known authority on mysticism, and Lorenzana, in his triple role as prior of a Dominican monastery, university professor, and censor for the Inquisition, was an expert on discerning people's spirits. The series of questions posed to Rosa moved quickly from an examination about suspect spiritual activity to using her as a springboard to discuss the authentic mystical path. The dialogic process ultimately uncovers a fundamental truth and serves as a vehicle to further church doctrine. Rosa becomes the unlettered authority about divine mysteries: "All were astonished by the responses of a simple, unlettered girl, when asked about the secret mystery of the Holy Trinity . . . and the fact that so many matters hidden from wise and prudent men, are revealed and made manifest to the humble, to children, and to the unlettered . . . it seemed to Lorenzana that he was seeing not a woman, but rather a mature professor of one branch or another of theology."[43] They all concluded "[that] the spirit of God worked through her, that she was filled with the gift of wisdom, that she was led by infused wisdom from Heaven."[44] Rosa had intuitive knowledge of God.

What hagiographers such as Hansen tended to ignore is that within ten years of this inquiry the same office severely undermined access to Rosa's own words and those of her followers. Biographers and witnesses rarely mention the Holy Office's second intervention in the 1620s, when it confiscated Rosa's works and began a systematic silencing of lay religious people close to her. This may appear to be a contradictory church response, but it served the single purpose of controlling direct public access to powerful laypeople's spiritual works. Ironically, Dr. Juan de Castillo, who had been instrumental in establishing Rosa's orthodoxy in the 1614 examination, was himself censored by the Inquisition ten years later. Notably, when Hansen wrote his biography of Rosa forty years later, he did not mention Castillo's encounter with the Inquisition. Rather, he presents the doctor as one of the most learned men in Lima, who, despite his lay status, was considered an expert on mystical theology. Because Castillo had officially authorized Rosa's mystical vocation, it was important to portray him as an authority on that topic and emphasize that his "life was a mirror of virtue."

The Inquisition also questioned Rosa's close companion, María Luisa Melgarejo, who had been a key witness in the 1617 *proceso*. In 1623, Inquisitors were particularly concerned about María Luisa's prolific spiritual journals (by some counts there were at least fifty-nine). Although María Luisa's confessor had already scrutinized the notebooks, they were later confiscated and may have been burned.[45] Nonetheless, María Luisa was called upon as a witness again for the 1630 *proceso* and later became the subject of hagiography herself. The most public message about curbing Rosa's influence were the actions taken against some *beatas* who claimed to follow the holy woman's example; they were processed by the Inquisition and convicted as *alumbradas* in the auto-da-fé that took place in Lima's Plaza Mayor in 1625.

During these same years, the Inquisition confiscated Rosa's own writings, including letters, poetry, and spiritual notebooks.[46] The future saint wrote at least several notebooks *(cuadernos),* one containing religious poetry and another her spiritual autobiography.[47] In the struggle to define sanctity and heresy, the Holy Office demanded these documents in 1624.[48] New research at the convent of Santa Rosa in Lima may uncover some of these lost texts.[49] Until such time, however, two autograph documents are significant. One of Rosa's letters, published for the first time in 1917, reveals that she was a capable organizer and worked hard to found a convent in spite of resistance from the Dominican order. Yet more revealing is the collage published for the first time in the 1930s: it suggests that hagiographic representations of Rosa focused on her penitential practices and downplayed her knowledge of the mystical life and texts.[50]

From the first, Hansen's biography downplays the extent of Rosa's learning. In a chapter dealing with her upbringing, he mentions "education" in the very title,[51] but the narrative only develops Rosa's physical suffering from an early age: she patiently endured deafening earaches, illnesses, and cuts. A handful of chapters later, we find out that Rosa did know how to read, but Hansen mentions it strictly in the context of Rosa learning how to imitate the lives of Catherine of Siena and the famous Mexican hermit and ascetic Gregorio López.[52] He privileges her mortification over her learning: "It is amazing that a body so emaciated and consumed by so many fasts, had enough room to receive lashes, and enough blood to flow from these. Nevertheless, so great was the desire and care that Rosa had in punishing her body that it was necessary that her confessors restrain her in this."[53] When talking about the prayers and songs Rosa composed, Hansen presents them only briefly and as spontaneous compositions inspired by God.

Other biographers and witnesses also describe Rosa's penitential practices and record Rosa's spontaneous composition of rather simple religious
songs and prayers. Confessors and family members note Rosa's habit of
singing devotional couplets and accompanying herself on the guitar:
"Leave me, little bird/flee the agile singer/but you are always with me/my
sweet Redeemer./Gentle nightingale/let us praise the Lord/you extol your
Creator/and I my Savior,"[54] and making wordplay on her names (Flores y
Oliva, flowers and olive trees): "Oh, Jesus of my soul!/How wonderfully
you appear/among the Flowers and the Roses/and the Olive groves of
green."[55] The prayers attributed to Rosa mention divine love, gratitude,
and God's magnificence. Based on the rosary, her "Angelic Exercise," for
example, praises the Holy Trinity.[56] Some of these devotional prayers were
edited (and perhaps significantly changed) by church officials and then
published as official texts.

Rosa's more elaborate work, the two-part iconolexic collage "The
Mercies" *(Las Mercedes)* and "The Mystical Stairway" *(La Escala Mística),*
however, was not published or mentioned in colonial texts (figure 13-1).
Through a series of cutout hearts pierced by arrows, crosses, and lances,
each surrounded by a written motto, the collage expresses Rosa's understanding of the mystic's journey of purgation, illumination, and union
with the divine. Based on the early modern use of emblems to unite
words with images to convey concepts, Rosa's work echoes ideas developed by Teresa and John of the Cross. *Las Mercedes* consists of three
hearts placed in a column to represent the stages to mystic union with
God: the heart wounded by love for God, the heart that carries the cross
and Jesus, and the heart in ecstatic flight to God and living in Him. Mot-
tos accompany each heart, and a lengthier written explanation frames the
lower part of the page (see figure 13-1). *La Escala Mística* continues the
representation of the heart's journey to God. The center of the page has
a cutout of a symbol of the fifteen "Levels of Divine Love," conceptual-
ized as a stairway based, as the image states, on "humility" and "perfection." Thirteen hearts on either side of the steps depict how continual
prayer leads to illumination and union with God. At the bottom of the
page a note in another hand (perhaps her Dominican confessor's)
explains: "Favors that Our Mother and Holy Patron St. Rosa de Santa
María received, what they mean is written in her own hand."[57] Not only
does the collage have an admirable primitive artistry, but it also reveals a

Figure 13-1

Rosa de Lima, "The Mercies" *(Las Mercedes)* and "The Mystical Stairway" *(La Escala Mística),* a two-part iconolexic collage. From Ramón Pinilla Mujica, "El ancla de Santa Rosa de Lima: mistica y politica en torno a la Patrona de America," in *Santa Rosa de Lima y su tiempo,* ed. José Flores Araoz et al. (Lima: Banco de Crédito de Lima, 1995), reproduced with the author's permission.

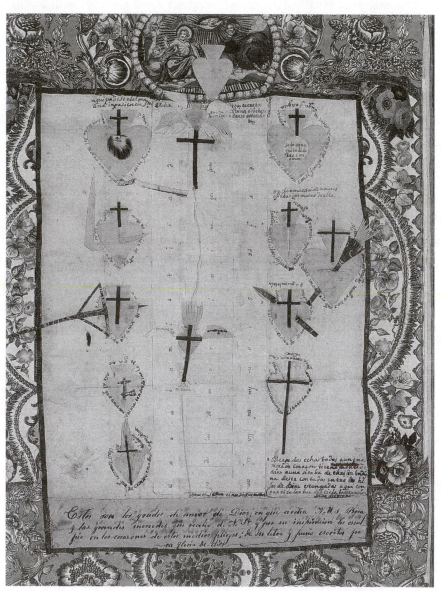

significant ingenuity and understanding of mystic theology and the emblematic tradition.

Like Teresa, Rosa opens her text on a paradoxical note: she is a woman writing under obedience to a confessor but who claims authority for her own mystical experience. The collages are part of the confessional process: "[Here is] that which I submit to Our Father as my only spiritual director, so that he might correct my errors, and emend that which the present work might lack or my ignorance. Many errors and faults you will find being explained by my own hand and if you find anything that is good, it will only be because of the grace of God."[58] Rosa explains further that God, rather than books, is the source of her mystic process: "I confess in all truth in the presence of God that all the mercies which I have recorded in this way in notebooks as engraved and painted on these two pieces of paper I have neither seen nor read about in any book, they are only worked through this sinner by the powerful hand of the Lord in whose book I read what is Eternal Wisdom."[59] This posture of holy ignorance and obedience to church superiors was essential for any woman mystic who sought to justify writing about her spiritual path. She further inscribed the work into the confessional process by saying that, after making a general confession with the Dominicans (ca. 1608), she composed the text:

> Out of divine mercy I received these three graces before a great tribulation that I suffered in the general confession [that I made] by order of that confessor, and it gave me so much that I deserved after having made the general confession and having suffered nearly two years of severe pains, tribulations, desolation, despair, temptations, battles with demons, the lies of confessors and of ordinary people. Illnesses, pains, fever, and, in short, all the greatest torments of hell that can be imagined during those final years, it would be five years since I received graces from the Lord that I have set down on this half sheet of paper, by the inspiration of my heart, although unworthy.[60]

Typical of most autobiographical spiritual writing by religious women in the period, this text is a result of its author enduring a period of suffering and working closely with a spiritual director. Rosa's work, although a hybrid artistic text that included both drawings and writing, is inscribed within Teresian mysticism and the "rhetoric of femininity."[61]

Yet Rosa's insistence on holy ignorance, confession, and obedience does not mean that she was literarily unschooled. Again, like Teresa, Rosa had worked closely with many learned men and listened carefully to church sermons and readings. One confessor testified that Rosa memorized entire sermons after hearing them only twice.[62] She studied doctrinal works in the *Devotio moderna* tradition by the sixteenth-century Spanish author Fray Luis de Granada, consulted with the learned Dr. Juan del Castillo, and participated in extended dialogues with well-educated Jesuit and Dominican confessors, several of whom were associated with the founding of Peru's first university, the University of San Marcos.[63]

In fact, the fifteen-step "stairway" or "ladder" and the imagery of the heart participate in long iconographic and textual church traditions,[64] and the idea of a ladder to the divine originated in the story of Jacob (*Genesis* 28:12). The two women mystics Rosa most admired, Catherine of Siena and Teresa of Avila, had both used the heart as the central metaphor for the soul flying to God.[65] Iconographic images frequently depicted Catherine with a cross embedded in a heart and Teresa with an arrow *(dardo)* piercing her heart; they symbolized the intimate relationship between the experience of divine love and the pain of surrender to it. In addition, meditation guides from the period, such as Ignatius of Loyola's *Spiritual Exercises,* encouraged the use of visual imagery in prayer, which in turn inspired the production of allegorical emblem books. Many of these books include images of the human heart.[66] By Rosa's time the human heart had become the key symbol for affective piety and mysticism. Rosa may have borrowed the imagery from her Limeño contemporary Alvarez de Paz, who published a work about a fifteen-step process of movement toward God and who had been one of Dr. Juan Castillo's authorities in determining Rosa's orthodoxy.[67] Or she may have read or heard about Fray Luis de Granada's popular translation of the seventh-century San Juan Clímaco's "Spiritual Ladder" *(Escala espiritual),* about a thirty-step spiritual process (1562).

Rosa's conceptualization of the prayer of union and ascent to God as a mystic marriage between a bride and a bridegroom came directly from church interpretations over the centuries of the biblical text *The Song of Songs.*[68] *Las Mercedes* quotes *The Song of Songs,* once in Latin. Because of the prohibition against laypersons reading the Bible, Rosa's source again may have been Teresa or John of the Cross. Using the spiritual analogy of God as a lover wounding his beloved to prepare her for union with him, Rosa's winged heart moves through the stages of being "wounded by an arrow of love," receiving the nails of Christ's painful Passion on the cross, being "sick with love, unto death," and, yet more deeply wounded by "a fiery spear" and "arrow of divine love." These stages open the way for the purification of the heart, the recognition that one must follow the way of the cross ("life is the Cross") and finally the "spiritual betrothal" in which the winged heart flies to God in a mystical union of the soul with the Holy Spirit in divine marriage.[69] As promised in the biblical source, and reiterated by both Teresa and John, this final stage is a sort of drunkenness and loss of self in a moment of ecstasy: "Ecstasy. Intoxication in the wine cellar. Secrets of divine love. Oh happy union, in the close embrace of God!"[70]

One of the confessors who later would be instrumental in the Inquisition cases of 1620 claimed that Rosa's understanding of church doctrine was so extensive that he would classify her as a "consummate theologian," able to speak the dogma of the Trinity and Incarnation, among other sacred topics.[71] If Rosa was indeed an accomplished mystic and writer, the question why she has been represented primarily as a woman who practiced extreme mortification is all the more insistent.

Although the hybrid artistic rendering of the mystic process in the *escala* may have marked the text for marginalization, a more likely cause was that the church wanted to control the representation of female sanctity and to redirect the growing lay religiosity that threatened to detract from the power of the institutional church. The Council of Trent had mandated the perpetual enclosure of nuns and encouraged women with strong religious vocations to seek the safety of the convent, where confessors and rules for daily life and spiritual practice monitored their spirituality. Although often ineffective in its efforts, the church wanted demonstrations of extraordinary feminine piety to be reserved for established institutions and carefully controlled. Confessors often ordered their spiritual daughters to write about their spiritual experiences, which clergy later used as the basis for posthumous male-authored biographies about religious women. As a result, after Teresa's time women's words rarely were published directly. In fact, Teresa's own *Vida* was in the hands of the Inquisition for many years before being released for publication.[72]

Nancy E. van Deusen and Fernando Iwasaki argue that popular lay religious movements in Lima undermined church efforts to set limits on spiritual behavior and lay authority. In fact, it is the setting of limits that made saintly behavior acceptable. The church recognized the power of Rosa's life for claiming a Christian identity for America, but it also reacted to an implicit threat to post-Tridentine Church efforts to enclose religious women, curb laypeople's access to theological books, and limit circulation of women's—and particularly pious laywomen's—writings.

Although the church considered women's spiritual texts to be valuable aids to confessors, the writings were dangerous to the welfare of both woman and church if they were made public without the editing (and censorship) of trained church clergy. Thus the more widely the news of a holy woman spread, the more control was needed over access to her works. Rosa's works caused alarm only after the first *proceso* was completed and popular veneration and emulation of her spread throughout Lima. As her case moved up the hierarchical ladder of the church, her original words were carefully selected and reinterpreted through hagiography and the process of canonization. The events of 1623–25 were recast. As one witness in 1630 explains, women were using Rosa's good name to authorize spiritual paths that the church did not allow: "Until today . . . although there had appeared in the said city certain women of whom it was said that they dedicated themselves to spiritual matters, it appeared afterwards that they were not on the right path for the service of God because some were punished and these women conversed with the said Sister Rosa in order to see if by chance this would authorize their actions and after their sins had been revealed this discredited somewhat the said Rosa . . . and after the noise died down and the said women were punished Sister Rosa's reputation was restored."[73] The portrayal of Rosa as a writer and a laywoman with a religious vocation was downplayed as posthumous representations fixed an image of her as the Catherine of Siena of the New World. Hagiographies omitted mention of Rosa's learning and emphasized her spontaneous experience of divine love and knowledge as the outcome of her penance and prayer and of God's mercy. The church that promoted Rosa was at the same time the church that codified and controlled her.

Just as Rosa had emulated the image of Catherine of Siena that had been promoted by the latter's influential confessor/biographer Raymond of Capua, so did girls attempt to emulate Rosa after her death.[74] Girls would model their lives on Rosa's extreme penances and preparation for mystical union. And just as Rosa's case often provoked contradictory official responses, so her imitators often encountered ambiguous dictates about holiness. Speaking to *beatas* about to become nuns at the new Convent of Santa Rosa in Puebla, Mexico, the Dominican Sebastián de Santander y Torres warned of the dangers of imitating Rosa's life. Using the metaphor of the mustard seed for women with a religious vocation, he says that three out of four seeds thrown into the ground outside the cloister will waste away, "as the most appropriate place for a virgin is the cloister of a convent."[75] Well aware of post-Tridentine efforts to enclose religious women, he is in a quandary as to how to exalt the virtues of the convent's patron saint, recognizing that she did not enter a convent. The women he addresses were to imitate their patron, but only to a point. Although enclosure ensured an easier road to virtue, it seemed to foreclose the possibility of achieving heroic virtue, for nuns would never be as sorely tested as their lay sisters. Only one nun from Spanish America, the Pueblan Carmelite María de Jesús Tomelín (1574–1637), advanced to the first stage of consideration for sainthood. The only other American woman to become a saint was Mariana de Jesus (1618–45), a *beata* who imitated Rosa in the city of Quito. But she was only canonized in 1950 (beatified in 1853), centuries after lay female piety had ceased to seem threatening. Even Teresa of Avila, who became the Counter-Reformation female saint par excellence, who had upheld the mandate for moderate penances and had advocated strict enclosure, did not herself always remain enclosed.[76] She frequently had to break enclosure to travel and set up new houses. These contradictory models for female holiness permeated the period.

Rosa de Lima's case illustrates the complex and intimate connections among hagiography, emulation, confessional life writings, canonization, and Inquisition practices. There was a dynamic interplay among local agendas, the court in Madrid, the institutional church in Lima and in Rome, individual confessors, hagiographers, and women's spiritual experiences and writings. At each level, the rules for holy behavior underwent reinterpretation. Hagiographic representation of Rosa's life united America with the Universal Catholic Church and attempted to control local lay movements. But the changing portrayals of her life over time also reflect the shifting official line between sanctity and heresy and the ever-narrowing role for religious women outside the cloister. The same circumstances that provided Rosa with an opportunity to undertake spiritually heroic acts also made her, or her imitators, a threat to the church. In the process of dissecting this elaborate weave, we gain a richer understanding of how holy individuals—in particular this Peruvian laywoman—played an essential part in defining the identity of the Counter-Reformation church and of Spanish-American colonial society.

NOTES

1. This is a shorter version of a chapter republished with permission from Oxford University Press, from my book *Neither Saints nor Sinners: Writing the Lives of Spanish American Women.*
2. See Fray Juan Meléndez, O. P., *Festiva Pompa, Culto Religioso, Veneración reverente, Fiesta, Aclamación, y Aplauso. A la Feliz Beatificación de la Bienaventurada virgen Rosa de S. María* . . . [1671], 20r–31r. For a twentieth-century narrative description of the event see Luis Eduardo Wuffarden and Pedro Guibovich Pérez, "Esplendor," in *Santa Rosa de Lima y su tiempo,* ed. José Flores Araoz et al. (Lima: Banco de Crédito del Perú, 1995), 29.
3. Fray Pedro de Loayza, O. P., *Vida de Santa Rosa de Lima* [1619] [hereafter *Vida*] (Lima: Iberia, S.A., 1965), chs. 27–29.
4. See Meléndez, *Festiva Pompa, Culto Religioso, Veneración reverente, Fiesta, Aclamación, y Aplauso,* for more information on the brotherhoods, 29r. Ramón Mujica Pinilla, "El ancla de Santa Rosa de Lima: mística y política en torno a la Patrona de América," in *Santa Rosa y su tiempo,* ed. José Flores Araoz et al. (Lima: Banco de Crédito, 1995): 156 describes the popularity of her portrait.
5. Fray Luis Getino, O. P., *La Patrona de América ante los nuevos documentos* (Madrid: Revista de las Españas, 1937). Also of note are Ruben Vargas Urgarte's *La flor de Lima: Santa Rosa,* 4th ed. (Lima: Ediciones Paulinas, 1983), a compendium of other biographies, and Domingo Angulo's *Santa Rosa de Santa María: Estudio bibliográfico* (Lima, 1917), an extensive bibliography of published sources.
6. While Frank Graziano, *Wounds of Love: The Mystical Marriage of Saint Rose of Lima* (New York: Oxford University Press, forthcoming) focuses on the role and significance of her "sacrificial body," Luis Miguel Galve, "Santa Rosa de Lima y sus espinas: La emergencia de mentalidades urbanas de crisis y la sociedad andina (1600–1630)," in *Manifestaciones religiosas en el mundo colonial americano,* ed. Clara García Aylurado and Manuel Ramos Medina, vol. 1 (Mexico: La Galera, 1993) and Fernando Iwasaki, "Mujeres al borde de la perfección: Rosa de Santa María y las alumbradas de Lima," *Hispanic American Historical Review* (1993): 581–613 argue that as a mature colonial city, Lima needed both a saint (Rosa) and scapegoats (Rosa's friends tried for *alumbradismo*) to establish its Christian identity. For his part, Luis Millones, *Una Partecita del cielo: la vida de Santa Rosa de Lima narrada por Don Gonzalo de la Maza a quien ella llamaba padre* [1617] (Lima: Editorial Horizonte, 1993) sees Rosa as being transformed into a symbol for Andean populations. Others, such as David A. Brading, *The First America: the Spanish Monarchy, Creole Patriots, and the Liberal State, 1492–1867* (Cambridge: Cambridge University Press, 1991), 369, suggest that Rosa's popularity and success stemmed from people associating her with the Virgen del Rosario, who had miraculously appeared during one of Pizarro's battles.
7. See the commemorative work edited by José Flores Araoz et al., *Santa Rosa de Lima y su tiempo* (Lima: Banco de Crédito del Perú, 1995).
8. For more information see Wuffarden and Pérez, "Esplendor."
9. Pinilla, *Santa Rosa,* 54. One account states that of the six thousand men of Spanish descent living in Lima, twenty-five hundred had taken religious vows, and one in four women lived in the convent, Galve, "Santa Rosa," 55, and Luis Martín, *Daughters of the Conquistadors: Women of the Viceroyalty of Peru* (Albuquerque: University of New Mexico Press, 1983), 176–80.
10. Toribio de Mogrovejo (1535–1606) and Francisco Solano (1549–1602) were beatified in the 1670s and canonized in 1726. Two other Dominicans, Juan de Macías (1585–1645) and Martín de Porres (1579–1639) were beatified in the nineteenth century. Martín de Porres was canonized in 1962. Galve lists other aspirants and venerables; more than sixty hagiographies were published during the period, "Santa Rosa," 62–63.
11. My portrait of Rosa is based on the two *procesos,* and the biographies by Antonio Gonzalez de Acuña, *Rosa Mística. Vida y Muerte de Santa Rosa de Santa María* (Rome, 1671), Leonard Hansen, *Vida admirable de Sta. Rosa de Lima: Patrona del Nuevo Mundo* [1664], trans. Jacinto Parrra (1671), Loayza, *Vida de Santa Rosa de Lima,* and Millones, *Una Partecita del cielo: la vida de Santa Rosa de Lima.*
12. Fray Pedro de Loayza says that Rosa memorized the saint's life story and that Catherine became Rosa's teacher in a spiritual path centered around imitating Christ's suffering, *Vida,* ch. 7. Another biographer, Fray Gonzalez de Acuña, also describes Rosa's close modeling of Catherine's life. *Rosa mística,* 158. Mujica Pinilla suggests that Rosa probably read Fray Fernando del Castillo's edition of Catherine's *Life* (Valdecebro, 1669), "El ancla de Santa Rosa de Lima," 43, 74. Hansen also notes that Rosa read and imitated the life of the new Spanish hermit Gregorio López (1542–1596), *Vida admirable de Sta. Rosa de Lima,* 100v.
13. Luis Millones studies this influential period of Rosa's life in "Los Sueños" in *Una Partecita del cielo.*
14. Accounts disagree on whether Rosa wanted to become a nun. She had three opportunities to enter a convent. While Loayza maintains that Rosa wanted to enter the Convent of Santa Clara, *Vida,* 23, other accounts say she refused to do so because of a vision in which Catherine of Siena prophesied the founding of a Dominican convent in Lima. See Mujica Pinilla, "El ancla de Santa Rosa de Lima," 64.

15. *Proceso ordinario. 1617–18,* Archivio Segreto Vaticano, *Riti,* vols. 1570, 1571, 1572, Lilly Library copy, Bloomington, Ind., fols. 138–39.
16. For a transcription of Gonzalo de la Maza's lengthy testimony about Rosa's life in the *Proceso ordinario* and *Proceso apostólico* see Millones, *Una Partecita del cielo,* 147–209. A selection of this testimony has been translated into English; see Kenneth Mills and William B. Taylor, *Colonial Spanish America: A Documentary History* (Wilmington, Del.: Scholarly Resources, 1998), 194–202; a portion of this is reproduced in appendix A.
17. For example, María Luisa Melgarejo testifies to having flown in an ecstatic state, *Proceso ordinario,* 28v (Lilly Library copy).
18. Testimony was recorded in 1670; see Teodoro Martínez Hampe, *Santidad e identidad criolla: estudio del proceso de canonización de Santa Rosa* (Cuzco: Centro de Estudios Regionales Andinos Bartolomé de las Casas, 1998), 70–71.
19. For an excellent chronology of the canonization process see Martínez Hampe, *Santidad e identidad criolla,* chs. 3–4.
20. *Proceso ordinario,* 1617–19. The 1617 *proceso* was begun by the prelates of Lima. The original is at the Convento de Santa Rosa in Lima. I consulted copies at the Lilly Library, Indiana University at Bloomington (a nineteenth-century copy) and the Secret Archives of the Vatican (a contemporary, notarial copy). All citations are from the Lilly Library copy. For more information on the *proceso* see Martínez Hampe, *Santidad e identidad criolla,* ch. 2.
21. A list of the witnesses is contained in the *proceso* itself. See Martínez Hampe's transcription of the list and his study in *Santidad e identidad criolla,* ch. 2. Loayza's *Vida* was not published until much later. I used the 1965 Lima edition by the Dominican Fray Carlos Aníbal Alvarez, which Frank Graziano graciously lent to me.
22. See Mujica Pinilla, "El ancla de Santa Rosa de Lima," 177, and Martínez Hampe, *Santidad e identidad criolla,* ch. 3. Bernard La Valle explains that two of Rosa's biographers, Bilbao and Meléndez, played important roles in the Dominican schism, *Las Promesas ambíguas: ensayos sobre el criollismo colonial en los andes* (Lima: Pontífica Universidad Católica del Perú, 1993), 180–85. In addition, while the order presented five Dominican candidates for sainthood, they were allowed to promote only one; Martínez Hampe also cites the astronomical costs of the canonization process as another reason for its being tabled, *Santidad e identidad criolla,* ch. 2. Also see Iwasaki, "Mujeres al borde de la perfección," 581, n. 1.
23. For more on the role of the inquisitor general see Mujica Pinilla, "El ancla de Santa Rosa de Lima," 63.
24. The *alumbrados* of sixteenth-century Spain were mystics who sought direct connection to God without the aid of the institutional church; they were accused of rejecting the sacraments of the church and were condemned by the Inquisition as heretics.
25. See Martínez Hampe, *Santidad e identidad criolla,* ch. 2, for a complete list of the witnesses and their biographical information. Twelve of the 147 witnesses also testified in the 1617 *proceso.*
26. It was translated into Italian, English, French, and Spanish. Domingo Angulo lists many of these editions, *Santa Rosa de Santa María.* The *procurador* for Rosa's canonization, Antonio González de Acuña, wrote a compendium based on Hansen's work, *Rosa Mística,* but it was not published until 1671.
27. José Toribio Medina's *Biblioteca extranjera de Santos y venerables* reveals Rosa's popularity as the subject of hagiographic biographies.
28. For a full discussion of Rosa's image and iconographic tradition see Mujica Pinilla, "El ancla de Santa Rosa de Lima," 54–214. Others have studied Rosa's influence on Andean populations. Waldo Ross argues that Rosa became associated early on with "fuerzas telúricas, cósmicas, astrales," "Santa Rosa de Lima y la formación del espíritu hispanoamericano." *Mercurio Peruano* 462 (1966): 187. Millones traces her role in Andean traditions that still take place in August every year, *Una Partecita del cielo,* ch. 4.
29. Meléndez, *Festiva Pompa, Culto Religoso, Veneración Reverente, Fiesta, Aclamación, y Aplauso,* 40r.
30. LaValle, *Las Promesas ambíguas,* discusses the important role of Dominicans in the criollo movement, with Rosa as perhaps their greatest symbolic success. For a history of this process with respect to Rosa see Mujica Pinilla, "El ancla de Santa Rosa de Lima," 158–71.
31. See esp. Cantos I and III, *Vida.*
32. Manuel de Ribero Leal, *Oración Evangélica en la beatificacón de Rosa de Santa Maria* (Lima, 1675). "Fragancias de buenos exemplos . . . han convertido en parayso de delicias santas esta selva antes inculta de nuestra Meridional America."
33. Meléndez, *Festiva Pompa, Culto Religoso, Veneracion Reverente, Fiesta, Aclamación, y Aplauso,* "Al lector."
34. See Richard Kieckhefer, "Imitators of Christ: Sainthood in the Christian Tradition," in *Sainthood: Its Manifestions in World Religions,* ed. Richard Kieckhefer and George D. Bond (Berkeley: University of California Press, 1998), ch. 1.
35. See Peter Burke, "How to Be a Counter-Reformation Saint," in *Religion and Society in Early Modern Europe 1500–1800,* ed. Kaspar von Greyerz (London: George Allen & Unwin, 1984), 46.
36. For a more thorough discussion see Kieckhefer, "Imitators of Christ," 24.

37. For a more thorough study of these *procesos* see Martínez Hampe, *Santidad e identidad criolla,* ch. 2. For a transcription of the questions, names of witnesses, and selected testimony see Alfred Anthony Brichta López, "The Roots of the Rose: A Sociohistorical Biography of St. Rose of Lima (Rosa de Santa María), 1586–1617" (Ph.D. diss., University of New Mexico, 1995), appendices.

38. Juan de Paz, "Presentación," in Hansen, *Vida admirable de Sta. Rosa de Lima,* unnumbered preliminary pages.

39. Rosa's first biographer, Loayza, *Vida,* 30–31, simply introduces the questioning as "Dios abrió el entendimiento a un singular varón seglar, doctor en medicina, excelente filósofo y buen teólogo, y en su teología mística admirable por tener esta ciencia no sólo con estudio, sino también de experiencia. . . . Como se vera del examen que se sigue. Preguntóle el dicho Doctor: 'Y de qué tiempo a esta parte se había dado a la oración?' Respondió, que de edad de cinco años." Nothing is said about it being conducted with an inquisitor present.

40. *Proceso ordinario,* first witness, Juan del Castillo.

41. For more on this examination and its representation in hagiographies see Mujica Pinilla, "El ancla de Santa Rosa de Lima," 108–13.

42. ". . . para que por su sanctidad conste," Hansen, *Vida admirable de Sta. Rosa de Lima,* 91.

43. Hansen, *Vida admirable de Sta. Rosa de Lima,* 99v–100v.

44. Ibid., 100v. "Se obrava con espiritu de Dios, que estava llena del don de sabiduria, que se governaba con ciencia infusa del Cielo."

45. See Iwasaki's important article on Malgarejo and the other women following Rosa. He quotes the Inquisition's notice that the notebooks had been falsified because of her confessor's censorship, "Mujeres al borde de la perfección," 96. See Mujica Pinilla, "El ancla de Santa Rosa de Lima," 58–61 and 202, n. 28. For more on the trials see Luis Galve, "Santa Rosa de Lima y sus espinas," Fernando Iwasaki, "Mujeres al borde de la perfección," and José Toribio Medina, *Historia del Tribunal de la Inquisición de Lima (1569–1820),* vols. I–II (Santiago: Fondo Histórico, 1956), 27–32.

46. See the reproduction of the letters in Domingo Angulo, *Santa Rosa de Santa María,* 334–39. See Luis Getino, *La Patrona de América ante los nuevos documentos,* for reproductions of the collages and some of the poetry and prayers. The *procesos* also record transcriptions of reported speech—that is, of the witness recalling Rosa's speech and citing it in the first person. One such example is the testimony by Juan del Castillo that cites Rosa's words during one of her raptures, as quoted in Getino, 52–55. The *proceso* also includes a list of hers, given to Gonzalo de la Maza, who had it transcribed in his testimony (it deals with the proper dressing of the Christ child), cited in Millones, *Una partecita del cielo,* 188–89.

47. The *proceso* includes the requests for Rosa's "papeles y particulas de sus habitos, huesos, o otras cosas tocantes a su persona" and the replies that state that the material had already been turned over, *Proceso ordinario,* folios 217–18. The request came from the Dominican Fray Luis de Bilbao, who was both one of Rosa's confessors and a censor for the Inquisition. Iwasaki also discusses the possibility of an autobiography having been written, "Mujeres al borde de la perfección," 594–95. Rosa herself mentions her notebooks when explaining her collages; see Luis Getino, *La Patrona de América ante los nuevos documentos,* 51, and Mujica Pinilla, "El ancla de Santa Rosa de Lima," 96. Wuffarden and Guibovich cite the records that discuss the censoring of her book of religious poetry, "Esplendor," 27–28.

48. In 1624, Fray Gabriel Zarate, prior of the Dominican Monastery, reports turning over Rosa's possessions and papers to the Inquisition, letter appended to the *Proceso ordinario,* f. 217.

49. Several Peruvian scholars made this suggestion at a conference organized by Frank Graziano and held at the John Carter Brown Library, Providence, R.I., May 1999.

50. See Luis Getino's reproduction of these in *La Patrona de América ante los nuevos documentos,* 15–55 and 73. The reproduction in this chapter is courtesy of Ramón Mujica Pinilla and is taken from "El ancla de Santa Rosa de Lima," 104–5.

51. Hansen, *Vida admirable de Sta. Rosa de Lima,* ch. 2. "Niñez, natural, educación, y voto de viriginidad."

52. Ibid., 43r.

53. Ibid., 37r. "Cosa es de maravillar que en cuerpo tan flaco, y consumido con tantos ayunos, hubiesse lugar donde recibir azotes, y sangre que derramar con ellos. No obstante era tan grande el deseo, y cuydado que Rosa tenia de castigar su cuerpo que fue necesario que sus confessores le fuessen a la mano en esto."

54. As cited in Getino, *La Patrona de América ante los nuevos documentos,* 66; also see Loayza *Vida,* ch. 19. "Déjame la avecilla,/huye el veloz cantor,/mas siempre esta conmigo/mi dulce Rendtor./Pajarillo ruiseñor,/alabemos al Señor;/tú alaba a tu Creador,/yo canto a mi Salvador."

55. As cited in *Proceso ordinario,* 45r. "Oh, Jesús de mi alma!/Qué bien pareces/entre Flores y Rosas/y Olivas verdes."

56. Other prayers attributed to her included "Alabanzas de Dios," which is also quoted in the *proceso,* and in *Actos de Contrición.* Several of these were published with some frequency in the latter part of the seventeenth century and the beginning of the eighteenth. See, for example, *Exercicio Angélico, empleo Celestial de Alabanzas a Dios por sus infinitas perfecciones . . . que inventó Santa Rosa de Santa María y pueden imitar*

las almas deseosas de aagradar a Nuestro Señor. Pr un Padre de la Compañía de Jesus (Lima, 1728) held at the Lilly Library, Bloomington, Ind.

57. "Favores que recibió N.M. y Patrona Santa Rosa de Santa María, como lo significan estos escritos de su letra y puño." Luis Getino suggests that this note may have been written by a nun at the convent, *La Patrona de América ante los nuevos documentos,* 18. More typically, confessors made written comments in religious women's texts. For other reproductions of the *Mercedes* see Caroina Ibáñez-Murphy, "Primera escritora colonial? Santa Rosa de Lima: Las Mercedes y la Escala Mística" (Ph.D. diss., University of Arizona, 1997) and Brichta López, "The Roots of the Rose."

58. As cited in Ibáñez-Murphy, "Primera escritora colonial?," 152.

59. As quoted by Mujica Pinilla, "El ancla de Santa Rosa de Lima," 97.

60. Cited by Ibáñez-Murphy, "Primera escritora colonial?," 153.

61. See Alison Weber's important work on the topic, *Teresa of Avila and the Rhetoric of Femininity* (Princeton, N.J.: Princeton University Press, 1990).

62. See Mujica Pinilla's quotes from biographies and *procesos,* "El ancla de Santa Rosa de Lima," 114–15.

63. For a list of Rosa's confessors see Iwasaki, "Mujeres al borde de la perfección," 591; Vargas Urgarte, *La Flor de Lima,* 27; and Mujica Pinilla, "El ancla de Santa Rosa de Lima," 51.

64. One scholar notes Hildegard of Bingen's illuminated works about her visionary life and John of the Cross's sketches of his visions, but neither of these authors place word and image in an intimate emblematic relationship. See Ibáñez-Murphy, "Primera escritora?," 128–34. See also Jeffrey Hamburger's study of heart imagery in the late fifteenth and early sixteenth centuries, *Nuns as Artists: The Visual Culture of a Medieval Convent* (Berkeley: University of California Press, 1997).

65. Catherine of Siena used the imagery of the ladder as well; see Suzanne Noffke's introduction to Saint Catherine, of Siena, *The Dialogue,* trans. Suzanne Noffke (New York: Paulist Press, 1980).

66. See Kristine Ibsen's work on the links among vision, meditation, and prayer in this period, and the popularity of the heart as an emblem, *Women's Spiritual Autobiography in Colonial Spanish America* (Gainesville: University of Florida Press, 1999), 102 and 114. See also Pedro F. Campa's study of Spanish emblem books, *Emblemata Hispanica: An Annotated Bibliography of Spanish Emblem Literature to the Year 1700* (Durham, N.C.: Duke University Press, 1990).

67. Leonard Hansen notes Juan de Castillo's use of Alvaez Paz's work, *Vida admirable de Sta. Rosa de Lima,* ch. 14.

68. For more on this topic see Ann Astell, *The Song of Songs in the Middle Ages* (Ithaca, N.Y.: Cornell University Press, 1990).

69. "Herido con flecha de amor"; "eferma de amores, que muero de ella"; "harpón de fuego"; "dardo de amor divino"; "la vida es cruz"; "deposorio espiritual," *Las mercedes* 5–14. For a more complete discussion of these steps and hearts see Brichta López, "The Roots of the Rose," 544–54; Luis Getino, *La Patrona de América ante los nuevos documentos,* 15–55; Mujica Pinilla, "El ancla de Santa Rosa de Lima," 98–107; and Ibáñez-Murphy, "Primera escritora colonial?," 182–205.

70. *Merced,* 15. "Arrobo. Embriaguez en la bodega. Secretos del amor Divino. Oh dichosa unión, abrazo estrecho con Dios!"

71. Cited in Pinilla Mujica, "El ancla de Santa Rosa de Lima," 113–14. "Teólogo muy hecho y consumado."

72. See Gillian T. Alhgren, *Teresa of Avila and the Politics of Sanctity* (Ithaca, N.Y.: Cornell University Press, 1996) and Carol Slade, *St. Teresa of Avila: Author of a Heroic Life* (Berkeley: University of California Press, 1995), for more about the politics of sanctity and the careful representation of Teresa's life and works.

73. Ramírez de Baldéz, *Proceso apostólico,* as cited in Mujica-Pinilla, "El ancla de Santa Rosa de Lima," 63.

74. See Karen Scott, "Urban Spaces, Women's Networks, and the Lay Apostolate in the Siena of Catherine," in *Creative Women in Medieval and Early Modern Italy: A Religious and Artistic Renaissance,* ed. E. Ann Matter and John Coakley (Philadelphia: University of Pennsylvania Press, 1994), 64–105.

75. Sebastián de Santander y Torres, *Sermón panegírico* (Puebla, 1692), 4–6. "Siendo para una Virgen el lugar mas apto la clausura de un monasterio."

76. For more on the creation of Teresa as a saint see Alghren, *Teresa of Avila and the Politics of Sanctity* and Jodi Bilinkoff, *The Avila of Saint Teresa: Religious Reform in a Sixteenth-Century City* (Ithaca, N.Y.: Cornell University Press, 1989). Karen Scott argues that Trent also successfully promoted Catherine of Siena as a model Counter-Reformation saint by altering certain biographical details, "Urban Spaces, Women's Networks, and the Lay Apostolate in the Siena of Catherine," 44.

14

Mexico's Virgin of Guadalupe in the Seventeenth Century: Hagiography and Beyond

WILLIAM B. TAYLOR

> I find the history [of the image and miracles of Our Lady of los Remedios] most difficult, not at all like a well full of stones that I could remove little by little. Rather, I find myself again and again on land that is filled with crags and barrens. It is a difficult thing to finally reach the water of truth there.
> —Luis de Cisneros [1616][1]

Catholic hagiography as sacred biography reaches beyond the lives of saints and other holy people to include the "lives" of images, relics, and places of a saint or Christ renowned as sites of divine presence and favor. This branch of hagiography for miraculous images, signs, and apparitions was especially important in colonial Spanish America. The New World of the sixteenth, seventeenth, and eighteenth centuries had very few saints of its own and was comparatively poor in certified relics of Old World saints. Not surprisingly, many of the most popular hagiographical and devotional texts that began to appear in New Spain in the 1620s concerned miraculous images and apparitions, especially of the Virgin Mary or Christ. Of the various images and shrines celebrated and promoted in printed hagiographies, sermons, and novena booklets, Our Lady of Guadalupe at Tepeyac eventually came to occupy a preeminent place in the devotional history and literature of Mexico. As Jeannette Rodríguez writes, "To be of Mexican descent is to recognize the image of Our Lady of Guadalupe."[2]

But were the early hagiographers of miraculous images, especially of Our Lady of Guadalupe, largely inventing a tradition in their texts, or were they mainly faithful scribes recording the tradition? Did they make memory or mainly capture and codify it? This is no small matter to historians of the Mexican Guadalupe because the first published hagiographies appeared more than a century after the events they purport to recount, and no manuscript versions of the tradition that definitely predate the published texts seem to have survived. If the published hagiographies of the mid-seventeenth century basically invented the tradition of Marian apparitions to a humble Indian at Tepeyac in 1531—as a main current of recent scholarship suggests—then the spotlight falls on the learned clerical inventors and their precocious seventeenth-century protonationalism. If the hagiographers were trying to catch up with and promote an already deep popular devotion, attention shifts to an older and more anonymous current of piety, perhaps all the way back to the 1530s.

In earlier work I tracked part of a history of devotion to Our Lady of Guadalupe during the eighteenth century with help from serial evidence of several kinds—baptismal records, published periodicals and journals, sermons, and some key figures and events, especially during the years 1731 to 1754.[3] I have come to regard those years as central to the broad appeal of *guadalupanismo* later. The sixteenth and seventeenth centuries remain more elusive, particularly the sixteenth century, with its long silences and few, glancing references that have been made to carry so much weight in later efforts to validate or dismiss an official story.[4]

Clearly, important changes occurred at the shrine of Our Lady of Guadalupe during the seventeenth century. A 1608 inspection of the municipal lands of Mexico City located a northern boundary at the "hermita [chapel, hermitage] de Nuestra Señora de Guadalupe" and planted the boundary marker on top of Tepeyac hill. No important settlement was described; only a "tiny pueblo" *(pueblecillo)* called Sancta Ysabel was said to be nearby, "antes de la subida del cerro de Tepeaquilla." In a similar inspection of 1690–91 that marked the municipal boundary on top of Tepeyac again, a more significant shrine and settlement had taken shape: "el santuario y hermita de Nuestra Señora de Guadalupe de el pueblo de Peaquilla."[5]

The story of Our Lady of Guadalupe first comes into bold relief in the mid-seventeenth century, in a cluster of studied little books by priest-devotees printed between 1648 and 1688: Miguel Sánchez's *Imagen de la Virgen María* (1648); Luis Lasso de la Vega's *Huei tlamahuiçoltica* (1649); Luis Becerra Tanco's *Felicidad de México* (1666, 1675); and Francisco de Florencia's *La estrella del norte de México* (1688). Not much is known about the history of the tradition during the seventeenth century beyond what scholars and devotees have inferred from these texts, several paintings and prints, building activity early and late in the century, and a set of testimonies about the tradition recorded in 1666. Hagiography effectively has passed as the seventeenth-century history of *guadalupanismo,* whether it is taken to validate a sixteenth-century story of early devotion or to express values and intentions of seventeenth-century authors.[6]

I mean *studied* little books in the double sense of self-conscious narratives that aspire to official standing, and texts that are repeatedly combed and cited by students of *guadalupanismo* seeking or debunking a kind of biblical certainty about beginnings. With this double meaning of "studied" in mind, Francisco de la Maza playfully but astutely called the authors of these seventeenth-century hagiographies the "four Evangelists," as if they succeeded in composing texts that were similar in aim and reception to the Gospels of the New Testament. They, along with Mateo de la Cruz's extract of Sánchez's book, were the first printed texts to tell the story of apparitions of the Virgin Mary at Tepeyac in 1531, as it has been retold countless times since:

> On Saturday, December 9, Juan Diego, an Indian from Cuauhtitlán, was on his way to attend Mass at the Franciscan convent of Tlatelolco. Passing the hill of Tepeyac, he heard celestial music and climbed up to encounter a resplendent Lady who instructed him to tell the bishop in Mexico City that she wished a church to be built there. The bishop received Juan Diego cordially, but did not promise to build the church. Juan Diego returned disconsolate to Tepeyac with this news, but the Lady instructed him to visit the bishop again with the same request. He did so on Sunday with a similar result—the bishop required a sign that Juan Diego was not speaking only for himself. When he returned to Tepeyac, the Lady appeared a third time, instructing him to go to his village and saying that she would provide a sign. Back in Cuauhtitlán he spent Monday looking after his uncle, Juan Bernardino, who had fallen gravely ill.

Early Tuesday morning, December 12, Juan Diego hurried toward Tlatelolco in search of a confessor for his uncle. He skirted the hill of Tepeyac to the east, but the Lady came down to him, calling him. Wanting to be on his way, he explained his urgent mission. The Lady responded that his uncle had already recovered from his illness and that Juan Diego should climb the hill and gather summer roses on this near-winter day as a sign to the bishop. Where the Lady appeared to him this fourth time a small spring of healing fresh water emerged. When Juan Diego spread the roses before the bishop, the image of the Lady—the Virgin Mary—was revealed on his cloak. The astonished bishop moved quickly to erect a church at Tepeyac and placed the image there shortly before his departure for Spain. Juan Diego and his uncle thenceforth devoted their lives to serving the Virgin Mary and practiced a vow of chastity. He received one last visit from Mary in 1548, informing him of his impending death, which would precede the bishop's by a short time. Thanks to the intercession of Our Lady, both the bishop and Juan Diego would receive their reward in heaven.[7]

Each of the four "Evangelists" approached the subject somewhat differently. Miguel Sánchez wrote for the learned, especially for fellow priests in Mexico City, as Florencia noticed when he wrote that Sánchez's book was "para hombres doctos."[8] Sánchez sprinkled his account of the apparitions and history of the image with providential biblical analogies and Latin phrases, and gave special attention to Mary's protection of the capital city. (Mateo de la Cruz's extract of *Imagen de la Virgen María*, published first in Puebla in 1660, was intended to bring the story to a wider audience.)[9] Lasso de la Vega's Nahuatl text does not have the learned references or many of the providential asides, and downplays the Mexico City connection. It lovingly elaborates on the apparition stories in ways that associate them with Indian believers.[10] His text, in contrast to Sánchez's, was evidently directed more toward priests in pastoral service among Nahuatl-speakers of central Mexico and perhaps a Nahua lay elite. Becerra Tanco gave more attention to the floods of 1629–34 as a sign and a benchmark of devotion, while Florencia offered a longer, survey treatment for a general audience, citing Sánchez and Becerra Tanco as his first sources for the tradition, and omitting the learned references. Florencia added some history of the *culto*[11] up to his own time, enlarged the standard list of miracles, and gave special emphasis to the incorruptibility of the image itself. His *La estrella del norte de México* amounts to a more elaborate, historical, and accessible version of Sánchez's text.

Despite their differences, the four "Evangelists" feature the apparition stories at Tepeyac and the culminating miracle of the image on December 12 in similar accounts. All four give special attention to Juan Diego and his uncle in the apparitions, a core set of miracles that favored both Spaniards and Indians, and Spaniards of Mexico City as the great benefactors of the shrine. All were written by American-born Spanish priests, expressing pride in "Mexico" (the vicinity of Mexico City) and America as places especially favored by the Virgin Mary. Sánchez, for example, referred to this image as *nuestra soberana criolla,* "our sovereign American Lady."[12]

The fact that no securely dated text for the Guadalupan tradition precedes those of the four "Evangelists" from 1648 to 1688[13] has led most recent scholars to a creole nationalist interpretation of the tradition. This interpretation holds that the four seventeenth-century hagiographies amount to the "invention" of the tradition as an expression of "creole consciousness"—expressing their love of their American homeland, and pressing for the religious autonomy of their American *reino* (kingdom).[14] In this interpretation, the story of apparitions and miraculous origin of the image amounts to a creole Spanish appropriation of a secondary, nearly moribund shrine in the mid-seventeenth century. Indians devotees are left out of the picture except as objects of a new evangelization, and the *culto* is assumed to have blossomed into a widespread, protonational devotion shortly after the publication of Sánchez's book. Sánchez and Lasso de la Vega, of course, firmly rejected such an interpretation, claiming that they were, as Lasso de la Vega put it, no more than "sleeping Adams" who had awakened to faithfully record a well-established tradition.

The seventeenth-century hagiographies give us the apparition stories, two Indian men of the Valley of Mexico as central to the tradition, and the makings of a December 12 feast day. But were their authors leading or mainly following an upward curve of devotion? And was it a single, steep curve? Did they essentially invent the tradition, or were they, as they claimed, simply publishing what was already widely known to the faithful? When was the tradition of apparitions known, celebrated, promoted, and widely accepted? Was there much Indian devotion to Our Lady of Guadalupe in the seventeenth century? Did the hagiographers want what other devotees wanted? We are left to wonder. The four "Evangelists" themselves do not provide many answers.

BEYOND HAGIOGRAPHY

Other seventeenth-century sources of recorded memory about Our Lady of Guadalupe and the history of veneration of the image are more prosaic and dispersed than these four hagiographies. No books of miracles or donations have come to light for this shrine—no long lists of donors or reported marvels recorded sequentially over many years, as one sometimes finds in Europe,[15] and no long series of ex-voto paintings for the seventeenth and eighteenth centuries, like the eye-catching collections for the late nineteenth and twentieth centuries. There is no long run of *gacetas* (periodicals) for the seventeenth century, as there is for much of the eighteenth century, but we do have Gregorio Guijo's and Antonio de Robles's *efemérides* (unofficial journals of public events from a Mexico City perspective) for the second half of the century,[16] and the minutes of the colonial *ayuntamiento* of Mexico City and the *cabildo eclesiástico* of the cathedral. Tepeyac appears in the sixteenth-century and early seventeenth-century minutes of the *ayuntamiento* mainly as a principal point of entry into Mexico City, with a heavily traveled road to be maintained. By 1586 Tepeyac was established as the resting place for new viceroys on their way from Veracruz to Mexico City. The viceroy lingered there for a day or two while the city government prepared his grand procession to the viceregal palace and offices on the main square. The shrine itself and the image of Our Lady of Guadalupe are not mentioned in the early references to these processions, but by the 1620s *casas de novenarios* (lodgings for visitors who came for a nine-day round of devotions) there doubled as the viceroy's quarters, as needed, although they were reported to be in poor condition in 1624 and the site of the viceroy's rest and grand entrance was moved to Chapultepec.[17] The shrine and image of Mary at Tepeyac are rarely mentioned in the *ayuntamiento* minutes before 1648, even during the period of the great flood from 1629 to 1634,[18] which some scholars and witnesses in the 1666 inquiry into the Guadalupan tradition have regarded as a pivotal date. Entries in the Guijo and Robles *efemérides* for 1648–1703 also have remarkably little to say about veneration of the image of Guadalupe. But, like the *ayuntamiento* minutes, they frequently mention another famous image and shrine in the Valley of Mexico, that of Our Lady of los Remedios.

The financial records prepared for official inspections *(visitas)* of the shrine at Tepeyac by delegates of the archbishop offer some additional information about seventeenth-century *guadalupanismo* that can be set alongside the four famous seventeenth-century texts. They amount to more than two thousand manuscript pages, including summary accounts and descriptions, and many individual receipts for expenditures and income, dating from 1634, 1648–51, 1653, 1664–69, and 1693–98.[19] It would be wonderful to have a continuous run of such records for the seventeenth century and beyond, but these four clusters come at convenient, even predictable intervals. Not surprisingly, they appear at pivotal points in the history of promotion and regulation of *guadalupanismo* by the cathedral and chaplains of the shrine, if not necessarily pivotal points in popular devotion.

Mainly, there have been two views about the history of *guadalupanismo* up to 1648. One, expressed first by Miguel Sánchez himself, sees a progressive series of steps culminating in a fully elaborated, widespread *guadalupanismo* in the 1650s. Jacques Lafaye pursued this idea in his book *Quetzalcóatl and Guadalupe,*[20] underscoring 1629—the year the great flood began in the Valley of Mexico—as a step near the top of this stairway. Serge Gruzinski has disagreed in a way that led him to place even more emphasis than do most creole nationalism interpreters on 1648 and the publication of Sánchez's text as the turning point of *guadalupanismo.* His intriguing hypothesis is that Sánchez and Lasso de la Vega were trying to rescue a devotion that had fallen on hard times and was about to disappear.[21] In place of Sánchez's and Lafaye's ascending stairway, Gruzinski would give us a sinking ship, not much more than a rowboat. David Brading also takes the publication of Sánchez's book to signal "the sudden efflorescence" of the tradition and popular devotion.[22] Stafford Poole's recent *Our Lady of Guadalupe: The Origins and Sources of a Mexican National Symbol, 1531–1797,* joins others in highlighting 1648, but he thinks that a *culto* had hardly developed by that time, especially among Indians, so there was little to revive. For Poole, the content of the tradition we associate with the Mexican Guadalupe was more or less invented by Sánchez and Lasso de la Vega.[23]

The half century or so after the first two "Evangelists" published in 1648 and 1649 has been associated mainly with the efforts of Miguel Sánchez, Luis Becerra Tanco, and the Mexico City Cathedral chapter to promote the *culto* and the shrine at Tepeyac. Those efforts culminated in appeals to Rome for recognition of the tradition, an official investigation for this purpose in 1666, Becerra Tanco's text, *Felicidad de México* (revised for publication in 1675 from his 1666 report), the various writings of the Jesuit Marian devotee Francisco de Florencia in the 1680s and 1690s—"the great orquestrator," as Gruzinski aptly calls him—the first cluster of published sermons, churches dedicated to the Virgin of Guadalupe in Querétaro, San Luis Potosí, and Mexico City, and the construction of a grand, new shrine to house the precious image, largely underwritten by Mexico City patrons.

In speaking of a history of *guadalupanismo* in the half centuries or so before and after Sánchez's and Lasso's books were published I want to touch on two historical issues in particular, about which there has not been much agreement or really much known. First is the tradition of apparitions occurring in 1531. Miguel Sánchez was the first to publish on this subject, but when was the tradition known and by whom? When was it widely accepted? How was it expressed and promoted? What, then, is the place of the 1648–49 publications and the 1666 investigations in establishing and shaping the apparition story and the *culto*? Second is the question of Indian devotion to Our Lady of Guadalupe in the seventeenth century. Here the literature is divided, more than silent or muffled. Poole infers that there was little Indian devotion to speak of before Sánchez and Lasso de la Vega published. Octavio Paz, Francisco de la Maza, and Lafaye, among others, think it was mainly a popular, Indian devotion until learned creoles began to catch up in the mid-seventeenth century, but offer little support for their conclusion. Those who have ventured into these two issues have been inclined to slight the special importance of Mexico City to the early history of devotion to Our Lady of Guadalupe.[24]

The decades before 1648 were a formative period for the development of regional miracle shrines in many parts of New Spain, including Izamal (Yucatán), Ocotlán (Tlaxcala), San Miguel del Milagro (Tlaxcala), Chalma (Estado de México), Tecaxic (Valley of Toluca, Estado de México), Cosamaloapa (Veracruz), Zapopan (Jalisco), San Juan de los Lagos (Jalisco), and los Remedios (Valley of Mexico), among others. The early years of the seventeenth century may well have been a formative time for Tepeyac and the Guadalupe story, too, but with a concentration of interest in Mexico City and among Indians in and near the Valley of Mexico, without yet becoming the widespread devotion and shared understanding that can be traced in considerable detail from the 1730s.

Was the shrine of Guadalupe at Tepeyac on the verge of collapse at the time that Miguel Sánchez's hagiography was published? The financial records of 1634 and 1648–53 suggest not, but neither do they support the teleological enthusiasm of Sánchez and nine other distinguished priests who spoke in 1666 of unbroken and widespread devotion since 1531. The 1634 financial records note that before the floods began in 1629 people frequented the shrine at Tepeyac on Sundays, including many priests, and that alms of about five silver pesos were collected on an average Sunday. During the flood years, from 1629 to 1634, when the image was removed from the shrine and taken to the cathedral in Mexico City, the Sunday collections dropped to less than half a peso. No wonder the shrine was said in 1633 to be "very poor."[25] Yet a new church had been completed in 1622, and the thoroughfare from Tepeyac to the city was enlarged under the sponsorship of Archbishop Juan Pérez de la Serna between 1613 and 1622;[26] at least one substantial bequest was received from a Spanish resident of the city:[27] the 1634 financial records note that *casas de novenarios* were under construction at the shrine before the floods; and by 1637 the shrine would gain a sumptuous new altarpiece donated by Doña Magdalena Pérez de Viveros of Mexico City that Sánchez, reaching for a suitably fulsome appreciation, called "precious, rich, splendid, magnificent, singular, rare, excellent, exquisite."[28] Unless the *casas de novenarios* were just retreat houses for devotees from the nearby capital or mainly maintained in anticipation of the arrival of a future viceroy, these lodgings suggest that visitors to the shrine were coming, or were encouraged to come, from more distant places.[29] This set of 1634 accounts also notes that during the flood years only "indios de la sierra" came to the shrine, and that the pastor there preached "en las dos lenguas" (Spanish and Nahuatl). So some Indian devotion beyond the city and valley is apparent in 1634, but just where Indian devotees were from and how many traveled to Tepeyac and when are not clear. The meager alms collections suggest small numbers, especially during the flood years.

The real estate belonging to the shrine in 1634 was limited to its compound. No properties in Mexico City were listed, no precious objects of silver and gold were acquired that year, and no collections by *demanda* were reported (i.e., no one was licensed by the archbishop and viceroy to go out on alms-gathering missions).[30] The property of the shrine amounted to the building and grounds, some religious art and furnishings, and 7,000 pesos in capital.

The 1634 accounts refer to important Semana Santa celebrations and a *fiesta de la cassa* that year, but they do not say when the fiesta took place. Was it December 12? The absence of a date here raises the question of when December 12 became the important feast day for the shrine. That would be solid evidence of when the apparition story as Sánchez, Lasso de la Vega, Becerra Tanco, and Florencia told it was widely known and celebrated. The fact that the image was moved to Mexico City during the floods of 1629–34 suggests that the tradition of its supernatural origin was not yet firmly in place. The image was not yet too precious to move. The absence of a centennial celebration in 1631, or any mention of December 12 or the Virgin of Guadalupe among the December religious events in Mexico City's *actas de cabildo* before 1648, also suggest that the apparition story as we know it had not yet become established, at least not officially.[31]

In 1634 substantial sums were spent at the shrine. In fact, the 1634 expenditures were exceeded only by 1648–50 in these seventeenth-century financial records. The outlays that year were mainly for construction of *casas de novenarios* and repairs of damage caused by the floods.

The next set of accounts and receipts, from 1648 to 1653, indicate that this was the period of highest annual income for the shrine during the seventeenth century, as well as a time of substantial expenditures on precious furnishings. With the peak of income and expenditures coming at mid-century, there was no continuous increase in income and property throughout the century, either from 1629 or 1648 onward, as one might expect; and apparently no great crescendo of popular devotion beyond Mexico City in the second half of the seventeenth century that a reading of the Evangelists would anticipate.

The growing expenditures evident in the 1648–53 accounts largely followed publication of Sánchez's book, but the growth in income *preceded* his book, which suggests that 1634–48 was an active and successful period for the promotion of the *culto,* and a time of growing popular devotion in Mexico City after the return of the image from the cathedral to the shrine as the floodwaters receded in 1633–34. By 1648 the shrine already had acquired most of the income-producing real estate it possessed during the seventeenth century. All of those properties were in Mexico City, and most of them were in the neighborhood of the Plaza de Santo Domingo. There was an increase in capital from wills and cash gifts in about 1648;

and in the years immediately following 1648 five *demandantes* collected for the shrine in various parts of the Archdiocese of Mexico. So 1648–53 stands out in the seventeenth-century financial records as a very active period of spending and getting (see tables 1 and 2), but it did not all follow publication of Sánchez's book, as one line of interpretation would imagine. That activity in 1653 was more the extension of a trend of promotion, devotion, and accumulation than a departure from the immediate past.[32]

The floods of 1629–34 were important to the history of *guadalupanismo* from 1634 to 1648, but not quite in the linear way that Lafaye and Sánchez imagined. (Lafaye was thinking of Guadalupe's sudden fame in protecting against floods, literally and figuratively, which clerical witnesses mentioned in the 1666 investigation.) Those years between 1629 and 1634 were, I think, a time of crisis for the shrine, if not for the reputation of the image in Mexico City. The new church of 1622, the *casas de novenarios* project, and the income of the shrine all suffered during the flood years. Alms collections at the shrine, and other donations, shriveled once the image was taken to Mexico City, and the physical plant deteriorated ("The buildings were crumbling," reports the 1634 account record).[33]

Table 1

Annual Income Tabulated from the Visita Records

	1634	1648–50	1651–53	1664	1693–98
Income-producing property	None listed	1,239p (11 houses, 15 *censos*)	1,312p (10 houses, 1 *hacienda*)	Information missing	1937p (10 houses, 6 *tiendas*, 11 *censos*)
Alms at the shrine	34p[i]	303p 6rr[ii]	475p 6rr[ii]	Information missing	581p 6rr
Demandas	—	C. 1,400p	C. 1,050p	Information missing	Less than 240p
Other income	867p[iii]	1,406p (4,218p 7rr total)[iv]	1,200p[v]	Information missing	223p 4rr[iv]
Total	901p	4,351p 6rr	3,237p 6rr	—	2,982p 2rr

i. 220–60p per year in the years immediately before the floods of 1629–34.
ii. Includes the alms box at the shrine and collections during the *fiestas principales.*
iii. Gifts of cash and kind.
iv. Includes wills, cash, sale of wax and oil.
v. Money owed by Lic. Muñoz.

Table 2

Annual Expenditures Tabulated from the Visita Records

	1634	1648–50	1651–53	1664–69	1693–98
Salaries	400p[i]	679p 6rr[ii]	600p[iii]	600p[iii]	781p[iv]
Upkeep and improvements	3,265p	964p 2rr	Information missing	500p (3,002p 2rr total)	513p 6rr[v]
Upkeep on rentals	—	—	577p (1,729p 5rr total)	185p 1r	Information missing
***Ornamentos* and vestments**	—	2,862p (8,587p total)	1,145p (3,435p total)	942p (5,651p total)	485p (2,912p total)
Liturgical costs	250p (*semana santa*)	C. 196p (*semana santa*)	—	—	—
Legal fees	—	52p 2rr[vi]	114p 5rr	—	C. 45p
Other	—	80p[vii]	137p	51p[viii]	—
Total	3,915p	4,834p	2,583p 5rr	2,278p 1r	1,825p

i. For vicario and sacristán.
ii. For vicario, mayordomo, sacristán, and procurador.
iii. For vicario, mayordomo, and sacristán.
iv. For vicario, mayordomo, sacristán, and ayudante de sacristán.
v. Incomplete. Only "gasto de esclavo" listed.
vi. Plus 438p legal fees concerning an obra pía attached to the shrine.
vii. Accountant's fee.
viii. Includes 216p paid for printing a novena booklet.

Then in 1634 there were substantial expenditures from the existing capital of 7,000 pesos, and the 1648 records indicate mounting donations for the shrine by Mexico City patrons in the preceding years, before Sánchez's book was published. Sánchez's emphasis on the apparitions and the supernatural origin of the image served as a powerful reason for keeping the image where it was and thereby securing the income of the shrine. This permanent residence of the image at Tepeyac after 1634 protected the shrine of Guadalupe from the erratic income cycles of the shrine of los Remedios because of that image's extended absences in Mexico City.

The financial records after 1649 shed some additional light on the history of the apparition tradition and popular devotion. Those from the 1660s and 1690s, in particular, yield a somewhat different story than the

extraordinary devotion suggested by the 1666 testimonies and the writings of the third and fourth Evangelists, Luis Becerra Tanco and Francisco
de Florencia. The 1660s records unfortunately do not include income,
but they register substantial payments for improvements to the buildings
and purchase of expensive silver and gold furnishings to dignify the *culto*.
These expenditures were almost as much as those of 1634. By contrast,
the income and expenditure figures for the early 1690s are surprisingly
modest. The alms-collecting initiatives produced much less in the 1690s
than they had at midcentury—less than 240 pesos a year, compared to
about 1,200 pesos a year from 1648 to 1653. The total income of the
shrine in 1693 was about 2,400 pesos compared to between 3,200 and
4,000 pesos annually from 1648 to 1653. And little new real estate had
been acquired by the shrine between 1653 and 1693.

Although the financial records for the 1690s showed mediocre returns
rather than the expected surge of income, property, and popular devotion,
other developments since the 1660s anticipated the *guadalupanismo* of
later times. The image had not been moved beyond its precinct; construction of a new and much grander church was planned by 1694; and
December 12 had become a significant holiday at the shrine, although the
popularity of this holiday seems to have come late in the century and was
less important than would be expected from Florencia's emphasis on it
in *La estrella del norte de México* (1688).[34] The 1660s may well be when
December 12 was introduced into the calendar of feast days.[35] The Capilla
del Cerrito, at the site where Juan Diego was believed to have gathered the
roses in his cloak, was dedicated in 1667,[36] and the 1666 investigation was
meant to win papal approval of the apparition story and a December 12
feast day. The pace of activity in Mexico City in support of the apparition
story and the shrine quickened in the 1670s. Reconstruction of the thoroughfare from the shrine to the city, with fifteen imposing monuments
to the mysteries of Mary, was begun in 1675 and completed in August
1676.[37] A few sermons about the apparitions began to appear in print; in
1676 Antonio de Robles's journal recorded for the first time a celebration
of the apparition, on the night of December 11; and the archbishop
ordered in 1677 that the glass case protecting the image should no longer
be opened for the faithful to kiss and touch the cloth.[38] Then in 1679
Doña Teresa de Aguirre of Mexico City established an endowment for an
annual December 12 fiesta at the Capilla del Cerrito.[39] In 1682, papal bulls

were published that permitted Masses at the main altar of the shrine, and granted indulgences to those who visited the shrine and prayed there.[40]

December 12 was an annual celebration by the 1690s, but the financial records of that time connect the celebration only to the Capilla del Cerrito, and they indicate that this date had not yet displaced what was called the *fiesta principal del santuario,* which was celebrated during a two-week period in November: one week for Spaniards and *castas,* and one week for Indians. While Robles had mentioned a celebration of the apparition in 1676, he did not mention it again as a significant event until 1703 when he wrote that "the fiesta of Nuestra Señora de Guadalupe" had been celebrated on December 12 "with great solemnity."[41]

Why was the seventeenth-century Guadalupan *fiesta principal* in November? The financial records do not say, but it could have been to honor Mary as Nuestra Señora del Patrocinio (Our Lady of Intercession), a generic devotion, much as the Virgin Mary in all her various representations also was called Queen of the Angels (la Reina de los Angeles). The feast of this advocation of Mary as Nuestra Señora del Patrocinio falls on the second Sunday in November, and it was observed in Mexico City (and elsewhere in New Spain) during the seventeenth century.[42] This *fiesta principal* in November for the shrine of Guadalupe is highlighted in the 1651–52 financial accounts. In 1651 the November fiestas represented fully half of the income of the shrine that year. In 1693 they still produced nearly twice the annual sum collected in alms at the shrine. The 1693 financial accounts unfortunately do not separate out the income from the December 12 events at the Capilla del Cerrito, but the monthly receipts from the alms boxes at the shrine show only a slight increase in donations during December.

These account records raise doubts about whether the story of Marian apparitions to a humble Indian at Tepeyac in 1531 was as widely known and celebrated as the seventeenth-century hagiographies seem to suggest. But neither do the account files support an emphatic creole nationalism interpretation that regards the hagiographers as inventors of the tradition and leaves Indian devotees out of the picture or only vaguely present until the second half of the century. By themselves, these financial records help to problematize the history of devotion to Our Lady of Guadalupe in the seventeenth century, but they offer only tantalizing suggestions of a deeper history of devotion.

Several more familiar seventeenth-century sources may contribute something new to historical study of *guadalupanismo* if they are approached with the financial records in mind. The best known of these sources are the depositions by nineteen elderly men and one woman in 1666 (eight Indian elders from Cuauhtitlán, one descendant of Moctezuma from Mexico City, and eleven distinguished senior priests based in the capital, including Miguel Sánchez). They were recorded to support an appeal by the councils of the archdiocese and the city of Mexico for papal recognition of the *culto*. Most of the witnesses said they recalled from their childhoods in the late sixteenth century stories of apparitions of the Virgin Mary to Juan Diego, the miraculous origin of her image on his cloak in 1531, and Indian devotion at Tepeyac.[43] And in the published version of his lengthy report to the 1666 commission, Luis Becerra Tanco claimed that he had witnessed Indian dances of a kind performed before the 1629 flood in which Indian elders sang of Juan Diego, the apparitions of Mary, and the miraculous image.[44]

Taken on their own, the 1666 testimonies may be doubted as pious hearsay and hindsight—expressing the ardent devotion of witnesses who were caught up in a high tide of promotion of the *culto* by cathedral dignitaries and priests attached to the shrine, without direct, personal knowledge of the sixteenth-century events of which they spoke.[45] But the 1666 testimonies should not be so easily dismissed as evidence only of the 1660s, rather than an earlier time. Most of the witnesses were testifying to practices and beliefs and conversations that they might well have witnessed or experienced long before Sánchez's book was published in 1648, if not from the sixteenth century. After all, Chimalpahin, the early-seventeenth-century Nahua chronicler and longtime resident of Mexico City, testified to a tradition of apparition when he wrote that Our Lady of Guadalupe had "revealed herself" on top of Tepeyac in 1556.[46] An artifact from the early seventeenth century that would seem to corroborate the 1666 witnesses' claims about an earlier belief in the miraculous origin of the image and Marian apparitions is the oldest signed and dated copy of the image, painted by Baltasar de Echave Orio in 1606. The painting depicts not only the image of the Mexican Virgin of Guadalupe but also the cloth on which the image appears, as if the cloth were as much the object of veneration as the image.[47] Echave Orio, a peninsular Spaniard, was the most celebrated artist in Mexico City at the time, and this painting would have been an important commission.[48]

But who commissioned Echave Orio's painting? Where was it displayed? What did such a painting of the cloth and image of Mary signify to its patron and viewers? Miguel Sánchez offered a possible clue, albeit thirdhand, in his testimony for the 1666 inquiry. He testified to having heard Lic. Bartholomé García (who served as chaplain of the shrine at Tepeyac from 1624 to 1646) say that Alonso Muñoz, dean of the cathedral chapter in Mexico City, had seen Archbishop Fr. García de Mendoza (1601–6) "reading with singular tenderness the legal records concerning the aforementioned apparition."[49] Was Archbishop García de Mendoza, in fact, the patron and owner of Echave Orio's 1606 painting of the image and cloth? Did it hang in the archepiscopal palace? If so, who beyond Juan Pérez de la Serna (archbishop from 1613 to 1625, responsible for completing the new church and thoroughfare, and promoting donations with prints of an image of Guadalupe as miracle-worker, known as the Stradanus engraving) shared García de Mendoza's enthusiasm for the image? Even if Sánchez's hearsay testimony can be trusted and the Echave Orio painting was commissioned by Archbishop García de Mendoza, who the devotees were and what they understood remain uncertain, even for high clergymen of the early seventeenth century. An undated note apparently written by or for García de Mendoza between 1603 and 1606 recalled a flood in the city the previous year but made no mention of appeals to Our Lady of Guadalupe for relief.[50] One sermon delivered at the Tepeyac shrine was published in 1622, but it did not concern Our Lady of Guadalupe directly. Only in the 1670s did sermons come to be published on Guadalupe and the apparitions theme. And the extant university theses abstracts from the colonial period that so often were dedicated to a patron saint or special advocation of Mary or Christ do not register dedications to the Virgin of Guadalupe until the 1650s.[51]

CONCLUSION

The years during and immediately after the publication of Sánchez's and Lasso de la Vega's hagiographies of Our Lady of Guadalupe (1648–53) were, indeed, a pivotal point in this history of faith, but there was not a sudden and definitive beginning then for the apparition tradition or Indian devotion, as creole nationalism hypotheses often suggest. Nor were the developments of 1648 to 1653 only the culmination of a swelling wave of popular devotion going back to 1531, as Sánchez claimed, though it is likely that Sánchez *was* building directly on developments in the 1620s and 1630s, and a still older tradition of miracles and apparition. Sánchez both built on a devotion in the making and actively promoted it in a way that eventually ensured the exceptional importance of the shrine at Tepeyac, the tradition of the apparitions to Juan Diego, and the December 12 feast. Sánchez, Lasso, and the other "Evangelists" brought together two devotional streams—an "Indian" apparitionist stream that remains something of a mystery in its details and devotees; and a "Spanish" stream situated mainly in Mexico City that was, in part, an expression of creole proto-nationalism (although peninsular devotees were prominent throughout the seventeenth and eighteenth centuries, too). Ritually, the two streams remained separate in their annual fiestas and much else, but the story of apparitions, as Sánchez and Lasso wrote it, would come to be shared by all devotees.[52] Sánchez's book and those of the other "Evangelists" were significant events in a story of devotion that had some momentum of its own and was actively promoted from the cathedral in Mexico City and priests at the shrine itself, both creoles and peninsulars. These printed texts were artifacts of an increasing devotion, but this momentum at midcentury did not quickly make December 12 and the apparition stories into the widespread *culto* we can trace from the 1730s.

The *visita* financial records and other sources that reach beyond the hagiographies into a more ample history of devotion do not reveal a wholly different seventeenth-century experience of *guadalupanismo*. However, they do suggest leads that place the famous texts of Sánchez, Lasso de la Vega, Mateo de la Cruz, Becerra Tanco, the 1666 testimonies, and Florencia into a process of devotion and promotion, rather than as the first or last words, standing in splendid isolation for a changeless past and present, or as largely irrelevant to that past except as manifestations of the aims and piety of their authors. Sánchez and Lasso de la Vega meant to order and publicize the tradition, and their books represent a kind of consolidation and elaboration—in retrospect, a codification—of an apparition story, but it was not yet the consolidation of a widespread tradition. An apparition tradition circulated from the late sixteenth century in some colonial Indian communities of central Mexico and among some leaders of the archdiocese in Mexico City. The Echave Orio painting, Chimalpahin's notation for 1556, and Sánchez's and Becerra Tanco's testimony in 1666 suggest as much. Just what that older tradition was (if, in fact, there was just one) is not clear. Judging by the silence about a December 12 feast day before the 1660s, and Chimalpahin's and the anonymous annals's reference to a Marian apparition at Tepeyac only in the 1550s, none of the traditions may have been as specific to apparitions during four days in December 1531 as the "Evangelists" suggest.[53]

These glimpses of a history of devotion in the seventeenth-century financial records and other sources suggest that the familiar tradition and practice were not firmly in place even at the end of the seventeenth century. The books of the "Evangelists" had not suddenly spread the word and awakened mass devotion. Florencia was still working on that project in his *La estrella del norte de México* of 1688. A transition toward the familiar tradition and practice comes into view in the 1690s financial records and the cluster of sermons published in Mexico City between 1695 and 1720, but it would take another concerted effort at promotion in the 1720s, the bicentennial in 1731, the great epidemic of 1737, Archbishop-Viceroy Vizarrón's active sponsorship, and the papal decree of 1754 to firmly establish the tradition and December 12 as *the* day of Our Lady of Guadalupe, and open a new era of popular devotion and promotion. The *fiesta principal* of Our Lady of Guadalupe in November is forgotten today, but it did not disappear even with the eighteenth-century surge of *guadalupanismo* and the by-then official story of the seventeenth-century hagiographers. Even in the mid-nineteenth century the popular calendars published by Galván Rivera listed the fourth Sunday of November as the "fiesta de los naturales en Guadalupe."[54]

In this chapter I have attempted to go to and a little beyond the "Evangelists'" hagiographies for a history of recorded memory about, and devotion to, Our Lady of Guadalupe in the seventeenth century. That memory appears rather fluid in the seventeenth century, despite the "Evangelists'" best efforts to capture and contain it. Projecting back to 1531 a timeless tradition of widespread belief and Indian devotion to an image of miraculous origin associated with apparitions of the Virgin Mary—whether it is Miguel Sánchez writing in 1648, Octavio Paz writing in the 1970s, Beverly Donofrio writing in 2000, or a pilgrim who will make the long trek to Tepeyac this December[55]—is likely to tell us more about memory and faith than about experience in the sixteenth and seventeenth centuries. The *guadalupanismo* glimpsed in the seventeenth-century financial records seems more incipient and open to substantial change later in the colonial period, but it was not just the invention of Sánchez and Lasso de la Vega, either.

History, says Richard White, is the enemy of memory. "Memory lives within us and cannot be separated from us without becoming something else. Memory constantly rearranges the past to make sense of the present."[56] Historians cannot eliminate or isolate memory and tradition as if they were simply untrue or irrelevant, or just more social facts to historicize. To do so would be to ignore or trivialize a vital part of human experience—*the* vital part, a devotee would say. Traditions like December 9–12, 1531, as the dates of Marian apparitions to Juan Diego cannot simply be explained away with the wave of a sheaf of documents that show no December 12 feast day before the late seventeenth century, any more than other kinds of convictions that give meaning to life can be easily suppressed with circumstantial evidence.[57] Such traditions have a life of their own. But they can be engaged in conversation with past experience and as past experience, and their differences from documented traces of experience and their connections to the history we write can be made clearer. In Carl Schorske's words, we can think *with* history, as well as think about history.[58] Or as White suggests, the limits of our reckonings with the past, as well as the limits of memory, need to be made clear. The limits of historical knowledge about the "lives" of sacred images are obvious enough, as Luis de Cisneros's distant words of 1616 about the barren, rocky plain of history remind us, though knowledge about them, like memory, is open to revision and, hopefully, to enlargement.

NOTES

1. "Hallo la historia dificultosísima y no como pozo lleno de piedra, que pudiera ir apartando, sino que me he obligado acabar de nuevo en tierra llena de peñascos y tepetates; que es cosa dificultosa llegar a dar en el agua de la verdad." *Luis de Cisneros, Historia de El Principio, y origen[,] progresos[,] venidas a México y milagros de la Santa Imagen de nuestra Señora de los Remedios . . .* (Mexico City, 1621), prologue. This was the first hagiography of a miraculous image and its shrine published in Mexico.

2. Jeannette Rodríguez, *Our Lady of Guadalupe: Faith and Empowerment among Mexican-American Women* (Austin: University of Texas Press, 1993), xxv.

3. William Taylor, "The Virgin of Guadalupe in New Spain: An Inquiry into the Social History of Marian Devotion," *American Ethnologist* 14, no. 1 (1987): 9–43.

4. Close examination of the sparse sixteenth-century record may be found in Edmundo O'Gorman, *Destierro de sombras: Luz en el origen de la imagen y culto de Nuestra Señora de Guadalupe del Tepeyac* (Mexico City: Universidad Nacional Autónoma de Mexico [hereafter UNAM], 1986); Stafford Poole, *Our Lady of Guadalupe: The Origins and Sources of a Mexican National Symbol, 1531–1797* (Tucson: University of Arizona Press, 1995); and Xavier Noguez, *Documentos guadalupanos: Un estudio sobre las fuentes de información temprana en torno a las mariofanías en el Tepeyac* (Mexico City: Fondo de Cultura Económica, 1993).

5. Bancroft Library Mexican manuscripts, M-M 272, fols. 12r, 89r.

6. Recent scholarship on the seventeenth century that begins to range beyond the texts of Sánchez, Lasso, Becerra Tanco, and Florencia includes Solange Alberro, *El águila y la cruz: Orígenes religiosos de la conciencia criolla. México, siglos XVI–XVII* (Mexico City: Fondo de Cultura Económica, 1999); Serge Gruzinski, *La guerra de las imágenes, de Cristóbal Colón a "Blade Runner" (1492–2019)* (Mexico City: Fondo de Cultura Económica, 1994); D. A. Brading, *Mexican Phoenix: Our Lady of Guadalupe: Image and Tradition across Five Centuries* (Cambridge: Cambridge University Press, 2001); Stafford Poole, *Our Lady of Guadalupe: The Origins of Sources of a Mexican National Symbol, 1531–1797* (Tucson: University of Arizona Press, 1995). Several essays by Alicia Mayer place *guadalupanismo* into the context of the Counter-Reformation and the ideas of seventeenth-century Mexican savant Carlos de Sigüenza y Góngora. See, for example, "Las corporaciones guadalupanas: Centros de integración 'universal' del Catolicismo y fuentes de honorabilidad y prestigio" in *Formaciones religiosas en la América colonial,* ed. María Alba Pastor and Alicia Mayers (Mexico City: UNAM 2000), 179–201; "El guadalupanismo en Carlos de Sigüenza y Góngora" in *Carlos de Sigüenza y Góngora: Homenaje,* 1700–2000, ed. Alicia Mayer (Mexico City: UNAM, 2000), 243–72; and "The Cult of Guadalupe and the Aims of the Counter-Reformation in New Spain" (unpublished paper, 2001). Jaime Cuadriello breaks new ground in his studies of the iconography and style of colonial paintings of Our Lady of Guadalupe. See esp. *Maravilla americana: Variantes de la iconografía guadalupana* (Guadalajara: Patrimonio Cultural del Occidente, 1989), and "La propagación de las devociones novohispanas: Las guadalupanas y otras imágenes preferentes," in *México en el mundo de las colecciones de arte,* ed. María Luis Sabau García (Mexico City: El Gobierno de la República 1994), III, 257–99. These authors lean toward the creole nationalist interpretation mentioned later in this chapter. Important earlier contributions include Francisco de la Maza's *El guadalupanismo mexicano* (Mexico City: Porruay Obregón, 1953, subsequent editions) and Efraín Castro Morales's "El santuario de Guadalupe de México en el siglo XVII," in *Retablo barroco: A la memoria de Francisco de la Maza* (Mexico: UNAM 1974), 67–77.

7. The "Evangelists'" story of the apparitions vary slightly. Here I paraphrase Agustín de Vetancurt's summary based on Sánchez, Becerra Tanco, and Florencia as a likely capsule version priests would have taught in the late seventeenth century. See Agustín de Vetancurt, *Teatro mexicano. Descripción breve de los sucesos ejemplares, históricos y religiosos del nuevo mundo de las Indias* (Mexico, 1698), pt. 4, tratado 5, ch. 3, 127–28.

8. Francisco de Florencia, *Estrella del norte de México. Historia de la milagrosa imagen de María Santísima de Guadalupe* (Guadalajara, Imprenta de J. Cabrera 1895), 74.

9. Mateo de la Cruz, *Relación de la milagrosa aparición de la Santa Virgen de Guadalupe* (Puebla, 1660).

10. A first English translation from the Nahuatl has recently been accomplished by Lisa Sousa, Stafford Poole, C. M., and James Lockhart, *The Story of Guadalupe: Luis Laso de la Vega's* Huei tlamahuiçoltica *of 1649* (Stanford, Calif.: Stanford University Press, 1998).

11. By *culto* I mean a particular form and content of worship, with a loyal following. I use the Spanish term to free the discussion from exuberant meanings and the pejorative edge of the word "cult" in American English.

12. *Imagen de la Virgen María* in *Testimonios históricos guadalupanos,* ed. Ernesto de la Torre Villar and Ramiro Navarro de Anda (Mexico: Fondo de Cultura Económica, 1982), 261.

13. The hypothesis that the "Nican Mopohua" printed in Lasso de la Vega's *Huei tlamahuiçoltica* (1649) was copied from a Nahuatl text composed by Juan Valeriano in the mid-sixteenth century has been advanced and explored, but not securely established. Among other sources see O'Gorman, *Destierro de sombras,* 48–60. In their recent translation of the *Huei tlamahuiçoltica,* Sousa, Poole, and Lockhart are persuaded that Lasso himself was the principal author, drawing mainly on Sánchez's book, perhaps with additions from oral traditions that may or may not have been written earlier, *The Story of Guadalupe,* esp. 43–47.

14. Jacques Lafaye, *Quetzalcóatl and Guadalupe: The Formation of Mexican National Consciousness, 1531–1813,* trans. Benjamin Keen (Chicago: University of Chicago Press, 1976; orig. 1974), 242; Poole, *Our Lady of Guadalupe,* 217, 223; D. A. Brading, *The First America: The Spanish Monarchy, Creole Patriots, and the Liberal State, 1492–1867* (Cambridge: Cambridge University Press, 1991), 3, 343–45; Richard Kagan, *Urban Images of the Hispanic World, 1493–1867* (New Haven, Conn.: Yale University Press, 2000), 131, 152, 162–68.

15. Pamela Sheingorn, ed., *The Book of Sainte Foy* (Philadelphia: University of Pennsylvania Press, 1995), provides a rich example of a European book of miracles in English translation.

16. Gregorio M. Guijo, *Diario, 1648–1664,* 2nd ed., 2 vols. (Mexico: Editorial Porrúa, 1986); Antonio de Robles, *Diario de sucesos notables (1665–1703),* 3 vols. (Mexico: Editorial Porrúa, 1946).

17. *Actas de cabildo,* Mexico City, September 15, 1586; Jan. 9, 1596; April 29, 1596; May 6, 1596; September 18, 1624. Chapultepec became the new site in 1624, according to Gustavo Curiel, "Fiestas para un virrey. La entrada triunfal a la ciudad de México del Conde de Baños. El caso de un patrocinio oficial, 1660," in *Patricinio, colección y circulación de las artes,* ed. Gustavo Curiel (Mexico: UNAM 1997), 166–68. In 1660, the conde de Baños insisted on paying his respects at the Guadalupe shrine before going on to Chapultepec (p. 167). Jorge Traslosheros' ongoing research on *guadalupanismo* in the

colonial period includes an examination of the colonial *actas del cabildo eclesiástico* for the Archdiocese of Mexico. We look forward to his findings on the seventeenth century from this source.

18. In the 1628–30 *actas*, the Virgin of Guadalupe was not listed among the *abogados*—divine advocates—of the city. The *abogados* mentioned most prominently in the *actas* during those years were San Gregorio *thaumaturgo*, San Hipólito, Santo Domingo, and Nuestra Señora de los Remedios.

19. Archivo General de la Nación (hereafter AGN), Ramo Archivo Histórico de Hacienda (hereafter AHH), 1202–2, exp. 1 (1648–1651), 2 (1634), 3 (1653), 6 (1664–68); AHH 1202–1, exps. 1, 2 (1693–98).

20. Lafaye, *Quetzalcóatl and Guadalupe,* 256, 292.

21. Serge Gruzinski, *La guerra de las imágenes,* 123.

22. Brading, *Mexican Phoenix,* 11.

23. Poole, *Our Lady of Guadalupe,* passim, but esp. p. 217. By contrast, Alberro, *El águila y la cruz,* considers Sánchez's text to be a culmination more than an early peak of creole nationalism.

24. Juan de Torquemada, *Monarquía Indiana,* 2nd ed. (Madrid, Nicolás Rodríguez Franco, 1723), II, 245–46.

25. AGN Acervo 49, caja 140, folder 24, Ruiz González petition.

26. Gonzalo de Hermosillo, *Sitio, naturaleza, y propiedad de la Ciudad de México . . .* (Mexico, 1617), fol. 109r.

27. For example, in 1618, Juana Palacios, widow of Gaspar López de Bajamonde, left her house in the Barrio de la Veracruz to the shrine. It was sold at auction for 1,100 pesos, AGN Civil 1839, exp. 7.

28. Castro Morales, "El santuario," 75.

29. Cisneros wrote in 1616 [1621] that the shrine at Tepeyac was "de gran devoción y concurso," *Historia de El principio,* fol. 20r.

30. A request for such a license to collect in Querétaro "and other parts" had been made in 1633, AGN Acervo 49 caja 140 folder 24.

31. For the period before 1648, *actas de cabildo* survive for 1524–1630 and 1635–43.

32. Gruzinski posits that 1653 was the first year of substantial income for the shrine, as if Sánchez's book triggered prosperity, *La Guerra de las imagenes,* 123–25.

33. "Iban desmoronándose los edificios."

34. *La estrella del norte de México,* 167–76. Lafaye, *Quetzalcóatl and Guadalupe,* 233, posits that as late as 1600 the Spanish Virgin of Guadalupe's feast day (September 8) or the Nativity of the Virgin on September 10 was the principal feast at the shrine, then supplanted by December 12. Neither the September dates nor December 12 appears in the early-seventeenth-century financial records.

35. A separate 1721–23 investigation mentioned this purpose of the 1666 *informaciones, Informaciones sobre la milagrosa aparición de la Santísima Virgen de Guadalupe recibidas en 1666 y 1723,* ed. Fortino Hipólito Vera (Amecameca: Imprenta Católica, 1889), 193, and the title of a 1661 sermon by Joseph Vidal de Figueroa suggests that an annual December 12 feast day at the shrine was being promoted then.

36. Robles, *Diario de sucesos,* I, 34, dedicated in February 1667. According to O'Gorman, *Destierro de sombras,* 283, "la primera pequeñita capilla del Cerrito" was erected in 1660. He does not cite a source.

37. Robles, *Diario de sucesos,* I, 189, 201.

38. The earliest published sermon about the image of Guadalupe (relying on Sánchez's text and the image as part of an apparition story) seems to be Joseph Vidal de Figueroa's "Theórica de la prodigiosa imagen de la Virgen Santa María de Guadalupe de México . . . el día 12 de diziembre en la fiesta anual de su milagrosa aparición en su hermita" (Mexico, 1661). It was followed a decade later by Juan de San Miguel's "Sermón . . . a nacimiento de Nuestra Señora y dedicación de su capilla de Guadalupe . . ." (Mexico, 1671); José Herrera Suárez's "Sermón . . . en la solemne fiesta . . . a la aparición milagrosa de la santa imagen de Guadalupe" (Mexico, 1673); and Juan de Mendoza Ayala's "Sermón que en el día de la Aparición de la Imagen Santa de Guadalupe, doze de Diziembre del Año de 1672 . . ." by Juan de Mendoza Ayala (Mexico: Francisco Rodríguez Lupercio, 1673). Robles, *Diario de sucesos,* I, 206 notes the December 11 celebration in 1676. AGN Acervo 49, caja 140, folder 8 has the order to keep the glass case closed.

The construction of shrines dedicated to Our Lady of Guadalupe outside the Valley of Mexico also follows the publication of the Sánchez text and gained momentum after the 1660s. The earliest distant shrine evidently was at San Luis Potosí, begun in 1654, followed by Querétaro, with a license of 1671 (under construction in 1674 and completed in 1680), Archivo Histórico del Arzobispado de México, caja for 1674, and Chalma in 1683, José de Olivares, "Oración panegyrica . . . de la nueva capilla que se consagró a Nuestra Señora de Gvalalvpe" (Mexico, 1683). For the failed attempt in 1674 by a devout Indian noble of Tepemajalco (near Tenango del Valle, modern Estado de México) to obtain a license for a chapel to Our Lady of Guadalupe, see AGN Indios 25 exps. 19, 23, and 76.

39. According to the 1690s financial records, AGN, AHH 1202-1.

40. Archivo Histórico del Arzobispado de México, caja for 1684, Archbishop Aguiar y Seixas granted permission in 1685 for these bulls to be published as a group.

41. Robles, *Diario de sucesos,* III, 303. According to Robles, the new shrine was dedicated on December 31, 1702. The *Gazetas de México,* which were published in series from 1722 to 1742, do not mention a major feast on December 12 until 1737, but the cofradía of Nuestra Señora de Guadalupe (founded in 1674) was reported to have celebrated its *fiesta titular* on December 12, 1735, and the bicentennial celebration in 1731 was held on December 12, too.

42. Guijo, *Diario,* II, 69; Robles, *Diario de sucesos,* II, 171.

43. *Informaciones sobre la milagrosa aparición . . . ,* 23–133.

44. *Felicidad de México,* fol. 14r–v.

45. See, for example, Stafford Poole's view of the 1666 testimonies as "literally a case of *post hoc ergo propter hoc,*" *Our Lady of Guadalupe,* 220.

46. "12 tecpatl xihuitl 1556. Auh ça no ypan in yhuac monextitzino yn totlaçonantzin Sancta Maria Guadalope yn Tepeyacac," Domingo Francisco de San Anton Muñon Chimalpahin Cuauhtlehuanitzin, *Die Relationen Chimalpahin's zur Geschichte Mexico's Text,* ed. Günter Zimmerman (Hamburg: Cram De Gruyter 1963), II, 16. These annals go up to 1615. Chimalpahin may have written them between 1615 and about 1620. Silvia Rendón translated this passage into Spanish without *ypan's* possible sense of "on top of": "También entonces ocurrió la aparición, dicho sea con respecto, de nuestra querida madre, Sancta María de Guadalupe en el Tepeyácac," *Relaciones originales de Chalco Amaquemecan* (Mexico: Fondo de Cultura Económica, 1965), 264. James Lockhart, *The Nahuas after the Conquest* (Stanford, Calif.: Stanford University Press, 1992), 247, refers to this passage in Chimalpahin, and on p. 551, n. 185, notes an earlier Nahuatl reference to Our Lady of Guadalupe appearing at Tepeyac (in an anonymous annals of Tenochtitlan, apparently dating from the 1560s.

47. Echave Orio's painting was first exhibited in the "Imágenes guadalupanas, cuatro siglos" show at the Centro Cultural/Arte Contemporáneo in Mexico City, November 1987–March 1988. For a color photographic reproduction see the catalog to the exhibition, *Imágenes guadalupanas cuatro siglos* (Mexico City: Fundación Cultural Televisa 1987), 31. Jaime Cuadriello provides a brief discussion of the painting in *Maravilla americana,* 33.

48. Writing in about 1610, Torquemada described Echave Orio as "un español vizcaíno . . . único en su arte" ("a Basque Spaniard, unmatched in his art"). Torquemada also noted that Echave Orio worked on the main altarpiece at Tlatelolco (completed in 1609). Tepeyac was within the political jurisdiction of Tlatelolco. *Monarquía Indiana,* III, 215.

49. *Informaciones sobre la milagrosa aparición . . . ,* 73.

50. Marqués de Montesclaros papers, Duque de Infantado Archive, Madrid. Microfilm in the DeGolyer Library, Southern Methodist University, roll 7, exp. 82.

51. The numbers of Guadalupan sermons listed in José Toribio Medina, *La imprenta en México (1539–1821),* 8 vols. (Mexico City: UNAM 1989) picked up after 1680, with a dramatic, sustained increase after 1737. Only 2 university theses out of 100 for the 1650s were dedicated to the Virgin of Guadalupe. Between 1660 and 1700 a total of 35 of 607 (5.7%) carried Guadalupan dedications. True to form, the peak period of Guadalupan dedications for university theses was 1750–1810, with 159 dedicated out of 1,750 theses (9.1%). Figures compiled from more than 4,000 theses from the 1590s to 1850 listed in *Catálogo de ilustraciones* (Mexico: Archivo General de la Nación, 1981), vols. 12 and 13.

52. Martinus Cawley, "The Four Evangelists of Guadalupe" (unpublished paper, 2002) provides a close reading of Becerra Tanco that points toward this confluence-of-two-streams interpretation of Sánchez's and Lasso's texts.

53. The principal traditions studied here were elaborated over a relatively long period, from 1521 to 1688, *Documentos guadalupanos,* 185.

54. *Calendario de Galván, para el año bisiesto de 1848. Arreglado al meridiano de Mégico* (México, 1847). But was the Indian fiesta different then, with different participants who understood it differently from their seventeenth-century predecessors?

55. Octavio Paz, *El ogro filantrópico: Historia y política, 1971–1978* (México: Joaquín Mortiz, 1979), 49; Beverly Donofrio, *Looking for Mary (or, the Blessed Mother and Me)* (New York: Viking Compass, 2000), 143–45.

56. Richard White, "History, the Rugrats, and World Championship Wrestling," *AHA Perspectives* (April 1999): 13.

57. As Hortensia, a devotee of the revered Niñopan—Baby Jesus—of Xochimilco put it when asked about the lack of historical evidence for the providential story of the image's origin in the sixteenth century, "Show me the document that says the opposite," Vania Salles and José Manuel Valenzuela, *En muchos lugares y todos los días: Vírgenes, santos y niños Dios. Mística y religiosidad popular en Xochimilco* (Mexico: El Colegio de Mexico, 1997), interview 7.

58. Carl Schorske, *Thinking with History: Explorations in the Passage to Modernism* (Princeton, N.J.: Princeton University Press, 1998), 3.

Select Bibliography

SAINTS AND HAGIOGRAPHY: EUROPEAN AND GENERAL WORKS

Brown, Peter. *The Cult of the Saints: Its Rise and Function in Latin Christianity.* Chicago: University of Chicago Press, 1981.

Burke, Peter. "How to Be a Counter-Reformation Saint." In *Religion and Society in Early Modern Europe 1500–1800,* edited by Kaspar von Greyerz, 45–55. London: George Allen & Unwin, 1984.

Bynum, Caroline Walker. *Holy Feast and Holy Fast: The Religious Significance of Food to Medieval Women.* Berkeley: University of California Press, 1987.

Certeau, Michel de. "A Variant: Hagio-Graphical Edification." In *The Writing of History,* translated by Tom Conley, 269–83. 1975. Reprint, New York: Columbia University Press, 1988.

Christian, William A. Jr. *Local Religion in Sixteenth-Century Spain.* Princeton, N.J.: Princeton University Press, 1981.

Heffernan, Thomas J. *Sacred Biography: Saints and Their Biographers in the Middle Ages.* New York: Oxford University Press, 1988.

Kieckhefer, Richard, and George D. Bond, eds. *Sainthood: Its Manifestations in World Religions.* Berkeley: University of California Press, 1988.

Reames, Sherry L. *The Legenda Aurea: A Reexamination of Its Paradoxical History.* Madison: University of Wisconsin Press, 1985.

Vauchez, André. *Sainthood in the Later Middle Ages.* Translated by Jean Birrell. 1988. Reprint, Cambridge: Cambridge University Press, 1997.

Warner, Marina. *Alone of All Her Sex: The Myth and the Cult of the Virgin Mary.* New York: Alfred A. Knopf, 1976.

Weinstein, Donald, and Rudolph Bell. *Saints and Society: The Two Worlds of Western Christendom, 1000–1700.* Chicago: University of Chicago Press, 1982.

Wilson, Stephen, ed. *Saints and Their Cults: Studies in Religious Sociology, Folklore, and History.* Cambridge: Cambridge University Press, 1983.

Woodward, Kenneth L. *Making Saints: How the Catholic Church Determines Who Becomes a Saint, Who Doesn't, and Why.* New York: Simon & Schuster, 1990.

Wyschogrod, Edith. *Saints and Postmodernism: Revisioning Moral Philosophy.* Chicago: University of Chicago Press, 1990.

Zarri, Gabriella. "Living Saints: A Typology of Female Sanctity in the Early Sixteenth Century." In *Women and Religion in Medieval and Renaissance Italy,* edited by Daniel Bornstein and Roberto Rusconi, 219–303. 1980. Reprint, Chicago: University of Chicago Press, 1996.

SAINTS AND HAGIOGRAPHY IN THE AMERICAS

Ahern, Maureen. "Visual and Verbal Sites: The Construction of Jesuit Martyrdom in Northwest New Spain in Andrés Pérez de Ribas' *Historia de los Triumphos de nuestra Santa Fee* (1645)." *Colonial Latin American Review* 8 (1999): 7–33.

Araoz, José Flores et al. *Santa Rosa de Lima y su tiempo.* Lima: Banco de Crédito del Perú, 1995.

Bercovitch, Sacvan. *The Puritan Origins of the American Self.* New Haven, Conn.: Yale University Press, 1975.

Berthiaume, Pierre. "Les *Relations* des Jésuites: Nouvel avatar de *La Légende Dorée.*" In *Les figures de l'Indien,* edited by Gilles Thérien, 121–39. Montreal: UQAM, 1988.

Brading, D. A. *Mexican Phoenix: Our Lady of Guadalupe: Image and Tradition across Five Centuries.* New York: Cambridge University Press, 2001.

Burkhart, Louise M. *Before Guadalupe: The Virgin Mary in Early Colonial Nahuatl Literature.* Austin: University of Texas Press, 2001.

Clissold, Stephen. *The Saints of South America.* London: C. Knight, 1972.

Cummins, Victoria H. "Blessed Connections: Sociological Aspects of Sainthood in Colonial Mexico and Peru." *Colonial Latin American Historical Review* 3, no. 1 (1994): 3–18.

Curcio-Nagy, Linda. *Saints, Sovereignty, and Spectacle in Colonial Mexico.* Albuquerque: University of New Mexico Press, forthcoming.

Davis, Natalie Z. *Women on the Margins: Three Seventeenth-Century Lives.* Cambridge, Mass.: Harvard University Press, 1995.

Dayan, Joan. *Haiti, History, and the Gods.* Berkeley: University of California Press, 1995.

Desmangles, Leslie G. *The Faces of the Gods: Vodou and Roman Catholicism in Haiti.* Chapel Hill: University of North Carolina Press, 1992.

García-Rivera, Alejandro. *St. Martin de Porres: The "Little Stories" and the Semiotics of Culture.* New York: Orbis, 1995.

Graziano, Frank. *Wounds of Love: The Mystical Marriage of St. Rose of Lima.* New York: Oxford University Press, forthcoming.

Greer, Allan. "Colonial Saints: Gender, Race, and Hagiography in New France." *William and Mary Quarterly,* 3rd ser., 57 (April 2000): 323–48.

Iwasaki Cauti, Fernando. "Mujeres al borde de la perfección: Rosa de Santa María y las alumbradas de Lima." *Hispanic American Historical Review* 73 (1993): 581–613.

Koppedrayer, K. I. "The Making of the First Iroquois Virgin: Early Jesuit Biographies of the Blessed Kateri Tekakwitha." *Ethnohistory* 40, no. 2 (1993): 277–306.

Laflèche, Guy. *Les saints martyrs canadiens.* 5 vols. Laval: Singulier, 1988–95.

Lavrin, Asunción. "La vida feminina como experiencia religiosa: biografía y hagiografía en Hispanoamérica colonial." *Colonial Latin American Review* 2 (1993): 27–51.

Morgan, Ronald. *Spanish American Saints and the Rhetoric of Identity, 1600–1810.* Tucson: University of Arizona Press, 2002.

Mott, Luiz. *Rosa Egipciaca, uma santa africana no Brasil.* Rio de Janeiro: Bertrand, 1993.

Myers, Kathleen Ann. *Neither Saints nor Sinners: Writing the Lives of Spanish American Women.* New York: Oxford University Press, forthcoming.

Perron, Paul. "Towards a Semiotics of Manipulation: Jesuit-Huron Relations in Seventeenth-Century New France." *Semiotica* 76 (1989): 147–70.

Poole, Stafford. *Our Lady of Guadalupe: The Origins and Sources of a Mexican National Symbol, 1531–1797.* Tucson: University of Arizona Press, 1995.

Rubial García, Antonio. *La santidad controvertida: Hagiografía y conciencia criolla alrededor de los venerables no canonizados de Nueva España.* Mexico City: UNAM, 1999.

Salles-Reese, Verónica. *From Viracocha to the Virgin of Copacabana: Representation of the Sacred at Lake Titicaca.* Austin: University of Texas Press, 1997.

Sampson Vera Tudela, Elisa. *Colonial Angels: Narratives of Gender and Sexuality in Mexico, 1580–1750.* Austin: University of Texas Press, 2000.

Villaseñor Black, Charlene. *Creating the Cult of St. Joseph: Art and Gender in the Spanish Empire.* Princeton, N.J.: Princeton University Press, forthcoming.

CHRISTIANIZING THE AMERICAS

Axtell, James. *Beyond 1492: Encounters in Colonial North America.* New York: Oxford University Press, 1992.

———. *The Invasion Within: The Contest of Cultures in Colonial North America.* New York: Oxford University Press, 1985.

Bastide, Roger. *The African Religions of Brazil: Toward a Sociology of the Interpenetration of Civilizations.* Translated by Helen Sebba. 1960. Reprint, Baltimore: Johns Hopkins University Press, 1978.

Caraman, Philip. *The Lost Paradise.* London: Sidgwick & Jackson, 1975.

Clendinnen, Inga. *Ambivalent Conquests: Maya and Spaniard in the Yucatán, 1517–1570.* Cambridge: Cambridge University Press, 1987.

Cohen, Thomas M. *The Fire of Tongues: António Vieira and the Missionary Church in Brazil and Portugal.* Stanford, Calif.: Stanford University Press, 1998.

Deslandres, Dominique. "Les femmes missionnaires de Nouvelle-France." In *La religion de ma mère: les femmes et la transmission de la foi,* edited by Jean Delumeau, 74–84. Paris: Le Cerf, 1992.

Dinan, Susan, and Debra Meyers, eds. *Women and Religion in Old and New Worlds.* New York: Routledge, 2001.

Farriss, Nancy M. *Maya Society under Colonial Rule: The Collective Enterprise of Survival.* Princeton, N.J.: Princeton University Press, 1984.

Grant, John Webster. *Moon of Wintertime: Missionaries and the Indians of Canada in Encounter since 1534.* Toronto: University of Toronto Press, 1984.

Greer, Allan, ed. *The Jesuit Relations: Natives and Missionaries in Seventeenth-Century North America.* Boston: St. Martin's Press/Bedford, 2000.

Griffiths, Nicholas, and Fernando Cervantes, eds. *Spiritual Encounters: Interactions between Christianity and Native Religions in Colonial America.* Lincoln: University of Nebraska Press, 1999.

Hall, David D. *Worlds of Wonder, Days of Judgment: Popular Religious Belief in Early New England.* New York: Alfred A. Knopf, 1989.

Hambrick-Stowe, Charles. *The Practice of Piety: Puritan Devotional Disciplines in Seventeenth-Century New England.* Chapel Hill: University of North Carolina Press, 1982.

Langer, Erick, and Robert H. Jackson, eds. *The New Latin American Mission History.* Lincoln: University of Nebraska Press, 1995.

MacCormack, Sabine. *Religion in the Andes: Vision and Imagination in Early Colonial Peru*. Princeton, N.J.: Princeton University Press, 1991.

Mali, Anya. *Mystic in the New World: Marie de l'Incarnation (1599–1672)*. Leiden, Neth.: Brill, 1996.

Megged, Amos. *Exporting the Catholic Reformation: Local Religion in Early Colonial Mexico*. Leiden, Neth.: Brill, 1996.

Mills, Kenneth. *Idolatry and Its Enemies: Colonial Andean Religion and Extirpation, 1640–1750*. Princeton, N.J.: Princeton University Press, 1997.

Mills, Kenneth, and William B. Taylor, eds. *Colonial Spanish America: A Documentary History*. Wilmington, Del.: Scholarly Resources, 1998.

Rapley, Elizabeth. *Les Dévotes: Women and Church in Seventeenth-Century France*. Montreal: McGill-Queen's University Press, 1990.

Ricard, Robert. *The Spiritual Conquest of Mexico: An Essay on the Apostolate and the Evangelizing Methods of the Mendicant Orders in New Spain, 1523–1572*. Translated by Leslie Byrd Simpson. 1933. Reprint, Berkeley: University of California Press, 1966.

Salisbury, Neal. "Religious Encounters in a Colonial Context: New England and New France in the Seventeenth Century." *American Indian Quarterly* 16 (1992): 501–9.

Taylor, William B. *Magistrates of the Sacred: Priests and Parishioners in Eighteenth-Century Mexico*. Stanford, Calif.: Stanford University Press, 1996.

Trigger, Bruce G. *Natives and Newcomers: Canada's "Heroic Age" Reconsidered*. Kingston, Ont.: Queen's University Press, 1985.

Contributors

Jodi Bilinkoff is associate professor of history at the University of North Carolina, Greensboro. She has published extensively on gender, religion, and urban culture in early modern Spain. The author of *The Avila of Saint Teresa: Religious Reform in a Sixteenth-Century City* (1989), she is currently at work on a book tentatively titled *Related Lives: Confessors, Their Female Penitents, and Catholic Culture, 1450–1750.*

Charlene Villaseñor Black, assistant professor of art history at the University of California, Los Angeles, publishes on Spanish, colonial Mexican, and Chicano/Chicana religious art. Her volume titled *Creating the Cult of St. Joseph: Art and Gender in the Spanish Empire* is forthcoming.

Julia Boss is a Ph.D. candidate in history and Renaissance studies at Yale University. Her research focuses on issues of community and identity in seventeenth-century New France. Her paper "The Life and Death of Mother Marie de Saint Joseph" appears in *Religions of the United States in Practice,* edited by Colleen McDannell (2001).

Joan Dayan, visiting fellow in the Program in Law and Public Affairs at Princeton University and professor of English at the University of Pennsylvania, is the author of *Fables of Mind: An Inquiry into Poe's Fiction* (1987) and *Haiti, History, and the Gods* (1995). She is completing a book on prisons and the law titled *Held in the Body of the State* (forthcoming). as well as a memoir called *Ezekiel's Bones,* which explores legal language and the supernatural.

Dominique Deslandres is professeure agrégée d'histoire, Université de Montréal, and adjunct professor of history at McGill University. Her research focuses on the history of Christian missions, holiness, and identity in Europe and America during the sixteenth and seventeenth centuries. She has published numerous articles and a book titled *Croire et faire croire: les missions françaises au 17e siècle* (2002).

Antonio Rubial García is a member of the Facultad de Filosofía y Letras at the Universidad Nacional Autónoma de Mexico and is a leading scholar in the social and religious history of colonial Mexico. His most recent publications include *La plaza, el palacio, y el convento* (1998), and *La santidad controvertida: Hagiografía y conciencia criolla alrededor de los venerables no canonizados de Nueva España* (1999).

Allan Greer is professor of history at the University of Toronto. He is the author of *The People of New France* (1997), *The Patriots and the People: The Rebellion of 1837 in Rural Lower Canada* (1993), and *Peasant, Lord, and Merchant: Rural Society in Three Quebec Parishes, 1740–1840* (1985). He is currently completing a volume titled *Mohawk Saint: Catherine Tekakwitha and the Jesuits.*

Kenneth Mills, associate professor of history and director of the Program in Latin American Studies at Princeton University, specializes in the colonial history of Latin America. He is the author of *Idolatry and Its Enemies: Colonial Andean Religion and Extirpation, 1640–1750,* and coauthor (with William Taylor) of *Colonial Spanish America: A Documentary History.* His current project is a book titled *Diego de Ocaña, Holy Wanderer: Evangelization and Experience in the Early Modern Spanish World.*

Kathleen Ann Myers is associate professor of Spanish at Indiana University. She has published numerous articles on women and religion in the New World and has coauthored *"A Wild Country out in the Garden": The Spiritual Journals of a Mexican Nun.* Her latest book, *Neither Saints nor Sinners: Writing the Lives of Spanish American Women* (2002), examines the lives of six women living in seventeenth-century Latin America.

Paul Perron, currently affiliated with the Department of French at the University of Toronto, has been principal of University College at the University of Toronto since 1997. He has edited and authored numerous articles and books on the semiotics of literature in Quebec and has published extensively on the writings of A. J. Greimas. His books include *A. J. Greimas and Narrative Cognition* (1993), *Towards a Semiotics of the Modern Quebec Novel* (1996), and *Narratology and Text: Subjectivity and Identity in New France and Québécois Literature* (forthcoming).

Carla Gardina Pestana, associate professor of history at Ohio State University, has published on the Quaker executions in various journals and in her book *Quakers and Baptists in Colonial Massachusetts* (1991). She is currently completing a book titled *The English Atlantic in an Age of Revolution, 1640–1661*.

William B. Taylor is Muriel McKevitt Sonne professor of history at the University of California, Berkeley. His research focuses on New Spain, including regional studies, *pueblos de indios,* church, and religion. He is the author of *Landlord and Peasant in Colonial Oaxaca* (1972), *Drinking, Homicide, and Rebellion in Colonial Mexican Villages* (1979), and *Magistrates of the Sacred: Priests and Parishioners in Eighteenth-Century Mexico* (1996). His current research centers on shrines and renowned religious images in Mexican history.

Dot Tuer is a professor at the Ontario College of Art and Design and associate graduate faculty at the University of Guelph. She has lectured and published extensively on the cultural history and contemporary art of Canada and Latin America. She is currently completing her doctorate in history at the University of Toronto.

Ronaldo Vainfas is professor of modern history at the Universidade Federal Fluminense in Rio de Janeiro. His published works include *A heresia dos indios* (1995) and *Confissoes da Bahia* (1997).

Index

A

Abad, 116
Abambá, 83
Abipones Indians, 89
Account of the Abipones (Dobrizhoffer), 89
"Account of the life, virtues, and death of
	Mother Marie de Saint-Joseph" (Incar-
	nation), 217
Acotundá, 103
Actas de cabildo, 286
Actes and Monuments (Foxe), 179
Acuña, Gonzalez de, 259
Adoration of the Eucharist (Ibarra), 205
Aguirre, Teresa de, 289
Ajofrín, Francisco de, 195
Alcácer-Quibir, Battle of, 105
Alexander VI, 202
Alexander VII, 258
Algonquins, 129, 154
Allegories of the Virtues of Palafox (Cabrera),
	198
Almedina, Fernando Yáñez de la, 6
Alumbrados, 120, 258, 262, 264
Alvarez, Baltasar, 203
Ambrose, St., 205
Ana de Casanate, 199
Ana de la Madre de Dios, Sor, 199
"Angelic Doctor, The," 101
Angelitos, 17
Angulo, Domingo, 253
Anne, St.
	daughters of, 4
	devotion in Spain and Mexico of, xvi, 3–29
	images of, 4–5
	marriages of, 4, 8–9
	teaching Mary to read by, 5, 6, 11–12, 20,
		26n.17
*Année bénédictine ou les Vies des saints de l'Ordre
	de saint Benoît pour tous les jours de l'an-
	née* (Blémur), 139
Anne of Austria, 134
Annonciades, 136
Antão, Santo, 100
Anthonians, 110
Anthony, Dom, 105

Anthony, St.
	career in Italy of, 100
	cult in Brazil of, xxi, 99–111
	as the "deparador" saint, 101
	as the "Hammer of Heretics," 101, 110
	military career of, 104–105
	as patron of "lost objects," xx
	as patron of the Portuguese Restoration,
		109–110
	thaumaturgic power of, 100
	death of, 100
Anthony of Lisbon, St., 100, 104
Anthony of Padua, xiv, xvi, xvii, 100
Antonio, 103
Aquinas, Thomas, 101
Arena Chapel, 4
Argentina, 77
Argentina (Barco Centenera), 80
Arrobamientos, 257
Arte y vocabulario de la lengua guaraní (Ruiz de
	Montoya), 80
Art of Painting, The (Pacheco), 9
Ashley, Kathleen, 4
Asuncíon, 79, 80
Audiencia, 56, 236, 237–238, 244
Augustinians
	activities in New Spain of, 68, 201
	cult of the Virgin of Guadalupe of, 53–54,
		59
Aymara, xv, xvii
Ayuntamiento, 282

B

Baca, Elena, 23, 24
Bagui, 45
Baillagon, Anne, 219
Baka, 37
Ballads, 106, 107
Bandarra, 106, 107
Bárbara, Santa, 103
Barbour, Hugh, 183
Barco Centenera, Martin de, 80
Barrois, Anne, 143
Bastide, Roger, 103

Beauvais, Anne de, 139
Becerra Tanco, Luis, "Evangelist" writings of, 279, 280, 283–284, 286, 289, 291, 293
Benedictine order, 136
Bermúdez de Castro, Diego Antonio, 195
Bernières, Jean de, 132
Berrueco, Luis, 200, 201
Berruguete, Pedro, 6
Besse, Joseph, 182–183
Bilbao, Luis de, 257–258
Bilinkoff, Jodi, ix, x, xiii–xxii, 115–128
Bishop, George, 177–179, 180, 181
Black, Charlene, xvi, xix, 2–39
Blackstone, William, 34–35
Blanes, Tomás, 62
Blémur, Jacqueline de, 139
Boco, 36
Bolivia, 53, 54, 56, 58–67, 69, 70, 71, 80
Bonaventure, St., 101
Bonner, Edmund, 179
Book of Common Prayer, 179
Borgoña, Juan de, 6
Borgraf, Diego de, 196
Boss, Julia, xvii, 211–233
Bourgeoys, Marguerite
   holy activities in New France by, 131, 134, 136, 137, 139, 142, 146
   narratives about, 215, 226
Boxer, Charles, 104
Boyarin, Daniel, 176
Boyer, Jean-Pierre, 40
Brading, David, 283
Brébeuf, Jean de, holy activities in New France by, 137, 155, 216, 217, 223, 225, 227–228
Bressani, François, 156
Brooksop, Joan, 185
Bulhões, Martim, 99
Bullion, Angélique Faure de, 134
Burkhart, Louise, 22
Bus, Cesar de, 136
Buteux, Jacques, 154, 215
Bynum, Caroline, 135

C
Cabildo, 236, 237
Cabildo eclesiástico, 282
Cabral de Mello, Evaldo, 110
Cacique, 87
Cadogan, León, 91
Calado, Manuel, 104, 110
Caldo, 6
Calundus, 103
Campaña, Pedro de, 10
Campo Tourinho, Pero do, 102
Canada, female holy activities in, xviii, 129–152
Candide (Voltaire), 81, 82
Canons Regular of St. Augustine, Order of, 99

Capilla del Cerrito, 289–290
Capitães-do-mato, 103–104
Capua, Raymond of, 270
Caraíba, 103
Carmelite order, 136, 197–201
Carmen, Virgin of, 200
Cartier, Jacques, 129
Casas de novenarios, 282, 286, 287
Casos de conciencia, 116
Castillo, Juan del, 258, 262–263, 268
Castorena y Ursua, Juan Ignacio de, 237, 244–245
Cataldino, José, 87
Catalina de Erauzo, 195
Catarina de San Juan, 196
Catherine de St. Augustin, 133
Catherine of Siena
   inspiration to Rosa de Lima by, 254, 255, 256, 259, 260, 264, 268, 270
   introduction to the New World of, xiv
   mystical writing of, 117
   as name saint of Catherine Tekakwitha, 247
Cayetano, Bruno, 253
Cécile de Ste. Croix, 132
Cemithualtin, 22
Cerro Rico, 59, 64
Chabanel, Noël, 225
Chaco Indians, 81, 82, 84
Chantal, Jeanne de, 136
Charlet, Étienne, 156
Chaumonot, Pierre, 226
Childbirth, patron saints for, xvi, 4, 6, 13, 23
Chimalpahin, 291, 293–294
Chiquito Indians, 80
Cholenec, Pierre, 224, 236, 247, 248
Christian, William, Jr., 4
Christian and Erudite Painter, or Treatise of Errors Frequently Committed in Painting and Sculpting Sacred Images, The (Ayala), 11
Cinco Señores, 14
Cinco Señores (Concha), 14, 15
Cinco Señores (Villalpando), 14
Cisneros, Luis de, 295
Clavis Prophetarum (Vieira), 107
Clement IX, 259
Clement X, 251, 259
Clement XIV, 207
Cleophas, 4
Coddington, William, 184, 186
Code civil des français, 37
Code Napoleon, 37, 38
Code Noir, 33, 37, 38
Code Rural, 40
Cofradías, 56, 60–61, 62, 64, 66, 69, 70
Colbert, Jean-Baptiste, 33
Collection of the Sufferings of the People called Quakers (Besse), 181
"Colonial Saints: Hagiography and the Cult of Saints in the Americas, 1500-1800," x
Color, people of, 17–19, 235, 236, 239–240, 242–245, 247, 249

Comedia, 62
Commentaries on the Laws of England (Blackstone), 34
Comontes, Antonio de, 6
Concepcion, Petronila de la, 245–246, 247
Concha, Andrés de la, 14, 15
Concilio Limense, 254
Concilios provinciales mexicanos (Lorenzana), 195
Congrégation Notre-Dame de Montréal, 134, 144
"Contact relics," 221
Cordero, Gil, 64
Córdova Megia, Pedro de, 69
Cornelius, 10
"Corporeal relics," 221
Corpus Christi, convent of, 236–240, 242, 244, 248–249
Correa, Juan, 17–18
Corregidor, 65, 69
Council of the Indies, 82, 237, 258
Council of Trent, 8, 12, 102, 221, 269
Counter-Reformation, 102, 243, 256, 260, 271
Cowland, Alice, 180
Cramoisy, Octave, 153
Cramoisy, Sébastien, 213–214
"Creole Catholicism," 49
Creoles, xvii–xviii, 42, 56
Criolla, Rosa de Lima as, 251–275
Cruz, Mateo de la, 279, 280, 293
Cuadernos, 264
Cuevas, Mariano, 125
Cusco, 67–70
"Custodian of the Courts of Heaven," 109

D

Danbala wedo, xvi, 46–48
Daniel, Antoine, 137, 217, 224, 225
Danto, Ezili, 49
David, King, 107
Dayan, Joan, xvi, xx, xxi, 31–50
Delbau, Jean-Claude, 39
Delectare, 193
Demandadores, 51, 62, 67, 68
Deslandres, Dominique, xviii, 129–152
Dessalines, Jean-Jacques, 37–38
Deusen, Nancy E. van, 269
Díaz de Talavera, Juan, 63
Diego, Juan, 281, 289, 291, 293, 295
Dobrizhoffer, Martín, 89
Docere, 193
Dolbeau, Jean, 133
Dominican order, 77, 252, 255, 257–260, 267
Donofrio, Beverly, 294
Dorothea of Montau, 121
Dyer, Mary, Quaker martyrdom of, xx, xxi, 169, 174, 175, 177–178, 179, 183, 186

E

Echave Ibía, Baltasar de, 20
Echave Orio, Baltasar de, 291–292, 293
Edict Regarding the Government and the Administration of the French Islands of America, and the Discipline and the Commerce of Blacks and Slaves in the Said Countries, 33
Efemérides, 282
"Elegies of some persons deceased in odor of sanctity at Montreal," 215
El pastor de Nochebuena (Palafox), 200
Encomendero, 53
Encomienda, 81, 84
Espejo, Vicente, 197
Esquisse Ethnographique, Le Vaudoun: Aperçu Historique et Evolutions (Trouillot), 42
Estampas, 60, 61
Estancias, 84
Estrada, Juan Manuel de, 16–17
Esturmio, Hernando de, 5
Eudes, Jean, 136
"Evangelists," 280, 281, 283, 289, 293, 294
Exempla, 193
Exus, 103
Ezili, 48–49

F

Fabian y Fuero, Francisco, 206
Father Baltasar Alvarez (Talavera), 204
Felicidad de México (Becerra Tanco), 279, 284
Felicité, St., 214
Feminist Triplex, 24
Fernandes Vieira, João, 110
Fernández de Toro, Blasco, 56
Fiesta principal del santuario, 290, 294
Firestone of Divine Love and Rapture of the Soul in Knowledge of the First Cause (Ruiz de Montoya), 92
"First Iroquois Virgin," 235–250
Flavian, St., 214
Florencia, Francisco de, "Evangelist" writings of, 201, 279, 280, 284, 286, 289, 293, 294
Flores, Gaspar de, 254
Flos Sanctorum, 174
Fort Orange, 167
Fourier, Pierre, 134
Fox, George, 173, 180
Foxe, John, 179
Foxe's Book of Martyrs, 179
France, 12, 136
Franciscans, 68, 77
Francis of Assisi, St., 99, 100
Freda, Ezili, 48, 49
French-Huron-Iroquois wars, 156
Friars Minor, Order of, 99
Friends, Society of. *See* Quakerism; Quakers
Frost, William, 183
Fuenleal, Sebastián Ramírez de, 200

G

Gacetas, 282
Galve, Luis, 275
Garcés, Julián, 205
Garcia, Andres Xavier, 238
García, Antonio Rubial, ix, xxi, 193–207
García, Bartholomé, 292
García Ferrer, Pedro, 200
Garnier, Charles, 217, 225
Gauchos, 78
Geertz, Clifford, 86
George, St., 104
Getino, Luis, 253
Giotto, 4
Golden Gate of Jerusalem, 4, 6, 11
Golden Legend, The (Voragine), 4, 174
González, Roque, 93
González Rosende, Antonio, 195, 197
Gospel of the Pseudo-Matthew, 4
Goupil, René, 153, 162, 225
Gracia triunfante, 237, 244, 245, 247
Granada, Luis de, 268
Grandissima devoçion, 57
Graziano, Frank, 275
Great Peace of Montreal, 130
Greer, Allan, xv, xviii, xix, 235–250
Gregory, Brad S., 174
Gregory XIII, 4, 8
Gregory IX, 100
Gregory XV, 12
Grim Reaper, 78
Gruzinski, Serge, 283, 284
Guadalupanismo, 278, 279, 283–284, 287, 289, 291, 293–295
Guadalupe, Our Lady of, 53–54, 59, 277–298
Guaraní, xv, xvi, xx, 77–97
Guaraní Wars, 82
Guaycurú Indians, 84
Guijo, Gregorio, 282
Guyart, Marie, 131–132, 132
Guy Fawkes' Day, 184
Guyon, Madame, 136
Guzmán, Ruiz de, 80
Gwo bon anj, 41

H

Hagiography, ix, xiii, xiv
  role of narratives in New France, 212–233
  See also specific saint
Haiti, xvi, xx, xxi
Haitian Creole, xv
Haitian *lwa*
  crise de lwa in, 45
  dehumanizing laws in slavery and, 33–36, 37–38
  practices of, 31–50
  saints in, 41–49
  white dog model of law in, 36–41
Hall, David, 175
Hallay, Barbe, 225

"Hammer of the Heretics," 101, 110
Hansen, Leonard, 256, 259, 261–262, 263, 264
Helena, St., 193
Henrique, Dom, 105
Herlihy, David, 13
Hermann, Jacqueline, 106
Hermitas, 54, 57
Hieratic scale, 5, 17
His Majesty, 108
Histoire d'un voyage fait en la terre du Brésil (Léry), 79
Historia de Nuestra Señora de Guadalupe (Talavera), 62
History of the Future (Vieira), 107
Holy Congregation of Rites, 203
Holy Cross Monastery, 99
Holy Family, images in Mexico of, 5, 20–21
Holy Family as "los Cinco Señores" (Concha), 15
Holy Family with a Little Bird (Murillo), 8, 9
Holy Grandparents, 6, 11, 20
Holy Kinship, 5, 8
Homo, Ecce, 245
Hospital Brothers of San Hipólito, 118
Hospitalières of Bayeux, 133
Hospitalières of La Flèche, 134
Hospitalières of Montreal, 137, 139
Hospitalières of Quebec, 137, 139
Hôtel-Dieu, 131, 133, 134, 137
Huei tlamahuiçoltica (Vega), 279
Hull, John, 186
Hurons, xv, 129, 153, 156

I

Iansã, Santa, 103
Ibarra, José de, 203, 205
Ignatius of Loyola, 79, 203, 262, 268
Illuminati, 120
Imagen de la Virgen María (Sánchez), 279, 280
Immaculate Conception, 6, 19
Incarnation, Marie de l'
  bones of, 225
  holy activities in New France by, xviii, 131–132, 135, 138–142, 144, 145–146
  letters of, 214, 217, 218, 222, 226
India, 235, 236, 239–240, 242–245, 247, 249
Inka, Melchor Carlos, 67, 68
Innocent XI, 11
Interián de Ayala, Juan, 11, 12
Iroquois-Huron wars, 153
Iroquois Indians, 129, 153, 154–156, 161, 163, 166, 235
Isidore, St., 217
Iwasaki, Fernando, 269, 275

J

Jansenists, 194, 203
Janvier, Louis-Joseph, 40
Jáuregui, Miguel de, 201

Jeanne Le Ber
 hagiographic narrative of, 215
 holy activities in New France by, xvii, 131,
  134–135, 136, 142–144, 146
Jeronymites, 51–52, 57, 60, 61, 62, 63, 67
Jesse, Tree of, 6, 11
Jesuit Relations, 153–158, 163–164, 216
Jesuits
 activities in New France by, 129–130
 activities in New Spain by, 77–97, 79–94,
  194
 archives in New France of, 211–212, 217
 order in Paris of, 79
Jesus, descent of, 5, 8
Jesus, Mariana de, 271
Jesus, Society of, 105, 206
Jesus Maria, 245, 246
Jesús Tomelín, María de, 195, 271
Joachim, St., 3, 4, 6, 8, 10, 14, 17–18
João IV, 107
Jogues, Isaac, holy activities in New France of,
  xix, xx, 137, 153–168, 216, 225
John, St., 102
John IV, 106, 109
John of God, St., 200
John of the Cross, 199, 200, 262, 265, 268
John Paul II, 93
John the Baptist, 197
John the Evangelist, St., 197
Jones, J. Canby, 173–174
Jorge, São, 103
Joseph, St., xix, 8, 13, 26n.21
Juana Inés de la Cruz, Sor, 243
Juan Clímaco, San, 268
*Juan de Palafox on Mount Carmel with Friars
  and Nuns* (anonymous), 199

K

Karai, 85, 86, 92, 94
Knott, John, 180
Ko kadav, 41
Kristeva, Julia, 5

L

La Ciudad Letrada (Rama), 83
La Conquista Espiritual del Paraguay (Ruiz de
  Montoya), 78–79, 80–82, 87, 92–94
La Cruz del Milagro, 77, 93
La Dauviersière, Jerôme de, 134
La estrella del norte de México (Florencia), 279,
  280, 289, 294
Lafaye, Jacques, 283, 284, 287
*La gracia triunfante en la vida de Catharina
  Tegakovita, india iroquesa,* 235
La Lande, Jean de, 156
Lalemant, Gabriel, 217, 223, 225, 227
Lalemant, Jérôme, narrative of, 155–158, 159,
  162–165, 167
Lamuerte, St., 77–78
Langdon, E. Jean Matteson, 86

"La Señora Chapetona", 61
Lasso de la Vega, Luis, "Evangelist" writings of,
  279, 280, 281, 283, 286, 292, 293,
  295
Las treinta doctrinas de guaraníes, 80
La tierra sin mal, 85, 91, 92, 94
La Troche, Marie de Savonnières de, 132
Laval, François de, 146
*La vida y excelencias y miraglos de santa Anna y
  de la gloriosa nuestra señora santa maria
  fasta la edad de quatorze años: muy
  deuota y contenplatiua nueuamente copi-
  lada,* 5
Lázaro, Diego, 201
Leclerc, Alix, 134
Leddra, William, Quaker martyrdom of, 169,
  175–176, 179, 183
Le Jeune, Paul, 136, 137, 154
Le mélange, 44
León, Luis de, 262
León, Martín de, 22
Léry, Jean, 79
Les Constitutions d'Haiti (Janvier), 40
Les filles du roy, 134
Lettered City, The (Rama), 83
*Letter to the Japanese Bishop, Hope for Portugal,
  Fifth Empire of the World* (Vieira),
  106–107
Lettres de la Vénérable Mère Marie l'Incarnation,
  212
Lettres nécrologiques, 217, 222
Life of St. John of God, The (Berrueco), 201
*Life That the Servant of God Gregorio López
  made in Several Places in This New
  Spain* (Losa), 116
Lily branch, 20
Limeños, 251, 254, 257, 258
Limosnero mendicante, 117
Limpia Concepción, 66
Limpieza de sangre, 242
Lizárraga, Reginaldo de, 57–58, 67
Loayza, Pedro, 255, 257
Lonb-kadav, 41
López, Gregorio, hermit wanderings of, ix, xvi,
  xvii, xix, 115–128, 264
López, Yolanda, 24
Lorenzana, Francisco Antonio de, 195
Lorenzana, Juan de, 262
Losa, Francisco, hagiographic account of López
  by, xvii, xix, 116–128
Losal, Diego de, 67, 70
Lost objects, patrons of, 101
Louis XIV, 33
Lozano, Pedro, 85
Lwa, practices of, xx, 31–50
Lyves of Holy Sainctes (Marbeck), 180

M

Macip, Vicente, 6
Maeder, Ernesto, 93

Maisonneuve, Paul de, 132, 134
Mamelucos, 81
Mance, Jeanne, holy activities in New France
       by, 131, 132, 133–134, 136, 213
"Manuscript of 1652," 211, 212, 215, 216,
       218, 222–224, 226–229
Marbeck, John, 180
Marcel, St., 217
Mariage blanc, 131
Mariana de Jesus, 271
Mariana of Austria, 259
Marie de Saint Joseph, 132
Marienwerder, John, 121
Marillac, Louise de, 136
Martin, Claude, 132, 214, 220, 225
Martínez Hampe, Teodoro, 275
Martínez Montañés, Juan, 6
Mary
    apocryphal "sisters" of, 8
    childhood of, 11
    conception of, 4, 6
    Nativity of, 3–4, 19
Massachusetts Bay Colony, 169, 170, 171,
       172, 181, 186
Masse, Enemond, 156
Masseta, Simon, 84
Maté, 84
Mater Dolorosa, 48
Mather, Cotton, 183–184
Mattos, Armando, 101
Mayordomo, 56, 63, 64, 68, 70
Maza, Francisco de la, 279, 284
Maza, Gonzalo de la, 256, 257
Mazerata, Bishop, 202
Mbyá-Guaraní, 91
McClintock, Anne, 240
McNaspy, C. J., 94
Meléndez, Juan, 251, 260
Melgarejo, María Luisa, 258, 263–264
Membra resque perditas, 104
"Memoires touchant la Mort et les Vertus des
       Pères Isaac Jogues, Anne de Noüe,
       Anthoine Daniel, Jean de Brébeuf,
       Gabriel Lallemant, Charles Garnier,
       Noël Chabanel et Un seculier René
       Goupil," 211
Mendoza, García de, 292
Mendoza, Lorenza de, 92
Mentalités, 253
"Mercies, The" (Rosa de Lima), 265, 266
Met tet, 42
Mexico
    cult of Our Lady of Guadalupe in, 277–298
    devotion to St. Anne in, 3–29
    hermit wanderings of López in, 115–128
    native artistic responses in, 14
    saint and patron of, 21
    tales of Catherine Tekakwitha in, 235–239,
       245–248
    War of Independence of 1808-1810, xxi
Middle Ages, hagiographies during, xiii, xxiin.1

Millones, Luis, 253
Mills, Kenneth, xv, 51–75
Miracle of St. Nicholas of Tolentino (anony-
       mous), 202
Missing people, patrons of, 101
Moctezuma, 291
Mogrovejo, Toribio de, 254, 255
Molanus, Johannes, 11
Montau, Dorothea of, 121
Montgolfier, Étienne, 146
Montúfar, Alonso de, 116
"Mother of the Mother of God," 3
Mott, Luiz, 102, 104
Movere, 193
Moya de Contreras, Pedro, 116, 117–118,
       119, 125
Mudéjar, 71
Mujica Pinilla, Ramón, 275
"Mulatresse," 48
Muñoz, Alonso, 292
Murillo, Bartolomé Esteban, 6, 7, 8, 10, 12
Myers, Kathleen, xviii, 141, 251–275
"Mystical Stairway, The" (Rose de Lima), 265,
       266, 268

N
Nahuatl, xv, 22, 241
Narváez, María, 203
Nassau, Maurice of, 104, 107
Nativity of Mary, 4
Nativity of the Virgin Mary, images of, 4, 5–6,
       10, 12, 17–20, 23–24
Nativity of the Virgin Mary (Correa), 18
Nativity of the Virgin (Murillo), 12
Nativity of the Virgin (Sánchez Salmerón), 17
Nayler, James, 172, 181
*New England Judged, Not by Man's, but by the
       Spirit of the Lord* (Bishop), 178–179
New France
    female holiness in, 129–152
    Jesuit archives in, 211–212, 217
    role of hagiographic narratives in, 211–233
New York Times, x
Nezú, 93
Nicholas of Tolentino, St., 201, 202
Norman Conquest, 34
Norton, John, 178, 181, 182
Noüe, Anne de, 156, 217
Nuestra Señora de Guadalupe, 278, 290
Nuestra Señora de los Remedios, 118
Nuestra Señora del Patroncinio, 290
Nuestra soberana criolla, xviii

O
Ocaña, Diego de
    paintings of the Virgin of Guadalupe by, 52
    travels in Peru and journals of, xv, xvii,
       51–75
    death of, 52

Ogum, São, 103
Olier, Jean-Jacques, 136
Oliva, Isabel Flores de. *See* Rosa de Lima
Oliva, María de, 254
Oración de unión, 262
Ordinario, 63
Oré, Luis Jerónimo de, 62, 66, 70
Orixás, 103
Orsua y Vela, Bartolomé Arzáns de, 71
Ounfo, 45, 49
Oungan, 36, 45
Our Lady of Copacabana, 59
Our Lady of Guadalupe, 277–298
Our Lady of Guadalupe: The Origins and Sources of a Mexican National Symbol, 1531-1797 (Poole), 283
Our Lady of Los Remedios, 282
Our Lady of Rosario, 102
"Our sovereign American lady," xviii
Oviedo y Herrera, Count, 259

P
Pacheco, Francisco, 9–10, 11, 17, 19
Paciencia, Señor de la, 78
Paine, Robert Treat, 183
"Painting of St. Anne No Longer in Use, A" (Pacheco), 9
Paje, 85
Palafox, Juan de, xvi, xxi, 103–207
Pantaleón Álvarez Abreu, Domingo, 205, 206
Paraguay, 78–94
Paraíso Occidental (Sigüena y Góngora), 245, 246
Paris Carmel, 133
Patrick, St., xvi, 46–47
Patroncinio de la Inmaculada Concepción (Magón), 206
Pauke, Florian, 91
Paul, Vincent de, 136
Paz, Alvarez de, 268
Paz, Octavio, 284, 294
Pedro de Osma, San, 203
Peirson, Peter, 174
Peltrie, Madame de la, 131, 132, 136, 145, 225
Pemberton, Isaac, 183
Pereyns, Simón, 14
Pérez de la Serna, Juan, 124, 285, 293
Pérez de Viveros, Magdalena, 285
Perron, Paul, xix, 153–168
Peru, 51–75
Pesquera, Diego de, 16
Pestana, Carla, xvii, xx, xxi, 169–191
Peterson, Jeanette, 61
Petit bon anj, 41
Philip II, 4, 51, 105, 108, 109
Philip III, 124
Philip IV, 109, 258
Philip of Jesus, St., 21
Pizarro, Francisco, 275
Pluchon, Pierre, 49

Pobres vergonzantes, 117
Poncet, Joseph, 228
Poole, Stafford, 283
Portals of Power: Shamanism in South America (Langdon), 86
Portrait of My Grandmother (Baca), 23
Portugal, 101
Posada, Fray Martín, 51
Potosí, xvii, 53, 54, 56, 58–67, 69, 70, 71
Pravia, Pedro de, 120
Pregnancy and childbirth, patron saints of, 4, 6, 13, 19, 23
Presentation of the Virgin in the Temple, 19
Price-Mars, Jean, 44
Printing press, xiii
Proceso apostólico, 252, 258
Proceso arzobispal, 252
Protoevangelium of St. James, 3–4
Puritans, xvii, xxi, 172

Q
Quakerism, 169–191
Quakers, martyrs of, xvii, xx, xxi, 169–191
Quechua, xv, xvii
Queen of the Angels, 290
Quetzalcóatl and Guadalupe (Lafaye), 283
Quilombolas, 104
Quiñones Osorio, Luis de, 71
Quiróz, Gutierre Bernardo de, 201

R
Rabasa, José, 94
Ragueneau, Paul, 133, 212, 216
Rama, Angel, 83
Ramírez de Vergara, Alonso, 61
Ramos Cervantes, Alonso, 57
Recollect, 129
"Recoverer of Lost Objects," 109
"Recoverer of Portuguese Sovereignty," 109
Reducciónes, 77
Reformation, xiv, 8
Regnault, Christophe, 223, 227–228
Regnouard, Marie, 225
Renovar, 68
Renty, Monsieur de, 213
"Responso das Coisas de Santo Antônio," 102–103
Retardataire style, 21
Réveillade, Antoinette, 136
Rey, Christo, 93
Rhys, Jean, 40
Richer, Cécile, 132
Rivera, Galván, 294
Rivero, Luisa de, 239
Robinson, William, Quaker martyrdom of, 169, 173, 174, 175, 176, 177, 178, 179
Robles, Antonio de, 282, 289, 290
Robles, Juan de, 5

Rodríguez, Jeannette, 277
Rodríguez Juárez, Juan, 18
Rodríguez Juárez, Nicolás, 16
Roelas, Juan de, 6
Romano, Alexandro, 238, 239
Rosa de Lima, life and miracles of, xviii, 251–275
Rosario, Our Lady of, 102
Rousseau, Marie, 136
Rubial, Antonio, 124
Ruiz de Montoya, Antonio
   experiences of, xv, xix
   Jesuit works with Guaraní of, 78–82, 84–85, 87–94
   slave-hunting by, xx
Ruysbroeck, John of, 117

S
"Sacred biography," xiii
Sacsayhuaman, 69
Sahagún, Bernardino de, 22
Saint Augustin, Catherine de, 222
Saint Bernard, Françoise de, 146
Saint Joseph, Marie de, 135–136
Saint-Méry, Moreau de, 46, 48
"Saint of Salt," 109
Salas, Ana de, 63
Salazar de Espinosa, Juan, 80
Saldivia, María de, 64
Salome, 4
San Blas Indians, 67, 68
Sánchez, Miguel, "Evangelist" writings of, 279–281, 283–287, 288, 291, 292–295
Sánchez Salmerón, Juan, 17, 19
Sancta Ysabel, 278
San José de Chiapas, 206
San La Muerte, xvi
San Pedro, Congregación of, 116
Santa María, Rosa de, 251–275
Santa María de la O, 5
Santander y Torres, Sebastián de, 270
Santiago, xiv
Santidade of Jaguaribe, 103
Santo Antônio de Barra, 104
Santo Cristo de la Veracruz, 59
São Jorge da Mina, 104
Sauvagesse, 144
Schorske, Carl, 295
Sebastian, King, 105, 106, 108
Sebastian, St., 102, 106, 108–109
Second Book of Kings, 107
Selbsdritt, 5
Sennacherib of Assyria, 107
Señora Chapetona, 65
Serna, Elvira de la, 57
Shamanism, in the Guaraní, 86–91
Sheingorn, Pamela, 4, 5
Sheriffs, 105
Sigüena y Góngora, Carlos de, 245

Simon de Longpré, Marie Catherine de, 133
Slavery
   civil death in, 33–36, 37–38
   concept of "blackness" of blood in, 34, 35–36, 38–39
   dehumanizing law codes in, 33–36, 37
   and Haitian lwa practices, 31–50
   and spirituality, xx
Société Notre Dame de Montréal, 134
Society of Jesus, 105
Song of Songs, The, 268
Southwick, John, 180
Spanish Succession, War of, 202
Speilberg, Janis van, 256
Spiritual Exercises (Ignatius of Loyola), 268
"Spiritual Ladder," 268
Spivak, Gayatri, 78
St. Anne Teaching the Virgin Mary to Read (Murillo), 7, 12
St. Anne Triplex, 5, 8, 12, 16–17
St.-Augustin, Catherine de, 131, 146, 226
St. Bernard, Anne Le Cointre de, 133
St. Bonaventure, Marie Forestier de, 133
St.-François Xavier, Marguerite de, 222
St. Ignace, Marie Guenet de, 133
St. Joseph, Madeleine de, 133
St.-Joseph, Marie de, holy activities in New France by, 145, 212, 216, 218–220, 227
St. Lawrence Valley, 129, 155
St. Vincent Monastery, 99
St.-Xavier, Mère Marguerite de, 139
Stevenson, Marmaduke, Quaker martyrdom of, 169, 175, 176, 177, 178, 179
Stratton, Suzanne, 6
Sulpicians, 215

T
Tablas, 71
Talavera, Cristóbal de, 200, 203, 204
Talavera, Gabriel de, 62, 63
Tauler, 117
Taveira, Teresa, 99
Taylor, William, xviii, xxi, 277–298
Teatro Angelopolitano (Bermúdez de Castro), 195
Tekakwitha, Catherine, holy activities in New France by, xv, xviii, xix, 215, 224, 235–250
Tekakwitha, Kateri, 211
Teresa, St., role in New Spain of, 199, 200, 203, 253, 265, 268
Teresa of Avila
   role in New France of, 138, 213
   role in New Spain of, 117, 198, 199, 262, 268, 271
Tesoro de la lengua guaraní (Ruiz de Montoya), 80
Ti bon anj, 41
Tinharé, 103

Titicaca, Lake, 59
Tlazolteotl, 23
Toci, xvi, 22–24
Treatise on Sacred Images (Molanus), 11
Treaty of Vervins, 129
Tree of Jesse, 6, 11
Tresguerras, Francisco Eduardo, 20
Tridentine, 8
Trinubium, 9
Trouillot, Duverneau, 42
Tuer, Dot, xv, xvi, xix, 77–97
Tupamba, 83
Tupí-Guaraní, 79
Tupí Indians, xv, xvi
Tupinamba, 79, 103
Turner, Victor, 86

U
Umbanda, 103
Universidad Nacional Autónoma de México, ix
Urban VIII, 196, 252, 258
Ursuline order, role in New France of,
    136–137, 138–139, 145, 146, 214,
    216–220, 222, 243
Urtassum, Juan de, 236, 248

V
Vainfas, Ronaldo, xvi, xxi, 99–111
Valdes, Joseph Francisco, 20
Valero, marqués de, 236, 237, 244
Valeroso Lucideno (Calado), 104, 110
Vallée, Marie des, 136
van Deusen, Nancy E., 269
Varón de deseos (Palafox), 199
Veinticuatro del cabildo, 63
*Vida de la Gloriosísima Madre de la Madre de
    Dios, y Abuela de Jesuchristo Séñora
    Santa Ana* (Valdes), 20
Vida (González Rosende), 197
Vie (Beauvais), 139
Vie de la Mère Catherine de Saint-Augustin
    (Ragueneau), 212
Vieira, Antônio, 101, 106–110
Vignerot Combalet, Marie de, 133
Villafranca Lezcano, Francisco Pérez de, 53
Villalpando, Cristóbal de, 14
Vimont, Barthélemy, 154, 155

Virgen del Perdón (Pereyns), 14
Virgin Mary, elements in vodou of, 48
Virgin of Carmen, 200
Virgin of Guadalupe
    cult in Peru of, xviii, 51–75
    paintings of, 52
    as patron of Mexico, 13
    skin color of, xv
Virgin of the Candlemas, 59
Virgin of the Immaculate Conception, 20
Visitadine Order, 136
Vita, Kimpa, 110
*Vita mirabilis mors pretiosa venerabilis Sororis
    Rosa de S. Maria* (Hansen), 259
Vivar, Juan Correa de, 6
Vizarrón, Archibishop-Viceroy, 294
Vodou
    Catholic practices in, 43
    le mélange in, 44
    origins in slavery of, xx, 32
    role of zombie in, 41
Voltaire, 81
Voragine, Jacobus de, 4, 174
"Vuestra Merced," 123

W
Wharton, Edward, 179
White, Richard, 295
Wide Sargasso Sea (Rhys), 40
Wilkie, Thomas, 175
Winthrop, John, Jr., 184
Women
    saintly role in New France of, 130–152,
        235–350
    saintly role in New Spain of, 3–29,
        251–275, 277–298
Woodworkers, patrons of, 13
"Writing and Evangelization in Sixteenth Cen-
    tury Mexico" (Rabasa), 94

X
Xaintonge, Anne de, 136

Y
Yerbales, 84
Yupanqui, Francisco Tito, 59